Jan H. Negenman

NEW ATLAS OF THE BIBLE

Edited by Harold H. Rowley, D.D., F.B.A.,
*Emeritus Professor of Hebrew Language and Literature
University of Manchester*

Translated by Hubert Hoskins and Richard Beckley

With a Foreword by Harold H. Rowley
and an Epilogue by Lucas H. Grollenberg, O.P.

Doubleday & Company, Inc.
Garden City, New York
1969

*Most of the colour photographs and many
black-and-white photographs were specially
taken for this book in Lebanon, Jordan, and Israel,
by Ad Windig of Amsterdam. He was
accompanied and advised by Lucas H. Grollenberg.*

Library of Congress Catalog Card Number 69-11566

Printed in The Netherlands

Originally published as "De Bakermat van de Bijbel"
Copyright © Elsevier Nederland N.V., 1968

FOREWORD

This volume traces in broad outline the growth of the Bible in the setting of the history out of which each of its parts came. For if the Bible is the Word of God, it must always be remembered that that Word was mediated through men who lived at particular times and who wrote first of all for their own contemporaries. To understand the situations out of which the various books were born is essential to any adequate Bible study.

No student of the Bible can ignore history. Israel looked back to a great moment of history when she experienced God's deliverance of her from Egypt and when she committed herself to him in the Covenant, and she looked forward to the age of universal peace and well-being when obedience to the will of God should be universal. Her faith was born in a historical setting and it had meaning for history. For the writers of the New Testament the life and death and resurrection of Jesus at a particular time of history are fraught with significance for all men of every age.

Yet it must be recognized that despite all our modern sources of knowledge there are many problems on which certainty is not possible, and the author of this volume would be the first to agree that there are many points where other scholars would disagree with him — often on details that do not seriously affect the general picture. From his wide acquaintance with modern study of both Testaments and of the history of the ancient Near East, he here sketches the history and, without attempting to pinpoint the origin of the various books in the way technical volumes of Old Testament and New Testament Introduction do, shares with the reader his own insight into their setting.

All of this will shed light on the Bible. The superb illustrations which abound in the pages of this volume will add greatly to that light, and will enable the reader to picture Biblical scenes and to see something of the culture and achievement of the people of the world in which the Bible was born. Maps, too, there are which will help him to follow the story in its geographical setting, and a feast for the eye and the mind will be found in these pages.

But why should we be interested in this ancient story, and why should the Bible still today be so widely studied and books about it find so many eager readers? That question Father Grollenberg, the author of the *Atlas of the Bible*, which had so remarkable and so well-deserved a reception, answers in the fine Epilogue he has written for this volume. If the Bible comes out of the past, it does not belong wholly to the past. Its message was addressed first to the generations out of which the books came: but it is addressed also to every generation, for it belongs to every age. It is not so much a book about Israel as a book about God, who spoke not only by lawgivers and prophets and psalmists but by His Son, and it calls men to a living encounter with the God who speaks. It is still the Word of God, leading men to the Word He speaks through Christ, in whom His greatest saving Word is spoken.

H. H. ROWLEY
Emeritus Professor of
Manchester University

CONTENTS

I. INTRODUCTION

A bird's-eye view of the Bible we know and its development, going back to the earliest manuscript fragments.

1. THE BIBLE WE KNOW

The Bible is unique in the world of books. Learned treatises on it and popular interpretations of it have been produced in a steady stream over the last sixteen centuries and will continue to be written. The Bible itself has been printed in greater quantity than any other book. The first printing of a recent translation was one million copies, probably the largest first edition in the history of publishing to that time.

Up to the end of 1967 the Bible had been translated into 1250 languages and had been disseminated to almost every country and region of the earth. The Protestant Bible Societies alone in 1965 distributed some 79,000,000 Bibles or parts of the Bible. Not only the main language areas have received attention, but also many small language regions where perhaps only ten thousand people speak a common tongue. Vietnamese, Swahili, Burmese, and Tamil Bibles are available, and Armenian, Cambodian, Korean, and Nepalese ones, and the New Testament is produced in Eskimo.

As life itself is constantly developing, so no Church can content itself with one definitive translation, if that no longer presents the meaning of the Bible in terms comprehensible to contemporary readers. For this reason continual effort is devoted to re-translating the Bible for the present day. Sometimes one translation is scarcely finished when a new version is being begun.

The word 'translation,' however, necessarily implies an original text to translate. On what text are our modern versions based?

2. THE PRINTED BIBLE

The history of the printed Bible begins in the fifteenth century. The era on either side of 1500 was in many ways similar to our own time, especially in being a time of unprecedented change and upheaval. The invention of gunpowder, which reduced the proud fortress towns of the Middle Ages to picturesque survivals, was its nuclear bomb; the invention of the compass and the dazzling voyages of exploration were its space travel; and then as now improvements in techniques of production and increased international trade brought increases in material well-being and increased leisure. The result was a wide-spread challenging of accepted values and standards. Galileo changed the image of the cosmos and man's understanding of his place in it, and Vasco da Gama forced Europe to face West as well as East.

A major contribution to this ferment of change was made by the invention of printing from movable type. Along with the

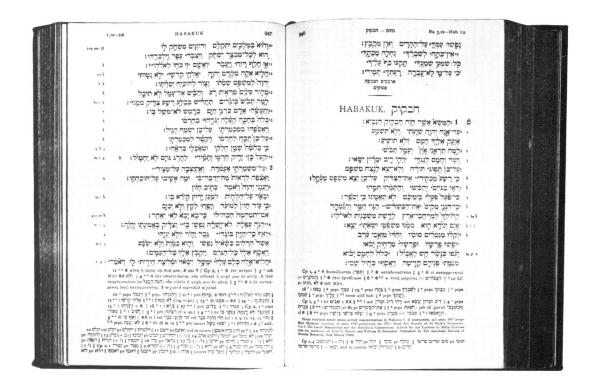

Nahum 3 : 18b-19 and Habakkuk 1 : 1–2 : 6a, from R. Kittel's *Biblia Hebraica*, the Old Testament in Hebrew, which is generally received at present as the basic text. Abbreviated in the margin are notes that were appended to the text in the manuscripts by the Masoretes, Jewish scholars of the 7th to the 14th centuries A.D. At the foot of the page is a critical apparatus in three parts. The first gives some less important textual variants, the second presents striking divergences which occur in other manuscripts and especially emendations proposed by the editor. The third part shows the variants in the Habakkuk Scroll discovered in 1947 at Qumran, which is at least eight hundred years older than the one used as the basic text above.

10

Luke 24 : 43-53 and John 1 : 1-14, from E. Nestle's *Novum Testamentum Graece* the New Testament in Greek, which provides what is nowadays the received basic text. The marginal references are to passages in the Old and New Testaments which in one way or another throw light on the verse facing them. The critical apparatus at the foot of the page gives the main variants from other manuscripts.

(Opposite, left) Exodus 1 : 1-20 according to the Bombergiana, the first Rabbinical Bible, published in 1517 by the printing-house of Bomberg in Venice. On the left is the Hebrew text, on the right the Aramaic version, and, below, the Rabbinical commentary in Late Hebrew.

(Opposite, right) Genesis 21 : 28-22 : 3 according to the Complutensian Polyglot, published 1520 at Alcalá (Complutum). Left, a Greek text with Latin translation; in the centre, Jerome's Latin text; right, a Hebrew text. Below, left, is an Aramaic version, and beside that the same in a Latin translation. In the margin are Rabbinical annotations.

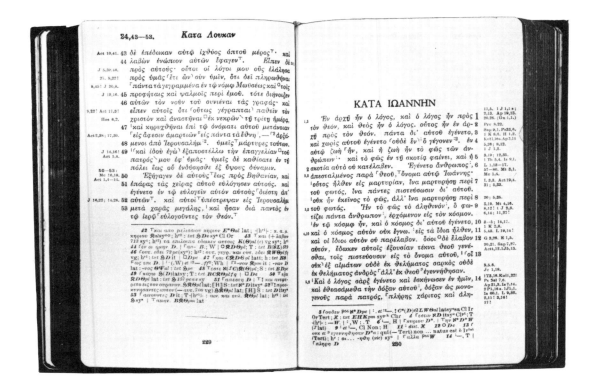

new knowledge, one of the first things to be given increased distribution was the Bible. At first, however, the quality of the printed texts was little improvement on the manuscript copies. Printer's errors and a haphazard choice of manuscripts for the basis of the text reduced the value of the first printed Bibles.

If the printing press, however, stimulated the reading of the Bible, another development made it possible for the quality of the texts to be improved. This was the rediscovery of the authors of classical antiquity which is one of the hallmarks of the Renaissance. The scholarly study of Greek and Latin was soon extended to Hebrew and Aramaic, along with Greek the original languages of the Bible writings.

As early as 1477 the Psalms were printed in Hebrew in Italy; in 1488 there followed the complete Old Testament. One of the most impressive of these early scholarly editions is the famous Bombergiana (1516–17) edited by Felix Pratensis and named after its Antwerp printer Daniel Bomberg, who had set up a printing house in Venice in 1515. The Bombergiana is what is known as a Rabbinical Bible, because on each page it has a Hebrew text of the Old Testament, together with an Aramaic translation, and, in addition, commentaries by famous Jewish scholars, above, below, and alongside the Bible text. The text of its second edition of 1524–25 was the basis of all printings of the Hebrew Bible up to modern times.

Of equal importance is the handsome Complutensian Polyglot which appeared in Alcalá (Latin name, Complutum) in 1520. This work has on each page of the Old Testament a Hebrew, Aramaic, Latin, and Greek text, and on each page of the New Testament a Latin and Greek text and marginal notes. The printing of the New Testament was complete in 1514, but as the Papal imprimatur did not arrive till 1520, the Basle printer Froben preceded the publication of the Complutensian Polyglot

with his less thorough edition of the Greek New Testament, the work of Erasmus of Rotterdam (1516).

In the history of printed texts of the Greek New Testament, the most important edition is the *Editio Regia* of the Paris printer Robert Stephanus. It contains the text of Erasmus slightly corrected to accord with the Complutensian Polyglot and a few MSS and is the first edition to have a critical apparatus. The next edition of this publication (1551) had for the first time the division of the text into verses which is still used today. (The traditional division into chapters had appeared soon after 1200 and is attributed to Archbishop Stephen Langton of Canterbury.) From the appearance of the second edition of 1633, printed by the famous Leyden printing family, the text of Stephanus was regarded as the 'textus receptus' till the nineteenth century.

Yet another feature of the Renaissance made an even more dramatic contribution to the critical study of the Biblical text—the Reformation. According to the great Reformers, the Bible had too long been a closed book to Christians. People should learn to live again from the Bible, *sola scriptura*, 'by the scriptures alone.' For this purpose, editions in the vernacular were necessary. The first English translation, that of Wycliffe, was completed about 1382. Tyndale's New Testament was issued at Worms in 1525, and the first complete printed English Bible was the beautiful version by Miles Coverdale (1535). The famous 'Breeches' Bible with lively notes appeared in 1560. These and various other versions were all largely replaced by the King James or Authorized Version of 1611. In 1466 there appeared the first printed German Bible, which was reprinted eleven times in twenty-four years. Soon there were a great number of different editions in many European languages. Thus in the time of the Reformation, the printed Bible was available in various vernacular editions as a commercial commodity.

The Catholic Church, too, became active in this respect. The theological quarrels with the Reformers required an authentic text. So, in 1546 at the Council of Trent, the Vulgate was declared to be authentic, that is to say, authoritative in matters of doctrine and morals. However, it was not till 1590–92 that there appeared a critical edition of the Vulgate. The third edition of this (1598) is still the valid Latin text of the Catholic Church today. After the two Popes who authorized it, this edition is called the Sixto-Clementina.

The next great era of Biblical criticism after the Renaissance began in the nineteenth century and has continued into our own day. The philologist Zeckmann, versed in ancient languages, was the first to attack the textus receptus, in his edition of the Greek New Testament of 1831, in which he applied the tried principles of textual criticism as laid down by classical philologists. After the wonderful discovery of the famous Codex Sinaiticus by von Tischendorf, there appeared in the course of a few decades those comprehensive editions of the Greek New Testament, which by their departure from the textus receptus, placed research into the Greek New Testament on a completely different basis. The most important of these was the *Novum Testamentum Graece* by Eberhard Nestle, universally used and known simply as 'Nestle.' The twentieth-century translations

are essentially based on this edition. In 1966 the United Bible Societies prepared an edition of the text in the *Greek New Testament* specially for translators. A definitive new revision of Nestle based on MS sources is being prepared in the University of Münster to take due account of recent finds of papyri and the early translations.

For the Old Testament the accepted text is that of the *Biblia Hebraica*, referred to as 'Kittel' after the nineteenth-century scholar who worked on the most widely used edition. The second edition of the *Biblia Hebraica* by common consent replaced the Bombergiana as the standard, and the third edition (1937) was able to use the Codex Leningradensis of 1008 and many old MS fragments. A new revision of this is being prepared taking into account the recent finds at Qumran near the Dead Sea; and in addition a new edition is being prepared in Jerusalem using the Aleppo Codex which is earlier than the Codex Leningradensis. Since 1907 the Benedictines of S. Girolamo in Rome have been working on an edition of the Vulgate, revised according to the principles of modern textual criticism.

All these editions are laboriously won from long and painstaking study of the manuscript sources which the devotion of monastic communities, chance, and the archaeologist's spade have given us. We must now glance briefly at these.

3. MANUSCRIPTS OF THE NEW TESTAMENT

Some 1500 years separate the earliest printed Bibles from the lifetime of Christ—a gap three times as long as that which separates us from the invention of printing. It is a gap that is only partially spanned by the MSS we possess, in spite of their number and (in many cases) marvellously high quality. Most serious of all, for the first hundred or even two hundred years of the existence of some New Testament books we have no written evidence whatsoever and are reduced to deduction and guesswork.

Until the third century A.D., writing was commonly on papyrus. This was made from the pith of the papyrus plant, cut into strips and glued together cross-wise like ply-board. The single sheets of papyrus were generally joined together to form rolls up to thirty feet long. These were mostly inscribed on the inner side only, where the fibres ran lengthwise. The text was written in narrow parallel columns, with a reed trimmed at the top, which was dipped in ink made from soot or gall.

Another form of book commonly chosen by Biblical scribes, was the codex, which in its basic form corresponds to the printed book current today. Four or more double-size sheets were laid on top of each other and folded in the middle, forming a 'codex' which then had only to be bound. The page of a codex was written in one to four parallel columns.

The title page of the Vulgate, Jerome's Latin translation of the Bible, revised by order of Pope Sixtus V. According to the publisher, Johannes Moretus, this edition appeared at Antwerp in 1603. On the right is Moses, and on the left, David, thought at that time to have been the principal authors of the Old Testament. Seated underneath are four Evangelists, representing the writers of the New Testament.

of the rabbinical school. But it is obvious that abbreviations of this sort could easily lead to variations in the text. This fragment gives the text of Isaiah 7 : 11—9 : 8.

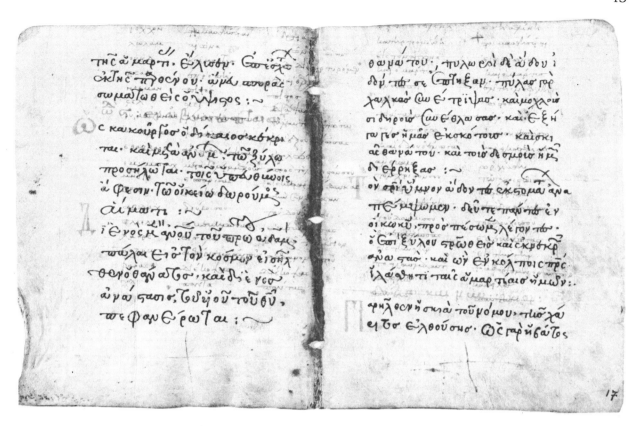

A page of a copy of Origen's ▷ Hexapla text, on which another text has been superimposed at some later time (palimpsest). In and among the thick letters of the more recent text, one can pick out, from left to right, the five columns of Origen, as follows: a Greek transcription of the Hebrew; a Greek translation by Aquila; a Greek translation by Symmachus; a Septuagint text; and finally an un-identified Greek translation known for convenience as Quinta, 'the fifth.' This extract of the Hexapla starts with the second word of Psalm 89, v. 38 and goes on to the second word of v. 41.

After about A.D. 200 the dearer but much more durable parchment gradually supplanted papyrus, which however continued to be used up to the eighth century for the production of New Testament MSS. Parchment is animal skin (from sheep, goats, calves, or antelopes) from which hair and grease have been removed, and which has been smoothed and whitened. This was quite different from papyrus, and could be written on on both sides. Parchment could also be scraped and written on again ('palimpsests'). It was particularly a Jewish habit to use rolls of skin rather than leaves for writing on. In the late Middle Ages parchment was gradually replaced by paper.

Up to the tenth century MSS were written in Greek characters in uncials or capitals and, moreover, without separating words and sentences. This, added to the peculiarities of individual scribes, makes the reading of them a specialized skill. From the ninth century onwards, writing in capitals was replaced by cursive writing in small letters. This had many advantages—less parchment and less time were needed and also less storage space.

The originals of the New Testament scripts are lost. The earliest MSS of the New Testament, all more or less damaged, and often only the remains of single leaves, originate from the second or third century A.D. The oldest fragment (found in Egypt) is a small scrap of parchment from the first half of the second century, with the text of John 18:31-33, 37. It proves that the Fourth Gospel was used at that time in a small provincial Egyptian town.

Two outstanding collections of papyri in Dublin and in Coligny near Geneva, contain the most important New Testament papyri. These have changed the course of modern textual criticism. To the Dublin collection of Chester Beatty belong several key papyri going back to the first half of the third century and containing parts of the Four Gospels, Acts, and almost complete texts of most of Paul's letters, and parts of the Revelation to John.

The Martin Bodmer collection in Coligny contains an interesting early papyrus fragment (parts of the Gospel of John) dating from A.D. 200 at the latest, an equally early series of fragments of the Gospel of Luke, and a papyrus of the second half of the third century containing the Letters of Peter and Jude.

Among the most important parchment MSS of the New Testament (mostly forming part of MSS of the whole or almost the whole Bible) are the following. The famous Codex Vaticanus and the no less famous Codex Sinaiticus, both of the fourth century and both wonderful uncial MSS of virtually the whole Bible, formed the bases of two nineteenth-century editorial traditions, ultimately combined by Nestle. The Codex Ephraemi rescriptus, from the fifth century, is the best-known palimpsest MS; this also originally contained the whole Bible. The Greek-Latin Codex Bezae Cantabrigiensis, which according to recent research may have originated in the fourth rather than the sixth century, contains the Four Gospels in the order Matthew, John, Luke, Mark, as well as the Acts of the Apostles. The Greek-Latin Codex Claromontanus from the fifth century contains Paul's Epistles.

Altogether we know at the present time of about 3100 MSS or fragments containing the New Testament in whole or in part, of which more than 80 are papyri and about 200 uncial MSS. In addition we have more than 2100 lectionaries or fragments of these, intended for the reading of Scripture in church services, which do not contain a continuous text but only services of the day, prescribed by the Liturgy. There are lectionaries in uncial and cursive script. Furthermore, there were made in the second and third centuries translations into Syriac, Latin, and various Coptic dialects, which are very important for the tradition of the New Testament text. From the fourth century we have the Gothic translations of Ulfilas. Finally, almost the whole New Testament has been handed down in quotations in the writings of early Christian Fathers and heretics such as Marcion and Tatian.

The material, though regrettably incomplete, is vast in extent. These few examples show how it is necessary to refer to and compare many sources if we are to arrive at the best text or in some cases at any text of every part of the Bible.

Even at the earliest date to which our material takes us—the second and third centuries in Egypt—we find no suggestion of a unified text. A century after most of the New Testament had been composed, individual MSS differed from each other in innumerable details. In Egypt it is clear we must reckon with at least three different forms of the text, each giving rise to its own textual tradition—the Egyptian, Western, and Caesarean. In addition there was the Byzantine text, fixed by the revision of the Presbyter Lucian (d. 312) in Antioch. This acquired in the Greek Church the same authority as the Vulgate in the Church of Rome.

The modern scholar reassesses these divergent witnesses and the complexity of the task can be seen from a study of the critical apparatus of any annotated version of the Bible.

The apparently arbitrary inclusion or exclusion of this or that item from any particular MS is generally a result of the uncertain situation prevailing in the Early Church and of variations in what books were accepted and used in this or that locality. As will be shown in chapters 11 and 12, it was not until late in the fourth century that the canon of the present twenty-seven books of the New Testament proposed by Bishop Athanasius of Alexandria in 367 was accepted as authoritative by both the Roman and Greek Churches. In the eastern national Churches it was accepted later still.

Real work on textual criticism of the Greek New Testament was no longer undertaken in the Eastern Church after the revision of Lucian but it continued in the Roman Church, and this produced a disastrous confusion in the old Latin translations. This state of affairs induced Pope Damasus in 382 to commission the famous Jerome to make a standard translation of the Bible. For the Gospels, Jerome revised an early Latin text, based on older Greek MSS. The basis of his revision of the other writings of the New Testament is not clear. For the Old Testament, Jerome made a largely new translation from Hebrew into Latin. In 405 this task was finished and the Vulgate created. But it was only slowly that it made headway. It was not till the eighth century that the exclusive validity of the Vulgate was assured, after a new interest in the Bible text was aroused by Charlemagne.

4. THE OLD TESTAMENT IN GREEK

When Jerome made a largely new translation of the Hebrew text into Latin, he by no means won the unanimous gratitude of contemporary Christianity. On the contrary, the mistrust and criticism that greeted his great work even culminated in accusations of deliberate forgery. Two things need to be remembered. In the first place, in his translation of the Old Testament Jerome went back to a language which none but he in the West could then understand; and secondly he broke with the tradition of

centuries, by which a particular Greek translation, the Septuagint (Lat. 'seventy') had for Christians in the West far outstripped the Hebrew text in authority.

Much of the regard for the Septuagint comes simply from the fact that few in the Early Church could read Hebrew. But this alone would hardly have made the Septuagint so unchallengeable, if, long before the first Christian communities emerged, the Jews of the Diaspora had not tried hard to show that the translation familiar to them was as valuable as the Hebrew text from which it came.

The first salvo of this campaign is the Letter of Aristeas. In this we are informed with a great show of authenticity how the translation into Greek of the five books of Moses came about. One day—so the writer informs his brother Philocrates—the Keeper of the famous Library in Alexandria had proposed to King Ptolemy II (285–247 B.C.) that he should have the Jewish Law (the Pentateuch or five books of Moses) translated into Greek, since the wisdom that it contained justified its being incorporated in the Royal Library. Ptolemy took up this suggestion and sent several envoys, including Aristeas, to the High Priest Eleazar in Jerusalem, with the request that suitable persons to undertake this translation should be made available. In response, seventy-two Jews from Palestine, six from each of the twelve tribes, came to Egypt. The King allocated the Pharos island for their stay. In seventy-two days they agreed upon the translation, which was subsequently deemed by the Jewish community to be 'beautiful, pious, and exact.' A curse was laid on anyone who dared to tamper in any way with this text, whether by additions, alterations, or omissions. After it had been laid

before the King, he too was deeply moved by the wisdom of the Jewish Law and sent the translators home with rich gifts.

This description was later considerably enlarged upon. According to the famous Jewish scholar Philo (ca. 25 B.C.–A.D. 40), the translators had worked quite separately and after seventy-two days each one had arrived independently at the same translation. This version of the story the Church Fathers took over and extended to the whole of the Old Testament. It is obvious that these later accounts at any rate are quite inaccurate. But so, in fact, is the original story in the Letter of Aristeas. There has long been agreement that the letter was written not in the lifetime of Ptolemy II, but probably some 150 years later. Furthermore it is scarcely credible that the sacred books were translated into Greek merely as a result of a royal wish. It is surely more probable that they were translated because of the decreasing number of Jews of the Diaspora who were familiar with the Hebrew language.

It is quite possible, nonetheless, that the beginnings of the Greek translation are to be sought in Alexandria, as one of the most important Jewish communities had certainly grown up in that town. A valid tradition, based on this fact, may be behind the Aristeas letter and its limitation of the translation to the Jewish Law, for the five books of Moses were, for the Jews, the most important part of the Old Testament. It is, therefore, probable that this part was translated into Greek first and the other books only subsequently.

It is generally accepted today that the Septuagint came into existence over a fairly long space of time. Only the vaguest indication of a date can be given for the beginning of this

(Opposite, left) A page of the Codex Alexandrinus, which dates from the beginning of the 5th century. The text is in Greek capitals, and the words are run together. This page contains 2 Peter 3 : 16b-18 and 1 John 1 : 1–2 : 9.

(Opposite, right) Luke 7 : 14b-38a according to Codex Vaticanus, which like Codex Sinaiticus dates from the 4th century and is therefore one of the earliest complete manuscripts of the Bible in existence.

The scroll of Isaiah from ▷ Cave 1 at Qumran, which is usually referred to as 1 Q Isᵃ. The current opinion among palaeographers is that this scroll dates from the 2nd century B.C. Here it is open at columns 32 (right) and 33 (left), which contain the text of Isaiah 38 : 8–40 : 28. Clearly visible to the left of column 33, is a seam where pieces of leather have been stitched together.

A part of the second column of the Hymns of Thanksgiving from Qumran 1 QH 2 : 20-30). This scroll from the first cave is usually denoted by the Hebrew word *Hodayoth*. These songs are in general harder to understand than our psalms. They often contain more specific allusions to historical situations and events which are now obscure. Furthermore, they employ a variety of Biblical phrases and expressions to formulate their characteristic ideas. In the translation of this psalm the main Biblical turns of phrase are italicized.

I give Thee thanks, O Lord,
For that Thou hast set my soul
In the bundle of life,
And hast fenced me about
From all the snares of the pit;
For *violent men sought my life*,
While I held firmly to Thy Covenant.
But they are a worthless throng,
A fraternity of Belial.
They know not that from Thee is my office
And that *Thy favour saves my life*,

For *Thou dost direct my steps*.
But by Thy will they strive against my life,
That Thou mayest be glorified by judgement on the
                                                    wicked
And show Thy power through me before the sons of
                                                    man,
For it is *Thy favour that maintains me*.
I said: Mighty men have encamped against me,
Surrounding me with all their instruments of war.
Arrows they let loose unceasingly
And javelins flashing like tree-devouring fire.
*Like the thunder of mighty waters is the uproar of their
                                                    clamour*,
A tempestuous cloud-burst for the ruin of many.
To the very skies break through *outcry and roar*,
While their waves mount high.
And I, my heart *melted like water*, I clung to Thy
                                                    Covenant.
But they, *their feet will be caught in the net they spread
                                                    for me*,
Into the snares they hid for me will they fall.
But my feet stand on level ground.
In the assemblies I will bless Thy Name.

process. Many investigators are inclined to accept the Aristeas letter on this point also and place the translation of the Pentateuch in the third century B.C. We are, however, on surer ground in fixing the later time limit, thanks to the prologue to the Book of Jesus Sirach (see p. 114). From this it emerges that not only the Law but also 'the Prophets and other books' were accessible in Greek by about 180 B.C.

The protracted origin of the Septuagint would in itself make one expect differences in style, and in fact a textual comparison between the Septuagint and the Hebrew text that has come down to us from the Jews shows that the individual translators set to work quite differently. A number of books are translated word for word, others are more freely rendered, and in some there are indications that the translation follows an original which now and then departs considerably from the Hebrew text known to us.

Conjectures of this nature received considerable support, following the discovery of numerous scrolls and fragments from the second century B.C. to the first century A.D. in the neighbourhood of Khirbet Qumran (p. 132). Amongst the discoveries were two Hebrew MSS of the Book of Jeremiah, one of which closely resembles a known Hebrew text, while the other confirms the shorter version known to us hitherto only from the Septuagint.

In the course of the first two centuries A.D., the Septuagint increasingly lost its importance amongst the Jews. Many factors contributed to this. After the destruction of Jerusalem in A.D. 70, the Jewish people developed a habit of intense retrospection into the heritage of their fathers. Amongst other things, this meant that from the various Hebrew texts of the Old Testament that had been used till then one particular version was chosen and proclaimed authoritative. Accordingly, the Jews of the Diaspora came to want a translation that reproduced as carefully as possible this text and no other. That the Septuagint could only imperfectly satisfy this need is clear.

In addition, owing to the rapid spread of Christianity to Gentile proselyte non-Hebrew-speaking communities, the Greek Septuagint became the Holy Scripture of the Early Church. In discussions between Jews and Christians, the latter were in the habit of quoting the Septuagint which, as a result of its very free renderings, sometimes incorporated changes of meaning. A famous example is found in Isaiah 7:14. As the Septuagint had rendered the Hebrew word 'almah by 'Virgin' the Christians saw in this passage a prophecy which found its fulfilment in the Virgin Birth of Jesus, whereas the Jews pointed out that the Hebrew text did not refer to a virgin but to a young woman. Finally, the value of the Septuagint was also diminished in Jewish eyes by the fact that the Christians regarded it as a living text that might be freely interpreted by additional writings.

All those factors finally led the Jews to reject the Septuagint and favour other translations. Two of these were to be carried out in the course of the second century A.D. by Aquila (ca. A.D. 130?) and Theodotion (ca. A.D. 190?). Whether the translation of Symmachus is to be seen in this context has been debated for some time. Various considerations, however, suggest that it is to be linked with Jewish-Christian circles, which in the first centuries A.D. played a not unimportant role in trans-Jordan, Syria, and Cyprus. Besides these translations known to us by name, there must have been at least three further translations,

Codex Aureus, from the monastery of St. Emmeran, ca. 870 (Bavarian State Library, Munich). Depicted here are Chris the four Evangelists, and four scenes from the Bible. Front board of oak, ornamented with gold leaf, precious stone pearls, and filigree work.

but we can no longer say whether they contained the complete Old Testament or only single books like the Psalms.

That we know anything at all about these translations, we owe entirely to the great Christian scholar Origen (185–254) who, it appears, gathered all the textual material of the Old Testament known in his time and presented it in a complete critical edition. The name Hexapla (Gk. 'sixfold') was given to this edition, because it presented the material gathered by Origen for the great majority of Old Testament writings, in six parallel columns. The first column contained the Hebrew text in the form familiar to us. The second column reproduced the Hebrew text in Greek transcription. Then followed the four translations of Aquila, Symmachus, the Septuagint, and Theodotion. In the case of some of the books, like the Psalms already mentioned, a further fifth, sixth, and seventh translations were drawn upon by Origen. These we usually designate as Quinta, Sexta, and Septima.

Unfortunately, except for a few fragments, this work, which would have been so informative for the Greek tradition of the Old Testament, has been lost. Presumably this unhappy outcome was a direct result of its vast size. According to an ancient tradition, the Hexapla is said to have numbered about 6000 pages and to have comprised 54 volumes. Few scribes would have had the courage to set about making a copy of such a monumental work. Generally they limited themselves to giving the text of the Septuagint from the fifth column. This was completely understandable. Origen had drawn on the rest of the textual material precisely because he wanted to revise the text of the Septuagint on the broadest possible basis.

If one contented oneself with the rendering in Origen's fifth column, then one sacrificed only the possibility of verifying, there and then, Origen's every decision on textual criticism. In modern terms, instead of an expensive, cumbersome complete edition, readers preferred an inexpensive working version, edited according to critical standards. This was completely sufficient for the daily use of the Old Testament. The Codex Colberto-Sarravanius from the fourth or fifth century offers us an example of a student's edition of this kind. It contains, with omissions, the Greek translation of Genesis 31 to Judges 21 in the version revised by Origen.

Origen's revision did not remain the only one in the history of the Septuagint. According to Jerome, there were three revisions about A.D. 400 in the Eastern Church. In the area between Constantinople and Antioch people followed the revision of Lucian. In Egypt the revision by Hesychius of the Egyptian text was commonly adopted and, in the provinces of Palestine that lay between, Origen's text had found general recognition. In the ensuing period, new textual forms developed. Readings of one revision infiltrated into another, and other re-revised texts mingled with texts that had undergone only a single revision.

All this makes it extraordinarily difficult to reconstruct the original text of the Septuagint. The manuscript tradition of the Septuagint unfortunately did not take shape till the fourth century A.D. Three great MSS especially may be mentioned here, of which two are already known to us from the previous section: the Codex Vaticanus, the Codex Sinaiticus, and the Codex Alexandrinus, which although they have considerable omissions, contain between them the whole of the Old Testa-

ment. We have admittedly a few fragments which are considerably older. These include the Chester Beatty papyri from the second to the fourth centuries A.D., mentioned in connection with the New Testament. In these several books of the Old Testament have come down to us in a more or less fragmentary form. Taking us much further back are two other papyri in the John Rylands Library in Manchester. Both may originate from the second century B.C. and so take us, if our reasoning above is correct, straight back to the time when we suppose the Septuagint to have had its origin. True, they contain only a few verses from Deuteronomy, only a tiny section from the whole Old Testament. So long as good fortune does not present us with new discoveries of texts from an earlier period, we are left to arrange the existing MSS in smaller or greater groups of related texts and, by comparison of those groups, to infer the possible original texts. This task was undertaken some decades ago by the Septuagint Commission of the Göttingen Society of Biblical Knowledge. Their findings are presented to us in the critical editions of the separate books of the Old Testament that have been published to date.

5. THE OLD TESTAMENT IN HEBREW

This section could with justification be called 'the Old Testament in the Synagogue,' for from soon after the return from the Exile till late in the Middle Ages, the Hebrew tradition of the Old Testament was limited to Jewish circles and there it was preserved by its ritual use in the synagogue (see p. 167).

The origin and shaping of the various parts of the Old Testament are more fully described in the chapters that follow. Here we may content ourselves with a few general comments.

In the centuries that followed the Exile the 'Jewish people' did not consist only of a small group within a certain area. Jerusalem was, and still is, the focal point, but beyond it there lived the millions of Jews of the Diaspora: in Egypt, Babylon, Syria, and in cities of the Roman Empire, indeed in the town of Rome itself. In all those communities an attempt was made to follow the Jewish way of life. Jews met in the synagogue to sing the Psalms, to read and expound the Law and the Prophets (and that included the Books of Joshua, Judges, 1 & 2 Samuel, 1 & 2 Kings, Isaiah, Jeremiah, Ezekiel, and the twelve Minor Prophets). The other books, known as the 'Writings,' with the exception of the Psalms did not enjoy the same esteem everywhere.

The history of the Samaritan Pentateuch provides us with one of our few firm reference points (p. 112). This establishes that by the fourth century B.C. the Pentateuch and probably the Former Prophets (the historical books Joshua to 2 Kings, excluding Ruth) and the Latter Prophets (Isaiah to Malachi, excluding Lamentations and Daniel) were a recognized collection of Holy Scriptures. Though the work of the Chronicler (1 and 2 Chronicles, Ezra, and Nehemiah) was set down soon after the Jewish-Samaritan schism, it was not accommodated in this part of the Old Testament. Each of these parts has in fact its own individual line of development, which stretches back in part to the time before the beginning of the monarchy. Thus many of the traditions which later became part of the Pentateuch underwent their first development in that early period. These include the

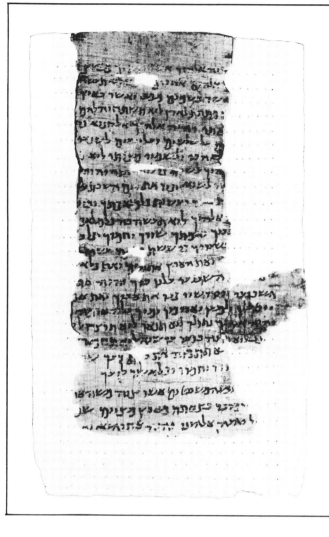

The Nash Papyrus cites the Decalogue as found in Exodus 20 : 2ff and Deuteronomy 5 : 6ff. Where the two traditions diverge, the text follows sometimes the version in Exodus (lines 9, 13, 14) and sometimes that in Deuteronomy (lines 17, 19). In some instances the papyrus gives its own version, departing from both Exodus and Deuteronomy (lines 1, 10, 11, 18, 24). With some differences lines 22-23 reproduce Deuteronomy 4 : 45. At the end of line 23 begins the well known Shema' Yisrael (Hear, O Israel).

1. . . . Yahweh, your God, who . . . out of the land of Eg . . . *(out of the house of bondage)*
2. . . . other gods before me. You must not make . . .
3. . . . that in heaven above and that in (the) earth . . .
4. . . . under the earth. You shall not bow down to them . . .
5. . . . I, Yahweh your God, am a jealous God, visiting . . .
6. . . . the third and fourth generation of those who hate me . . .
7. . . . of those who love me and keep my commandments. You shall not
8. . . . your God in vain, for Yahweh will not hold (him) guiltless . . .
9. . . . his name in vain. *Remember* the sabbath day . . .
10. . . . you shall labour and do all your work, but *on* the day . . .
11. . . . your God, *in it* you shall not do any work . . .
12. . . . your manservant and your maidservant, your ox and your ass and all
13. . . . in your gates, for *in six days Y(ahweh) made* . . .
14. . . . *and earth, the sea and all that* . . .
15. . . . the seventh. Therefore Yahweh blessed . . .
16. . . . the seventh and he hallowed it. Honour your father and your mother
17. . . . *it go well with you* and that your days may be long in the land . . .
18. . . . Yahweh, your God, gives you. You shall not *commit adultery*. You shall not *kill*
19. . . . You shall not bear false witness against your neighbour. You shall not covet . . .
20. . . . You shall not covet your neighbour's house, his field . . .
21. . . . his ox, or his ass, or anything that is your neighbour's . . .
22. . . . and the ordinances, which Moses laid upon . . .
23. . . . in the wilderness, when they came out of the land of Egypt. Hear . . .
24. . . . Yahweh is our God, Yahweh, *it is he* alone. Well now . . .

stories about the Patriarchs, their sojourn in Egypt and the Exodus, the reoccupation of the Promised Land, and the origin of the world. Those 'sacred stories' lived in the hearts and minds of the people long before they were established in writing for the first time.

This amorphous unity of the sacred books was not sharply defined till the Synod of Jamnia ca. A.D. 100. Perhaps as a reaction against the growth of Christianity, the Palestinian experts in the Scriptures, after long deliberations, drew up a list of sacred books, in which a number of writings are lacking which were apparently held in esteem by other groups of Jews. This excluded not only all the Apocalyptic books (with the exception of the Book of Daniel) but also a number of books which had found their way into the Septuagint. As part of the Septuagint, these have long been regarded in the Christian Church as a definite part of the Old Testament.

The Synod of Jamnia also chose one of the variety of texts that were circulating and pronounced it alone to be authentic. This has come to be known as the Masoretic Text and from the date of its establishment only insignificant differences appear in the codices of the Hebrew Old Testament, which can be regarded as all representing the same basic text. This is the text underlying all printed copies of the Hebrew Old Testament up to Kittel's second edition of the *Biblia Hebraica* (above).

A characteristic of this text was that, in accordance with contemporary custom, it reproduced only the consonants and not the vowels of the words. One and the same sequence of consonants, *m-l-k* (say), could therefore convey various meanings, and it depended on a given context whether it was read for example, as *melek*, 'king' or *malak*, 'he ruled.'

This required from anyone who was to read a passage of the Scriptures at a service a high degree of literary acumen, familiarity with the text, and a knowledge of Hebrew. In the course of time the necessity grew to determine clearly the pronunciation of the old Hebrew text. Probably under the influence of Syriac and later also of Arabic, in which vowels were indicated by dots and strokes below and above the consonants, a similar system was devised for Hebrew (we speak of 'pointing' the text). It took many years, however, before an agreed system established itself amongst Jewish scholars, who were traditionally called Masoretes (from Heb. *Masorah*).

In this the greatest share of the credit is rightly accorded to the Ben Asher family, who for several generations devoted themselves to clarifying these contentious questions. Some MSS of the eighth to tenth centuries bear witness to their work. Among these are the Codex Cairensis from 895 and, in particular, the famous master Codex from Aleppo, dating from 930. At one time this last contained the whole of the Old Testament. In spite of its eventful history—it was in Jerusalem from the eleventh century, later in Cairo, and from the beginning of the Middle Ages in Aleppo—it survived the centuries unscathed. At present it is back in Jerusalem. Unfortunately the beginning and end of this

Fragment of a page from a Coptic Gospel, representing the Baptism in the Jordan. This 'evangeliarium' was produced between 1178 and 1180 and is a translation from Greek into Coptic by Michael, Bishop of Damietta. It comes from the library of Cardinal Mazarin (Bibliothèque Nationale, Paris).

unique MS were damaged in the confusion of the post-war era. Both these codices were pointed by relatives of the Ben Asher family, and provided with comments both in the margins of the various books of the Old Testament and at the end.

In addition, we possess still another series of MSS, which according to the colophon (the tailpiece added by the scribe) were based on the codices of the Ben Asher family. To these MSS belongs the Codex Leningradensis of 1008, which as we have already seen in the second section, is the basis of the third edition of the *Biblia Hebraica*.

The services of another Masoretic school have with the passage of time been overshadowed by the fame of the Ben Asher family. This school was founded by the Ben Naphtali family, which had participated over several generations in the elucidation of the system of pointing. In certain details each family went its own way, but we have much less evidence of the manner in which the Ben Naphtali family pointed its texts. The Codex Reuchlinianus from 1105 reflects their influence.

In the course of the Middle Ages, the MSS of both schools influenced each other, and then one version of the text appeared which smoothed out the differences and it was this reconciled version that made its way into all printed copies of the Old Testament up to the second edition of the *Biblia Hebraica*.

The reliability of the Masoretic tradition was long contested. Certainty seemed unattainable as scholars could not get further back even with their oldest MSS than the end of the eighth century. With the help of fragments found in the old Synagogue of Cairo the time limit could be pushed back to the seventh century. But still between this point of time and the emergence of the books of the Old Testament stretched a gap of over ten

centuries. This was only inadequately bridged when, at the beginning of this century, W. L. Nash discovered in Egypt a strip of papyrus which probably dates from the first century A.D. It contains Deuteronomy 6:4ff and the Decalogue which partly follows the wording of Exodus 20:2ff, partly the version of Deuteronomy 5:6ff.

It was therefore a sensation of the first order when, from 1947 onwards, a great quantity of MSS and fragments dating from the second century B.C. to the first century A.D. was discovered in the surroundings of Khirbet Qumran (see pp. 132ff). Amongst the MSS, which are unfortunately in very many cases extremely fragmentary, there were many transcriptions of books of the Old Testament. In addition, the investigators also came upon Hebrew fragments of Tobit (hitherto unknown in Hebrew) and the Wisdom of Jesus the son of Sirach (hitherto known in Hebrew only in fragments found in Cairo at the beginning of this century). The texts of many of these finds, like the famous Isaiah scroll from the first cave to be discovered, approximate closely to the Masoretic text that is known to us. But there are also some MSS which belong to other textual traditions. To these belong the fragments of the Book of Jeremiah already mentioned, which confirm the shorter version of the Septuagint. One partly preserved scroll of Exodus throughout represents a type of text otherwise known to us only from the Samaritan version of the Pentateuch.

Only some of the MSS discovered have so far been published, and it is very possible that further publications will allow us to penetrate into the early history of the text that is the common ancestor of them all. The value of the MSS published to date consists in the fact that, in the majority of cases, they confirm the great antiquity of the Hebrew text that has come down to us. That many passages were composed in early times is certain. One of the earliest is the Song of Deborah in Judges 5:

> Most blessed of women be Jael,
> the wife of Heber the Kenite,
> of tent-dwelling women most blessed.
> He asked water and she gave him milk,
> she brought him curds in a lordly bowl.
> She put her hand to the tent peg
> and her right hand to the workmen's mallet;
> she struck Sisera a blow,
> she crushed his head,
> she shattered and pierced his temple.
> He sank, he fell,
> he lay still at her feet;
> at her feet he sank, he fell;
> where he sank, there he fell dead.
> Out of the window she peered,
> the mother of Sisera gazed through the lattice:
> 'Why is his chariot so long in coming?
> Why tarry the hoofbeats of his chariots?'

Our introductory survey has led us back from the Bible today, through the printed version and the MSS traditions to its first beginnings. In the following chapters, the many factors which made possible the origin, growth, development, and final form of the Bible will be investigated at greater length.

II. THE BIBLE - A WRITTEN BOOK

The development of writing that made the Bible as a book possible.

1. THE MIRACLE OF HUMAN COMMUNICATION

Throughout the ages man's desire to give expression to his thoughts, feelings, and experience of life has been an essential part of his nature, and it is nowadays taken for granted that language and writing should play a principal part in the realization of this need. Yet the art of writing emerged relatively late in the history of man's development, and does not in fact appear to go back much further than about 3000 B.C. Before this there was no written literature of any kind and no means of literary expression though man had long since learned to communicate with his fellow-beings through the medium of speech. For this reason the period which preceded the emergence of a written language is known as the 'pre-literary' or prehistoric period.

Perhaps the most striking proof of the faculty for expression developed by early man is the large number of drawings which have been found in caves and on rock faces. These drawings by the ancestors of modern man date from the period of the last Ice Age, and have been discovered in more than a hundred caves, mostly in Spain and France. The entrances to these caves are usually very narrow, but many of them open out into a spacious area resembling a hall or chapel. The walls and sometimes even the ceilings of these chambers are covered with figures of animals scratched on to the surface and then coloured in black, red, white, or brown. They are the mammoths, bison, reindeer, wild horses, and other animals which primitive man hunted or tamed. The oldest drawings consist of little more than outlines, but later ones are executed in much greater detail. From these drawings we can deduce something of how men lived in the last Ice Age.

The caves themselves do not appear to have been their permanent dwelling-places, because excavation of the cave-floors has revealed a total absence of any real signs of occupation. The tribe probably lived in primitive huts or tents just outside the caves or against their entrances. The underground chambers at the end of the narrow entrances were possibly sacral areas, where cultic rites and ceremonies took place. Underlying the whole cultic practice would be the notion that word and action, image and actuality, were intimately connected with one another, and that the drawing or representation somehow influenced the thing represented. If you damaged the likeness of an object, you struck at the object itself. This is why the numerous hunting-scenes often exhibit wounded, dead, or trapped animals.

A sense of everything constituting an interrelated whole finds positive expression as well, particularly in the pictures of pairing animals and in figurines of the female form with very pronounced sexual characteristics. These were probably attempts to ensure the fertility so desperately needed in real life. Some drawings seem to depict cultic activities. More than seventy of those which have been found represent sorcerer-like figures wearing animal-masks and dancing to the sound of the flute.

In prehistoric times man fashioned most of his implements out of stone. This period is therefore known as the Stone Age, and is sub-divided into the Old, Middle, and New Stone Ages (Paleolithic, Mesolithic, and Neolithic, see diagram, pp. 22-3). Within prehistory as a whole the first stage (the Paleolithic) is again sub-divided into an early, a middle, and a late period.

Since 1964 an American expedition led by J. B. Pritchard has been investigating the mound at Tell es-Sa'idiyeh in the Jordan valley. This entails working very slowly and meticulously so that the remains of ancient civilizations are brought to view in as sound a condition as possible. The smallest find may be of considerable value. Pottery, which made its first appearance in Neolithic times, has a particularly important role to play, as its material, method of manufacture, shape, and decoration can be used to date this or that layer of habitation with a fair degree of accuracy, and also to indicate how the site is related in certain respects to other ruins already investigated.

The early Paleolithic period saw the development of stone tools from rough, almost wholly unfashioned flints, to implements with somewhat ragged but sharp cutting edges. These were produced by using one stone to strike chips off another. They were made by creatures who did not belong to the human species proper, who have left behind them no signs of artistic or religious expression, not even of the most primitive kind. The material yielded is classified as belonging to the group known as Pithecanthropus, which included Java, Peking, and Heidelberg man.

The middle Paleolithic period saw the development of tools of pared or rubbed stone. These are well shaped and have a comparatively smooth cutting edge. They seem to be the work of two groups of manlike creatures. (1) The pre-sapiens group, including Swanscombe, Steinheim, Ehringsdorf, and Fontechevade man. The last of these is regarded as already belonging to the species of *Homo sapiens* and is identified with the Tayacine. (2) The neanderthal group, including Rhodesian, Palestine, and Neanderthal man. The last of these was responsible for the Mousterian culture. Although of these only Neanderthal man buried his dead, he nevertheless appears to have had fewer human characteristics than the pre-sapiens group. He too, therefore, does not rate as one of modern man's direct ancestors.

All these cultures were produced by small itinerant communities of hunters.

The late Paleolithic period ushered in the age of *Homo*

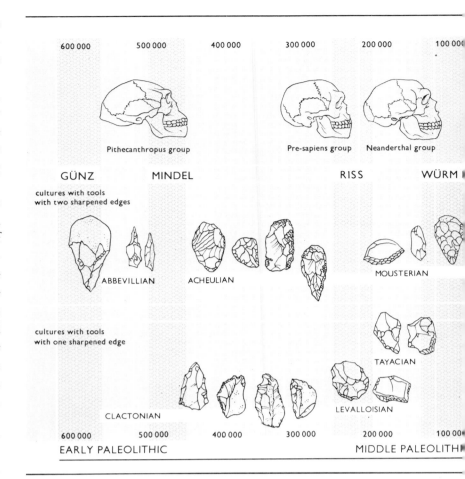

Small sack-shaped jugs with loop handles, that is, handles protruding a fair way above the rim, are among the earthenware of a people who, with two other groups of nomads, entered Palestine from the east and north at about 3200 B.C. They settled in villages out of which towns were to develop several centuries later. They would bury a number of corpses in one cave and would provide them with utensils, including these small sack-shaped jugs. Graves of this sort have been discovered at Tell es-Sultan (Jericho), Tell en-Nasbeh (Mizpah?), Tell el-Far'ah (Tirzah) and Tell el-Mutesellim (Megiddo).

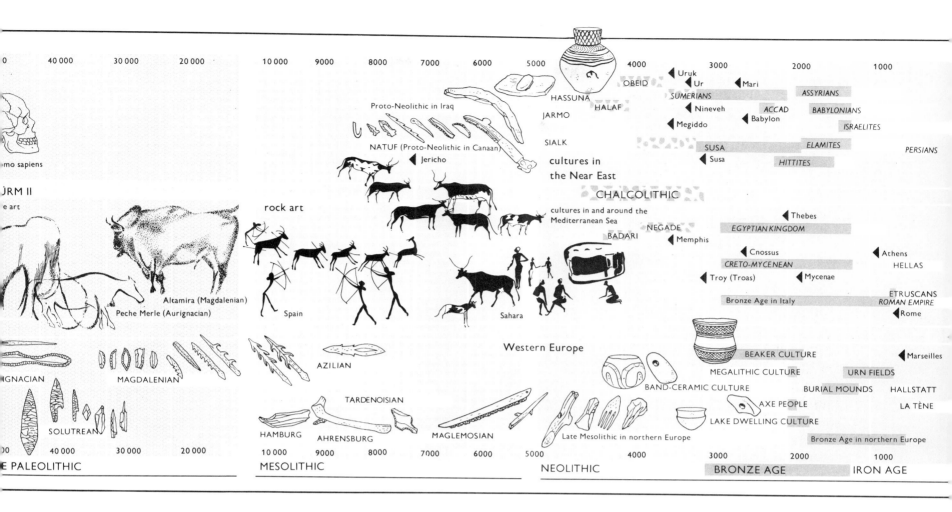

The chart shows a timeline from 40 000 to 1 000 with various cultures and artifacts:

Top scale: 40 000, 30 000, 20 000, 10 000, 9000, 8000, 7000, 6000, 5000, 4000, 3000, 2000, 1000

Proto-Neolithic in Iraq
NATUF (Proto-Neolithic in Canaan)
Jericho
cultures in the Near East

HASSUNA, JARMO, SIALK, HALAF, OBEID, SUMERIANS, Uruk, Ur, Mari, Nineveh, ACCAD, Babylon, Megiddo, SUSA, Susa, ASSYRIANS, BABYLONIANS, ISRAELITES, ELAMITES, HITTITES, PERSIANS

CHALCOLITHIC

cultures in and around the Mediterranean Sea
NEGADE, BADARI, Memphis, Thebes, EGYPTIAN KINGDOM, CRETO-MYCENEAN, Cnossus, Troy (Troas), Mycenae, Athens, HELLAS, Bronze Age in Italy, ETRUSCANS, ROMAN EMPIRE, Rome

rock art
Altamira (Magdalenian)
Peche Merle (Aurignacian)
Spain
Sahara

Western Europe

BEAKER CULTURE, MEGALITHIC CULTURE, URN FIELDS, BAND-CERAMIC CULTURE, BURIAL MOUNDS, HALLSTATT, AXE PEOPLE, LA TÈNE, LAKE DWELLING CULTURE, Bronze Age in northern Europe, Marseilles

mo sapiens
ÜRM II
e art

AURIGNACIAN, MAGDALENIAN, SOLUTREAN
AZILIAN, TARDENOISIAN, HAMBURG, AHRENSBURG, MAGLEMOSIAN
Late Mesolithic in northern Europe

Bottom scale: 40 000, 30 000, 20 000, 10 000, 9000, 8000, 7000, 6000, 5000, 4000, 3000, 2000, 1000
PALEOLITHIC, MESOLITHIC, NEOLITHIC, BRONZE AGE, IRON AGE

sapiens and is represented by the finds at Cromagnon, Combe Capelle, Predmost, and Grimaldi. The artistic skills manifested by man in this period reveal him as being already in full command of his faculties. A corresponding development is reflected in the finds belonging to the Aurignacian and Magdalenian periods. Tools now exhibit a high degree of workmanship, and no longer consist exclusively of flint. Implements of horn, bone, and ivory have been found in plenty, and their shape suggests that they were meant to be fitted to a haft or handle. The centre of this culture lay in southern France and Spain, where the prevailing climate, influenced by the retreating glaciers of the last Ice Age, was arctic, and where the tundras supported large herds of reindeer, bison, aurochs, mammoths, and horses. With this food supply, and with the numerous caves which abound in this area as his winter retreat and refuge, man was able to maintain himself extremely well.

Characteristic of the Mesolithic Age which followed is an abundance of microliths, small fragments of flint fitted together to form a cutting-plane along the length of a shaft of bone, horn, or wood. This period began in Europe with the retreat and disappearance of the glaciers of the last Ice Age. The milder climate favoured the growth of thick forests, which became the haunt of other kinds of game. The Magdalenian culture was impoverished by the disappearance of the big game herds. It was succeeded by cultures hunting smaller wild animals and fish (Azilian, Tardenoisian). The first animal to be domesticated was the dog, possibly in this period.

Meanwhile, the descendants of the herd-hunters clung to the steppes uncovered by the ice-caps, which were now retreating farther to the north. These people established the Hamburg and Ahrensburg cultures in central Europe. When this area also became covered with forest, there appeared a new culture of forest hunters, known as the Maglemosan culture. A typical product of this period was the strong stone or horn axe, with a hole for the insertion of a handle. This was stout enough for felling and splitting trees.

Elsewhere, the great volume of melt-water from the glaciers brought abundant rain. The Sahara, which was for this reason an area rich in game, became the habitation of tribes who continued the artistic tradition of the Magdalenian culture. Here, as in Spain, there emerged a culture which continued into the Neolithic Age, with rock drawings illustrative of the transition from a culture of hunters and food-gatherers to one of a pastoral type.

In Palestine the Natuf culture (so called because of the finds made at Wadi en-Natuf, northwest of Jerusalem) is likewise characterized by the use of microliths. This came into being at the same time as the Tardenoisian culture in Europe, but is distinguished from it by the special care which was taken in the burial of the dead. From three to six people were usually buried side by side. The head, neck, and arms of some of the deceased were ornamented with bone beads, and they were frequently laid in a doubled-up position, with the knees touching the chin. They were a people of small stature, approximately five feet tall. Their eyes were set wide apart; and they were long-headed, or dolichocephalic. There are clear indications that these people were in a process of transition from a nomadic to a settled mode of life.

The Neolithic Age saw the appearance of polished stone tools of a highly efficient kind. It was in this period that the biggest and most revolutionary change ever accomplished by man took place. He freed himself of his dependence on hunting and gathering as his sole means of livelihood, and exploited on a large scale those sources of food and material which have been of such great importance to him ever since. He began sowing and reaping crops, breeding animals from stock, and mining the earth for flint. He also developed his technical skills, and learned how to tame animals and harness their energy for his own purposes, to make pottery, and to weave.

The development of land cultivation appears to have come about in Iraq, where the find at Jarmo has disclosed the earliest known settlement of this kind. The Iraq region was also perhaps the cradle of the megalithic tomb culture, which was probably spread by traders along the seaboard areas of Europe (as witness the *hunebedden*, 'graves of the giants,' in the Netherlands). The enormous improvement in living conditions brought about by settled farming was followed by a steady increase in population. This meant that small groups were constantly breaking away and moving off in search of fresh territory. In this way the new culture spread through Asia Minor, Egypt, Asia, and, by way of the Danube valley, eventually to Europe (Band-ceramic cultures). Another route taken by the spreading agricultural economy ran through Spain. Among the places settled by these cultivators was the region of the Swiss lakes. On the sites of their lake dwellings many remains have been found, including implements of stone and bone, remnants of woven fabrics, fishing nets, and plain undecorated earthenware.

In the Chalcolithic period the swiftest development occurred in the villages of the Nile valley and the basin of the Tigris and Euphrates. The growth of large populations in these comparatively small areas meant that barter could make all sorts of equipment generally available and that progress could be made in a variety of specialized skills.

It was out of this development that in the early part of the Bronze Age there emerged the city culture which in the course of time spread from the Near East to other parts of the world. The city culture of Jericho, which had come into being about 7000 B.C., was exceptional in developing outside Egypt and Mesopotamia. It was in the Bronze Age, too, that the art of writing made its appearance, an event that for the Near East marked the close of the prehistoric period. In western and northern Europe progress did not take place till centuries later. In fact, it was not until the Iron Age that a city culture emerged there.

2. THE DEVELOPMENT OF WRITING

About 4500 B.C., when the Stone Age was being superseded by the Chalcolithic Age in the Near East, Egypt and Mesopotamia very slowly began to emerge as the two main centres of civilization in the world of that time. Another thousand years were to elapse, however, before this civilization reached the point at which it was able to develop the art of writing.

Although the art of the Stone Age offers remarkable instances of how primitive man envisaged life and reacted to it, the pictures and drawings which he made were only an indirect way of conveying his thoughts and feelings. He was no doubt able to communicate these by means of the spoken word, but he could not record them. In order to do this he would have needed to discover some way of 'congealing' speech, by finding graphic symbols to represent sounds. Such a system of representation could only be developed at a much later stage in man's history.

Troas
ca. 2700 city with walls and gates

HITTITES
ca. 1600 Hittite hieroglyphic and cuneiform systems

Karabel *bas-relief on rock of Hittite god ca. 1400*

Izmir
ca. 2500 city culture

Sardis
capital of Lydia ca. 600

Ephesus
ca. 650 temple of Artemis-Cybele

Cnossus

CAPHTOR = CRETE
ca. 1900 Cretan hieroglyphs
ca. 1600 Linear-A script
ca. 1400 Linear-B script

ALASHIYA = CYPRUS
in 2nd millennium trade relations with Syria, Asia Minor, Egypt, Crete, and Greece

PHOENICIA
trade relations with Egypt, Assyria, Babylonia, Syria, Palestine, Asia Minor, Crete, and Greece

MEDITERRANEAN SEA

"GREAT SEA"
"UPPER SEA"

Tanis

EGYPT
ca. 3200 beginning of hieroglyphic writing

On this and all subsequent colour maps the present-day ground cover is shown by the following sequence of colours:

- forest, shrub, steppe, and mountain vegetation
- cultivated areas
- mixed dry forest
- mixed temperate forest
- irrigated valleys and plains
- desert and arid regions
- cultivated Mediterranean areas
- ruins
- swamp

Memphis

Nile

Oxyrhynchus

Akhetaton
Tell el-'Amarna

Thebes
ca. 1370 clay tablets with Mesopotamian cuneiform

BLACK SEA

CASPIAN

SEA

Alaça Hüyük *royal tombs 2400*
Hattushash (Boghaz Köi)
Hittite capital 1600-1200

Alishar Hüyük
city culture ca. 2400

(Kültepe) Kanish
city culture ca. 2400

Halys

Karatepe
bilingual inscription ca. 900

Zenjirli

Haran *flourishing city ca. 1700*

Carchemish
important Hittite base

Halba (Aleppo)
Nerab

Nineveh
*destroyed 612;
important library of
Ashurbanipal (668-629)*

ASSYRIA

Orontes

Ugarit
*ca. 1500 Ugaritic cuneiform and Egyptian and Hittite hieroglyphs,
Sumerian, Babylonian, and Assyrian cuneiform*

Ashur
city culture 2500-612

Hamath

Tadmor

Mari
important city 3000-1700

Tigris

Kadesh
*ca. 1285 battle between
Egypt and the Hittites*

Euphrates

Byblos
1300 pseudo-hieroglyphic script

Tell Asmar
alabaster praying figures ca. 2500

Sidon

Damascus

Accad?
*early cuneiform called Accadian after this city;
flourished ca. 2300*

Tyre

Acco

ACCAD

Babylon
centre of culture 1750-450

Susa

Tabor
Megiddo

BABYLONIA

Nippur

Shechem

Deir 'Alla

Isin

Lagash
city culture 3000-2000

abne Yam
Ashkelon

Gezer
Jericho
Jerusalem
Beth-shemesh

Uruk
ca. 3000 city culture

Gaza
Hebron

Ur
ca. 2400 royal tombs

SUMERIA
*ca. 3000 cuneiform ; taken over by Semitic conquerors
ca. 2400 and gradually spread throughout the Near East*

SINAI

PERSIAN
GULF
"LOWER
SEA"

rabit el Khadim
1500 proto-Sinaitic inscriptions

Oasis of Teima
residence of Nabonidus of Babylon ca. 550

0   50   100   150   200 km.

0   50   100   125 mls.

RED
SEA

To the west of modern Jericho rises the mound of Tell es-Sultan, which is about 70 feet high and has a surface area of about 10 acres. Between 1952 and 1958 a British expedition unearthed in this mound a tower that is still 30 feet high. This tower was part of the defences of a settlement which existed there at around 7000 B.C. At the eastern base of the tower is a low entrance, giving access to a steep flight of steps, twenty-two in all, leading to the upper level of the tower. A building like this shows that, if only intermittently, men had already begun the transition from the nomadic life of the hunter to a settled existence based on farming by about 7000 B.C.

Archaeological investigations have shown that writing as a skill was first practised in the earliest type of city culture which flourished simultaneously in both Egypt and Mesopotamia. Whether it also originated in this area is a question which has not so far been satisfactorily answered. It could be argued either that writing developed independently in both regions, or that one took it over from the other. Contacts had existed between them from an early date. Another possibility is that there may have been a third, unknown culture which influenced both regions, but has since vanished without trace. The future will perhaps bring a solution to this problem.

In spite of the lack of concrete evidence, it is possible to reconstruct in broad outline the process by which writing must have originated. With the passing of time, the growth of population in the basins of the Nile and the Euphrates encouraged more complex social and economic organization. Specific tasks became the responsibility of individual members of the community, and this division of labour made men dependent on each other for their daily needs. They were tied not only to each other, but also to the soil, which they cultivated for their food. The productive capacity of the land therefore became a vital issue, and as the population increased under settled conditions, the fertility of the land had to be increased also. Religious ceremonies, aimed at invoking the help of those supernatural powers which regulated the seasons and sent the rain and the flood-waters—factors which men depended on but had no control over—now became an essential part of social life, in which priests played a leading role.

Where man could help himself in these matters, however, he did so. The annual floods were only a blessing to him so long as he could control them. Otherwise there was always the danger of too much or too little water, with famine as the consequence either way. He therefore devised a system of regulating the flow of water by directing it through channels and, incidentally, irrigating a much larger area of land. On the one hand these measures led to the establishment of a religious cult of state proportions, with a priestly caste enjoying increased power and prestige. On the other hand, the development and maintenance of the irrigation system, which required the use of hydraulic works, called for considerable technical expertise.

The same developments took place in other spheres of life. All kinds of specialized occupations, trades, and crafts now became necessary: state officials for the public works, temple ministers for the practice of religion, hydro-engineers, brickmakers, house-builders and shipwrights, leather-workers and tool-makers and so on. Very soon there was a growing number of traders and merchants, whose business was to use the surplus production of a given article to supply another area.

In a growing society of this kind there was an ever-increasing need to mark goods and possessions more clearly. This accounts for the large number of seals, in the form of cylinders and rings, that have been discovered. The supply of goods to the temple, and more especially to one's fellow citizens and to other countries, required that some sort of tally should be kept by both parties. Trading on any considerable scale would not otherwise have been feasible. At first, such records were simple enough—merely a picture of the article or animal traded, plus strokes or notches to indicate the numbers involved. But the more large-scale and complicated commerce became, the more these methods of 'book-keeping' had to be simplified. It was as a result of this

The Nile with Luxor and Karnak, site of the capital city of Thebes in the period of the New Kingdom (1575-1087 B.C.). The celebrated Tombs of the Kings are situated near the mountains on the west bank. The photograph shows why after the last Ice Age the lower course of the Nile offered conditions favourable to permanent agricultural settlement. The annual flooding deposited rich alluvial mud over a great part of the low-lying valley floor. In the valley, some 5 to 16 miles wide, it was possible for men to live in relative security, because the mountains and deserts to the east and west formed natural barriers against invasion. Furthermore as the river facilitated communications between settlements, it was not long before a centralized state emerged.

need that more abstract, functional written symbols gradually emerged.

Exactly how these symbols were developed into a system of writing is uncertain. What we do know, however, is that by the year 3000 B.C. or thereabouts writing was practised in both Egypt and Mesopotamia.

In the southern part of the Euphrates and Tigris basin the system was what is nowadays known as cuneiform. The symbols were composed of one or more strokes imprinted on wet clay by means of a stylus. This was held at an angle as a pencil is nowadays, and the tapered point, pressed into the clay, left a wedge-shaped mark (cuneiform means 'wedge-shaped'). Though this system represents a stage in the art of writing which is comparatively advanced, no examples of earlier methods have so far been discovered, perhaps because they were made on more perishable material, such as wood.

It is generally agreed, notwithstanding, that some kind of picture-writing must have preceded the cuneiform system, and that this had probably been developed by about 3500 B.C. Picture-writing would, however, mean using curves, and curves are troublesome to inscribe in soft clay. This is probably why small

set strokes of a linear kind gradually replaced other symbols. Any connection between these and the pictorial symbols out of which they developed was quickly lost. Writing was now free to become wholly abstract in its representation of what it had to communicate—a script based solely on deliberate choice and common agreement as to its use of symbols.

This Mesopotamian cuneiform system, also called Accadian, after the ancient city of Accad, survived for many centuries as an international written language, and did not disappear until the sixth century B.C., when the Persians began to use Aramaic as the official language of their empire. There were, of course, local variations, and in the course of the centuries the system underwent certain modifications. Literary documents of the Sumerian period dating from about 2600 B.C. therefore look very different from texts of a later date. The same is true of the texts of the Babylonian period (1700 B.C.), and of the Assyrian period (800 B.C.). These are not written with exactly the same symbols, though the script itself remained basically unchanged, and they may all therefore be quite properly classified as texts in the cuneiform script.

The Nile area has preserved a totally different system of

It is difficult to be sure of the purpose of this cylinder seal from Mesopotamia *(opposite, centre);* but after rolling on wet clay the figures on it, somewhat difficult to distinguish in intaglio, stand out sharply enough in relief *(left)*. In the middle one can see a crowned and bearded figure, grasping two upstanding bulls by the necks. To the right stands a half-animal creature flanked by two lions. On the left a similar creature is depicted, grasping the front paws of a lion with both hands whilst looking behind him. The scene may have been inspired by the ancient legends about Gilgamesh and his friend, the half-animal Enkidu, who was supposed to have slain the celestial bull. It would seem more likely, however, that this is a representation of the kind of tutelary god who according to Babylonian belief was assigned to each and every individual to protect him from demons, who were the cause of evil and disease. *Right:* the impression of a cylinder seal on which the sun-god, Shamash, and other gods are seen ascending and descending among the mountains of the east and of the west. The scene is probably based on the idea that in the course of his daily journey across the sky Shamash would descry and punish every evil deed. Notice also the river and the fish behind the second figure on the right. Both seals date from the third millennium B.C.

Fragments of two clay tablets from Uruk in Babylonia. The symbols still have partly recognizable shapes (e.g., an ear of corn and a star)—a clear indication that even cuneiform was originally a kind of picture-writing. As the symbols are not as yet reduced to the straight, angular lines of the cuneiform of Hammurabi's time (ca. 1700), these two fragments must date from the third millennium B.C., and probably from the Accadian dynasty (ca. 2300 B.C.).

A stele, 15 inches high, on which the Assyrian king, Ashurbanipal (668-629) is depicted in relief. On this commemorative stone the monarch is portrayed in a very traditional style. The basket of stones resting on the head was as early as the third millennium B.C. a symbol of building activity; but the script is formed in a manner typical of the last Assyrian period. The text first of all lists the building operations which the king had already carried out. Then comes a detailed account of how the king restored, with cypress and cedar, the main temple of the supreme god, Marduk—that is, the famous Esagila ('the house with the high top'), which stood close by the zikkurat in Babylon. He fitted new doors and gave vessels of gold, silver, copper, and iron. The text concludes with the usual curses against any who might venture to violate the sanctuary.

writing. Whereas in Mesopotamia people had to depend mainly on clay as their writing material, in this region the discovery was made that the papyrus plant, which grew in abundance along the banks of the Nile and was already used for making ropes, mats, and sandals, needed only a minimum of preparation before it was suitable for writing on with ink (see Chapter One). This probably occurred as early as the first dynasty, about 3000 B.C. It was the ancient Greeks who later gave this Egyptian writing the name of hieroglyphics ('sacred scratchings'), probably because they encountered this script mainly on the walls, pillars, and rock-faces of the holy sites of ancient Egypt, long after the papyrus scrolls had decayed or been buried beneath the dry sand.

This script remained in use for a very long time, and it was not until about A.D. 300 that it disappeared entirely. Perhaps the main reason for its continued existence was that it gradually underwent a simplifying process, which later produced two different kinds of script. The first was the hieratic script, which remained fairly close to the original and was used by the priests for religious purposes. The second was the demotic, an adaptation of the hieratic script to suit the every-day needs of the community. The fact that the Egyptians evolved modified scripts out of their ancient hieroglyphics rather than adopt an entirely new system is a sign of their sturdy traditionalism. In this respect the palace and the temple played a prominent part, by preserving over many centuries the use of the hieratic script for most of the official documents.

Hieroglyphics are more obviously a kind of picture-writing than the cuneiform script. But even in Egypt men were searching after new and simpler ways of writing. Three short undulating lines, for example, gave a stylized representation of water. In old Egyptian this was 'mw,' pronounced *moo*. Very soon these became modified to three notched strokes, which were then used to denote the two letters 'mw.' This sign could now be employed to indicate something which had no connection with water, for

Papyrus is a water-plant that was once very common in Egypt and still grows even today along the Blue Nile and the White Nile and also in the Jordan valley, as this photograph shows. The plant can reach a height of six or seven feet. In earlier times the leaves were used as a vegetable, the fibrous inner bark for rope, and the stalks for making small, lightweight boats. From the beginning of the third millennium B.C. people had known how to process the pith so as to obtain sheets on which one could write with ink. Papyrus remained in use as a writing material until the 3rd or 4th century A.D. Although frail and highly perishable, many papyri have been preserved, especially in the sand of such a dry country as Egypt.

instance 'Sh-m-w,' meaning summer, which was the very season when the water-level of the Nile was at its lowest. This process developed even further, and the Egyptians eventually had a different sign for each separate consonant. They might have evolved an alphabet out of this system, had it not been for their strong pictorial bent, which seems to have prevented them from accepting a totally abstract system of sign-writing. Instead, they continued to prefer a more figurative script, and left it to other nations to invent an alphabet.

By about 1900 B.C. the island of Crete had already developed a hieroglyphic script of its own. Archaeological finds have revealed that by this date trade relations already existed between Crete and the kingdom of the Pharaohs, but it is not possible to demonstrate any direct influence of the Egyptian hieroglyphics on the script of Crete, which seems to have evolved quite independently. Future investigations may be able to clarify this. Up to the present, however, this Cretan hieroglyphic script has not been deciphered, and the seal-stones which bear its symbols are too few in number to allow any philological conclusions to be drawn.

At a subsequent period other systems of writing were employed in Crete. These are known as Linear A, dating from about 1600 B.C., and Linear B, which made its appearance about 200 years later. The first has not so far been definitively deciphered, but the key to the second was discovered in 1950, when to the surprise of most philologists, it was found to represent a primitive Greek. Both systems are described as 'linear' because they consist more of short simple lines than of hieroglyphics or cuneiform symbols. This linear script was fairly short-lived. Natural disasters or political upheaval seem to have put an end to its development.

Mention must also be made of the systems of writing in use amongst the Hittites, whose power extended over the whole of

The Development of Cuneiform

From picture to symbol in Mesopotamia
The first sign is the representation of an *ox-head* (ca. 3500?). The second—for reasons unknown—has been given a quarter turn and is already somewhat more angular (3000). The third is cuneiform script of ca. 1700, already well developed. The fourth and last is the symbol used in the 8th and 7th centuries. *Meaning:* all these signs denote the word *alpu,* 'ox' or 'bull.'

The development of the pictorial representation of 'water'
The first sign depicts a stream or watercourse (ca. 3500?).
The second, for some obscure reason, has been given a quarter turn (ca. 3000).
The third and fourth are almost identical and date from the second and first millennia B.C.
Meaning: all these signs basically represent *mu,* 'water'; but the last two can also denote the sound 'aa'.

Examples of Cuneiform

The word 'Hezekiah,' as it appears on the Prism of Sennacherib

(III, 18), an Assyrian record of a military expedition to the west. The symbols are to be explained thus:
1. A single wedge ('arrowhead') as a symbol of 'one.' This wedge is also used to indicate that a personal name is about to follow, denoted by a small 'm.'
2. The syllable *ha,* and also *ku.*
3. „ „ *za,* and also *sa.*
4. „ „ *qi,* and also *qin* or *kin.*
5. Ideogram for *mu,* 'water,' but also the sound 'a.'
6. The sound 'u,' and also the syllable *sam* or *sha.*
 Consequently, the word runs: ᵐHa-za-qi-a-u. He was king of Judah from 716 to 687.

The word 'Jerusalem' as it appears on the Prism of Sennacherib (III, 28). Explanation of the symbols:
1. Ideogram for *alu,* 'city.' The function of this symbol here is simply to indicate that the name of a town or city follows. In transcription this is expressed as 'al,' in small letters.
2. The syllable *ur;* but also *liq, das,* etc.
3. The syllable *sa.*
4. The syllable *li* or *le.*
5. Ideogram for *sharu,* 'wind,' but also the syllable *im* or *em.*
6. Ideogram for *shumu,* 'name,' but also the syllable *mu.*
 Thus the word reads: ᵃˡUr-sa-li-im-mu.

A fragment from the temple at Medinet Habu, a small mound on the west bank of the Nile, near what was once Thebes. Rameses III (ca. 1180) built this sanctuary and in hieroglyphics and pictorial carvings left on the walls and pillars a permanent record of all his undertakings. On this fragment an unidentifiable god from the underworld proffers life (the knotted loop with the cross) to a Pharaoh, recognizable by the 'uraeus' (the small serpent) on his forehead. The text is too fragmentary to admit of any precise translation. On the righthand side it says something about life, good fortune, and prosperity being given. To the left are two cartouches. In the right hand one is R'-mn-hpr, meaning 'Ra's coming to be is constant.' In the cartouche on the left is Dhwty [the god Thoth]-ms-nfr-hpr.s, that is to say, 'Thoth has caused her coming-to-be in beauty.' It is not clear, however, to whom these names are meant to refer. Above the right-hand cartouche can be seen the cane or reed-stem, the symbol of Upper Egypt, and the bee, symbol of Lower Egypt. The technical execution of these hieroglyphics and of the scene represented is very remarkable. Intaglio as deep as this is not common, and is met mainly in the period of the New Kingdom.

central Turkey during the second millennium. The Hittites employed both hieroglyphics and the cuneiform script, and each appears to have evolved under the stimulus of the systems already in use in Egypt and Mesopotamia. Once again it was trade relations which made such influences possible. As early as 1900 B.C., or thereabouts, Assyrian merchants were travelling the length and breadth of Turkey, and it was not long before these people settled there and established themselves in colonies. Archaeologists carrying out excavations in Turkey have constantly come across clay tablets inscribed with Assyrian cuneiform. As a result of this influence the Hittites later developed a cuneiform script of their own, which it first became possible to read at the beginning of this century.

As may be gathered from this short account the peoples of the Near East all displayed a remarkable facility for developing methods of writing. The stimulus of trade, which encouraged the spread of these various systems, was bound in the long run to lead to their simplification also. As might be expected, this simplification first took place in the land which lay between the two great kingdoms of Egypt and Mesopotamia, in Canaan.

3. THE INVENTION OF THE ALPHABET

Greater Canaan embraces Palestine, western Syria, and the Lebanon. Because of its situation the area inevitably became a focal point between the major powers of the ancient Near East, and it was in or through this region that the peoples of Mesopotamia, Egypt, and Hatti generally made contact with each other. The Phoenicians, a seafaring people who inhabited the northern coastal strip with its many natural harbours, became the intermediaries between these great powers. The methods of writing first used by the Canaanites were adopted from the dominant cultures by which they were surrounded, but archaeological evidence suggests that by about 1500 B.C. they had begun to develop a simpler system of their own.

The best-known example of this system is the cuneiform alphabet of Ugarit. This city, which since excavation began in 1929 has been made to disclose so many of the secrets of its past, stood on the Syrian coast, facing the north-eastern point of what is now Cyprus. Its inhabitants made extensive use of the art of writing, as is evidenced by the discovery of a library belonging to the temple, some texts from the palace archives, and a private

collection of documents. These consist of thousands of clay tablets bearing inscriptions in several different languages, written in several different types of script. There were also a number of stone slabs with Egyptian hieroglyphics carved on them. Assyrian, Babylonian, and even Sumerian cuneiform texts were found, along with examples of Hittite hieroglyphics.

The commonest script, however, was one which was found to contain a total of thirty different cuneiform symbols. A study of these soon revealed that they made up an alphabet of thirty letters. Another remarkable discovery was that the letters followed the same order as those in the much later Hebrew alphabet. The source of this Ugaritic alphabet has not yet been discovered. Does it represent an ingenious combination and adaptation of the Egyptian and Mesopotamian systems? This is unlikely. The order of the Egyptian letters was extremely variable, if indeed it existed at all; and the script from Mesopotamia, possessing as it did more than 250 symbols, can have no more than a remote connection with Ugarit's thirty letters. The two great language areas may well have provided some stimulus, but the Ugaritic alphabet remains essentially an original invention. It was probably used elsewhere in Canaan too. A brief inscription from Beth-shemesh and some symbols on a copper dagger from the neighbourhood of Mount Tabor suggest that this was so.

Another indication of this general tendency to evolve a simplified system of writing is provided by the letter-symbols which have been found carved on some rocks in the Sinai peninsula. As early as the period of the Old Kingdom (ca. 2600 B.C.) the Egyptians had explored this area and discovered large quantities of copper, which was so essential to their civilization. Considering Egypt's domination of Canaan at this time, it is quite possible that the Egyptians used prisoners-of-war from Syria and Palestine to mine this metal. On boulders in the neighbourhood of the mines a number of inscriptions have been carved alongside some Egyptian hieroglyphics, and the supposition is that these were the work of the prisoners or their overseers. So far something in the region of twenty-five such inscriptions have been discovered, but the deciphering of them still presents a major problem The symbols are indistinct, and the letters are few in number. Nevertheless, it is generally agreed that they reveal a tentative effort at a simplified, and possibly an alphabetic, script. If this is in fact the case, we may fairly safely assume that these written symbols were known in Canaan as well, especially since other inscriptions have been found in Palestine which appear to be written in a kind of linear-alphabetic script. The most important of these finds were made at Lachish, Shechem, Gezer, Megiddo, and in the vicinity of Beth-shan. They are too fragmentary to allow of any definite conclusions as to what they might signify, but it can be said with a fair degree of certainty that they date from 1500–1000 B.C.

The el-Amarna letters (see p. 48) offer indisputable proof that the Canaanites of this period were already well practised in the art of writing. They show that the language and cuneiform script of Mesopotamia had at the beginning of the fourteenth century B.C. acquired an international status. They also show that there were people living in Canaan who were masters of this complicated script, with its enormous number of characters, though we must remember that writing was still mainly the province of professional scribes.

Scribes must have been highly-respected members of the

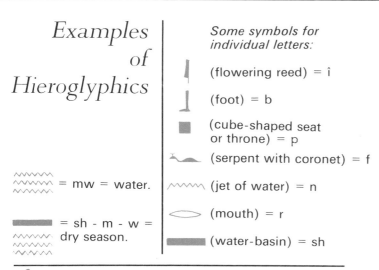

Examples of Hieroglyphics

Some symbols for individual letters:

| (flowering reed) = î
| (foot) = b

■ (cube-shaped seat or throne) = p

(serpent with coronet) = f

(jet of water) = n

(mouth) = r

(water-basin) = sh

≈ = mw = water.

= sh - m - w = dry season.

= *Thothmes* (name of various Pharaohs from ca. 1550).

Explanation of the symbols:

ibis on supporting shelf: symbol for the God *Thoth*
apron of three fox skins: passive form of the verb *ms* = to be born.
crook: the consonant *s* = repetition and confirmation of the preceding s.
Meaning: Thoth is born.

= *Nefertiti* (consort of 14th century Pharaoh Amenhotep IV = Ikhnaton).

Explanation of the symbols:

heart + windpipe: the letter-combination *nfr* = good, fine.
serpent with coronet: the consonant *f* = repetition and confirmation of the preceding 'r'.
small loaf: the consonant *t;* indicates the female sex.
flowering reed with legs in motion: the verb *ii* = come back.
flowering reed: the letter *i* = repetition and confirmation of the preceding 'i.'
two small strokes + legs in motion: the letter *y;* indicates the adjectival use of the verb 'to come.'
pestle: the letters *ti* = the feminine ending of the third person sungular, indicating that the verb denotes a condition.
flowering reed: the letter *i* = repetition and confirmation of the preceding 'i.'
Meaning: the beautiful (one) has come.

UGARITIC ALPHABET

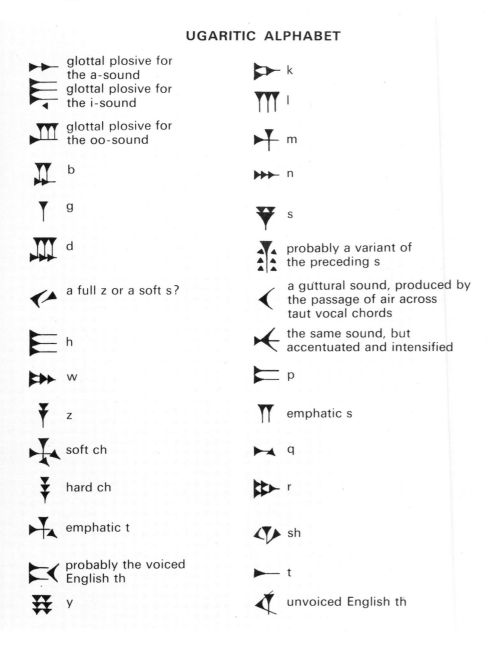

glottal plosive for the a-sound	k
glottal plosive for the i-sound	l
glottal plosive for the oo-sound	m
b	n
g	s
d	probably a variant of the preceding s
a full z or a soft s?	a guttural sound, produced by the passage of air across taut vocal chords
h	the same sound, but accentuated and intensified
w	p
z	emphatic s
soft ch	q
hard ch	r
emphatic t	sh
probably the voiced English th	t
y	unvoiced English th

temple three clay tablets were discovered bearing a hitherto unknown script. The symbols in this case seem to represent the letters of an alphabet, but it may be impossible to decipher them unless more texts of the same kind are found.

All this evidence proves without any shadow of doubt that the art of writing was practised extensively in Canaan in the second millennium, and that there was constant pressure to evolve simpler ways of conveying language through written symbols. Though we do not have evidence for all the intermediate stages of this evolution, we know what its final outcome was. In 1923 a large stone coffin was discovered at Byblos. Carved along the edge of its lid is a lengthy text, most of which is written in an alphabetic script. When this was deciphered with the aid of the Hebrew language, it was found to read as follows: "This is the sarcophagus made by Itba'al, son of Ahiram, king of Gebal [Byblos], for his father, Ahiram, as his lasting abode. If there should be a king among kings, or a governor among governors, or any army commander in Gebal, who opens the sarcophagus, that man's staff of authority will be broken, his royal throne will be overturned. Peace will depart from Gebal; and he himself will be destroyed." Since this text was chiselled in hard stone and was meant to endure, we may assume that the script in which it is written was already well established and had been in general use for some considerable time. This enables us to set the date for the

An ostrakon found in 1932 east of the ancient city of Samaria. This potsherd is therefore not part of the collection discovered in 1910 near the royal palace on the acropolis. The letters are not in ink but are engraved on the sherd. Their form belongs to the 8th century B.C. Decipherment is difficult. Several letters are not clear; and some words have perhaps been abbreviated. From right to left one may make out the following consonants:
1. . . . b r k s   2. b r k . . . h d 'm h q s b w   3. y m n h s' r m . . .
In translation this could be:
1. . . . Baruch . .   2. your grain 2 (measures), let them know, listen and 3. let there be counted measures 2 (or 3) . . .

community in the harbour towns of Phoenicia, if only because their services were essential for the commercial transactions on which these places depended for their continued prosperity. This must have been particularly true in the case of Byblos, which, because of its richly forested hinterland, enjoyed close commercial ties with Egypt, a country poorly endowed with wood. There is an Egyptian travel-story, dating from the twelfth century B.C., in which reference is made to some inscribed papyrus rolls kept in a 'record office' at Byblos. We do not know what kind of writing appeared on these rolls, but it is unlikely to have been Egyptian hieroglyphics. They may have been in the script known as pseudo-hieroglyphic, of which various examples have been found at Byblos on blocks of stone. It comprises more than a hundred symbols resembling simplified hieroglyphics. These have not as yet been deciphered, but they probably constitute a syllabic script, that is to say, a script in which each symbol represents a syllable, or a vowel plus a consonant.

Another find which illustrates this tendency towards the simplification of writing was made in 1964 during excavations at Deir 'Alla in the Jordan valley. Among the remains of an ancient

writing. There was no longer any need to acquire the difficult skill of distinguishing between the hundreds of hieroglyphs and cuneiform symbols and their multiplicity of meanings, which up to this time had made writing the preserve of a few specialists. The number of letters contained in this new alphabetic script was small. There were only thirty in Ugaritic, and even less in Hebrew and Greek. Professional scribes continued to exist, of course. In fact, it was not until the invention of printing, twenty-six centuries later, that they became superfluous. The really important change brought about by the invention of the alphabet was that from now on the art of writing could be acquired much more quickly and by many more people, with the result that it became a natural part of everyday life not only in the large commercial centres but even in small towns and villages.

There was, in addition, another advantage. Cuneiform and hieroglyphic scripts had been closely tied to the languages they were designed to express. To use these same symbols for another

◁ In 1887 more than 250 clay tablets with texts in cuneiform script were discovered in the mound at Tell el-'Amarna on the east bank of the Nile, almost 200 miles south of Cairo. They were nearly all letters addressed to the Pharaohs Amenophis III and Amenophis IV (Ikhnaton). The language is Accadian, even in the 14th century B.C. apparently the language of diplomacy. Some of the letters were written by the king of Babylon, Ashur, Mitanni, and Hatti; but more than 300 of them were dispatched from Canaan. The senders included the rulers of Jerusalem, Lachish, Hebron, Gezer, Ashkelon, Megiddo, Acco, Tyre, Sidon, Byblos, and Ugarit. The clay tablet shown above bears a letter from King Tushratta of Mitanni to Pharaoh Amenophis III. Tushratta informs him that he has sent him a number of gifts and that he now expects the Pharaoh to send him a large quantity of gold.

A miniature sphinx, about 6 in. high, from Serabit el-Khadim, a place in the Sinai peninsula, where Semitic slaves worked under Egyptian direction in the copper-mines. The six symbols on the side show what was probably one of the earliest attempts at a linear alphabet. This script has been dated at about 1500 B.C. So far only nineteen different symbols have been discovered—too slender a basis for any assured interpretation.

invention of the linear alphabet at about 1100 B.C. or perhaps a little earlier.

The text discovered at Byblos is not the only example of its kind. Three other inscriptions, carved on blocks of stone, seem to be almost as old as the epitaph for Ahiram. One of these appears on a commemoration tablet, and reads as follows: "This is the house built by Yehimilku, king of Gebal, who has also repaired all the ruins of the houses. May Ba'al-shamin (and) the Lord of Gebal and the council of the holy gods of Gebal multiply the days and years of Yehimilku; for he is an upright man and a righteous king in the sight of the holy gods of Gebal."

With these texts, which date from the tenth century B.C. we find we have reached the age of David and Solomon. As will be seen later, it was during this period that the court historians of Israel produced the first of those documents which were later to be incorporated into the Bible.

4. THE LANGUAGES OF THE BIBLE

With the perfecting of the linear alphabet it became possible, in theory at least, for everyone to master the art of reading and

34

A small granite figure of an Egyptian scribe, dating from the fourth ▷ dynasty (ca. 2600 B.C.). The scribe sits cross-legged, his left hand holding on his lap an unrolled papyrus. His right hand has lost the pen with which he was writing from right to left. From the posture one can deduce that he was using what is known as the hieratic script, a more cursive form of hieroglyphics, as this was invariably written from right to left. The figurine was certainly a likeness of some prominent Egyptian. People liked to have themselves portrayed in this fashion, because the profession of the scribe was held in great respect.

A clay tablet discovered in 1964 by a Dutch expedition led by H. J. Franken at Deir 'Alla in the Jordan valley. The tablet was found with two others beside a sanctuary which must have been destroyed by an earthquake about 1200 B.C. The symbols on this tablet undoubtedly represent a script, probably even an alphabetic one. It can be seen from the form of the imprint in the clay of the various strokes and signs that the author wrote from right to left and from top to bottom. More than that, however, one cannot say, in view of the scanty amount of material.

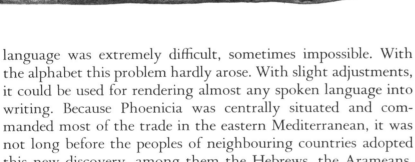

language was extremely difficult, sometimes impossible. With the alphabet this problem hardly arose. With slight adjustments, it could be used for rendering almost any spoken language into writing. Because Phoenicia was centrally situated and commanded most of the trade in the eastern Mediterranean, it was not long before the peoples of neighbouring countries adopted this new discovery, among them the Hebrews, the Arameans, and the Greeks. The languages of these three peoples were later to play an important part in the growth of the Biblical tradition.

When the earliest Hebrew tribes first penetrated into southern Canaan, they came into contact with a culture superior in most respects to their own. When they eventually established themselves in the land, therefore, it was natural that they should acquire some of the skills and accomplishments of the people they had conquered or assimilated into their own communities. The extent of this influence may perhaps be judged from the fact that the Hebrews adopted the language and script of the Canaanites. As semi-nomadic tribes they must originally have spoken an old Aramaic dialect. This would account for the passage in Deuteronomy 26:5, which says "You shall make response before the Lord your God, 'A wandering Aramean was my father.'" In the Book of Isaiah (19:18) Hebrew is therefore rightly described as 'the language of Canaan,' because the language which we now call Hebrew must have come about through the adaptation of the dialect of the invading nomads to the Canaanite tongue.

Outside the Bible, one of the chief pieces of evidence for this development is the Farmer's Calendar from Gezer. This is an inscription scratched on a fragment of limestone measuring 4¾ in. × 2¾ in., which was found in 1908 among the remains of the ancient town of Gezer. The text, which dates from the tenth century B.C., and is carved in rather primitive fashion, reads:

Two months gathering,
Two months sowing,
Two months cutting grass,
One month cutting flax,
One month the harvest of barley,
One month harvesting and measuring,
Two months pruning,
One month summer-fruit.

Such simple texts suggest that even ordinary people could write. Quite recently, in 1960, yet another inscription of this kind was unearthed south of Yabne-Yam in the modern state of Israel. Somewhere around 620 B.C. a labourer addressed to a magistrate a short letter on a potsherd, a material much used for writing in ancient times. The writer seems to be complaining that he has been falsely accused of not carrying out the work demanded of him, and has had his clothing confiscated as a consequence:

May my lord the magistrate give ear
to the business of his servant. Your servant,
with harvesting was your servant occupied in the
garden of 'sm. And your servant harvested
and measured and stored away as (he did) every day before

going to rest.

As soon as your servant had weighed his crop and

had stored it away, there came Hashabyahu, the son of Shobai,

and he took away the garment of your servant, I who had stored away

my crop, that is, my daily crop. He took the garment from your servant.

But all my brethren are witnesses for me, they who harvested with me in the heat.

My brethren witness on my behalf, truly I am innocent of . . .

. . . . .my garment, and so . . .not . . . .

. . . . .your servant, and do not turn away from . . . . .

Right down to the time of the Exile in the sixth century B.C., the sacred texts of Israel continued to be written in this language and script which the Hebrews had adopted from the ancient Canaanites. It is extremely unlikely that these texts were recorded on stone slabs or earthenware sherds, but rather on rolls of papyrus or leather. Jeremiah 36, for instance, would lead one to suppose that people wrote on leather. In the course of excavations recently carried out at the Wadi Murabba'at in the Judean desert a piece of papyrus was unearthed bearing a number of names and figures which must have been written down during the eighth or seventh century B.C. It seems likely, therefore, that papyrus was in fact used at this time .Yet there is little hope of our recovering any Biblical texts written on this material before the period of the Exile. Leather and papyrus do not stand up well to the wet winters of Palestine. It is only in the dry desert caves that a few fragments may still have been preserved.

The second language of the Bible, which is used in parts of Ezra and Daniel, is Aramaic. The people who spoke this language are known to us mainly from the Biblical accounts of events that took place in Aram-Damascus in the ninth and eighth centuries B.C. (See 1 Kings 20 and 2 Kings 5.) The Arameans had not always

lived in and around Damascus, however. Originally, they had all inhabited the Syro-Arabian desert, from where they periodically penetrated into the more civilized regions of Mesopotamia and Canaan. In the eleventh century B.C., when the power of Assyria was declining, they began to abandon their nomadic way of life, and to set up city states, such as Damascus, which acted as buffers between Assyria and Israel. Like the early Hebrews, the Arameans were quick to adopt the Phoenician alphabet, and a number of inscriptions dating from about 900 B.C. can be attributed to them. One particularly interesting example from the seventh century B.C. is an epitaph that was unearthed at Nerab, near the modern town of Aleppo. Its text reads as follows:

> From the deceased Sinzirban, priest of Sahar in Nerab.
> And this is his monument and tomb. Whoever you be who sweep away this monument and this tomb from its place, Sahar and Shamash and Nikal and Nusek [the names of gods] will cut off your name and your place from life and with a baneful death will they visit you and they will put an end to your lineage.
> But if you treat this monument and tomb with respect, then another will respect yours.

Like the Northern Kingdom of Israel, all these small Aramean states were wiped out in the eighth century B.C. by the Assyrian overlords. Yet their language persisted, and what is much more surprising, gradually spread over all the culturally advanced regions of the Near East, from Persia to Egypt. It was a process which must have taken place over several centuries, but this makes it no less remarkable. We have an early and important proof of the prestige of Aramaic in the well-known passage in 2 Kings 18:26 (= Is. 36:11), where the chief men of Jerusalem ask the Assyrian king's representative to speak to them not in Hebrew but in Aramaic, because, unlike the common people, they are as familiar with that language as with their own.

During the two centuries of Persian domination (ca. 540–330 B.C.) Aramaic was the language used for diplomatic purposes throughout the empire. Some Aramaic texts in the Old Testament, such as Ezra 4:8ff, for example, come from this period. Also worth mentioning are the papyri from Elephantine, the small island in the Nile where in the fifth century B.C. a number of texts were written in Aramaic by a community of Jews. Later on, the process of hellenization inaugurated by Alexander the Great, which made Greek the new 'lingua franca' of the ancient world, could not oust Aramaic entirely. In the Book of Daniel, for instance, which appeared in the second century B.C., there is both

The 'Farmer's Calendar' of Gezer is more or less universally assigned to the 10th century B.C., and so to the period of David and Solomon. It is impossible to be sure whether this fragment of limestone is really evidence that the art of writing was practised by the Israelites. Gezer was never firmly in David's hands. It was Solomon who first acquired administrative control of the town from the Pharaoh of Egypt. This may possibly be the work of someone practising or learning to write; for the tablet has been used more than once. Traces of earlier letters are still visible underneath the existing text. It has been argued that the letters, bottom left, which are vertically inscribed, can be made to yield the name of the writer. The first letter could be an 'aleph (the initial letter of the Hebrew alphabet); and the second is certainly a beth. In the third sign some are inclined to see a yod. In that case the name could be constructed as 'byhw: this would be 'Abiyahu ('Yahweh is my father'). But then one might also read 'Abiezer, 'Abibaal, and so on. However, the first and especially the third letters are not sufficiently clear to establish any of these conclusions.

Part of the Aramaic papyrus (lines 1-17) from Yeb (Elephantine), a small island in the Nile near Aswan. In the Persian period a Jewish garrison was stationed here, charged with protecting the southern frontier of Egypt. The texts found at the site do not reveal, however, when and under what circumstances this group of Jews came there. From the letter reproduced here, which dates from 408 B.C., it would appear that the island housed a Jewish sanctuary in honour of Yaho, which was destroyed in 410 at the instigation of some Egyptian priests. The event prompted Jedoniah, the leader of the Jewish group, to write to Bagoas (probably Nehemiah's successor as governor of Judah), requesting permission to rebuild the sanctuary. The first two lines of the letter run:

> To our lord Bagoas, governor of Judah, your servants Jedoniah and his colleagues, the priests who are in the fortress of Elephantine. May the God of Heaven seek after the welfare of our lord exceedingly at all times and give you favour before King Darius . . .

In lines 8-9 comes the actual complaint:

> Nafayan thereupon led the Egyptians with the other troops. Coming with their weapons to the fortress of Elephantine, they entered that temple and razed it to the ground. The stone pillars that were there they smashed.

a Hebrew and an Aramaic section, the latter being in all probability the older of the two. It is also quite certain that among the Jews Hebrew was slowly but surely obliged to make way for Aramaic, and although the ruling classes long continued to cultivate the Hebrew tongue, it went completely out of use amongst ordinary people. This is why, at the beginning of our era, the divine revelation was conveyed to the world in the language of the Arameans. Students of the Greek New Testament try to explore the Aramaic background to the Scriptures, for the Christians of the Early Church not only spoke and wrote Aramaic, but thought in it too.

During this period of Aramaic influence the Hebrews also ceased to use their old Canaanite script, and adopted the square-shaped letters of the Aramaic script. In the last centuries of the pre-Christian era this square script, as it is called, was used even for sacred texts. The Hebrew Bible is today still published in characters of this kind.

The third language of the Bible is Greek, which grew in importance as an international language from the time of Alexander the Great onwards (ca. 330 B.C.). The Greeks had already adopted the Phoenician alphabet as early as 800 B.C. This may be seen from the shape of many of the Greek letters, and from the names given to them. In the Hellenistic period so many Jews of the Diaspora knew no Hebrew that it became necessary to translate the Law, the Prophets, and the Writings into Greek. Some of the sacred books were in fact written in Greek in the first place, for example the deutero-canonical Book of Wisdom. The Early Christian Church, which, as mentioned earlier, was primarily Aramaic-speaking, had to translate its message into *koinē*, or common Greek, when it ventured out of the province of Judea and took to the highways of the Roman empire. With the spread of Christianity, all the books of the New Testament had eventually to be translated into the current Greek of the time. It was the language most commonly used throughout the Near East in the early years of the Christian era. This is illustrated admirably by the following text, in which colloquial forms of expression determine the style of the language. It is a short letter which an Egyptian boy, writing about A.D. 200, sent after his father, who had gone off on a journey. It was discovered at Oxyrhynchus, where the dryness of the Egyptian sand had ensured its preservation.

> Theon to his father Theon. Greetings.
>
> A fine thing you did to me! You didn't take me with you to the town. If you won't take me with you to Alexandria, then I'm not writing you any more letters; I'm not going to talk to you or greet you any more. And if you are going to Alexandria by yourself, then I shan't stick up for you any more, I shan't even say hullo. If you won't take me with you, that's what will happen!
>
> My mother too would say to Archelaus: "He makes me fed up; off with him."
>
> Yes, it's a fine thing you've done to me! You have sent me presents, big ones: pips to you! [The boy is too grown-up apparently, to be coaxed with sweets and dainties.] They tricked me, on this twelfth day, the very day that you have taken yourself off. Well now, have me fetched, I beg of you. If you don't have me fetched, I shan't eat and I shan't drink. That's what I'll do!
>
> I hope that things may go well with you.
>
> The eighteenth of the month Tybi.
>
> Deliver it to Theon. From his son Theon.

III. ISRAEL'S PRECURSORS

Historical and cultural developments in the ancient Near East that were important in the origin of Israel and of the Bible: 3000-1000 B.C.

INTRODUCTION

From about 3000 B.C. onwards the rise of a new culture can be traced in the Near East. Copper, the soft and malleable metal used during the preceding period, no longer met the needs of peoples who were becoming increasingly urban. In time, therefore, it was replaced by the harder bronze.

The Bronze Age lasted until about 1200 B.C., and it is divided like the Stone Age into three periods. In the first period, the Early Bronze Age (3000–2100 B.C.), the main civilizations were the Old Kingdom in Egypt, and the Kingdom of Sargon of Accad, and the Sumerian empire in Mesopotamia. These reached their peak about 2500 B.C. After a confused interim period, the culture of the Middle Bronze Age (2000–1600 B.C.) produced the civilization of the Egyptian Middle Kingdom and that which flourished in Mesopotamia under the ascendancy of Hammurabi (ca. 19th and 18th centuries B.C.). It was during the Late Bronze Age (1600–1200 B.C.) that international contacts were established between Egypt, Canaan, the Hittites, Assyria, and Babylonia.

Individual elements in the history and culture of the regions occupied by these powers deserve closer attention, in view of their significance for the emergence of Israel and of the Bible.

1. MESOPOTAMIA

The peoples of the Tigris and Euphrates valleys began to develop a written language of their own at a very early stage in their history, and countless texts are extant which give us an insight into their religious thought and feeling.

The Sumerians have handed down to us a story dealing with the origin of various gods and describing a 'celestial paradise.' Such myths usually have little or no significance as documents of historical fact, but they are valuable inasmuch as they frequently reflect the conditions of the people and the country at the time they were written. For instance, in the narrative just referred to it is the freshwater god, Enki, who fertilizes the goddess Ninhursag, the earth-mother. It is his seed to which the various kinds of trees owe their origin. This myth thus illustrates the importance accorded to the water which irrigated the Sumerian countryside and is appropriately called 'the Paradise Myth.' The scene of the action is called Dilmun, a district or a city ideally placed.

The land Dilmun is pure, the land Dilmun is clean;
The land Dilmun is clean, the land Dilmun is most bright…
The place, after Enki had lain with his wife,
That place is clean, that place is most bright;…
In Dilmun the raven utters no cries,
The ittidu-bird utters not the cry of the ittidu-bird,
  [a frightening noise?]
The lion kills not,
The wolf snatches not the lamb,
Unknown is the kid-devouring wild dog,…
The dove droops not the head,
The sick-eyed says not 'I am sick-eyed,'
The sick-headed (says) not 'I am sick-headed,'
Its old woman (says) not 'I am an old woman,'
Its old man (says) not 'I am an old man'…

The intense longing for an all-embracing peace, so often encountered in the Scriptures, is already falteringly expressed here. Another story presents the clash between a pastoral and an agricultural way of life, as in the conflict of Cain with Abel in the fourth chapter of Genesis. But the action of the Sumerian myth is set in the world of the gods, and in contrast to the Biblical story the conflict between Dumuzi, god of shepherds, and Enkimdu, the farmers' god, ends happily with a reconciliation.

The Sumerians were also acquainted with a story of a flood. The main character is not called Noah, but Ziusudra. He receives a message from heaven that the gods intend to send a deluge to cover the earth. In order that he may escape destruction he is counselled to build himself a ship. The myth ends with the words:

After, for seven days (and) seven nights,
The flood had swept over the land,
(And) the huge boat had been tossed about by the windstorms
  on the great waters,
Utu [the sun-god] came forth, who sheds light on heaven
  (and) earth.
Ziusudra opened a window of the huge boat,
The hero Utu brought his rays into the giant boat.
Ziusudra, the king,
Prostrated himself before Utu,
The king kills an ox, slaughters a sheep.

The passages quoted all come from Babylonian or Assyrian

The sequence of civilizations in the Near East

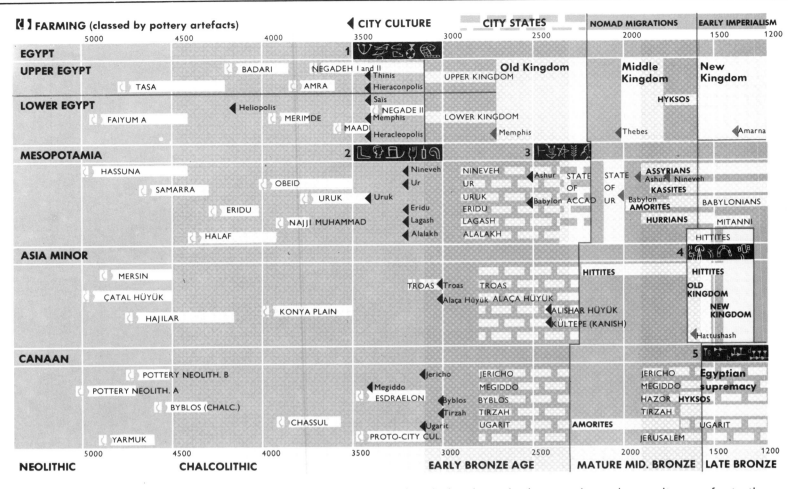

Along the top of this chronological table are placed the economic and political periods; along the bottom the various cultures refer to the vertical brown undertints. The flowering of a particular civilization is indicated by a window cut in the overall grey tint and the name of the civilization or period (as under Egypt). In decline the grey tint returns. By about 600 B.C. metal-based culture (Iron Age II) is universal and from then on the name of the dominant power is used instead of a division into periods.
1. Primitive pictography in Egypt. 2. Primitive pictography in Sumeria. 3. Ideographic script of the Accadian period. 4. Ideographic script of the Hittites. 5. Cuneiform alphabet from Ugarit. 6. Linear alphabet.

'libraries' of clay tablets, but they are written in Sumerian. The texts to which they belong were apparently regarded as divinely inspired, and provided a standard or norm which determined later religious tradition. It is not surprising, therefore, that even in Ugarit and Asia Minor clay tablets have been found which contain Sumerian texts, and that in the ancient Hittite capital itself Sumerian-Hittite glossaries have been discovered.

Those who succeeded the Sumerians in the Mesopotamian basin—the Accadians, the Babylonians, and the Assyrians—carried on their literary and religious traditions. They not only adopted the old Sumerian myths for their own purposes, but created new myths of their own. King Sargon, for example, who founded the Accadian kingdom about 2300 B.C., became in later tradition a supernatural creature of mysterious origin. The myth recounting his birth is reminiscent of the story of Moses in the bulrushes, as recorded in Exodus 2:1-10. The opening lines are:

> Sargon, the mighty king, king of Agade, am I.
> My mother was a changeling [?], my father I knew not.
> The brother(s) of my father loved the hills.
> My city is Azupiranu, which is situated on the banks of the Euphrates.
> My changeling mother conceived me, in secret she bore me.
> She set me in a basket of rushes, with bitumen she sealed my lid.
> She cast me into the river which rose not (over) me.
> The river bore me up and carried me to Akki, the drawer of water.
> Akki, the drawer of water lifted me out as he dipped his e[w]er.
> Akki, the drawer of water, [took me] as his son (and) reared me.
> Akki, the drawer of water, appointed me as his gardener.
> While I was a gardener, Ishtar [goddess of love] granted me (her) love...

There is also an ancient Babylonian myth regarding the origin of man. It describes how the mother-goddess forms man out of clay and brings him to life with the blood of a god who has been slain. Man is given the name of Lullu, and receives the task of serving the gods. This text, however, has come down to us in a very fragmentary state, and the details of the story remain obscure. World-famous, on the other hand, is the Babylonian epic that deals with the origins of the earth and the birth of man, an epic called after the first two words of the text: *Enuma elish*, 'when on high.' This is probably a cultic text which had a wide-

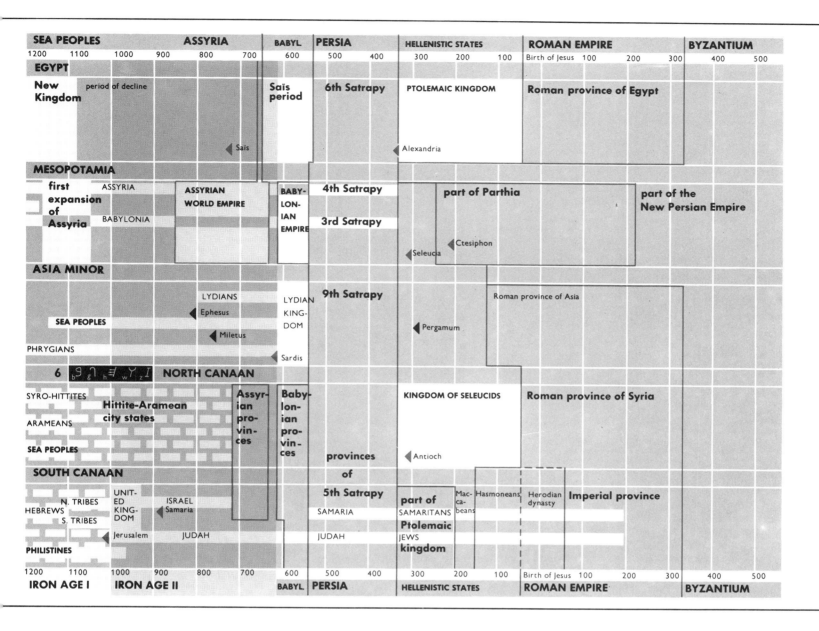

spread use at the time of the new-year festival. It is not surprising, therefore, that several varying versions have been recovered. This is how the opening lines of the poem run:

When on high the heaven had not been named [did not exist],
Firm ground below had not been called by name,
Naught but primordial Apsu [fresh water], their begetter,
(And) Mummu-Tiamat [salt water], she who bore them all,
Their waters commingling as a single body;
No reed hut had been matted, no marsh land had appeared,
When no gods whatever had been brought into being,
Uncalled by name, their destinies undetermined.

Out of this chaotic, nameless, primeval water the first gods emerged, and these in turn gave birth to new gods. By their intrigues and quarrels, however, they caused complete disruption, and it was in order to restore harmony that the wise god Ea begat Marduk, the chief god of Babylon. Marduk assumed the role of redeemer and creator. He annihilated the fractious elements in the divine world, and eventually, with the blood of a rebellious deity, he made man, upon whom was enjoined the duty of serving the gods. At the end of this epic, which is really a eulogy in honour of Marduk, all his names and activities are solemnly listed.

The Gilgamesh epic ought not to pass unmentioned in this connection, because although it is a poem more profane than sacred in character, it touches upon profound themes in human life, and was copied and recast many times. It celebrates the glory of man, nature, love, friendship, battle, and adventure; and running through it all is the persistent theme of the relativity of human existence. Gilgamesh, the hero of the story, sets out in search of 'everlasting life.' Crossing the waters of death on this journey, he meets with his ancestor, Utanapishtim, who tells him about a ruinous flood that had once swept over the earth. Here we have an echo of the Sumerian Ziusudra and yet another predecessor of the Biblical Noah. At the behest of the wise god Ea, Utanapishtim had built a ship and so had escaped destruction. The old man then continues thus:

When the seventh day arrived,
I sent forth and set free a dove.
The dove went forth, but came back;
Since no resting-place for it was visible, she turned round.
Then I sent forth and set free a swallow.
The swallow went forth, but came back;
Since no resting-place for it was visible she turned round.
Then I sent forth and set free a raven.

An alabaster figure from Chorsabad, a small village just north of what is now Mosul and was once Nineveh. King Sargon II (721-705) established a new residence there, which his successor, Sennacherib, later abandoned. The figure, some 15½ feet high, may represent the hero Gilgamesh. With his left hand he holds captive a lion and in his right hand he carries a weapon. Uncertain though the identification is, the object is generally referred to as 'Gilgamesh with the lion.'

> The raven went forth and, seeing that the waters had dimin-
>   ished,
> He eats, circles, caws and turns not round.
> Then I let out (all) to the four winds and offered a sacrifice.
> I poured out a libation on the top of the mountain.
> Seven and seven cult-vessels I set up,
> Upon their pot-stands I heaped cane, cedarwood, and myrtle.
> The gods smelled the savour,
> The gods smelled the sweet savour,
> The gods crowded like flies about the sacrifice.

Utanapishtim was rewarded by the gods with immortality. But Gilgamesh is unable to obtain this privilege, because he cannot retain mastery over sleep, the shadow of death. On his departure the hero does indeed secure the plant of life which will enable him and every man to recover youthfulness, but on the return journey, while he is bathing in a limpid stream, a snake creeps up and snatches the plant away. The whole expedition has been in vain!

All these themes appear again, in modified form, in the traditions of Israel. Formerly, it was assumed that the Biblical versions were direct borrowings from these myths. An explanation more in favour nowadays is that they were common currency in the ordinary day-to-day life of all the peoples of the Near East. They offered an answer to the questions men asked about the origin of the world and the human race, about the enigma of suffering and death, and so on. At a certain stage in its development every human community reaches the point where it asks these questions, and the outward form given to the answers is often influenced by the outlook current at the time among neighbouring peoples.

The same common background has to be acknowledged in the case of numerous ancient laws, with regard both to their form and content. Urban culture, with its concentration of people living and working together, soon called for specific rules of conduct sanctioned by the authority of the state. Compilations of laws appeared very early on in Mesopotamia. The most famous is the 'lawbook' or code of the Babylonian monarch Hammurabi, which dates from about 1700 B.C. It was not the first, for even before this time laws had been codified. We must not regard any of these collections as being comparable with the legal codes or statute-books of modern times. The main thing the princely rulers of the ancient East succeeded in doing was to establish the law of custom and jurisprudence.

On the strength of what is depicted on the 'stone of Hammurabi' the opinion has been advanced that the king was believed to have received the law at the hand of the sun-god, Shamash. But this is incorrect. The sceptre and ring which the god clasps in his hand are the effective symbols of divine power. The text on the black pillar of Hammurabi denotes the same thing: the king is appointed by the deity to maintain law and order, but not to decree a divine law. On this point, therefore, there is a difference of view from that of Biblical writers. The following are some striking examples of the ancient Babylonian laws of Hammurabi. The first offers protection in matters of religion:

> 6: If a seignior stole the property of church or state, that seignior shall be put to death; also the one who received the stolen goods from his hand shall be put to death.

The expansion of commerce calls for practical protective measures. Hence:

> 7: If a seignior has purchased or he received for safe-keeping either silver or gold or a male slave or a female slave or an ox or a sheep or an ass or any sort of thing from the hand of a seignior's son or a seignior's slave without witnesses and contracts, since that seignior is a thief, he shall be put to death.

Stealing was—as it still is in the Near East—a serious crime, and so:

22: If a seignior committed robbery and has been caught, that seignior shall be put to death.

Even unforeseen circumstances in everyday life were taken into account. For example, if for unexpected reasons there was a bad harvest, a debtor would be allowed to wet the clay tablet on which his debt for that year was inscribed and rub it smooth. The debt for the year in question was then wiped out:

48: If a debt is outstanding against a seignior and Adad has inundated his field or a flood has ravaged (it) or through lack of water grain has not been produced in the field, he shall not make any return of grain to his creditor in that year; he shall cancel his contract-tablet and he shall pay no interest for that year.

The institution of marriage in an urban culture was exposed to more risks than it was in a family-centred nomadic way of life, so when a marriage was arranged, a contract was drawn up:

128: If a seignior acquired a wife, but did not draw up the contracts for her, that woman is no wife.

And for the dissolution of a marriage the law stood thus:

138: If a seignior wishes to divorce his wife who did not bear him children, he shall give her money to the full amount of her marriage-price and he shall also make good to her the dowry which she brought from her father's house and then he may divorce her.

The formulation of the following laws is reminiscent of the Old Testament:

196: If a seignior has destroyed the eye of a member of the aristocracy, they shall destroy his eye.
200: If a seignior has knocked out a tooth of a seignior of his own rank, they shall knock out his tooth.

But alongside this we read:

201: If he has knocked out a commoner's tooth, he shall pay one-third mina [a certain weight] of silver.

There are two archaeological sites in Mesopotamia which have attracted a great deal of attention during the past few decades. The first is Nuzi, a town on the upper reaches of the Tigris. Excavations there have shown that over a long period during the second millennium B.C. the dominant class in the population were Hurrians, a people who at that time were scattered over large areas of the Near East. According to certain passages in the Bible they also lived in Canaan. The writings on the thousands of clay tablets found at Nuzi often reflect an unwritten,

customary law when dealing with the subjects of adoption, slavery, inheritance, and wedlock, and these offer fairly close parallels with incidents in Old Testament stories about the patriarchs. A literary connection between Nuzi and the Bible, however, is highly unlikely. The length of time which elapsed before the latter was established in written form is too great. Here again it is the widely disseminated law of custom that constituted the common background.

Another important town was Mari, on the west bank of the Euphrates. This mound, known nowadays as Tell el-Hariri, has been under investigation by archaeologists since 1933. About 1700 B.C. this city was razed by Hammurabi of Babylon and was never afterwards rebuilt. Since then, the desert sands have preserved the remains of the city intact. In places, the ruins of the palace of Zimrilim, last king of Mari, are still 16 feet high. On its walls mural paintings have been found with their colours preserved. But the most valuable remains to have been unearthed in Mari consist of more than 20,000 clay tablets with texts in Babylonian cuneiform.

Because of its situation Mari came into contact a great deal with wandering nomads, and consequently the texts that have been dug up throw light on the political and social situation of the Syrian desert areas in those days. It is noteworthy, for instance, that mention is made of the 'Bene-yamina,' a name that resembles Benjamin, but is probably meant to refer to a certain tribe as 'sons of the south.' Even more frequently occurs the word 'dawidum,' which probably means 'defeat.' Is this the origin of the name 'David'? In Mari reference is also made to 'prophets,' but it is not possible to learn much from the texts concerning their position and function. The total picture afforded by the finds at Mari confirms once again how much the culture of those days was common property and how much Canaan, and later Israel, were a part of its heritage.

On the political plane the rulers of Babylonia and Assyria

A clay tablet from the library of King Ashurbanipal (668-629) at Nineveh. The measurements are 5.8 by 5.3 in. It is a fragment of tablet 11 of the Gilgamesh epic in the late Assyrian version. This narrative was current among the Sumerians as early as the third millennium B.C. During the reign of Ashurbanipal it was set down, along with many other traditions, in the Assyrian of the time. The right-hand column of the side visible in the photograph contains verses 165-214. In this fragment Utanapishtim, the man who survived the legendary flood, is telling Gilgamesh how he was rescued, thanks to the intervention of the wise god Ea, and how the god Enlil took him and his wife up into the world of the gods.

A small silver boat from the 'Tombs of the Kings' at Ur in Babylon. These tombs belong to the Sumerian period and are dated, at present, about 2500 B.C. They are said to be the last resting-place of a certain King Meshkalamduk and his consort, Shubad. The gold and silver utensils and ornaments and the precious stones found there are evidence of an advanced civilization. Remarkably enough, these treasures show some affinity with the burial gifts from the graves at Troy and Alaça Hüyük, which come from the same period. Why this little silver boat was put into the tomb it is hard to say. It was probably intended as an object for use in 'the other life,' along with the gold and silver dishes, goblets, ornaments, and weapons.

were long restricted to the Mesopotamian basin. The pressure to expand westwards, which was eventually to put an end to Israel's existence as a nation, was admittedly there from the start, but only occasionally did it result in actual penetration. Sargon of Accad (ca. 2300 B.C.) and Hammurabi of Babylon (ca. 1700 B.C.) and also the rulers of the Middle Assyrian kingdom (15th to 13th centuries B.C.) made political and military contact with the Canaanite peoples on the Mediterranean Sea. But Tiglath-pileser I, king of Assyria about 1100 B.C., was the first really to succeed in pushing through to the coast of the 'upper sea' (a name used in Mesopotamia for the Mediterranean Sea, in contradistinction to the Persian Gulf lying to the south). This king had cedars on Mount Lebanon felled for the temples of the Assyrian gods, and he exacted tribute from Byblos, Sidon, and Arvad. After Tiglath-pileser Assyrian power once more rapidly declined. Not until centuries later did the monarchs of the New Assyrian kingdom (9th-7th centuries B.C.) and the neo-Babylonian empire (625-539 B.C.) obtain a firm foothold on the shores of the 'upper sea.' By that time Israel had already long existed as a nation in her own right.

During the third and second millennia, therefore, Canaan remained free from political domination by the Assyrians and Babylonians. Nevertheless, the eastern end of the 'fertile crescent' did influence the regions to the west of it. The fact, mentioned earlier, that the kings of the Canaanite towns around 1400 B.C. had their letters to the Pharaohs of Egypt written in the Accadian cuneiform script is cogent enough evidence of the cultural influence of Mesopotamia.

Throughout the Near East the number seven frequently recurs. This should probably be seen as the sum of three, the divine number, and of four, the number which in the four quarters of the wind comprehended the earth. Seven would then be that which pre-eminently represents plenitude, perfection, and totality. Also, three multiplied by four yielded the synonymous symbol 'twelve,' which played such a major role in the Israelite nation, made up as it was of twelve tribes.

2. EGYPT

The mystery of death has a significant role to play in every man's existence. The people of ancient Egypt were no exception. In fact, the Egyptians were concerned with the hereafter to a degree which is unparalleled anywhere else. It is mainly to this overriding concern with death that we owe the relics and remains which make it possible to reconstruct the life of ancient Egypt. It is true that the earlier towns and villages have for the most part disappeared beneath the mud of the Nile or beneath modern buildings. But on the edges of the desert which stretches out to the east and west on each side of the Nile, the pyramids and other burial places still offer an imposing witness to the way in which the Egyptians regarded death.

It contrasted sharply with the way men felt about life in Mesopotamia and Canaan. In those areas men envisaged the

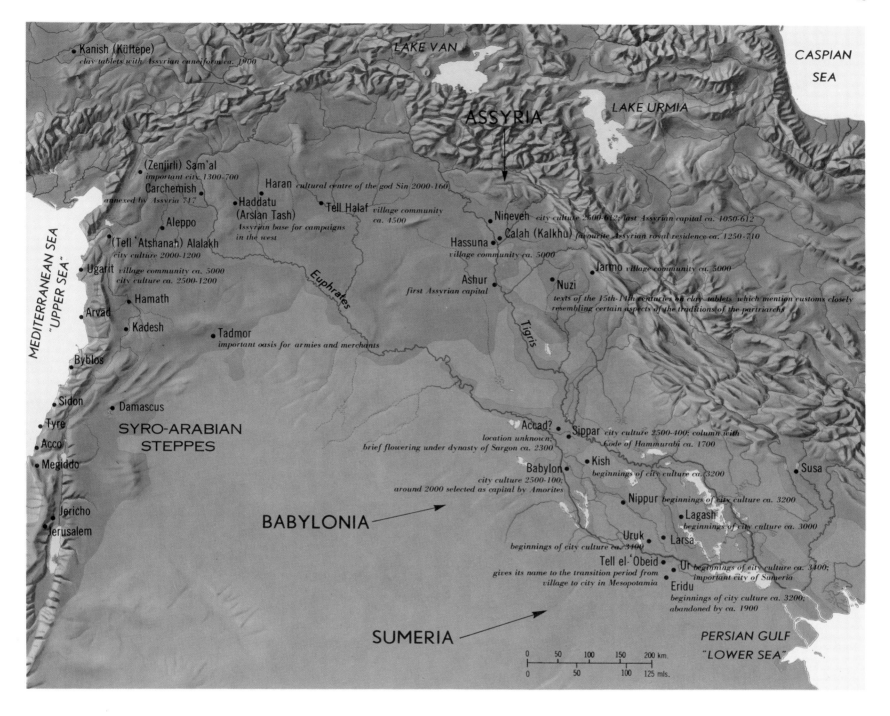

Important political events in Mesopotamia

ca. 3500: From the north-east the *Sumerians*, a non-Semitic race, pressed forward into the southern part of Mesopotamia. They established a number of wealthy city-states, which flourished until—

ca. 2300: A powerful wave of Semitic nomads from the Syro-Arabian desert region poured over the civilized areas. They laid the foundation for the *Accadian kingdom*.

ca. 2100: The *Sumerians* regained the upper hand; and their civilization enjoyed a brief renaissance.

ca. 2000: The Amorites, Semites from the Syro-Arabian desert, settled in Mesopotamia.

ca. 1900: First show of power by Assyria. Assyrian merchants made their way into Asia Minor.

ca. 1750: Under Hammurabi's leadership the *Old Babylonian kingdom* took its rise. Because of the continuous inroads made by the Cassites from the north-east, its power quickly declined.

ca. 1620: The Hittites conquered Babylon but were unable to hold the city.

ca. 1500: The Hurrians in northern Mesopotamia formed the kingdom of *Mitanni*, conquered by the Assyrians about 1300.

ca. 1100: For a brief period *Assyria* took the lead in Mesopotamia. However, Arameans pressing in from the Syro-Arabian desert soon crippled the power of this kingdom.

ca. 850: Under Ashurnazirpal II (883-859) the *Assyrian world empire* emerged.

ca. 630: Assyria declined and Babylon was strengthened, thanks to the Chaldeans (East Arameans), who settled in southern Mesopotamia.

ca. 610: End of the Assyrian empire and growth of the neo-Babylonian empire.

ca. 540: End of the neo-Babylonian empire. The *Persians* under Cyrus assumed world domination.

ca. 330: Alexander the Great put an end to the Persian empire.

An aerial view of the ruins of the palace at Mari. Prior to excavation the town was known only from a number of texts. Since 1933 the mound at Tell el-Hariri on the west bank of the Euphrates has been thoroughly investigated by archaeologists. We know that urban culture had started in Mari as early as the fourth millennium. The town twice enjoyed periods of great prosperity: about 2700 and then almost a thousand years later around 1800 B.C. During the latter period Mari was in the front rank as a cultural centre. Its kings resided in the enormous palace complex, which covered an area of more than six acres and included about 260 apartments and courtyards. The palace had only a single entrance, which was in the north. By passing through several corridors the visitor reached the great inner court (140 by 108 ft.), the centre of all official activity and of the administration. Adjoining this court was the hall in which the king gave audience. His private apartments were in the north-east corner.

hereafter as a kind of shadowy existence in a vague underworld. Such a negative vision made of life after death a worthless 'copy' of life on earth. In Egypt, on the other hand, a more positive conception prevailed. There the hereafter was envisaged as a festive continuation of this earthly life. What is rather surprising is that this optimistic view did not penetrate into Israel and influence the Bible. The Egyptians called the grave 'the house of eternity.' Life on earth simply continued in the hereafter.

That is why the body had to be securely protected against corruption, against beasts of prey and desecrators. That is why the dead person was provided with as many as possible of the things he had need of on earth: furniture, casks, victuals, clothing, ornaments and similar things. And because of the ancient belief that there existed an identity between a thing and its pic-

A bronze figurine of a worshipper from the temple at Larsa, about 30 miles north of the ancient city of Ur. The figurine is 7¾ inches high. The face and hands are still partly gilded. On the base are a number of figures and an inscription in which mention is made of King Hammurabi (ca. 1700 B.C.).

A wall painting from the palace at Mari, customarily entitled 'the investiture of the king of Mari.' The painting dates from the beginning of the second millennium; and its measurements are 8ft. by 5ft. 8 ins. It is obviously a triptych, the symmetrical panels to left and right looking in toward the middle. In these side panels one can distinguish in succession: a praying goddess; a palm tree with two gatherers seated in it; three mythological figures, from the top downwards, a winged lion, another winged beast, and then a bull with what is probably a human head. Then come two ornamental trees. In the lower part of the centre panel are two goddesses clasping a vase which has water flowing out of it. The upper part is the real core of the painting. In the centre standing, left, the king and, right, the goddess Ishtar, holding in her right hand a sceptre and a ring and in her left some kind of weapon. Behind them are two more goddesses, their hands raised in supplication; and in the right-hand corner a god stands looking on.
It is impossible to say for certain just what this painting signifies. It may indeed depict the investiture of the king; but it is also possible that the painter's subject was some ritual ceremony which took place rather more frequently, perhaps annually, in the temple.

torial representation, all sorts of diagrams, images, and pictures with texts were painted or carved on the coffins, the sides of the tombs, and the walls and pillars of the temples. It is these burial customs that make it possible to give some account of the civilization of ancient Egypt.

Yet despite these abundant remains it is not altogether possible to interpret accurately and in detail the ways in which men thought and felt about their religion. When in 3000 B.C. or thereabouts Egypt was unified, the varying religious ideas and customs current in the numerous small communities were not synthesized to form an intelligible system of belief. Local traditions were merged, but did not disappear. Thus religion became, to our Western eyes, a jumble of discrepancies. Where, for example, was the abode of the dead? Was it somewhere in the west, where the sun, too, vanished daily? The dead were indeed known as

'the western ones,' and the deceased were for preference interred on the edge of the western desert. Even in very early times it was the custom to lay the dead on their sides, with their heads to the south and their faces to the west.

Yet elsewhere, especially in the myth of the god Osiris, we come across the idea that the dead dwelt in an underworld through which the life-imparting sun made its nightly journey. The realm of the departed was also located in the north-eastern quarter of the celestial spheres, in 'the field of nurture' or 'sustenance,' as it was called. It was also believed that the burial-place itself was of prime importance in the afterlife. The richest tombs were made to look like dwellings equipped for some festivity.

The same diversity of contradictory notions is found in the world of the gods. Again, these cannot be contained within a single system. Each village and town had its own local deities before the country was unified, and they continued to remain in being when Egypt became a single kingdom. As a result, the total number of principal gods alone amounted to more than fifty. It was of course impossible to produce an ordered and logical system out of this confusion. Nevertheless, as authority became centralized, certain gods came to occupy a predominant position. For example, in Memphis, the capital during the time of the Old Kingdom, Ptah, the god of arts and crafts, was treated with special veneration, and in Thebes, for a long time the chief city of the Middle and New Kingdoms, the god Amon assumed particular importance, whilst from the fifth dynasty (ca. 2200 B.C.) onwards the sun-god Re was generally accorded pre-eminence in the Egyptian pantheon.

It is, however, hardly possible to re-construct a complete hierarchy of the gods. The confused and conflicting ideas which existed in this respect find expression to some extent in a fragmentary creation-myth of the god Atum.

"I am Atum when I was alone in Nun [the chaotic, primeval water], I am Re in his (first) appearances, when he began to rule that which he had made."
Who is he? This "Re, when he began to rule that which he had made" means that Re began to appear as a king, as one who was before the liftings of Shu [the god who holds aloft the vault of heaven] had taken place, when he was on the hill which is in Hermopolis...
"I am the great god who came into being by himself."
Who is he? "The great god who came into being by himself" is water; he is Nun, the father of the gods. Another version: He is Re.
"He who created his names, the Lord of the Ennead."
Who is he? He is Re, who created the names of the parts of his body. That is how these gods who follow him came into being.
"I am he among the gods who cannot be repulsed."
Who is he? He is Atum, who is in his sun disc.
Another version: He is Re, when he arises on the eastern horizon of heaven.
"I am yesterday, while I know tomorrow."
Who is he? As for "yesterday," that is Osiris.
As for "tomorrow," that is Re on that day on which the enemies of the All-Lord are annihilated and his son Horus is made ruler...

Even better known is the *Book of the Dead*. This modern sounding title is the name given to a number of papyri on which are inscribed magic formulae supposed to protect the dead from all kinds of evil powers. As a compilation this *Book of the Dead* dates from the New Kingdom, but many parts of it had a long tradition behind them even then. At first reading they might appear to be texts of a high ethical content. But they must be approached with caution. It is true that the Egyptian of the classical period does seem to be a more humane figure than the ancient Assyrian. His grief for the dead was tempered with the hope of an eternal life. But in the New Kingdom the feeling became more and more prevalent that all kinds of demonic forces were menacing man, and it was felt to be increasingly necessary to exorcise these powers by magic formulae. For that purpose innumerable amulets were used, for instance, in the form of scarabs. In addition, 'ready-made answers' were felt to be needed, in order to ensure entry into the world of eternal life, and these were given to the departed in the text of the *Book of the Dead* to accompany them on their journey.

What is said on reaching the Broad-Hall of the Two Justices, absolving ...[name of the dead man] of every sin which he has committed, and seeing the faces of the gods: Hail to thee, O great god, lord of the Two Justices! [Osiris] I have come to thee, my lord, I have been brought that I might see thy beauty. I know thee; I know thy name and the names of the forty-two gods who are with thee in the Broad-Hall of the Two Justices, who live on them who preserve evil and who drink their blood on that day of reckoning up character in the presence of Wennofer [Osiris]. Behold, "Sati-mertifi, Lord of Justice," is thy name. I have come to thee; I have brought thee justice; I have expelled deceit for thee.

Then the dead person had to enumerate a long list of misdeeds that he had not done. Here are some of them:

(A1) I have not committed evil against men.
(A2) I have not mistreated cattle.
(A8) I have not blasphemed a god.
(A9) I have not done violence to a poor man.
(A11) I have not defamed a slave to his superior.
(A12) I have not made (anyone) sick.
(A14) I have not killed.
(A15) I have given no order to a killer.
(A20) I have not had sexual relations with a boy.
(A22) I have neither increased or diminished the grain-measure.
(A32) I have not built a dam against running water.

The injunctions contained in the *Book of the Dead* presuppose a belief in the myth of Osiris, the god of new life. As a righteous king, Osiris had once ruled on earth as deputy of the sun-god, Re. His wicked brother, Set, had then robbed him of his life. Isis, Osiris's sister and spouse, succeeded after much difficulty in obtaining possession of his corpse. So passionate were her tears of sorrow that the dead man came back to life. But Osiris could not continue to live on the earth, and was therefore made lord of the underworld. Thus the ancient Egyptians gave expression in the myth of the risen Osiris to their belief in a new life. This god, they held, decided the future existence of every human being. Consequently, his tomb, to which a locale was ascribed at Abydos, was much frequented and venerated. People liked to be buried in its vicinity, and when that was not practicable, they achieved it symbolically by having stone pillars erected there with their names inscribed on them.

It is not only the Egyptian idea of the hereafter that contrasts sharply with that of Israel. There is a similar contrast when it comes to representing the likeness of a god. As we know, Greek and Roman writers were hardly able to contain their ridicule when they observed the Egyptians, whom they regarded as an intelligent people, actually according divine honour and worship to various animals. This cult is, however, of a late date. It is true that as far as is known certain animals had played an unusually important role in the lives of the Egyptians from the earliest

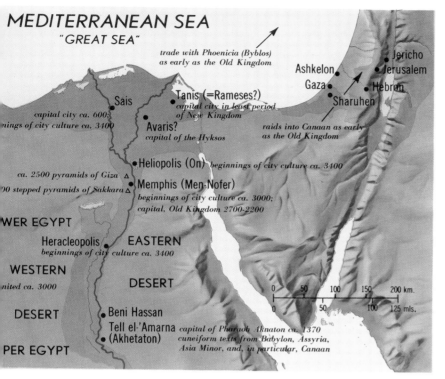

MEDITERRANEAN SEA
"GREAT SEA"

trade with Phoenicia (Byblos)
as early as the Old Kingdom

Ashkelon
Gaza
Sharuhen
Jericho
Jerusalem
Hebron

Sais
capital city ca. 600;
ings of city culture ca. 3400

Tanis (=Rameses?)
capital city in least period
of New Kingdom

Avaris?
capital of the Hyksos

raids into Canaan early
as the Old Kingdom

Heliopolis (On) beginnings of city culture ca. 3400

ca. 2500 pyramids of Giza

00 stepped pyramids of Sakkara

Memphis (Men-Nofer)
beginnings of city culture ca. 3000;
capital, Old Kingdom 2700-2200

WER EGYPT

Heracleopolis
beginnings of city culture ca. 3400

EASTERN

WESTERN

nited ca. 3000

DESERT

DESERT

Beni Hassan

Tell el-'Amarna
(Akhetaton)
capital of Pharaoh Aknaton ca. 1370
cuneiform texts from Babylon, Assyria,
Asia Minor, and, in particular, Canaan

PER EGYPT

0   50   100   150   200 km.
0   50   100   125 mls.

Important political events in Egypt

ca. **3000**: Upper Egypt and Lower Egypt, where city-states had already been highly developed for centuries, were united under a single authority.

ca. **2700**: Start of the *Old Kingdom*. This lasted till—

ca. **2200**: The first interim period; the country was split politically, and enfeebled.

ca. **2000**: Unity was restored; and the *Middle Kingdom* appeared.

ca. **1780**: The second interim period; Lower Egypt fell under the domination of the Hyksos, who entered the delta from Canaan.

ca. **1580**: The Hyksos were expelled from Egypt. Use of the war chariot enabled the Egyptians to reach the Euphrates. The *New Kingdom* began. For a long period Canaan remained politically within the Egyptian sphere of influence. Egypt enlarged her territory to the south, as far as the Fourth Cataract of the Nile.

ca. **1370**: *The Amarna period;* over several decades Egypt lost her political power.

ca. **1285**: Indecisive battle between Egyptians and Hittites near Kadesh; the 'eternal peace' was constituted.

ca. **1200**: Egypt confronted the 'sea peoples,' including the Philistines, and drove them back into Canaan.

ca. **1080**: *End of the New Kingdom*. Egypt lost her prosperity and split up.

ca. **660**: Temporary occupation of Lower Egypt by Assyria.

ca. **600**: Brief period of prosperity under the dynasty from Saïs.

ca. **525**: *The Persians* subdued Egypt and controlled it until—

ca. **330**: Alexander the Great annexed Egypt to his empire.

times, and as a result it has been assumed that animals were regarded as tribal totems.

The admiration, reverence, and fear experienced by man when faced with the mysteriousness of the animal nature and his inability to communicate with it, is a phenomenon found among many peoples and races in ancient times. But the Egyptians actually cultivated this sense of mystery. Among them, more than anywhere else, various animals came to be living symbols of different gods, creatures in whom divine forces were revealed. As a result, they tended to portray the gods in the form and aspect of an animal, or of a human being with an animal's head. Despite this, it is not possible, at least with regard to the classical period of Egypt, to speak of an 'animal cult' in the full sense of the term. The actual worship of, for instance, the Apis-bull, which people have from time to time connected with the golden calf of the Bible, arose only about the year 600 B.C.

Whereas the Egyptians, like the Sumerians, regarded the king as the son of a god, the Babylonian and Assyrian princes thought of themselves more as the deity's appointed governors. In Israel, too, men always remained conscious of the distinction between Yahweh and their king. In Egypt, it seems the king was conceived of as a divine being from the very outset, and this conviction persisted for wellnigh 3000 years. The Pharaoh ('Pharaoh' really stands for *per-a*, 'great house') eventually came to be regarded as the 'embodied' son of the god Re, who impregnated the queen. For that reason the ruler was the real priest, the person who, above all others, represented a link between the gods and men. The absolute character of his dominion found expression particularly during the New Kingdom, when the whole country was his personal property and every subject lived in total dependence on him. The story of Joseph in the Bible attributes this authority to the Pharaoh, but has an explanation of its own to offer (Gen. 47:13ff).

Egypt's contacts with the surrounding peoples were strongly influenced by the natural boundaries of the country. To the west and east extensive desert areas protected the Nile valley. To the south the border was secured by rocky, desert uplands; and in its upper reaches the Nile was difficult to navigate because of rapids. The northern frontier was defined by the Mediterranean Sea. Thus the people were able to live in safety along the fertile banks of the Nile. Only to the north, where the Nile formed a delta, did the habitable area fan out to east and west. The natural isolation of this land bordering the navigable reaches of the Nile very soon made one nation of the people living there. At first were two kingdoms, Lower and Upper Egypt—the delta region and the territory between the delta and the First Cataract near Aswan. But by about 3000 B.C. Egypt had already become one great nation, although the names and symbols of the northern and southern kingdoms were to remain in use for a long time to come. Thus one of the regular titles of the Pharaoh was 'ruler of the two lands.'

From this position of natural safety the Egyptians ventured into the world outside. At first a tentative and incidental movement, it later became more bold and more systematic. To the south of the cataracts the Egyptians invaded Nubia, chiefly to carry off ivory, animal hides, ebony, and, in particular, slaves. There was not much here in the way of honest trading, but their dealings with the Asiatic countries were quite different. The first contacts established in this direction were with the seaports of Phoenicia. With ships that hugged the coast from port to port, they built up a lively trade based on barter and exchange. Even as early as the period of the Old Kingdom the Pharaohs were sending their votive offerings to the 'mistress of Gebal,' the chief goddess of the city of Byblos. These sacrificial gifts have been found in the remains of her temple. Also, the names of most of the Egyptian princes of the third millennium have been found recorded at Byblos, and the inhabitants were even at this early date using the hieroglyphics of Egypt.

About the year 2000 B.C. relations became less friendly. The whole of the Near East, including Canaan, was then in a state of upheaval. From their base in the eastern delta the Pharaohs of the Middle Kingdom were making inroads into Asian territory, and it is to the resulting conflicts that we owe the so-called anathemas or 'execration formulae.' Egyptians would write the names of hostile states in Canaan on small earthenware statues and pots. Believing as they did in the mysterious connection between the representation and the object represented, between the name and the person to whom it belonged, they thought that by smashing the inscribed pots and images they were actually striking at their adversaries. The texts of these execrations show that by the nineteenth century B.C. certain well-known places in Canaan—Jerusalem, Shechem, Hazor, Byblos, and Beth-shemesh, for example—were already in existence. When the Middle Kingdom fell into decline, organized bands of Asiatics forced their way into northern Egypt via the eastern delta, which had been both the launching point for surprise attacks and the weak spot in the natural defences.

These Asiatics are something of an enigma. In the Graeco-Roman period it was thought that 'Hyksos'—the name by which they were known—meant 'shepherd kings.' In fact this was simply the name the Egyptians used when referring to any people who lived beyond their borders, though it was especially applied to Asiatics. Very little information has come down to us regarding this mixed group of conquerors. When in the sixteenth century B.C. the Hyksos were expelled, the Egyptians did their utmost to wipe out all traces of their alien culture.

The confrontation with these Asiatic powers intensified Egypt's concern with the Canaanite area. With the aid of the war-chariot—the new weapon taken over from the Hyksos—it penetrated as far as it could into Canaanite territory. Pharaoh Thothmes III, in particular, won fame from his achievements in this field. In his first campaign, possibly during the year 1479 B.C., he marched by Gaza through the plain of the Shephelah and Sharon straight to Megiddo, where he defeated an alliance of the Canaanite rulers. During his sixth campaign he overran Kadesh, which as the only remaining city of the once mighty Hyksos empire still occupied a leading position in the north of Canaan. The following year he even succeeded in crossing the Euphrates at Carchemish, an accomplishment of which he was particularly proud. It was on this occasion that the king of Babylon and the ruler of the powerful 'Kheta' people in Asia Minor (probably the Hittites) sent him gifts.

All these events were celebrated in Egypt with wild exuberance. In Karnak two obelisks were erected, one of which stands today in Istanbul. On it is written: 'Thutmosis, who crossed the great river of Naharin (the Euphrates) as a mighty conqueror at the head of his army.' This ruler appeared with his army some sixteen or seventeen times altogether in the north of Canaan, a fact which testifies to the pre-eminence of Egypt at this time.

A little after 1400 B.C. the situation changed somewhat. Egypt was then entering upon the Amarna period, in which the Pharaohs adopted a passive attitude in the sphere of foreign politics. This is borne out by the letters which various Asiatic rulers addressed to the Pharaohs Amenhotep III and IV. The first batch of these was discovered accidentally in 1887 at Tell el-'Amarna and consists of nearly four hundred clay tablets which throw light on the contemporary political situation in Canaan. At that time, apparently, there were a considerable number of more or less independent city states, with little unity obtaining between them. The Amarna letters mention among others the cities of Ashkelon, Hebron, Jerusalem, Gezer, Shechem, Megiddo, Acco, Damascus, Tyre, and of course, Byblos.

Most of the rulers in Canaan, however, appear to have received no replies to their letters. Pharaoh Amenhotep IV, especially, showed little interest in the political troubles of other nations. He preferred instead to concern himself with a religious movement which even today arouses no small wonder. A monotheistic strain had existed in Egypt well before his time, but it was he who developed it further and gave it a new form. For him, the essential nature of the godhead consisted in 'the force of all life,' with its centre in the sun. This he worshipped under the name of Aton. He changed his own name to Ikhnaton (possibly 'servant of Aton'), and he removed his capital from Thebes, the city of the god Amon, to Akhet-Aton ('horizon of Aton'). After his death the city he had built was soon ravaged and abandoned, and the ruined remains are known nowadays as Tell el-'Amarna. According to the new belief the god Aton revealed himself in the sun, and its energizing rays were depicted as a solar disc with beams radiating out from it and terminating in tiny hands. The famous 'hymn to the sun,' which gives expression to this new belief, contains themes and turns of phrase akin to those we find later in Psalm 104 (103).

Finally, there is another remarkable parallel between Egyptian literature and the Bible. At the end of the second millennium in Egypt Amen-em-Opet, the sage, put on record a number of wise counsels. The text of these has been transmitted to us on a papyrus, probably of the seventh or sixth century B.C. The instruction given by this Egyptian bears a strong resemblance to the Book of Proverbs, and in particular to Proverbs 22:17–24:22. Compare, for instance, Proverbs 22:17-18a with Amen-em-Opet's preamble:

> Give thy ears, hear what is said,
> Give thy heart to understand them.
> To put them in thy heart is worth while,
> (But) it is damaging to him who neglects them.

As with the Mesopotamian parallels (p. 37), so here we should not immediately assume direct literary indebtedness. It was the predominance of the New Kingdom during the century immediately preceding the rise of Israel that enabled Egyptian culture to affect Canaanite civilization, which in its turn later influenced Israel. Moreover, the Pharaohs had a number of military bases in that area, where Egyptian soldiers were stationed. For example, one such garrison was located at Beth-shan, a town to the south of the lake of Gennesaret. Among other things the remains of Egyptian temples have been found there, along with monuments commemorating the Pharaoh Seti I (ca. 1300 B.C.) and his successor, Rameses II. Again, when some centuries later Israel had become an independent state with a king, a royal household, and public offices of various kinds, a close contact existed between Solomon and his successors and the Egyptian court. Such evidence goes to show that the culture

This papyrus is from the tomb of an Egyptian priest who died about 1100 B.C. In 1960 this specimen was unrolled at the British Museum and turned out to be some 23 feet long. At the beginning is a picture of Osiris, god of the underworld, and of Ma'at, the goddess of justice. Osiris is wearing the high crown and holds the sceptre in his hand. With her right hand Ma'at offers him a feather, the symbol of truth. It was in the New Kingdom that the custom arose of giving the deceased person a collection of proverbs on a roll of papyrus. They are 'saws' of a magical and religious character, intended to assist the dead man on his journey in the hereafter. The name given to collections of this kind is *Book of the Dead*, even though the selection and number of proverbs, and the order in which they occur, may be different in each case.

of the 'fertile crescent'–the way its inhabitants thought and felt, wrote and spoke–provided the general background for certain Biblical ideas and forms of expression.

3. THE HITTITES

Right up to the beginning of this century it was still not at all clear how important the Hittites were for the history of the Near East. Ancient Egyptian and Mesopotamian documents intimate that the Hatti, as this people were then called, played a prominent part on the stage of international politics during the second millennium B.C. But the evidence is limited to brief allusions. In addition they are mentioned in several stone inscriptions found in northern Syria, which no-one could at first decipher.

It was the Bible that seemed to offer the plainest clues. Here, the Hittites were assumed to be inhabitants of Canaan. Abraham is said to have bought a cave at Hebron from 'the sons of Heth' (Gen. 23), and Esau to have taken to wife some Hittite girls (Gen. 26:34; 36:2). One of David's soldiers, Uriah, was apparently a Hittite (2 Sam. 11:3). Solomon numbered Hittite princesses amongst his wives (1 Kings 11:1), and also traded with Hittite kings (2 Chron. 1:17). When the Arameans were besieging the city of Samaria, they took flight on hearing the rumour that the Hittite kings were coming to the aid of Israel (2 Kings 7:6). Furthermore, the Bible mentions the Hittites along with

the Kenites, Rephaim, Amorites, Canaanites, Jebusites, and other inhabitants of Canaan in several lists of nations–for example, in Genesis 15:19-21 and Joshua 3:10. Thus the eponymous father of the tribe, Heth, was regarded in Genesis 10:15 as a son of Canaan. Even during the Exile this idea was still current. When Ezekiel wanted to drive home the insignificant origin of Jerusalem, he said: "Your origin and your birth are of the land of the Canaanites; your father was an Amorite, and your mother a Hittite." (Ezek. 16:3) The Biblical writers believed, therefore, that the Hittites belonged in Canaan, and more especially in the northern parts.

This view has been somewhat modified in the present century as a result of excavations carried out in central Turkey. The Biblical authors are partly right, inasmuch as there were indeed small Hittite kingdoms in northern Syria during the first millennium. But as usual, these authors presented the situation as it appeared in their own day, even when dealing with the remote past. During the patriarchal period the historical position of the Hittites in fact presented a very different picture. Throughout the second millennium they were a world power, and their true homeland at that time was in Asia Minor. It was centred on the ancient city of Hattushash, whose ruins have been discovered near the small village of Boghaz Köi, east of Ankara.

Furthermore, the Hittites were not Semites but Indo-Europeans, coming originally from the interior of Asia or Europe. Pushed outwards by one of the many migrations of peoples in earlier times, they gradually settled, around the year 2000 B.C.,

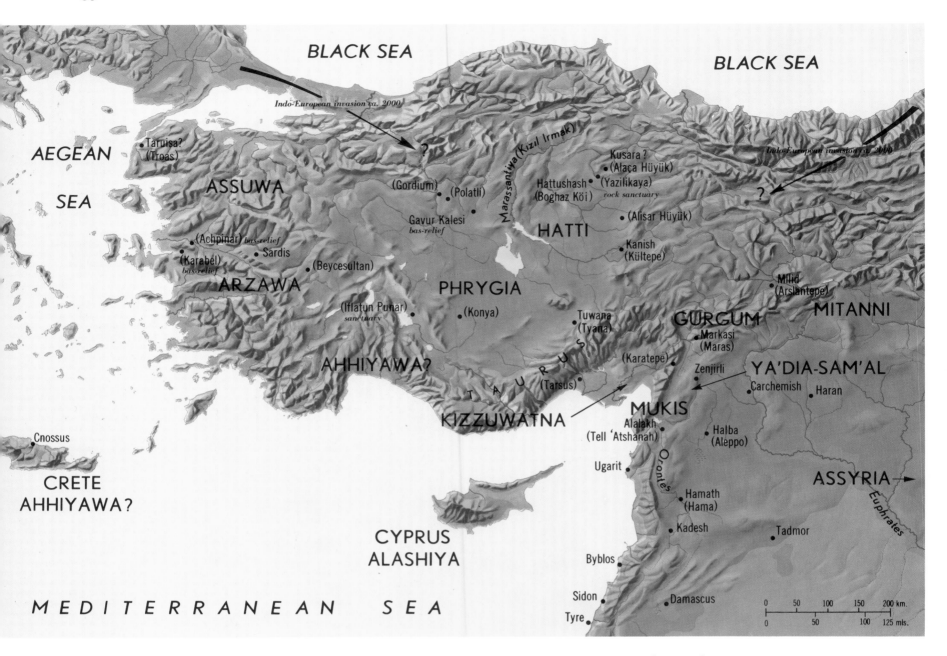

Important political events in Asia Minor

ca. 2300: According to legendary stories of a later period King Sargon of Accad is supposed to have led a military expedition deep into Asia Minor.

ca. 2200: According to a popular tradition King Naram-Sin of Accad, the grandson of Sargon, fought a coalition of seventeen kings from Asia Minor, including Pamba, King of Hatti.

ca. 2000: Indo-Germanic tribes from the Caucasus or from the Balkans settled peacefully in Asia Minor, especially around the basin of the Kızıl Irmak (Halys).

ca. 1900: Assyrian traders made their way through Asia Minor. In Kanish (Kültepe) they even built their own quarter, where numerous clay tablets have been discovered, inscribed with Assyrian texts in cuneiform.

ca. 1700: The Indo-Germanic tribes who had settled among the indigenous peoples seized power. From the town of Kusara (Alaça Hüyük?) King Anittas and his successor Labarnas, governed the central part of Asia Minor: start of the Old Kingdom.

ca. 1630: The Hittites, led by Hattusilis I, marched to the Euphrates and into Syria for the first time. They were defeated at Halba (Aleppo).

ca. 1600: Mursilis I moved from Kusura to Hattushash, where he took up permanent residence. He conquered Aleppo and pushed on as far, even, as Babylon, thus bringing about the collapse of Hammurabi's dynasty. The Hittite kingdom was still not secure enough, however, to consolidate these successes. Moreover, the Mitanni kingdom, which was to develop fully in the north of Mesopotamia a few decades later, proved an obstacle to any lasting expansion in the direction of Syria.

ca. 1455: For a number of years the power of Mitanni was broken by Pharaoh Thothmes III during his eighth expedition into Syria.

ca. 1450: Start of the New Kingdom. King Tudhaliyas II conquered and destroyed Aleppo. Outlying states such as Assuwa, Arzawa, Ahhiyawa, and Kizzuwatna gradually came under the authority of Hatti.

ca. 1370: King Suppiluliumas I razed the capital city of Mitanni, conquered Aleppo and Alalakh, and penetrated as far as Kadesh. During the Amarna period Egypt remained a powerless onlooker.

ca. 1340: Another expedition into Syria. Suppiluliumas subjected even Carchemish to the power of Hatti. Tutankhamon's widow in Egypt asked for a Hittite prince to be her new consort. Because Suppiluliumas hesitated too long, the widow's opponents in Egypt were able to put their own plans into execution and murdered the young prince at the Egyptian frontier.

ca. 1285: Indecisive battle between Egypt and Hatti at Kadesh.

ca. 1270: Egypt and Hatti concluded the 'eternal peace,' perhaps with an eye to the growing power of Assyria.

ca. 1200: Owing to a large-scale migration of peoples from the north-west the kingdom of Hatti crumbled and collapsed, never to recover. In the southeastern corner a few minor neo-Hittite states, such as Milid, Gurgum, Ya'dia, Mukis, Halba, and Hamath managed to survive. Assyrian and, later on, Aramean influence within these small states gradually increased.

ca. 800: In various military campaigns Assyria subdued the small neo-Hittite kingdoms.

ca. 750: For a brief period there emerged in Asia Minor the Kingdom of the Phrygians, who had reappeared in this area during the major shift in population about 1200.

ca. 600: In the western part of Asia Minor King Croesus ruled the state of Lydia, conquered by Cyrus of Persia in 546.

CANAAN
to ca. 1200 B.C.

It is difficult to sum up in a few sentences the main points in the history of Canaan up to ca. 1200 B.C. There was no central authority to give any consistent direction to events: each tribe or town went very much its own way. About 3000 B.C., under the stimulus of developments in Mesopotamia and Egypt, urban culture made its appearance. In the north of Canaan the cities managed to survive despite repeated incursions of bands of nomads. In the south, in Palestine, urban culture suffered an interruption about the year 2000 that was to last for several centuries: invading nomads took possession of the country. In the 19th century urban life gradually revived; and, during the centuries that followed, this continued, in spite of domination by the Hyksos (17th century) and the Egyptians (16th-13th centuries). Outside the towns and villages, however, there was still room enough for nomads to roam; and it was to the latter group that those Hebrew tribes belonged who in the second half of the second millennium established themselves in the hill country of Palestine.

MEDITERRANEAN SEA
"UPPER SEA"

"GREAT SEA"

city culture as early as ca. 3000;
many contacts with Egypt in 3rd
millennium; earliest text in linear
script on sarcophagus of King
Ahiram ca. 1000

Ugarit

Hamath

Byblos

rock inscriptions
Dog River

Berytus

LEBANON   highest peak
10,000 ft.

BEQA

ANTI-LEBANON   highest peak
8000 ft.

much traffic with Egypt during
the New Kingdom (1575-1087)   Sidon

Damascus
Aramean city state ca. 1000

Hermon 9232 ft.

Tyre

Litani

the site was a rocky off-shore island
until Alexander (332) built a causeway
to link it to the mainland

MOUNTAINS
OF
GALILEE
highest peak
4000 ft.

SYRO-

Canaanite temple (Nahariya)

Acco

Hazor
Canaanite city of large area;
100 acres of cultivated land

SEA OF
CHINNERETH

-690
ft.

ARABIAN

CARMEL

PLAIN
OF
JEZREEL

Yarmuk

GILEAD
(fertile area)

Dor

Mesolithic culture
in Wadi el-Mughara

Megiddo
important
crossroads

Taanach

Dothan

Beth-shan
Egyptian garrison till ca. 1000

Jordan

Tell es-Saidiyeh (Zarethan?)

Ebal 3084 ft.
Shechem
MOUNTAINS
OF
EPHRAIM

Gerizim
2860
ft.

Deir Alla (Succoth?)

Jabbok

SHARON

Wadi Farah

AMMONITES ca. 1100 Semitic state

TJEKER
ca. 1200

Shiloh

PHILISTINES

mesolithic culture
in Wadi en-Natuf

Bethel

Gezer

Jericho

Ammon

DESERT

mesolithic culture ca. 9000;
neolithic culture;
wall and towers ca. 7000

Ashdod

Jerusalem
height ca.
2300 ft.

ca. 1200
HEBREW
TRIBES

difficult to cross before
domestication of the camel

Ashkelon
important port

SHEPHELAH

MOUNTAINS
OF
JUDAH

Lachish

Hebron

WILDERNESS OF JUDAH

-1290 ft.

Arnon

Gaza

En-gedi

DEAD SEA
SALT SEA"

Tell el-Far'ah

Beer-sheba

Kir-Hareseth

Sharuhen? Egyptian garrison
town in New Kingdom (1575-1087)

MOABITES ca. 1100 Semitic state

Zered

N E G E B

ARABAH

Bozrah

EDOMITES ca. 1100 Semitic state

SINAI

GULF OF AQABA

0   20   40 km.

0   5   10   15   20   25 mls.

The Battle of Kadesh
according to Egyptian sources

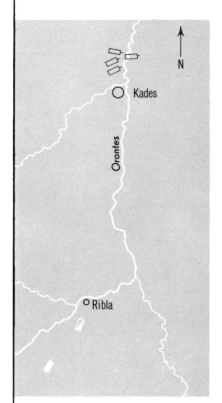 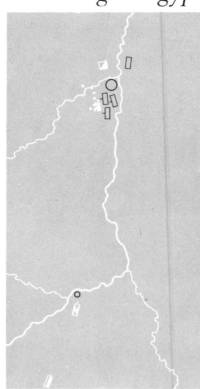 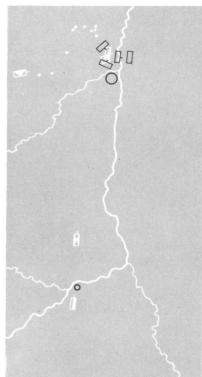 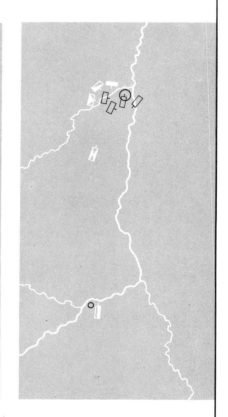

Key to Symbols

⊑▸ *Hittite army unit, moving in the direction indicated.*

The remaining symbols refer to the Egyptian forces;

◣ Amon division	◩ Re division	⊠ Ptah division
▭ Seth division	◪ Western recruits	

Map 1: Toward noon on a summer's day in the year 1285 (?) the vanguard of the Egyptian army, under Rameses II, reached the river Orontes near Shabtuna, a place later referred to in the Bible (2 Kings 23 : 33; 25 : 6) as Riblah. There two prisoners from the Hittite camp were brought to Rameses. These two duped the Pharaoh by telling him that the Hittites had made a hurried withdrawal and that, as Canaanites, they both wanted to desert. Thereupon Rameses hastily crossed the Orontes with the Amon division to take the town of Kadesh and then surprise the Hittites. These were lying hidden north of the town and at the enemy's approach crossed under cover to the east bank of the river.

Map 2: Rameses' army had already been some weeks on active service; and fatigue was making itself felt. The Amon division therefore pitched camp north of the town, when it was realized that the place could not be taken by surprise. Meanwhile the Re division was approaching too. At that moment the Hittite cavalry crossed back over the Orontes south of the town. The Re division was surprised and completely routed.

Map 3: The Hittite chariots then turned to attack Rameses' camp, which was already in a state of chaos: A number of Egyptians fled northwards; the remainder, including the Pharaoh, were encircled. Rameses saw at once that the weakest point in the Hittite circle was in the direction of the river. Against this sector he launched his attack; and thanks to his bold action the enemy were soon forced into the river. The ring enclosing Rameses was broken. Even so, the situation was still critical for the Egyptians. In front of them were ranged the Hittite chariots; and in their rear, on the far side of the river, were the rest of the enemy forces. Then fortune came to the help of Rameses and his troops.

Map 4: Distracted by the spoils of the Egyptian camp, the Hittite cavalry failed to press home their attack. Just then help arrived unexpectedly from the west. A division known as the 'recruits' had been ordered to march on Kadesh by a different route. They put in an appearance just in time. With the 'recruits from the west' and the men of the Amon and Re divisions who had fled but were now returning Rameses was able to form a new battle order. The battle continued for several hours. As darkness closed in and the Ptah division drew near, the Hittite cavalry withdrew into the town. The battle was over. Both sides had apparently suffered great losses. Without laying siege to Kadesh, Rameses, with what remained of his army, began his way back to Egypt; and for their part the Hittites did not—indeed could not—venture in pursuit.

in the mountainous parts of Asia Minor among the races already living there. For historical reasons which are still obscure, they were able to subjugate this entire area about 1700 B.C., from which time the beginning of their Old Kingdom is usually dated. The strength of the Hittites at this time is evident from the fact that about 1600 B.C. their king, Mursilis I, pushed forward into the more civilized regions of Syria and Mesopotamia and conquered the mighty city of Babylon. The Babylonian chronicles report the incident thus: "In the time of Samsuditana the men of Hatti advanced against the country of Accad."

Militarily, economically and, above all, politically however, the Hittites were not then in a position to maintain a world empire. Consequently the Old Kingdom soon withered away. In the fifteenth century B.C., a new phase of expansion began, and for a time the Hittites were the strongest power in their part of the world. This is evident from the fact that just after the Amarna period, the widow of Tutankhamon sought the hand of a Hittite prince in marriage. However, this opportunity of gaining control over Egypt was lost because the Hittite king took too long in accepting the proposal. As a result, the hostile faction in Egypt were able to muster their opposition, and the prospective husband was killed at the Egyptian border.

One particular event, which took place considerably later, was of very special importance for the subsequent history of Israel. After the lax Amarna period Egypt had rallied her strength once more and attempted to put an end to Hittite domination in Syria. In the fifth year of his reign—probably in 1286–1285 B.C. —Pharaoh Rameses II marched north-eastward with his army, intent on driving the Hittites out of Syria once and for all. The battle between these two world powers at Kadesh on the river Orontes profoundly influenced the future course of events in Canaan. Egyptian stories, poems, and pictures commemorating this engagement have long been known, but the discovery of the remains of the ancient Hittite kingdom at Hattushash and elsewhere has made it possible to interpret the Egyptian accounts more impartially.

It is now clear that the battle at Kadesh weakened both sides to such an extent that very soon afterwards other forces were able to come to power. Total victory on the part of either Egypt or the Hatti would probably have prevented the invasion of Canaan by the 'sea peoples' (among whom were the Philistines) and also the conquest of the highlands of Palestine by Hebrew tribes. As it was, the outcome of the battle remained indecisive, even if the Egyptian account of it does portray Rameses II as a mighty warrior and hero. About 1270 B.C., out of respect for each other's power—and probably out of concern for their own weakness as well—the two sides concluded their renowned pact of 'everlasting peace.' In Egypt and in the Hittite kingdom the text of this treaty was engraved on a tablet of silver, and in both countries copies of it have been recovered which run roughly parallel. The restrained opening of the Hittite version reads:

> Treaty of Rea-Mashesha mai Amana [Rameses, beloved of Amon], the great king, the king of the land of Egypt, the valiant, with Hattusilis, the great king of the Hatti land for establishing (good) peace (and) good brotherhood (worthy of) great (king)ship forever.

Promises were exchanged to refrain from attacking each other and to defend each other against any third party. Moreover, there was an attempt to render conspiracy difficult in either country by undertaking that one ruler should never give asylum to political opponents of the other. In the Egyptian version the treaty was ratified thus:

> As for these words of the regulation (which) the Great Prince of Hatti (made) with Ramses (Meri-Amon), the great ruler (of Egypt), in writing upon this tablet of silver —as for these words, a thousand gods of the male gods and of the female gods of them of the land of Hatti, together with a thousand gods of the male gods and of the female gods of them of the land of Egypt, are with me as witnesses (hearing) these words...

This famous alliance was cemented by the marriage between Rameses II and a daughter of the Hittite king. Chaperoned by her father and his powerful army, the girl was brought to Egypt. She was given the Egyptian name of Maat-nefru-Re and became the first lady of the royal harem. The Egyptian chronicler comments: "And so it was that, if a man or a woman proceeded on their mission to Djahi, they could reach the land of Hatti without fear around about their hearts, because of the greatness of the victories of his (maj)esty."

This peaceful situation did not last for long. About the year 1200 B.C. the peoples settled round the eastern Mediterranean began to move inland. It was a migration that put an end to the Hittite empire and the city of Ugarit, and pushed the Egyptians back as far as the delta. The Syrian part of the Hittite kingdom, however, remained safe from the onset of these sea peoples. This area then split up into a number of small states—a situation with which the Biblical authors were well acquainted.

In 1947 there was discovered at Karatepe in the south-east of Turkey an inscription in two languages, at each of two entrances to an ancient fortress. On the right-hand side were Hittite hieroglyphics, and on the left a parallel text in the language and script of ancient Phoenicia. Since then it has been possible to decipher thousands of Hittite texts found on clay tablets and rock inscriptions with a fair degree of accuracy. Once again an ancient centre of civilization has been rescued from the obscurity of the past. But whether the culture of the Hatti had any influence on Israel is not so easy to determine, although scholars have in recent times directed attention to the Hittite treaties and laws as a possible example.

The Hittite kings were apparently more given than other rulers to making treaties with their vassals and with the peoples they had conquered. The texts of these nearly always follow the same plan. The pact starts off with an historical introduction, listing in particular the benefits conferred by the high prince of the Hittites on his vassal. Then come the orders and regulations with which the defeated party must comply. At the end the gods are invoked as witnesses. All who observe the provisions of the treaty are duly blessed, while those who break them are threatened with a curse. It is obviously tempting to link these texts with those of alliances mentioned in the Bible which show certain similarities (as, for example, in Josh. 24).

The Hittite laws are conspicuously humane, and they contain no indication, at least not in any literal sense, of the

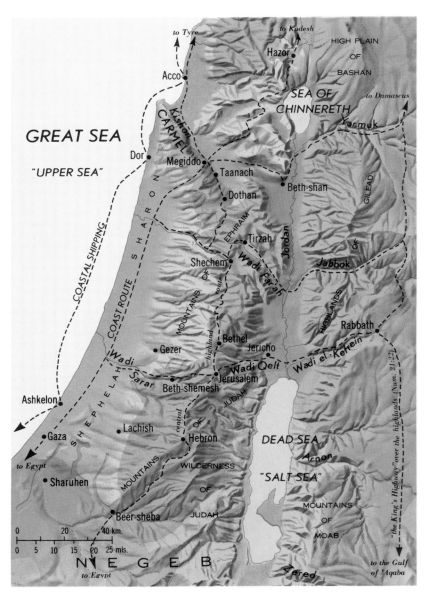

oriental attitude of 'an eye for an eye, a tooth for a tooth.' As a penalty for theft, the inflicting of bodily harm, etc., no physical punishment was imposed except, in certain cases, on a slave. As a general rule, material reparation was held to be sufficient. Only for what were considered the most serious crimes—sexual intercourse with animals, rape, sexual intercourse with certain close relatives, and sedition—was the death penalty imposed, but even here the king could exercise his prerogative of mercy.

Scholars have pointed to yet other elements which it is possible to link with the Bible, but the most striking remain the treaty formulae and the respect for the individual embodied in the laws. It is not to be inferred from this, however, that the Hittite texts had any direct influence on the Bible, because the empire of Hatti had already vanished long before Israel became a nation. What does need to be recognized is that the Hittite civilization helped to form the general cultural climate of the Near East, and it was within this cultural framework that Israel found its place and the Bible acquired some of its features.

4. CANAAN

The development of written language and the course of history in the Near East make it clear that Canaan—that is to say, Syria-Palestine—was an area where many political and cultural trends met and clashed. These influences, emanating from Egypt, Babylonia, Assyria, Hatti, and other nations, effectively prevented the political unification of Canaan. Even without invasions from outside, it would have been difficult for this territory to develop into a single state of any considerable size. Its physical features, conditioning as they did the settlement of the

Trade routes through Palestine

Through Palestine ran the main trade routes between Mesopotamia, Syria, Phoenicia in the north and Egypt in the south. These routes followed the fairly level, straight course that nature had provided.

Generally speaking, the east-west connections were less important. They also made for less easy travelling, because they had to follow the twists and turns of the uneven beds of the wadis.

Megiddo was centrally situated in the north, on the edge of the plain of Jezreel. As a junction, this town dominated the whole movement of trade; and to a somewhat smaller extent the same applied to Shechem. In the highlands, Jerusalem came to have a strategic position. The city commanded the lines of communication between the northern and southern Hebrew tribes.

Lachish, Gezer, and Sharuhen were less centrally situated, on the borderline between the highlands and the level plain. As a result, they did not profit so much from the commercial traffic; but on the other hand they were more secure when hostile armies were traversing the country.

Among the natural trading-routes the Jordan valley had no very considerable place. In summer, because it lay almost 1000 feet below sea level, it was broiling hot. In winter the eddying waters of the wadis entering from east and west made the banks difficult and treacherous. Furthermore, the remarkably tortuous course of the Jordan forced travellers to cover many more miles than was necessary.

The cedar is one of the most widely reputed trees in the world of the Bible. Its wood is highly durable; and it was used in the countries of the Near East in the construction of temples, palaces, and ships. At one time these trees must have covered the slopes of the Lebanon and the Anti-Lebanon, above 3000 feet, in vast numbers. Nowadays only a few small clumps remain. Some specimens are about 100 feet in height, and their girth at the foot of the trunk can be from 50 to 65 feet. The age of the largest is estimated at more than 2000 years.

(Opposite) The Jordan in the north of Palestine. Four springs which rise on the southern spurs of the Lebanon and Anti-Lebanon mountain ranges supply the water for the river. The point where the springs join is still 156 feet above sea-level; but the river soon drops below sea-level, which is why the whole Jordan valley has a warm, damp climate. Because of the relatively small difference in level between its source and its mouth in the Dead Sea the river is both very winding and shallow. It is only in the spring, when the rainfall is abundant and the snows melt on the Lebanon, that the water rises and the river floods its banks. As a result of all this, the river and its valley were little used by travellers.

Between the Gulf of 'Aqaba and the Dead Sea runs a broad valley, known nowadays as the Arabah. In the Bible this word usually signifies an infertile region. The name is sometimes used to denote the whole cleavage which divides Canaan from north to south. Thus the Dead Sea is itself described as 'the sea of the Arabah' (Deut. 3 : 17, etc.). The valley called Arabah today was long disputed territory between Judah and Edom, because of the iron and copper in the mountains to the east and west.

country, hindered a unification from within. Some description of the land of Canaan may help to explain this situation.

Canaan is a roughly rectangular area between the Mediterranean and the Syro-Arabian desert. Nature divides this rectangle into four narrow strips running north and south. In the west, bordering the sea and stretching from Ugarit to south of Gaza, lies a coastal plain. It would make a convenient route for armies on the move, were it not for the fact that in several places mountainous rock formations run right across it, thrusting their impassable headlands into the sea. This is especially the case north of Beirut at the 'Dog River.' Numerous armies in the past have found this a critical point. On the rocky walls along the river not a few army leaders have had their memorial tablets inscribed. Egyptian, Assyrian, Babylonian, Greek, Latin, Arabic, even French and English inscriptions are to be found there. The coastal plain is again interrupted to the south of Tyre and yet again at the celebrated Mount Carmel, where armies and caravans were obliged to detour inland past the town of Megiddo, which thus occupied a position of strategic importance.

To the east of this long coastal plain the second strip runs from north to south—an extensive series of mountain ranges stretching, with some breaks, from Ugarit as far as Sinai. Inland from Ugarit are the mountains which culminate in the Zaphon peak, where according to Ugaritic texts the god Baal had his throne. Inland from Byblos is the mountain range of the Lebanon with its cedars, and in northern Palestine the Galilean range, which at its southern point suddenly becomes the plain of Jezreel. Then come the hills of Samaria and Judea, and far to the south the rocky wastes of the Negeb and the Sinaitic range.

The third strip again offers a marked contrast to the second. The peaks of the Lebanon often rise to 6500 feet or more, but less than five miles east of this the valley near Hazor falls below sea-level. In the northern part of this strip lies the fertile plain of Syria, with Aleppo as its centre. Further south, the area of low ground narrows to become the Beqa', a valley between the ranges of the Lebanon and the Anti-Lebanon. Through this valley, in a northerly direction, flows the river Orontes, while the Litani, which reaches the sea just above Tyre, takes a southerly course. Then one after the other come the Jordan valley, the Dead Sea, and the Arabah. They constitute a deep depression, in which, at the lowest point on the earth's surface, the shores of the Dead Sea reach almost 1300 feet below sea-level.

East of this deep rift valley towers yet another mountain-range, forming the fourth strip. In the north lie the Anti-Lebanon and Hermon, with its eternal snows. Further south stretch the hills of Gilead, Moab, and, in particular, Edom. It is only to the east of these two ranges that the country becomes less rugged. Here a broad and smooth plateau slopes down to the Syro-Arabian desert, where the shortage of water gives but meagre opportunity for life to flourish.

These four elongated strips, themselves broken up by mountains, valleys, rivers, and wadis, divide Canaan into a number of areas contained within natural barriers. The northerly coastal strip is very narrow, but it has some natural harbours. Protected by the inhospitable mountain range to the east, powerful sea-towns like Ugarit, Arvad, Byblos, Sidon, and Tyre were able to develop. Further inland, in the plain behind the mountains, towns like Aleppo, Hamath, Kadesh and, to the south, Damas-

cus came into being. In Palestine, the southern part of Canaan, the situation was different. The coastal plain is indeed wider here than in Phoenicia; but no ports of any note were able to develop because the coast was flat and the coastline straight. The mountains of Galilee, Samaria, and Judea, on the other hand, are lower than the Lebanon and Anti-Lebanon. Even during the wet winter season people could still live there. The third strip, the narrow valley of the Orontes, the Litani, and the Jordan, is also subject to considerable climatic variations. Thus in summer-time the valley between the Lebanon and the Anti-Lebanon enjoys an agreeable temperature, whereas the Jordan valley and the Dead Sea become a veritable furnace.

One result of all these geographical factors was that small, independent states, each centred on a town of some importance, sprang up all over Canaan. It was a situation highly favourable, of course, to nomadic tribes like the Hebrews who wanted to settle in this territory. No central authority existed which might have barred their way. Again, the density of the population varied greatly owing to the local differences in climate. The rainfall in particular, which varies considerably from west to east and from north to south, was a controlling factor. Around Jerusalem the annual rainfall is about the same as, for example, in London or Amsterdam. The coastal plain receives roughly three-quarters as much, the Jordan valley only about one-quarter, while the mountainous region of trans-Jordan receives about the same amount as Jerusalem.

The area between the line Taanach-Jerusalem-Hebron and the Jordan valley is especially short of rain, because it lies in the rain-shadow of the hills to the west. Permanent settlements in this region were rare, therefore, especially to the south, where the wilderness of Judea stretched out along the shores of the Dead Sea. The annual rainfall in Palestine is in fact adequate, but the rainy season is relatively brief. In the winter months of December, January, and February heavy showers of rain are usual. During the autumn and spring there is only the occasional shower, and in the summer the land dries up altogether. Moreover, since it is difficult for the rainwater to penetrate the rocky surface of the hills, most of it runs away through the clefts in the mountains to the Mediterranean, the Jordan, the Dead Sea, and the Arabah.

Soil and climate determined where the people of Canaan lived. So long as they had no means of catching the rainwater and storing it, they had to settle near a spring. Consequently, most towns stood on the edge of the hill country, as did Megiddo, Beth-shan, Hazor, Dothan, Taanach, Shechem, Gezer and Hebron. Places such as Jerusalem, Jericho, Ashkelon and Dor were, for specific reasons, exceptions in this respect. The

To the east of Jerusalem lies the Kidron valley which is continued as the Wadi en-Nar, shown opposite. This wadi runs south-eastwards and reaches the Dead Sea between Qumran and the mouth of the Wadi Murabba'at. Like many other valleys the Wadi en-Nar therefore presents an obstacle to north-south traffic through Palestine. It is, in fact, almost impossible to cross, for its precipitous walls in places reach a height of 260 feet. During the rainy season in the winter a little water often flows along the bed. Then it is too dangerous to use the wadi as a route from east to west; for after a heavy downpour a torrent of water may suddenly rush, with a roar like thunder, in the direction of the Dead Sea.

central highlands were therefore not densely populated, and this, too, was favourable to the Hebrew settlement of Canaan.

Another factor with which the Hebrew tribes had to come to terms was the religion of the Canaanites. Despite the lack of political integration it is still possible to speak of a 'religion of Canaan.' These city states depended very largely for their continued existence on the cultivation of the fields that surrounded their towns. In Egypt and Mesopotamia permanent sunshine and the abundant water for irrigation provided by the annual floods gave the land what it needed to make it fertile. In Canaan the situation was quite different. The Jordan was too low-lying to be used for irrigating the more elevated mountain country, and there were no other rivers of any size. The coastal plains and the valleys between the mountains had to depend entirely on rain falling to make them fertile.

During the dry summer months the fields lay barren and deserted. Only in the autumn, when the 'early rain' had fallen, was it possible to begin sowing and planting. Then the earth became green once more, the wild flowers gave colour to the countryside, and the herdsmen could lead their sheep and goats to pasture even in the so-called desert places. But one year the rain would come early and in abundance, another year late and in meagre quantity. Against this capriciousness on nature's part the Canaanite was powerless. In Egypt and Mesopotamia the flood-waters were controlled by canals and dams, but in Canaan it was a case of waiting for what nature might give. This conditioned the Canaanite attitude to religion and made of it a typical nature cult.

Until recently our knowledge of Canaanite religion was very limited. The sources were mainly secondhand, and the most important of these were the anti-Canaanite passages in the Bible. We find such passages in Exodus 34:13; Deuteronomy 12:2; 16:21-22; 18:9-11, and especially in 2 Kings 17:9-17. Although substantial progress has been made in this field since the Ugaritic cuneiform script was deciphered in 1930, our knowledge still remains fragmentary, and we cannot take the information contained in the Ugaritic texts as applying without qualification to the whole of Canaan. Nevertheless, the stories of the gods from Ugarit do help to shed some light on the matter.

In the Bible God is frequently denoted by the term 'El,' but this can just as well be a proper name as a generic noun. In Ugarit it is the same. The god supreme over all the gods of Canaan was likewise called 'El.' Besides this, he was given other names, such as 'father of the gods,' 'father of men,' and 'maker

A stele of Baal from Ugarit. This piece of white limestone is 4ft. 7 in. high, 18 in. broad, and 11 in. thick. The god is wearing a headpiece with a pointed tip. Rising from his forehead are two horns, representing, probably, the bull which is the symbol of Baal. He has two long locks of hair hanging down and a pointed beard. He wears the typical short apron of the warrior; and from his belt hangs a dagger. In his right hand he brandishes a club, possibly symbolizing thunder. With his left hand he clutches a lance, which signifies lightning and early vegetation. The god is standing on a double plinth, on which undulating lines are engraved. The top line probably represents the mountains on which Baal has his throne, and the bottom line the water, which Baal has subdued. The small figure in front of the god is hard to identify: it may perhaps represent a ruler of Ugarit, seeking refuge with the god. It is conjectured that this stele dates from the 19th or 18th century B.C.

of what is made.' His authority was indicated by the title of 'king,' his goodness by 'the merciful,' and his primal energy by 'the bull El.' But as elsewhere in the Near East, this supreme god lost his paramount position. As a venerable, aged figure he continued to occupy his throne, but other deities took his place as rulers over the earth.

According to a Ugaritic myth the struggle for power was protracted. The first to come to the fore was Yam-Nahar, god of the water that lays waste and destroys. Against him the mountain god, Baal, who 'rides upon the clouds,' had to wage a life-and-death battle. Thanks to the goddess Anat, Baal, whose name means 'owner, master, or possessor,' was the victor. Then the god of the storm, thunder, lightning, and, above all, rain assumed dominion, and the earth entered upon a period of fecundity and well-being.

As yet, however, Baal possessed no palace and no temple. His authority was not as yet definitively established. It remained for him to conquer Mot, the god of scorching heat, of drought, and of the planted corn. Baal sought out Mot in the latter's own domain. The clay tablets do not give us full details as to the course of the battle, but it is clear that for a time Baal fell into Mot's power. Athtar, god of springs and irrigation, then took Baal's place on the earth, but was unable to maintain it. In fact the earth was without life, and Mot reigned supreme for a while. Eventually, however, to the joy of all the other gods, Baal returned and re-established his authority.

Unfortunately, the beginning and end of this myth have not been preserved, and it is therefore impossible to clarify its meaning. The experience of one particular natural disaster, a protracted drought or something similar, may lie behind it, or it may be an attempt to represent the annual cycle of the arid, barren summer and the wet and fruitful winter season. Whatever its origin, we find in this and other Ugaritic myths features which are typical of Canaanite religion as a whole.

One rather striking instance is the role played by the female deity. For example, Anat, Baal's sister and consort, the goddess

of battle and love, is always ready to lend him aid, and in other texts frequent mention is made of the goddess Astarte. As the goddess of fertility she acquired a pre-eminent position in the religion of Canaan. Numerous figurines of her, with pronounced sexual characteristics, have been recovered in the course of excavations in Palestine, even in layers of Israelite occupation. Another feature of Canaanite religion was its primitive character. The anthropomorphic gods, with their passions and their amorous adventures, closely resemble the gods of the later Greek stories in Homer. Furthermore, the sex of the various deities is not always clearly defined, and they are not always sufficiently distinguished from their animal symbols. Thus El is referred to as 'the bull,' and Baal as 'the bull-calf.'

The sexually oriented and primitive character of Canaanite religion made a considerable impact on the simple Hebrews when they exchanged their semi-nomadic existence for an agrarian way of life. It is clear from Old Testament accounts that right up to the time of the Exile such a nature cult must have remained a constant threat to the religion of Israel.

What has been said is enough to show that the inhabitants of Palestine had by this date attained a considerable level of cultural and economic development. In contrast, those Hebrew tribes that in the second millennium pushed into the inhabited area were distinctly less advanced. They were simple nomads rather like the Bedouin of yesterday. Their conquest of Palestine is, therefore, not to be compared with that by Babylon or Rome in later times: these powers incorporated Palestine into their world empires through their professional armies.

Moreover, the Hebrews did not move into the country in one organized group. This merits some explanation. Until recently the story of the Exodus was often taken much too literally. The traditional narrative was regarded as recorded history—the Hebrews were held all to have come from Egypt and to have quit it at one specific hour under the leadership of Moses. Together they then roamed the wilderness, with Mount Sinai and the oasis of Kadesh as resting-places. Eventually they invaded Palestine from the east and conquered the country.

This simple presentation cannot survive close scrutiny of the texts. Thus it is a major question-mark, whether the ancestors of *all* the countrymen of David dwelt in Egypt and were there oppressed by a Pharaoh. The texts reveal distinct groups that only later merged to form the people of Israel.

Even the route of the Exodus does not remain unchallenged. It is shown, it is true, on many maps, but it can only be hypothet-

(Right) An image of the Canaanite Astarte, who more even than the Babylonian Ishtar was the goddess of love and fertility. She is therefore often portrayed naked, with pronounced sexual characteristics. Excavations in Palestine have shown that even in the period of the monarchy many Israelites kept small images of this kind in their houses and so were worshippers of this goddess.

(Left) This dark-brown stone figurine, about 4 inches high, is more recent by many centuries than the familiar representations of Astarte. This is evident, for example, from the head-dress, which belongs to the Hellenistic period. It comes from the vicinity of Petra, the country of the Nabateans. Underneath the figurine is a hole. It was probably an amulet, fixed to a staff as its headpiece, and carried about in that way. The emphasis here falls on the parturition stage in the fertility process.

ical. Even the locality in which the fleeing Hebrews made good their escape from the pursuing Egyptians is not precisely known. The traditions of Sinai are likewise problematical; they do not fit harmoniously with other traditions. It is noteworthy that even in the period of the monarchy the position of the holy mountain could not be certainly identified (see p. 87).

We must accept that various more or less independent memories of the Exodus and the wandering in the wilderness were later woven together. The same holds good for the conquest of Palestine. It is more sensible, indeed, to speak not of conquest but of penetration; and that was a process that lasted several centuries. The Book of Judges provides further evidence of the complexity of the process.

This historical appreciation, however, must not blind us to the underlying religious truths that lived on in the traditions. It becomes even clearer as we probe that the decisive factor was not military might or economic pressure but the exceptional religious heritage that the various Hebrew tribes brought with them from their nomadic existence. This it was that enabled them to form in Palestine the nation of Israel under the leadership of David and Solomon.

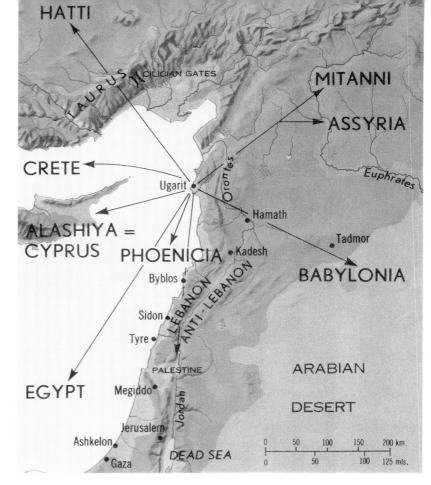

The northern coastal area of Canaan, better known as Phoenicia, possessed various inlets which made excellent harbours. Along this coast there sprang up a number of towns which served as links between the cultural centres of Egypt, Mesopotamia, Asia Minor, and Crete.

In the third millennium the most prominent of these was Byblos; in the second millennium power was concentrated in Ugarit, and, in the first, in Sidon and Tyre. The Phoenicians, famous sea-farers, were able to reach as far as present-day Tunis, where they founded the city of Carthage. Punic, the language of early Carthage, has many points of similarity, therefore, with Phoenician.

Excavations in Ras Shamra, the hill beneath which ancient Ugarit lies concealed, have shown that about 1500 B.C. this city was in close contact with neighbouring civilizations, a point established beyond doubt by texts from the temple archives, from the four palace archives, and from the libraries of private persons.

The Wadi el-Mujib, the Biblical Arnon, has its source in the desert almost 20 miles east of the Dead Sea. After a mile or two, this tiny stream has already become a deep and rocky chasm which in the rainy season is likely to put the traveller in danger of his life. Even in the dry summer season the crossing is extremely hazardous: the distance between the two 'banks' is some $2\frac{1}{2}$ miles in some places. As far back as the end of the second millennium this chasm formed a natural frontier between two spheres of influence: Moab to the south of it and the 'Amorites' to the north. The Arnon figures, too, in those Biblical traditions which tell of the journey of the Hebrew tribes through trans-Jordan into Canaan: the Hebrews are said to have passed not across the Arnon but around it to the east.

IV. THE BIRTH OF THE BIBLE

The origins of the Bible against the background of political, cultural, and religious life in the time of David and Solomon: 10th century B.C.

1. THE KINGDOM OF DAVID AND SOLOMON

About the year 1000 B.C. events that were later to be of far-reaching significance for the whole world were taking place in the little land of Canaan. Under the leadership of David the Israelites were able to gain the advantage over their weaker neighbours and establish a kingdom that was to become one of the most powerful of those times. A whole series of factors were conducive to this development. The 'world powers' of the second millennium had withdrawn to their own territories and no longer showed much interest in Canaan. After the downfall of Hammurabi's dynasty, Babylonia had become impotent as a state and was to remain so for several centuries. Similarly Assyria, despite a temporary phase of aggrandizement under Tiglath-pileser I, had relapsed into insignificance by about 1000 B.C., and around 1200 B.C. the Hittite kingdom had been swallowed up by the mass migrations of the 'sea peoples,' among whom were the Philistines. Only in northern Syria did a few remnants of the once mighty Hatti empire survive.

Egypt, whose control over southern Canaan had been so tight in earlier centuries, now relaxed its hold. After its temporary repulse of the 'sea peoples' about 1170 B.C.—its last conspicuous achievement—it had no choice but to stand back and watch them gain a firm foothold in the south of Syria. This situation is well illustrated by the report of the Egyptian Wen-Amon, who some time in the eleventh century made a journey to Byblos. En route he stayed at the harbour town of Dor, some 15 miles south of Mount Carmel. Settled in Dor at that time were the Tjeker, who like the Philistines, had migrated from the eastern Mediterranean. The ruler of this people did not give Wen-Amon the reception due to the representative of a sovereign prince, but simply treated him like any other guest. In the account of his journey Wen-Amon gives it to be understood that he was received in a similar way by the king of Byblos.

Not only in the neighbouring countries but in Canaan itself the situation was greatly in David's favour. The invasions of the sea peoples had not in fact put an end to the centuries-old internal divisions in Canaan. Only in the south had the Philistines been trying for some time to bring a large part of the country under their control. In the central highlands of Palestine they found themselves facing Hebrew tribes who had invaded the country some time before them.

At this time the Hebrews were far inferior to the Philistines. They had no territorial borders and no area of land they could call their own. Nor had they as yet developed a social structure with different strata, out of which a military caste might have arisen. They seem to have infiltrated in small groups into the inhabited parts of the land from the south and east and even possibly from the north.

As is clear from the Old Testament stories of Abraham, Isaac, and Jacob, the forbears of the Hebrew tribes had been

A view of the modern el-Khalil (Hebron). The Biblical Hebron lay to the west of this small town, on the hill where olive trees now grow. Since the Arabian period Hebron has been concentrated around the caves, east of the town. The spot played an important role in the traditions about the patriarchs. Abraham is said, according to the Bible, to have purchased the cave of Mach-pelah as a tomb for his wife Sarah (Gen. 23). Abraham himself (Gen. 25 : 9), Isaac (Gen. 35 : 27-29), Rebekah (Gen. 49 : 31), Leah (Gen. 49 : 31), and Jacob (Gen. 50 : 12-14) were later buried there as well. The place was venerated even in the time of Herod the Great. To oblige the Jews that monarch built a massive wall around the cave, a great part of which is still intact (centre, above the olive trees). On top of the cave the crusaders constructed a church which was eventually converted into a mosque.

semi-nomadic. They moved backwards and forwards between the mountains and the lowlands with their small herds of animals according to the seasons of the year, until an opportunity arose of adopting a more settled existence. This may have come about in various ways—for example, as the extension of an agreement about watering rights already made with a local tribe (Gen. 26), or as the result of some commercial transaction with the Canaanites (Gen. 38:1-5). The right of settlement may just as easily have been obtained in exchange for unpaid labour (Gen. 49:14-15), by land-purchase (Gen. 33:17-20), or by clearing the land and cultivating virgin soil (Josh. 17:14-18).

At the time when the Philistines were established in the coastal plain at the foot of the mountain ranges of Judah and Ephraim the process of settlement was already far enough advanced among the Hebrew tribes for them to be able to form a union, which was called Israel. According to traditional belief, which we find reflected in the story of Jacob's blessing (Gen. 49) and the birth of his sons (Gen. 29:31; 30:24), this consisted of the twelve tribes of Reuben, Simeon, Levi, Judah, Zebulun, Issachar, Dan, Gad, Asher, Naphtali, Joseph, and Benjamin.

In the light of our present knowledge, however, it is doubtful whether all these tribes were simultaneously united at this precise time. It is likely, for instance, that the tribes of Reuben and Simeon had not only been powerful and independent before the tribe of Gad had even settled in the valley of east Jordan,

The mountains of Gilboa seal off the southern extremity of the plain of Jezreel, which extends from Megiddo to Beth-shan. Thus they are the northernmost hills of the mountains of Ephraim in central Palestine. Their name has been perpetuated by the battle fought between the first Israelite king and the Philistines: Saul was decisively defeated there by an enemy with superior weapons. Inside the cave in the foreground rises a spring, known today as 'Ain Jalud. These waters are identified with the Spring of Harod which figures in the story about Gideon (Judges 7:1ff).

but had already long since declined. But although the number twelve has the air of being contrived there is no doubt that a union of some sort existed before Israel was welded into a nation. This was, of course, a union of a particular kind. It was not bound by political ties, but by its cultic activities, which had grown up around a common sanctuary.

Such unions or leagues were not unusual in the ancient world. There was one among the tribes of the Ishmaelites, who were Israel's immediate neighbours (Gen. 25:13-16), and also among the Arameans (Gen. 22:20-24). They were organized in the same way as in Greece where the temple of Apollo at Delphi and the sanctuary at Delos were similarly each the centre for the cultic activities of twelve tribes joined together in a league or amphictyony. It is from ancient Greece, in fact, that we gain the clearest indication of the meaning and purpose of these religious confederacies. As a league they shared the responsibility of protecting the sanctuary, and it was at the sanctuary that they met together for the yearly festivals and claimed mutual respect for their rights as individual tribes and as a nation.

The Israelite league was almost certainly similar. Its first sanctuary was in the vicinity of the old Canaanite city of Shechem, and there is an Old Testament story which was once supposed to commemorate the founding of this league by Joshua (Josh. 24). Nowadays, however, it is thought that the league existed before his time and that Joshua was responsible for converting the tribes who worshipped at Shechem to the belief in Yahweh. As in Greece, military actions undertaken in common against outsiders to the league do not seem to have been part of its original purpose. It is true that the stories about Ehud (Judges 3:12-30), Gideon (Judges 6–8), and Jephthah, in the form handed down to us, give the impression that these men saved the whole nation of Israel from the hands of its enemies, but on closer inspection these figures appear to have the characteristics of local heroes rather than great military commanders.

These must have been the conditions prevailing amongst the Israelite tribes settled in the highlands of central Palestine when the Philistines began their territorial expansion. At first, it was an unequal conflict, because the Philistines were technically more advanced than their opponents and were already skilled in the working of iron. (The beginning of the Iron Age in Palestine is dated from 1200 B.C.) Thus the assembled Hebrew farmers and shepherds had to do battle using the sling and spear, the bow and arrow, against the Philistines and Canaanites, with their chariots and armour of iron. The situation is described in 1 Samuel 13:19-22: "Now there was no smith to be found throughout all the land of Israel; for the Philistines said, 'Lest the Hebrews make themselves swords or spears'; but every one of the Israelites went down to the Philistines to sharpen his ploughshare, his mattock, his axe, or his sickle." It is no wonder the Philistines were able to penetrate so far into the highlands. The Ark of the Covenant—the Hebrews' sacred object—was lost, and Shiloh, the sanctuary of the tribe of Ephraim and possibly of the whole league, was devastated.

Some considerable time later the Philistines suddenly found themselves confronted, by a combination of circumstances, with a really formidable adversary, the Benjaminite Saul. An assault by the Ammonites on the trans-Jordanian town of Jabesh brought all the Hebrew tribes together, probably for the first time, under

An earthenware coffin, the lid of which has the form of a human head and arms. This method of interment was comparatively rare. So far, such coffins are known only from Lower Egypt and a few places in Palestine. The coffin pictured here is 6 feet in length and was discovered in a fragmented condition at Beth-shan. It dates from the 12th or 11th century B.C. and is a product of Philistine culture with Egyptian influence. That is not surprising, because an Egyptian garrison was stationed at Beth-shan till some time in the 11th century B.C.

Saul's leadership. So inspired were the people by his victory over the Ammonites that, supported by Samuel, their religious leader, they proceeded to the ancient sanctuary of Gilgal near the Jordan, and there, before Yahweh, affirmed Saul's kingship over Israel. From that moment Israel began to resist Philistine domination in a more organized way.

Small-scale encounters now ensued at regular intervals, and it was in one of these that David distinguished himself by his bravery. Saul, however, saw the new hero as a competitor, and, as a result, David was gradually forced on to the side of the Philistines. At first, he appeared to be siding with Israel's greatest enemy, but in reality he was undermining the strength of other foes in the Negeb, such as the Amalekites, and protecting the Israelites in the south. When in the end Saul's army was decisively defeated by the Philistines on the mountains of Gilboa and the king himself committed suicide, the southern tribes proclaimed David their king. He accepted this title and the dignity it conferred on him, probably with the approval of the Philistine rulers.

From the accounts of David's rise to power in the first book of Samuel, it appears that everyone, apart from the jealous Saul, was in his favour. He apparently possessed many outstanding qualities—bravery, honesty, friendliness, shrewdness, dignity, and enthusiasm. Something of his generous personality is revealed in the probably authentic elegy in which he mourns the death of his enemy, Saul, and his friend, Jonathan (2 Sam. 1:19-27).

After the south had elected him, David succeeded, by proceeding gradually, in winning the support of the northern tribes. At first, the situation looked unpromising. The whole of the north continued to support Saul's son, Eshbaal, or Ishbosheth, and it was during these years of separation that the terms 'Judah' and 'Israel' acquired political connotations. David was king over the southern tribes, among which Judah came to occupy a leading position. It could therefore be said with justification that David was 'king of Judah.' For his part, Eshbaal continued to call himself 'king of Israel,' although in fact he ruled only over the northern tribes. Thus the name 'Israel' was given a narrower meaning to denote only this latter group. Even so, the religious implications of the word 'Israel' as a concept were still preserved inasmuch as it continued to be used in writings of the more prophetic kind when referring to 'the chosen people' as a whole.

Eshbaal's power was more apparent than real. The highlands west of the Jordan had been drawn once more into the Philistine sphere of influence, and Eshbaal had been forced to withdraw across the Jordan and settle in Mahanaim. It was really Abner, Saul's commander-in-chief, who held the reins of power in the Northern Kingdom. This is implied in 2 Samuel 2:8–"Now Abner had taken Ishbosheth, son of Saul, and brought him over to Mahanaim; and he made him king over... all Israel." It was not long before this general opened negotiations with David, probably because he realized that Eshbaal was not fit for the kingship. But Joab, the commander of David's forces, murdered Abner in a corner of the gate at Hebron to avenge the death of his youngest brother, Asahel, whom Abner had struck down in the course of a brief engagement. The ambitious Joab may also have been anxious about his position in David's army. After Abner's death negotiations broke down. When some time later

The United Kingdom

The union of the northern and southern tribes enabled David to push the Philistines back to the coastal plain and to consolidate his authority throughout Palestine.

Thanks to the military weakness of Egypt, Mesopotamia, and Asia Minor and to his own gifts as a strategist, David succeeded in extending the power of the united tribes far beyond Palestine itself. Amalek, Edom, Moab, Ammon, Geshur, Damascus, and Zobah all in some measure acknowledged his overlordship. That is why a passage like 2 Samuel 24 could refer to Aroer and Jazer in the east, Kadesh, Tyre, and Sidon in the north, and Beer-sheba in the south as border towns of the kingdom. The same applies to 1 Kings 5 : 1-4 (for example), where it says that Solomon ruled 'from the River [Euphrates] to the border of Egypt.' Statements of this sort serve to indicate the true sphere of influence of David and Solomon's kingdom.

The actual territory of the United Kingdom did not extend beyond the borders of Palestine—which is why, from that time on, the expression 'from Dan to Beer-Sheba,' meaning the whole kingdom, obtained general currency. It occurs, for instance, in 1 Samuel 3 : 20; 2 Samuel 3 : 10; 17 : 11; 24 : 2, 15; and 1 Kings 5 : 5.

Eshbaal was murdered, the heads of the tribes of 'Israel' thereupon made a treaty with David and acknowledged him as their king. Judah and Israel were united under the personal leadership of David.

After this inter-tribal strife, which according to the Bible (2 Sam. 2:11) lasted for about seven years, that monarch was able to confront the Philistines openly. His gifts as a military commander soon decided the issue; and from then on, the Philistines remained a weak and insignificant nation living on the borders of Israel. David subsequently deprived the Moabites, various groups of Arameans, the Edomites, and the Ammonites of their independence, one after another. In this way he extended his power over the greater part of Canaan. Only the north Syrian plain, the Phoenician coast, and the territories remaining in the hands of the Philistines did not fall directly under his authority. His power extended, in fact, from "the river of Egypt to the great River, the river Euphrates." (Gen. 15:18; 1 Kings 5:1)

As soon as David had been proclaimed king of all Israel in Hebron, he turned his attention to Jerusalem. This city stood on a small eminence in a valley ringed by mountains. On three sides the inhabitants were protected by ravines. Only to the north was the site connected with the surrounding countryside by a high spur of land which rose to a small plateau measuring no more than about ten acres. It was in this direction that the city had first started to expand. At the foot of the eastern slope an abundant spring provided it with the necessary water. Thus it lay hidden and secure in the central highlands.

The city already had a long history behind it. There are references to it in the Egyptian execration texts of the 19th and 18th centuries B.C. There is mention of it again some centuries later in the Amarna period, when 'Abdu-Heba, the ruler of 'Urusalim,' as it was called at that time, sent a number of letters to the Pharaoh. One of these contains the following passage:

Say to the king, my Lord: thus speaks 'Abdu-Heba, the king's servant. At the feet of the king, my Lord, I fall seven and yet seven times. Behold what Milkilu [the ruler of Gezer] and Shuwardata [the ruler of Hebron] have done to the land of my lord the king. They have caused troops to march out from Gezer, Gath, and Keilah [a town between Hebron and Gezer]. They have occupied the country of Rubutu [possibly a town in central Palestine]; the king's land has gone over to the people of 'Apiru [semi-nomadic groups]. But now even a city of the country of Urusalim, called Bit-Lahmi [Bethlehem?], a city of the king, has gone over to the people of Keilah. Let the king listen to 'Abdu-Heba, his servant. Send him bowmen to win back the royal land for the king. But if no bowmen come, then the king's land will pass into the hands of the people of 'Apiru. This has happened at the command of Milkilu and of Shuwardata. Therefore, let my king have a care for his land.

Whether the ruler of Jerusalem was telling the truth is doubtful, for the man he accused, Shuwardata of Hebron, wrote to the Pharaoh making precisely the same allegation about 'Abdu-Heba. It is difficult to ascertain which of the two was telling the truth. What does appear plainly enough from several of the Amarna letters is that Jerusalem was a city of considerable importance in the Canaan of those days. In the centuries that followed, its

Canaanite inhabitants, called Jebusites in the Bible, managed to hold their own amid the Hebrew intruders. Their sphere of authority had indeed shrunk, but they still formed a wedge in the middle of Israelite territory. In the past this had always created something of a gulf between the southern and northern tribes. David, therefore, acted wisely in making Jerusalem the capital city of his kingdom. It was much more centrally situated than Hebron, and this enabled him to parry the growing rivalry between north and south, since the city could not be claimed by either side as its own. Thus it became the personal possession of the king, and ever since has been honoured with the title of 'the city of David.'

Whereas circumstances compelled David to devote most of his attention to military and political matters, his son and successor, Solomon, found himself free to concentrate on more peaceful pursuits. Solomon regulated and organized the country's administration, taxes, legal system, and trade. The tranquil and indeed prosperous state of affairs under Solomon is described in I Kings 4:25 as follows: "And Judah and Israel dwelt in safety, from Dan even to Beer-sheba, every man under his vine and under his fig tree, all the days of Solomon." His particular achievements are well known. He brought Phoenicians to Jerusalem to erect the Temple on the spot where the Mosque of Omar stands today. He had copper smelted in the Jordan valley between Succoth and Zarethan, and provided cities like Jerusalem, Hazor, Megiddo, and Gezer with new walls and gates. He also had barracks built for the troops, and stables for the horses. One of his most spectacular enterprises was to fit out a fleet, which sailed from Ezion-geber, near Elath, to the mysterious land of Ophir, in order to bring back costly timber, precious stones, and, above all, gold. He even used Phoenicians to man his ships (1 Kings 9:27). As time passed Solomon's wealth became proverbial. In the Bible it reaches mythical proportions, as, for example, in 1 Kings 10:14-29.

The social and economic expansion of the kingdom under Solomon was accompanied by the rise and growth of an indigenous literature. Professional scribes were soon engaged at the royal court (2 Sam. 8:17; 1 Kings 4:3), and one of the main works to appear from their hands is known as the Court History. It was written in reaction to a remarkable development in the law of succession in Israel, and concerned Solomon's hereditary right to the kingship. Past leaders, such as Moses, Joshua, Gideon, Samuel, and Saul had been acknowledged and accepted as such because people clearly saw in them the power of Yahweh at work. The question of heredity, therefore, did not arise until the Benjaminite Saul desired to have the same authority as the kings of other nations. In the ensuing conflict of opinion two groups were formed, a conservative party which considered such innovations as the kingship to be incompatible with the old religious traditions, and a more modern faction which wanted to adapt to the changed circumstances. Echoes of both schools of thought are detectable in 1 Samuel 8-12.

It is clear from this controversy that the conception of the kingship in Israel before Saul's time was quite different from that in neighbouring countries. There, it was accepted as a self-evident, indispensable, and even divine element in the national life. In Israel, too, the king was accorded a religious status, but at the same time the idea was stressed that at a particular moment in

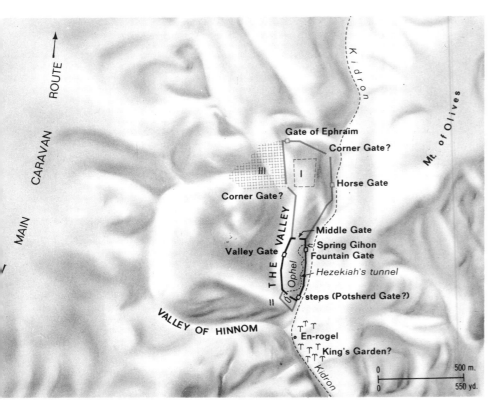

Jerusalem in the period of the monarchy ca. 1000-587 B.C.

The earliest city (black) was built by the Canaanites on a small eminence at the foot of which the water caught by the higher slopes emerged from the rock (the spring of Gihon). To the west of this stronghold, crossing the ridge of the mountains from north to south, ran the main line of communication between the tribes in the north and those in the south. This gave the city its exceptional strategic importance; for this potentially hostile stronghold stood between Judah and the central Highlands. David's conquest of Jerusalem in about 1000 B.C., therefore, made possible unified control of the United Kingdom—a unity which, however, was lost immediately after Solomon. Solomon (ca. 950) annexed to the city the northern hill, with which the Ophel ('hump') of David was connected. On this spot arose the Temple and the palace (I).

About 700 King Hezekiah extended the city in a southerly direction (II). The occasion for this was the construction of a tunnel through the rock, to bring waters of the Gihon into the city. The pool in which the water collected was enclosed within the city by walls.

Toward the end of the monarchy refugees from the conquered Northern Kingdom (721) and a further expansion of the Southern Kingdom added substantially to the population of Jerusalem. Hence a new district sprang up on the high ground outside the city on the north-west (III). This began the gradual filling up of the valley.

In 587 the city was laid in total ruin by the Babylonians. It has (so far) proved impossible, therefore, to trace with any degree of certainty the line of the city walls and the positions of the various gates. Generally, excavation on the spot is difficult. In view of 2 Kings 14 : 13, one may suppose that the Gate of Ephraim was located in the north-west. The Corner Gate must in that case have stood some 200 yards to the east or south. There is mention of various gates in the Book of Jeremiah. Is one to suppose the Middle Gate (Jer. 39 :3) to have stood between the Davidic and Solomonic parts of the city? The Potsherd Gate (Jer. 19 : 2) was situated in the neighbourhood of the Valley of Hinnom. Is it permissible to locate this gate at the spot where, some decades ago, steps hewn out of the rock were discovered? According to Jeremiah 31 : 40 the Horse Gate stood a good distance upstream in the Kidron valley. In parts of the Bible that have preserved post-exilic traditions (e.g., Neh. 2 : 11-15), reference is made to a Valley Gate and a Fountain Gate. For the Fountain Gate, the only likely position is the vicinity of the Gihon; and with regard to the Valley Gate there is the meagre supporting evidence afforded by an excavation undertaken some decades ago.

Finally, there are the King's Gardens (2 Kings 25 : 4). These must have lain to the south of the city along the bed of the Kidron, as the waters from the Gihon flowed in that direction. (See plate, right.)

(Opposite) On the acropolis of Hazor, just to the east of the Solomonic gate of the town, stands a building known nowadays as 'the storehouse of Hazor.' It was built in the 9th century B.C. (layer VIII) and continued in use for about a century (layer VII). The heights of Hazor commanded the Jordan valley. Toward the north-east the view extended as far as the spurs of the Anti-Lebanon.

The drawing, based on archaeological data, is intended to give an impression of 'the storehouse of Hazor.' The building was a rectangular one divided down its length by two rows of columns into three levels. The rectangle measures approximately 60 by 35 feet. All nine columns on the left-hand side are 5 feet high and are still to be seen in position; to the right, five of the ten blocks remain, together with a short stump (see photograph). The columns presumably had a superstructure of mud bricks. Their function was undoubtedly to support a roof; but whether there was originally a further floor above them one cannot be sure. No other building like this is known as yet in Palestine. It was definitely not used as stabling for horses, because no trace has been found of anything that would point in that direction. One must assume, therefore, that it was a storage-place (for grain?), although in that case the building must have been practically empty when it was razed. This storehouse stood against the north-east wall of the town, a wall dating from the 10th century (layer X) and still in service when the building was put up. It is a typical instance of the 'casemate wall' that came into vogue in the time of Solomon (two parallel walls connected by transverse partitions). Small doors in the inner wall gave access to the 'casemates,' which were utilized as magazines for weapons and other material. This provided, without any great expense, a good, thick wall and at the same time some extra space in the confined area of the little town.

(Below) The situation of the Ophel. In the distance can be seen the south wall of the former Temple court, with the dome of the Mosque of Omar. On the ridge in front lies the Ophel, on which a number of small Arab houses stand today. To the right stretches the always impressive valley of the Kidron. The Tyropoeon or Valley of the Cheesemakers has more or less disappeared. In earlier times it ran from the small wood to the left of the Ophel northwards towards the left-hand minaret. In the foreground are orchards surrounding the spring of Rogel. In former days the Kings's Garden probably stood there.

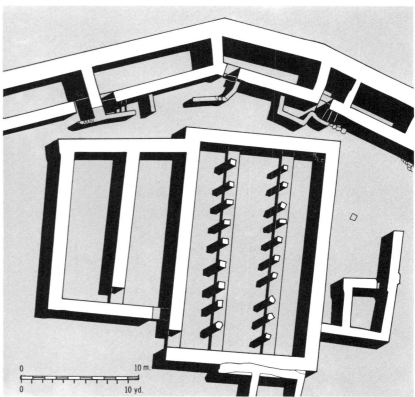

the history of the nation the king had been picked out from the community by God. He was still thought of as essentially an ordinary mortal who had been made king for the purpose of serving the people. In the critical situation at the time of Samuel it was the more modern current of opinion which prevailed. After Saul, David was accepted as king readily enough, because for the God-fearing Israelite the spirit of God was palpably manifest in this heroic figure. By the time of David's death, however, the kingship had already become something taken for granted, although it was still possible for its hereditary character to be disputed.

In fact Solomon's enthronement was not unattended with difficulties. The final outcome was a demand that Solomon's kingship and the position enjoyed by the 'House of David' be given a religious basis, and it is to this that we owe the existence of a masterly Court History, which for its frankness and sincerity stands alone among the annals of the ancient East. Unfortunately, the narrative was later interspersed with other documents, but the story of the royal succession can nevertheless in large measure be reconstructed from the text as it now stands. (It is contained in the following chapters: 2 Sam. 7 and 9–20, together with 1 Kings 1–2.)

The author's purpose in writing this work was probably to demonstrate the political and religious legitimacy of Solomon's kingship. With this in view he directed his attention to certain past events centred on the person of David. He gave a distinctive form to the data he gathered and selected, yet without doing violence to the historicity of his facts. We would not expect that during Solomon's reign anyone would ascribe discreditable actions to his father, the mighty David. It is therefore surprising that the latter's faults and deficiencies should have been listed with such candour.

The outline of the chronicle is as follows. The first part of the narrative offers an emphatic assurance regarding the hereditary succession; God himself promises David that one of his sons will succeed him and will build a temple for Yahweh (2 Sam. 7). After David's piety has been mentioned, an example of his magnanimity is given: a potential rival, Mephibosheth, an invalid son of Saul's, is brought to the court to be cared for (2 Sam. 9). It must be added that this may also have been a skilful move on David's part to enable him to keep an eye on a possible rival. David's weak moments are also mentioned. By the adultery with Bathsheba and the murder of her husband, Uriah, he brings the wrath of God upon his house (2 Sam. 11–12). Then comes one disaster after another. Amnon, David's eldest son, rapes his half-sister, Tamar, and her brother Absalom takes revenge by murdering Amnon during a festal celebration on the mountain of Baal-hazor (2 Sam. 13). Although David eventually forgives Absalom, the latter shows no gratitude. He attempts to seize power by stealth, but God protects David. Absalom puts off for too long his pursuit of his father's army, and this costs him his life (2 Sam. 14–19).

David seems to be partial, if not weak, in dealing with members of his own family. He is ready to spare Absalom, and yet he has Sheba, a rebel of far lesser stature, put to death (2 Sam. 20). Thus it is open to doubt whether the great king was a very able father. David betrays the same weakness when it comes to providing for the succession. He cannot choose between Solomon and Adonijah, and only the efforts of the prophet Nathan and his queen, Bathsheba, finally bring him to a decision in favour of the youngest son (1 Kings 1). The chronicle ends with an account of the first measures Solomon took as king. As was customary in the ancient East, he started by exterminating potential enemies. David had never had to do such a thing, but apparently he anticipated the difficulties his son was to encounter. However matters may have stood in reality, the author has David advising Solo-

Shiloh played a leading role in the life of the Hebrew tribes at around 1100 B.C. It was during this period that the Ark of the Covenant was deposited there. However, in the 11th century the town was razed to the ground, probably by the Philistines. From then on Shiloh was of little importance, although there have always been a few people living there. Consequently, no 'tell' has arisen on this site: it is rightly referred to as Khirbet Seilun, that is, ruins of Shiloh. Men have been repeatedly attracted to the place, probably because of its sacred character. Pointers to this sacredness may be seen today in the remains of a Muslim sanctuary, of two Christian churches, and of a synagogue, south of the mound of rubble. In the photograph are two unfinished churches, built during the 'thirties on Byzantine foundations. On the sky-line behind them lie the ruins of what was probably once a synagogue.

Types of City Gate

In the course of the centuries various types of city gate were used in Canaan. These five sketches give an impression of what they were like. The arrow indicates in each case how entrance to the city was obtained.

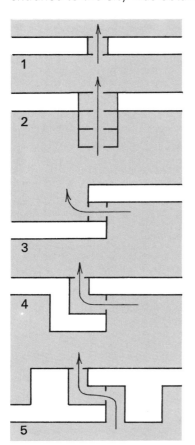

1. The direct type. This is undoubtedly the most primitive form. An example is the east gate of ancient Shechem (Tell Balata), built in the 16th or 15th century B.C.

2. The direct type, further developed. The direct type was gradually elaborated: three and sometimes four sets of pillars appeared, instead of two. By Solomon's time the intervening spaces were being used as stances for the guards. Examples of this type are the gates at Megiddo and Hazor.

3. The indirect type *(a)*. This construction was arrived at by overlapping the town walls at a particular spot. A gate of this kind was easier to defend. The enemy was obliged to approach alongside the wall and thus to expose himself to the arrows and stones launched by the defenders from the wall above him. Furthermore, as most of the attackers would be right-handed, and so would be carrying their shields on the left arm, they offered an easy target. This type of gate, dating from the 7th or 6th century, is to be found at Tell en-Nasbeh (Mizpah?).

4. The indirect type *(b)*. This concealed the actual gate behind a bastion. One might regard this as a combination of Nos. 1 and 3. Like No. 2, this type was developed especially during the Israelite period. The 7th-century gate of Lachish is an instance. But the system itself, though in a simpler form, had been known at an earlier time, as is evidenced by a gate at Tirzah, dating from the third millennium.

5. The indirect type, further developed. This type also goes by the name of 'zigzag gate.' Later on, it was a system used particularly where the terrain was flat. The existing Damascus Gate in Jerusalem, which dates from the 16th century A.D., is a splendid illustration. This type, in a simpler design, also occurred in earlier times: for instance, the gate of Ugarit, dating from the 15th century B.C.

mon to eliminate a number of adversaries as speedily as possible (1 Kings 2). The narrative ends with the words: "So the kingdom was established in the hand of Solomon."

It was not long before this chronicle was added to the perhaps even earlier record of David's successes as a young man which we find in 1 Samuel 16:14 to 2 Samuel 5:10. It was also later adapted and revised on theological grounds. Nevertheless it is still possible to regard this Court History as one of the earliest parts of the Bible to be written.

2. THE RELIGIOUS REVIVAL

David chose Jerusalem for his political capital, but it must be remembered that in ancient times there was no clear distinction between secular and religious affairs—or, to put it in modern terms, between state and church. That is why David's city was also the religious centre of Israel. The latter consideration was of far greater importance than the former.

Since the destruction of Shiloh by the Philistines the Israelites did not in fact have any central sanctuary, even though it was its religion which above all else held Israel together. This kind of religious vision called for some practical expression, a concrete cult. In earlier times it had been centred in particular on the Ark of the Covenant, which during their desert wanderings the people had always carried with them. But this wandering was now a thing of the past. The Hebrews had long since abandoned their semi-nomadic way of life and had settled down as farmers or city-dwellers. The Ark of the Covenant, too, had needed to have some kind of permanent home. To begin with, it had probably stood in the old Canaanite sanctuary at Shechem, but it was very soon afterwards transferred to Shiloh.

According to the accounts given in 1 Samuel 1–3, there must already have been a 'house of Yahweh' there. Why the choice fell on this particular place is still something of an enigma, though the Ark was undoubtedly less exposed there to attacks by the Canaanites. Shiloh, known nowadays as Khirbet Seilun, lay on the edge of the cultivated area, whereas Shechem was situated in the middle of a fertile plain, at a point of intersection for caravans. It is highly unlikely that the Hebrew tribes would have brought the Ark of the Covenant to a place that was not for one reason or another already regarded as 'holy,' though no such reasons are mentioned anywhere in the Bible. Shiloh remained a centre of cultic activity for a long time. When Samuel was still a youth, perhaps about the year 1050 B.C., the Ark had fallen into the hands of the Philistines, and Shiloh had been destroyed. The

leading priestly family disappeared from the scene, only to turn up later in Nob, a place possibly situated just north of Jerusalem. Because Saul thought that they were in league with David, he had them put to death. Only one man, Abiathar, escaped. He fled to David, who with his men was then roaming the rocky wilderness of Judah.

When David came to power, therefore, Shiloh, the centre of cultic activity, lay in ruins. The Ark of the Covenant was standing at Kiriath-jearim, a forgotten spot west of Jerusalem, and Abiathar, the refugee priest, moved around as a member of the king's retinue. As soon as David had consolidated his power he had the Ark transferred to Jerusalem with great solemnity and

In the centre of this picture stand the remains of the temple consecrated to the Baalath of Byblos ('the Mistress of Byblos'). Nothing of her sanctuary remains standing but some small sections of wall. The archaeologists who have been excavating at this site since 1921 (the house on the shore in the background was built for them to live in) have established that this temple was already in use by about 2700 B.C. Gifts offered by several Pharaohs of the Old Kingdom have been found in the sanctuary, which confirms that close relations existed between Byblos and Egypt as early as the third millennium B.C. The temple continued to function well into the Roman period. It must have been flourishing during the lifetime of Solomon; but on the evidence of the foundations, it can be said that this building had little or no influence on the architecture of Solomon's Temple.

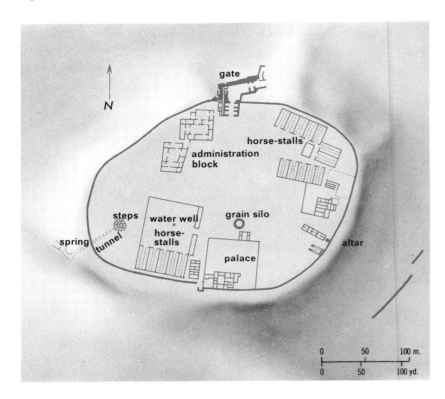

Megiddo was already a town at the start of the Early Bronze Age. But the mound, which is about 12½ acres in size and an average of 65 feet high, has not as yet been fully excavated. Only on the eastern side, where the Canaanite open-air altar dating from the beginning of the second millennium is situated, have the deepest levels of habitation been explored.

About 1150 Megiddo was totally destroyed (layer VII), so that buildings of the Late Bronze Age were left. After this calamity the town was soon rebuilt (layer VI). The steps and the tunnel which gave access from the town to the spring date from this period. About 1100 unknown assailants sacked the town again: and the site was then uninhabited for about a century.

In the year 1000, or thereabouts, a new group settled on the hill (layer V). They were probably Israelites. The walls were restored and the town gate was rebuilt at the traditional spot on the north side of the hill. No large public buildings of Solomon's time have been found; so that Solomon's building activities were probably more restricted than the text at 1 Kings 9 : 15 would suggest. In any case, the Solomonic town was subsequently swallowed up almost entirely.

Megiddo's heyday came in the 9th century (layer IV). The hill was more or less built over with stabling for horses, a palace, and governmental offices, the masonry of which closely resembles that of Samaria, dating from the same period. For security the steps leading to the tunnel were cut away and the tunnel was deepened, allowing the water to flow through to the foot of the shaft within the town, where it was then hauled up by means of pitchers on ropes. The city was enlarged and fortified, and gives the impression of having been a garrison town and the seat of a governor.

In the 8th century the Assyrians razed the city. The next phase was very primitive (layer III). The big grain silo may date from this period. Access to the tunnel was made simpler too; a new set of steps was built inside the shaft. The Assyrian period was followed by a Babylonian (layer II) and then a Persian one (layer I). By then, however, Megiddo was no longer a city, but at most a large village. In the Hellenistic period it ceased to exist.

(Right) A sense of religion was not exclusive to the people of Israel—a fact evidenced by this monumental open-air altar at Megiddo. It was in use as early as 1900 B.C., and may even date from the third millennium. The distance across the platform is as great as 26 feet; and the height is approximately 4½ feet. This stone construction was undoubtedly an altar; for in the debris on the upper surface many animal bones and potsherds, probably the remains of sacrificial offerings, were unearthed. The layer of rubble behind the altar illustrates splendidly how the level of the town rose in the course of roughly a thousand years.

even made plans for housing it permanently in an imposing temple. These ambitions were in fact only to be realized by his son Solomon, but David did enough to ensure that Jerusalem should be not only the political, but also the religious centre for the Israelites and the Jews of a later time. It is thanks to him that 'the city of David' is still for a countless number of people 'the holy city.'

The crowning point of the religious revival, and at the same time the source of the power needed for future growth and development, was the building of the Temple. Since in the architectural field the Israelites had no long tradition, Solomon obtained the help of Hiram, king of Tyre. In Canaan, people had been building temples for many centuries. At Byblos, for example, the foundations of a sanctuary for 'the Mistress of Byblos,' dating from about 2700 B.C., have been discovered. In Megiddo today one can admire an immense altar made of stone slabs, which belonged to a Canaanite temple of the 19th century B.C. Near the modern town of Nahariya, about 19 miles north of Haifa, an accidental discovery in 1947 revealed the remains of another temple dating from about 1500 B.C. There are also the remains of other Canaanite temples in, for example, Hazor, Lachish, Beth-shan, and Deir 'Alla. Scholars have shown considerable interest in these temples, not only because their style undoubtedly influenced the construction of Solomon's building, but because, in spite of the detailed description of this building given in the Bible (1 Kings 6), it is still difficult to gain a clear impression of what it looked like. Furthermore, although we know for certain just where the building stood, it is impossible to carry out any archaeological investigations, because the site is a holy one for Muslims.

From the account given in the Bible the interior of the Temple was twenty cubits in width and seventy cubits in length, including the porch. (A cubit probably measured about eighteen inches.) The entrance was in the short wall on the east side. The inside was divided into three apartments. First came the small

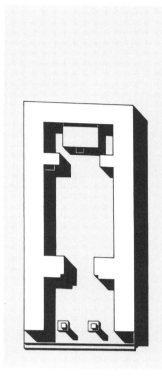

In 1 Kings 6 and 2 Chronicles 3–4 there is a description of Solomon's Temple. On the architectural side, however, these accounts are so poor that it is impossible to reconstruct this sanctuary with any real degree of completeness; it is only possible to determine the course of the main walls. A remarkable parallel has been found at Tell Tainat on the Orontes, although in the case of the Solomonic Temple the proportions are somewhat different. The accompanying drawing gives a diagrammatic ground-plan of the sanctuary in Syria. The division into entrance-hall, holy place, and holy of holies is clear to the eye. The over-all measurements are about 80 by 40 feet. Yet this temple can have had no influence on Solomon's 10th-century building, as it is in fact more recent (9th or 8th century B.C.).

porch or antechamber, ten cubits in length, then the principal room, forty cubits in length. In this room stood an altar for incense, the table with the showbread, the ten candlesticks, and an altar for burnt offerings. Last of all came the rear chamber, twenty cubits deep, where the Ark of the Covenant was housed beneath statues of the cherubim, and where Yahweh was thought to be present. Built right up against the outer walls were a number of side chambers. Like most Semitic sanctuaries this Temple stood in a spacious court surrounded by a wall. This was the sacral area proper for the people, whose religious activities were conducted mainly in the open air. It was in this court that the massed liturgical ceremonies and festal gatherings took place. There the psalms were sung, songs of thanksgiving in times of happiness, laments on days of sorrow and distress. Although it had long been a custom in Israel to compose religious songs—as the Song of Deborah and David's elegy show—the Temple cult did much to encourage this mode of expression. It may even be said that the Book of Psalms had its beginnings in the pre-exilic Temple, and found its completion in the Temple of the post-exilic period.

So far the search for a close parallel among the Canaanite sanctuaries has been in vain. One or other of these buildings sometimes has this or that feature in common with the Temple of Solomon. The temple at Lachish, for instance, also has three apartments, but they are not in line with one another. Two temples have recently been excavated in northern Syria which, to judge from their foundations, had more or less the same ground plan as Solomon's buildings. But perhaps the temple at Hazor (now Tell el-Qedah, southwest of the former Lake Huleh) is still the best example of what it must have looked like. Here again there are three chambers, standing in line and running from east to west, and the bases of two columns have been discovered, reminding one of the two pillars of Solomon's Temple which bore the enigmatic names of Jachin and Boaz. But there are differences too. The two pillars of the sanctuary in Jerusalem stood *in front of* the antechamber, in the open air, whereas at Hazor the bases

stand within the antechamber, at the entrance to the principal room. Moreover, in the rear chamber of Solomon's Temple, later known as the Holy of Holies, no liturgical ceremonies ever took place, whereas the finds in the equivalent room at Hazor suggest that it was much used for cultic purposes.

After the building of the Temple at Jerusalem, Israel did not entirely ignore the other local sanctuaries, such as Bethel, Shechem, Dan, Beer-sheba, and Gilgal. These continued in existence for a long time to come. Nevertheless, with the Temple at Jerusalem the foundation had been laid for the centralization of all cultic activities, and a school of thought soon arose which proceeded to lay this down as a principle. Centuries were to pass, however, before it was generally accepted.

3. THE ESTABLISHMENT OF A BIBLICAL TRADITION

Israel's political and religious development naturally had an effect in the sphere of culture too. The need for ornamentation in the Temple and the royal palaces was a challenge. The copper and gold objects required for cultic purposes, the reliefs of lions, oxen, cherubim, and palms, the lining of walls with costly cedarwood, the music and dance which must have been part of the solemn liturgical observances in the Temple court and must also have graced festive occasions at the royal palace—all served to stimulate the growth of artistic talent. Turning to the archaeological finds, however, one is struck by the fact that they are few and unimpressive. One main reason for this, very probably, is the injunction, known to us from the Decalogue, which forbids the making of 'images.' The development of the plastic arts suffered as a result. It is less surprising, therefore, that in the ebullient life of the tenth century B.C. a different kind of artistic expression—religious literature—developed at a more than ordinary rate.

Even in the old sanctuaries there had been a need for liturgical texts, but the demands of the impressive Temple cult inspired some very ambitious attempts in this field. People began to reflect on the unexpected greatness and prosperity of the nation. With that in mind they gathered together many ancient folktales about the journey through the wilderness under Moses' leadership, about specific events in the lives of the patriarchs, and about the origin of the world, of man and of evil. But they were not content just to collect this material. Inspired by their religious vision, which brought all things into focus, they wove from the old stories a connected narrative with a coherent meaning.

By viewing the past from the standpoint of the new historical situation the ancient traditions of the various tribes were given a religious interpretation in terms of a united Israel. This method is nowadays spoken of as 'prophecy in retroverse,' because these texts were meant to make clear to the Israelites of the tenth century B.C. what Yahweh had been doing in past history. In this way the ancient stories became, in effect, a means of guidance (*torah* in Hebrew) for the pious Israelite. The matter may be summed up by saying that the tenth century B.C. produced a kind of religious retrospection which resulted in a profounder vision of the past—one which was meant to bear upon the present and shape the future.

It follows that if we are to have a right understanding of the ancient Biblical texts we need to exercise a measure of discrimination. More specifically, there is a considerable divergence between the actual course of events and subsequent accounts of them, between the bare fact and the later interpretation. It has always been beyond the reach of the present to grasp directly the 'bare facts' of the past. The so-called 'objective' writing of history is never a feasible proposition. The historian who testifies to this or that event will invariably reflect his own particular standpoint. The further away he is from an event and the more personally involved he and his generation are with the issue, the more subjective his account is likely to be. In the case of the Biblical texts there can be no question of their representing an impartial or purely factual account. The Bible is a collection of religious testimonies, of faith-motivated viewpoints on particular events and circumstances, and what we find in it is much more in the nature of a 'proclamation' or a series of 'instructions.'

Again many parts of the Bible—among others, the stories concerning the prehistory of Israel—are the product of a people or a group rather than of a single person. The traditions having to do with the journey through the wilderness and the lives of the patriarchs sprang up and were passed on in the family or the tribal community. They cannot be compared with an account written by a present-day reporter. Thus it was that these stories acquired the particular characteristics which we term 'epic.'

In epic narratives there is usually a marked tendency to simplification. For instance, events that took place at different times and in different localities are often run together. Similarly, many personages who may have had an important part in the action are reduced to minor roles or even disappear altogether. The leading figure becomes, as it were, a solo performer. More often than not—and certainly in the Biblical documents—the actions of the main character and the places he frequents become specially significant for the nation which evolves such an epic. They create a national consciousness and determine the national way of life by providing a point of reference, and because of this contemporary value attaching to the feats of the main character some of them come to be seen larger-than-life. Consequently, the Biblical accounts often contain unconscious exaggerations and repetitions. A good example of this may be found in Exodus 1:7: "But the descendants of Israel were fruitful and increased greatly; they multiplied and grew exceedingly strong; so that the land [Egypt] was filled with them." Such an utterance in no way precludes the inadvertent remark in Exodus 1:15ff, that a mere pair of midwives were sufficient to cope with the birth of every Hebrew child!

Moreover, precisely because it is the *living* community that gives an epic its shape, it is more often than not the current situation of the community that informs it. That is why, according to the Bible, the patriarchs were already worshippers of Yahweh (Gen. 12:8), whilst side by side with that we have the statement that it was Moses who first induced the Hebrew tribes to regard Yahweh as their God (Ex. 6:3), a view, incidentally, which would seem to accord with the facts, if one is considering only that group of Israelites who once dwelt in Egypt. Nowadays we regard this kind of statement as an anachronism, but people in ancient times had a different approach to the matter. Without consciously intending to do so, they projected their own situation into the traditions of the past, because they felt themselves to be intimately involved with the main characters and with the events of which those characters were the protagonists. The story would otherwise have been incomprehensible to them and would have lost its purpose. For the function of the epic was to provide a foundation for the communal life of the tribe or nation. That explains why at first reading this sort of narrative often gives the impression of being simple and schematic, and yet as soon as we try to ascertain the exact course of the events recounted, we find ourselves faced with an impossible task. An example of this already mentioned is the route of the Exodus from Egypt and the subsequent journey through the wilderness.

If we bear in mind this proclamatory and epic character of so many of the stories of ancient Israel, we may begin to understand the Bible. The question will then no longer be: what actually happened? but rather: what religious proclamation does this text embody?

The school that during the tenth century B.C. collected together the extant oral and written traditions of Israel, and arranged and edited them, was what is nowadays called the Yahwist school, because the writers belonging to it nearly always call God Yahweh, in contrast to a later school of writers who used the term Elohim. These texts have other distinctive characteristics, too. For instance, we know that there is often a strong anthropomorphic element in the Yahwist conception of God, and we do not, therefore, ascribe the first creation-story (Gen. 1:1–2:4a) to this current of thought, since it presupposes a much more developed view of God. We would, however, ascribe the second one (Gen. 2:4b–3:24) to it, though to go into the reasons for doing so would involve a detailed discussion of the differences which is beyond the scope of the present study.

In seeking to interpret the significance of events which took place in the Israel of Solomon's time the Yahwist tradition looked primarily to the more recent past. There were old stories which reported that in earlier times a group of ancestors under the leadership of a certain Moses had fled from Egypt. During their wanderings in the desert they (or some of them) had accepted Yahweh as their God on the holy mountain of Sinai. Next they had tarried for several years at the oasis of Kadesh. Eventually, after having made a considerable detour, they (or some of them) had approached Canaan from the south-east. There their leader had died.

Out of these traditions the Yahwist school created a powerful narrative with a cogent message. Yahweh had demonstrated his power by causing various calamities to descend upon Egypt, because the Pharaoh was persecuting Israel. Yahweh's superiority became evident when he led Pharaoh and his forces to destruction and brought Israel safely across the Red Sea and through the rocky wilderness. Time and again Yahweh had assumed an active role in the affairs of men. Thus the past showed that Yahweh was stronger than any other power. He had revealed his might and his will in the past, and continued to do so in the present, now that through its covenant with him Israel had become a great nation and a mighty people. This was to last for as long as Israel remained true to his will and his law.

But the Yahwist tradition also sought to account for this goodness of God toward Israel and to assess what it portended for the future by reference to the more remote past and the traditions regarding Israel's progenitors. According to these, an

The ruined mound of Hazor (Tell el-Qedah) covers an area of about 175 acres, which makes it the largest tell in Palestine. It consists of two parts: the lower town and the acropolis. The lower town (left, in the photograph) would seem to have been inhabited only from ca. 1700 to ca. 1250 B.C. A temple and various other buildings have been discovered there. During that period the lower town was probably not fully built over, so that the place afforded space for horses and chariots and also a refuge for the neighbouring villagers in time of war. On the acropolis there was a town in existence as early as the third millennium. In the Israelite period, too, the summit was inhabited. To that period belong the city gate of the 10th century (Solomon) and the storehouse of the 9th century B.C. (Ahab). See also page 67.

ancestor called Abraham, who originally came from far-off Mesopotamia, had made the journey to Canaan with his family and his entire possessions. For many years he and his descendants had wandered about this country as semi-nomads, until famine forced some of them to migrate to Egypt.

The Yahwist school deduced the following meaning from these events. God in his goodness chose Abraham out of all men as the one to be brought into the land of Canaan. In trusting obedience Abraham followed God's call. God responded by making known to Abraham all the saving acts he himself would one day perform. Abraham was given a threefold promise: he would possess the land, his descendants would become a great nation, and in him all the peoples of the earth would be blessed. God immediately set about implementing his promise. He hal-

lowed the country by his presence at Shechem, Bethel, at the spring between Kadesh and Bered, at Mamre near Hebron, at Gerar in the Philistines' country, at Beer-sheba, on a mountain in the region of Moriah, and at Penuel on the far side of the Jordan. God then also took care to ensure that Abraham's descendants would become a great nation. He gave Jacob, Abraham's grandson the ideal number of twelve sons—a figure implying abundance and fullness—out of which a mighty nation must arise.

This was how the Yahwist writers proclaimed that not only in the present, but even in the remote past God had already been active on Israel's behalf. More emphatically still, the prosperity of Solomon's day was shown to rest on the threefold promise God had made. Abraham's descendants now ruled 'the promised land' and had become a people as numerous as 'the grains of sand

A number of dressed stone blocks, discovered in or around the temple in the lower town of Hazor. Various fragments were found in the rearmost apartment, from which it would appear that this room did not have the same function as the Holy of Holies of the Solomonic Temple. Some of the stone blocks have been worked over more elaborately. On the left a male figure is depicted, seated on a chair, with his hands stretched out in front of him. He probably held a bowl or container for sacrificial gifts. In the centre is a small pillar or pedestal with a pair of hands in an attitude of prayer. Above them appear what are probably the symbols of several deities: a half moon (for the moon god?) and a sun or star (for the sun god or the goddess Ishtar?). On the right is a roaring lion, carved in relief on a block of basalt, found beside the holy of holies. It was probably a mural decoration.

by the sea shore.' Since in these two respects the promise of salvation had been fulfilled, Israel's greatness seemed to augur much good in store for all men.

With regard to the third promise, the Yahwist tradition set about placing the idea of universal salvation on a sure foundation with the aid of folk-legends about the origin of the world, of man, and of evil. A wide variety of tales dealing with these themes were current both in Israel and the Near East in general. They contained such features as the tree of life, paradise, demonic powers, floods, and so on. The Yahwist writers modified these stories to propound their message, though it is likely that this process of adapting legends to accord with Israel's religious views had already begun some time before.

The Yahwist account of the creation went approximately as follows. Initially, the earth had been a place where no kind of life was possible, a wilderness without shrub or plant, for God had not as yet caused it to rain, and there was as yet no human being to work the cultivable land. Then God caused water to well up out of the earth to irrigate it. Next he formed man out of the soil, 'the dust of the earth,' and set him in a secluded, well-watered garden, to tend it and to watch over it (Gen. 2). But with the creation of man, evil, too, appeared on the earth. All the pain and misery with which mankind has since been perpetually beset were there from the beginning, because then as now man was unwilling to comply with the will of God. Even so, neither demonic powers nor blind fate were to prevail over mankind, for God was to remain constantly active and give him the promise of salvation (Gen. 3).

A rectangular piece of earthenware from Beth-shan, dating from the 12th or 11th century B.C. It probably represents a two-storeyed house with windows. On it appear several human and animal figures, too vague to admit of any definite interpretation. Only the snake, slithering out of the lower right-hand window toward the first storey, is clearly discernible. It illustrates the popularity of the snake in Canaan as a creature bringing life. This item undoubtedly had some religious function; it may have been a bowl in which incense was burnt.

In spite of this promise man soon fell into yet greater evil and committed fratricide (Gen. 4). From that moment evil spread, eventually culminating in the mysterious intercourse of the 'celestial' beings with the daughters of men (Gen. 6). God resolved to exterminate mankind by flood. Only Noah, the man of righteousness, and his family were spared (Gen. 7). But this act of beneficence on God's part miscarried too. Noah's descendants also turned away from God. The summit of evil, literally and figuratively, came with 'the tower of Babel.' It was then that God decided to scatter men abroad over the whole earth and to choose one person out of all races, so that in him and his posterity, in Abraham and Israel, he could bring to pass his salvation.

The Yahwist tradition, therefore, taught in a vague and imperfect way, that 'the Solomonic peace' was meant to bring salvation to all peoples. True, this happy state had not as yet been completely achieved. Evil continued to do its work in Israel through, for example, the snake cult of the Canaanites. Sickness and pain, drought and famine—these still threatened the very existence of the Israelites. But it was comfort to the pious to be told that Yahweh's power extended beyond all these perils.

The way these ancient traditions were assembled and adapted presented the Israelite with the past as something he could grasp and lay hold of in terms of the present. The business of selecting from the traditions did not, of course, involve any study of sources or use of textual criticism, as it does today. It cannot be said, therefore, that the Yahwists were historians in the modern sense of the word. To equate what they did with present-day historiography would be to misunderstand their intentions entirely. This does not mean to say that these writers did not themselves believe in what they wrote. They doubtless thought that the facts were as tradition painted them. Their main concern, however, was not so much with what had actually happened as with the religious meaning that the traditions held for the Israelite community in the tenth century B.C.

In selecting from the great number of traditions current, the Yahwist writers most certainly exercised a deliberate choice. There were yet other stories in circulation regarding the patriarchs, such as, for example, the account of how God put Abraham to the test in the matter of his son, Isaac, on Mount Moriah (Gen. 22). Again, certain traditions relating to the period spent in the wilderness (one of which, at least, was an abbreviated Decalogue), and popular traditions about the penetration into Canaan under Joshua, and its defence under the Judges, were not included in the Yahwists' work. Texts such as the Book of Jashar (the Just One) (cf. Josh. 10:13 and 2 Sam. 1:18) and the Book of the Wars of Yahweh (cf. Num. 21:14) were not used, and were eventually lost. Moreover, accounts had already been written of the great leader, Samuel, of the first king, Saul, of David's youth and his successful reign, accounts such as the Court History mentioned earlier.

It was not the aim of the Yahwist redactors, however, to incorporate every extant tradition into their work. Their purpose was to trace a clear line through the course of the events by which Israel had come into being. According to them it was one which had been determined by Yahweh, their God. In this they succeeded remarkably well. Their literary efforts proved to be of inestimable value for the later growth of the Bible, for they laid foundations on which subsequent writers were able to build.

V. GROWTH OF THE BIBLE

The growth of the Bible against the background of the disruption of the Solomonic kingdom and the advance of Assyria: 9th and 8th centuries B.C.

1. THE POLITICAL SITUATION IN JUDAH AND ISRAEL

King David had succeeded in bringing about a union between Judah and Israel under his personal leadership. But a political structure of this kind called for rulers of real stature, which the house of David was subsequently unable to provide. Even under Solomon, David's successor, the kingdom was already beginning to disintegrate, and soon after his death it was split in two. The foolish policies of Solomon's son, Rehoboam, accelerated this process. Rehoboam wanted to continue the monarchy in the same style as his father, whereas the northern tribes were anxious to see restored the conditions that had prevailed in David's time. They considered, reasonably enough, that Solomon had paid insufficient attention to ancient and venerated tribal traditions.

In assertion of their own dignity and independence they made Rehoboam come to the ancient sanctuary of Shechem in order to discuss with him his accession to the throne. Overestimating his own strength, the young prince rejected their proposals, refusing to ease the burdens on them or abolish compulsory labour. As a result he was obliged to flee in haste from the disaffected territory, and the split which had existed for some years now became a definite rupture. The northern tribes immediately declared their independence from the house of David and soon appointed one of their own people king over Israel. From now on there was a Southern Kingdom of Judah

over which Rehoboam ruled, and a Northern Kingdom of Israel.

In the subsequent period the two kingdoms developed very differently. Judah enjoyed a much more stable order than the Northern Kingdom, largely owing to the fact that right up to the time of its destruction in the sixth century B.C. it accepted the principle of hereditary succession, and remained loyal to the house of David. There were, from time to time, risings against individual rulers, but there was never a general revolt against the Davidic dynasty.

When, for example, in 841 King Ahaziah was murdered

Between Jerusalem and Bethlehem stands a hill, known nowadays as Ramat Rahel ('heights of Rachel'). Excavation has shown that a fortified country house was built here about 700 B.C. The inner court of this 'villa,' which was exceptionally spacious, was surrounded by a colonnade. Several proto-Aeolian capitals, now in the museum at Jerusalem, were unearthed there. Round about the villa itself stood a number of labourers' cottages. It was thought at first that what had been discovered here was King Uzziah's (Azariah's) 'free house,' mentioned in 2 Kings 15:5. But as this meant, in effect, assigning the building to an unacceptably early date, the preference now is for identifying this place with the Biblical Beth-haccherem ('house of the vineyard') of Jeremiah 6:1 and Nehemiah 3:14.

Judah and Israel

- - - - - - - *Principal trade routes*
— · — · *Approximate frontiers*

After the rupture of the Solomonic kingdom, David's grandson had only an unimportant and infertile region left under his control. At first, Edom also remained under the authority of the king in Jerusalem; but when, about 845, that nation regained its independence, the Southern Kingdom found itself hemmed in by the mountains of Judah. It did not count for very much, therefore, either militarily or in the economic and political sphere. Despite this weakness Judah was able to keep going tolerably well. The fact that in the dynasty of David and the city of Jerusalem the nation possessed a religious and political focal point had a good deal to do with this.

In Israel the situation was exactly the reverse. Through that country with its fertile valleys and plains ran the trade routes from Philistia, from Judah, Edom, and Moab, and from Egypt to Phoenicia, to Damascus and the Aramean states in northern Syria, and to Assyria and Babylonia. This through trade brought Israel considerable prosperity: but for that very reason the Northern Kingdom was deeply involved in any political changes that occurred in Canaan at large. As a result, there were endless clashes with the Philistines, with Moab, with Assyria, and especially with Aram-Damascus. Almost annually the forces of Damascus were on the march through the countryside of Gilead and Galilee. It was only with Tyre and Sidon that Israel enjoyed constantly good relations. The interest of these port towns was a maritime one; so that they had no territorial ambitions. Continuous fighting weakened the favourable economic position of Israel; and then, too, the many palace revolutions and the strife and confusion over religious issues were bad for the country's stability. After two centuries of this, the Northern Kingdom therefore fell an easy prey to Assyria.

Capitals of the Northern Kingdom

After 931 B.C. it was some time before the Northern Kingdom acquired political stability. The first king established his residence in Shechem, a town that had always played a leading role in politics as in religion (931).

The offensive launched by Pharaoh Shishak (ca. 925) obliged the king to move his seat to Penuel, east of the Jordan. However, this town lay on the fringe of the Northern Kingdom; and so, when the Egyptian forces had left Palestine, King Jeroboam abandoned Penuel and settled once more in the hill country of Ephraim.

As the ancient town of Shechem stood on the edge of a plain and was vulnerable from the south, he chose Tirzah as his new capital. Tirzah was situated on a plateau jutting out rather like a peninsula; and was protected to the south by a mountain ridge. Furthermore, there was an easy escape route eastwards along the Wadi Far'ah.

A few decades later it began to become evident that the hill of Tirzah was too small to accommodate the royal residence. Moreover, the threat from Damascus to the north-east was becoming increasingly serious. Consequently, King Omri (885-874) moved his capital to a hill on the western side of the mountains of Ephraim. On this bare summit he built the new city of Samaria.

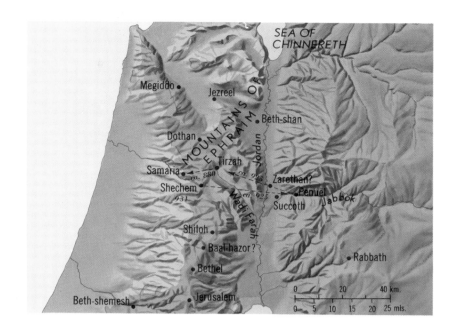

during a visit to the Northern Kingdom, and his mother, Athaliah, seized power in Jerusalem, the whole nation came out on the side of the priests, who refused to support this new régime. Some years were to elapse before the situation could be changed, but when the opportunity finally arose Athaliah was deposed, and Ahaziah's son, Jehoash, was set on the throne in her place. On another occasion, when King Amaziah (796–781) fell victim to a conspiracy and was murdered, the whole of Judah came out on the side of his son Uzziah—known also as Azariah—and unanimously endorsed his succession to the throne.

It was during the reign of Uzziah that Judah gave a remarkable demonstration of its loyalty towards the house of David. The King contracted a skin disease, and because of the stigma of uncleanness traditionally attaching to such a complaint, he was obliged to withdraw from public life and live in isolation in a house which had been set apart for him. (A current theory is that this was situated at Ramat Rahel, a little to the south of Jerusalem, where an eighth-century citadel has recently been excavated.) Uzziah's sickness, which in accordance with the religious beliefs of the time was thought to be a punishment from Yahweh for some sin he had committed, caused less dismay amongst the people of his realm than might have been expected. In his absence his son, Jotham, assumed the position of regent without any opposition.

This sense of loyalty seems to have increased rather than diminished with the passing of time. When, a hundred years later, King Amon (642–640) was killed in a palace rising, the members of the old-established families in the country acted with one accord, and firmly defended the traditional order by slaying the murderers and immediately enthroning the eight-year-old Josiah as his father's successor.

This remarkable fidelity to the ruling dynasty was probably due mainly to the enormous prestige which the capital city possessed in the eyes of the population. Since the days of David and Solomon it had housed the principal sanctuary of Yahweh. Temple and palace stood side by side in the northern part of the 'city of David.' In both a literal and a metaphorical sense they

formed a single whole. Defection from the house of David would therefore have amounted to disloyalty to Yahweh.

The Northern Kingdom found itself in a markedly less favourable situation. It lacked everything that had favoured the continuance of the dynasty in Judah. Although attempts were made to establish the principle of hereditary succession in North Israel, they failed signally to obtain the assent of large areas of the population. The latter held obstinately to the traditional view, that the kingship could be claimed only by some-

A view of the hill on which the city of Samaria was built in the 9th century B.C. Since the 12th century A.D. this eminence has been more or less uninhabited. Only the name of the small village of Sebastiyeh on the eastern slope (right, in the photo) enshrined up to the start of this century the memory of Sebaste, the name given to Samaria by Herod the Great in honour of the Roman emperor. Excavation has disclosed remains dating from the Israelite monarchy (9th to 8th centuries B.C.), from the Hellenistic period (3rd century B.C.), and the Roman period (1st and 2nd centuries A.D.)

Among the remains of the royal palace of Samaria, destroyed by the Assyrians in 721 B.C., more than two hundred pieces of ivory, large and small, have been discovered. Against the background of Near Eastern culture there is nothing very surprising about that; for Egyptian and Mesopotamian texts dating from as early as the second millennium make reference to elephant-hunting. The above fragment is part of a band of inlaid work. It is a representation of a not very well-known god, Hah, the god of unbounded time—a fact remarkable in itself; for one would rather have expected to find, in Israel at any rate, a better known Egyptian god. In each hand the seated god holds a palm tree, the symbol of years, to which is attached an ankh symbol (= life). As in the case of the fragmentary figure on the right, his right elbow rests upon an unidentifiable object. On his head is a fillet with long strands. He is wearing a broad necklace, a shoulder-strap, and a belt. The clusters of palmleaves on the upper rim evince Phoenician infuence. Above the head of the god these are interspersed with the rays of the solar disc. The measurements are $20\frac{1}{2}$ by $12\frac{1}{4}$ inches.

one who had been promised it by a prophet. In practice this led to Israel's enjoying only a few periods of internal tranquillity. If a prophet proclaimed someone as a future king, the first thing he did was to seize the throne by violence. The kingship thus became devalued, and this made it easier for those to reach for power who were unsuited to wield it.

Hence at least eight kings were murdered, and in the short space of two hundred years members of nine different families occupied the throne. The first dynasty (931-909 B.C.) comprised only two kings, Jeroboam I and Nadab; the second (909–885) likewise. Then came the assassin Zimri, who reigned for only seven days. He committed suicide after his defeat by Omri, whose dynasty, comprising four kings, lasted for about forty years (885–841). After that came the royal house of Jehu, with five monarchs, who between them reigned for nearly a century (841–743). In the last twenty years of Israel's history one palace revolution followed another. Four different families came and went on the acropolis of Samaria, and the nineteen kings of Israel reigned on an average scarcely eleven years each. Since a revolution was inevitably accompanied by the wholesale slaughter of all the blood-relatives and supporters of the previous king, it is not surprising that this constant change of dynasty hindered the social and economic consolidation of the country.

The favourable development of the Northern Kingdom was also hindered at the outset by another factor. Under David and Solomon Jerusalem had been not only the religious centre, but a proud and beautiful capital city. There was no such political focal point in the north. Its first king, Jeroboam, chose Shechem as his capital, but an attack by the Egyptian ruler Shishak forced him to change it for Penuel, in the territory beyond the Jordan. When the danger from Egypt had passed, he recrossed the Jordan, but did not return to Shechem. Apparently he did not consider it sufficiently safe, situated as it was on the edge of a broad plain. Instead, he settled at Tirzah, a small town probably to be identified with Tell el-Far'ah, about six miles north-east of Shechem. Tirzah lay on a hill and was protected on all sides by mountains, the Wadi Far'ah offering a quick escape route to the Jordan. Although it occupied an area of barely ten acres, subsequent rulers of Israel retained this unpretentious little place as their capital, until King Omri (885–874) decided on a change for both political and economic reasons. Tirzah was in fact too small and could not be enlarged. What is more, the Arameans were exerting increasing pressure from the east. The obvious thing was to move the capital further west.

It says something for Omri's originality and boldness that he did not choose an already existing town, but an imposing uninhabited hill about six miles north-west of Shechem. Here he founded the new royal city of Samaria. This hill had been occupied since the beginning of the Bronze Age, but only intermittently, and no fixed settlement had ever been established. In the pre-exilic period it had an area of about twenty acres, and was, therefore, at least twice as big as Tirzah. It is a fortunate circumstance for Biblical archaeologists that Omri chose to build his capital on ground that had not previously been the site of a Canaanite settlement, for it is now possible to say with some degree of certainty what an Israelite town of that time was really like. Moreover, the imposing and open situation of the place indicates that in those days the Northern Kingdom was no longer a loosely-knit collection of a few tribes, but a strong and prosperous nation with its own culture.

The relations between Judah and Israel had a very chequered history. At first the kings of Judah tried to win back control over the northern tribes, but they were soon forced to realize that they had underestimated the strength of the Northern Kingdom. Later hostilities were generally aimed at gaining small territorial advantages, and fighting was limited to border incidents. Thus the third king of Israel, Baasha, occupied the stronghold of Ramah so that he could restrict the movements of the king of the Southern Kingdom. King Asa of Judah did not have enough power of his own to prevent this, but he made a very skilful move by calling in the help of the Arameans, who during the preceding centuries had set up a state around the city of Damascus. David had at one time annexed this region to his kingdom, but even under Solomon Damascus had recovered its independence. Ever since that time the Arameans had been waiting for a favourable opportunity to extend their kingdom to the south and west. They responded, therefore, to Asa's appeal and invaded Israel from the north. Baasha of Israel had to evacuate Ramah at once in order to hold back the invader, and Judah took advantage of this opportunity to raze the fortress and remove the wood and stones to reinforce the defences of the border villages of Mizpah and Geba in Benjamin, to the north. The sole consequence of this war between Judah and Israel was that the frontier was moved a few miles.

At one point this fratricidal conflict threatened to take a tragic turn. When Amaziah of Judah, about the year 790 B.C., had defeated his feeble neighbour Edom, and wanted to match his strength with Jehoash of Israel, the latter accepted the challenge and marched straight to Beth-shemesh in Judah, where he succeeded in taking Amaziah prisoner. Next, he marched on Jerusalem, demolished a stretch of the city wall four hundred cubits in length, plundered the Temple and the palace, and finally returned to Samaria with a number of hostages. Oddly enough, he released Amaziah, who continued to rule as king over an independent Judah. His people, however, eventually turned against his warlike policies, and he was forced to flee from Jerusalem. At Lachish he was overtaken and put to death.

Of course Judah and Israel were not always fighting against each other. On various occasions they supported each other in wars against the surrounding nations. There was even a brief period when the two ruling houses found themselves related by blood. A daughter of Ahab of Israel (874–853) was given in marriage to Joram of the house of David. Twenty years later their son, Ahaziah, was paying a visit to his ailing uncle, Joram of Israel, and both monarchs were slain by Jehu, a rebel general in Israel's army. A new dynasty now came to power in the Northern Kingdom, and the close bond between the royal houses of Judah and Israel was once more severed.

The development of the two countries was decisively influenced by their different geographical positions. Unlike Judah, Israel was transit territory, a situation that brought with it many advantages, for through it ran the great caravan routes to and from Egypt and Syria, Mesopotamia and Asia Minor. The country was, therefore, of some consequence in the world of that time, and trade brought it wealth and prosperity, especially during the long reigns of Ahab (874–853) and Jeroboam II (783–743). The ivory carvings discovered in the acropolis of Samaria, for instance, are renowned. These costly panels were used to decorate couches and walls, and there are a number of scriptural references to them. Thus in the Book of Amos we read (3:15), "I [Yahweh] will smite the winter house with the summer house; and the houses of ivory shall vanish." In the same book there is a threat against those who "lie upon beds of ivory" (6:4). Similarly, a passage in 1 Kings 22:39 speaks of the palace of Samaria: "Now the rest of the acts of Ahab, and all that he did, and the ivory house which he built, are they not written in the Book of the Chronicles of the Kings of Israel?"

Excavations at Megiddo and Hazor have confirmed these activities of Ahab and his successors. Ruins of palaces, fortifications, and houses of the period can now be seen at these places.

A stone feeding-trough on the ruined mound at Megiddo. Among the remains of the ancient town there are several of these troughs, which belonged to the famous stables or mews. During the excavations carried out in the thirties these stables were attributed to King Solomon, on the basis of 1 Kings 9:17-19. Further investigation, however, has revealed that the remains are more recent by a century. It is now believed that King Ahab (874-853) built the stables; but this does not mean that Solomon could not have erected something similar on this spot a century earlier.

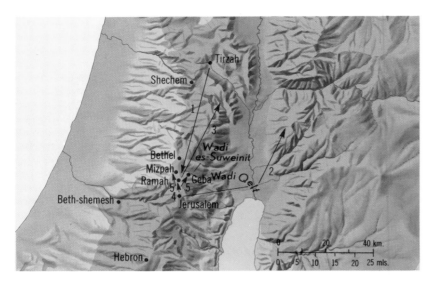 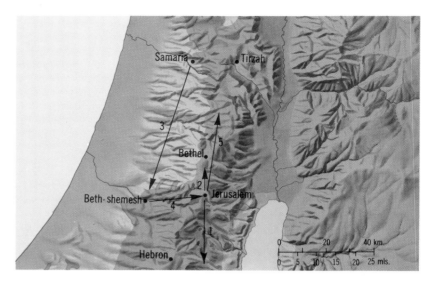

Border war between Israel and Judah, I

1. King Baasha of Israel (909-886) advanced on Ramah and turned the town into a strongly fortified frontier post. He thus deprived Jerusalem of its last natural defence to the north.
2. King Asa of Judah (911-870) could not on his own ward off the danger from the north. He asked the ruler of Damascus to invade north-eastern Israel, which that prince readily did.
3. King Baasha of Israel quickly withdrew his troops from Ramah to put them in the field against Damascus.
4. Thereupon King Asa of Judah went to Ramah, dismantled the fortifications and—
5. With the materials thus obtained he strengthened Mizpah and Geba, two towns situated a little further north.

Border war between Israel and Judah, II

1. King Amaziah of Judah (796-781) defeated a persistently rebellious Edom.
2. This victory made him rash enough to declare war on the king of Israel too.
3. King Jehoash of Israel (789-783) immediately took the initiative and marched southwards along the mountains of Ephraim. By using this route he took the southern army by surprise, defeated it at Beth-shemesh, and took King Amaziah prisoner.
4. Jehoash then marched on Jerusalem, broke down the north wall of the city, and sacked the palace and the Temple.
5. After this Jehoash returned to Samaria with a number of hostages. He did, however, set King Amaziah of Judah free.

The rulers of Israel also enlarged and beautified the famous stables at Megiddo which Solomon had built. Some remnants of them are still visible today. Among the tumble-down walls of the royal fortress in Samaria a large number of inscribed potsherds have been discovered. In the absence of papyrus and leather it was on this material that notes were kept of goods delivered to the palace. Unfortunately these brief records are often hard to decipher.

The Southern Kingdom was not so favourably situated. It lay right off the main trade routes, shut away in the mountains of Judah, with the Philistines to the west, Israel to the north, and the desert and the Dead Sea to the east. Its only connection with the outside world was towards the south, for there lay Edom, even weaker and less important than Judah itself. This situation explains why the Assyrian armies left Jerusalem unmolested for so long. Even so, Judah was not a poor country. Its relative isolation, together with its political and religious stability, made for a certain prosperity. This is evidenced by the fact that throughout its existence as a kingdom the palace and Temple treasures were stolen or had to be handed over on at least seven occasions. The silver and gold went once to Egypt, twice to Damascus, once to Israel, twice to Assyria, and on the last occasion to Babylon. Yet Judah always recovered from the blow, which suggests that it is not necessary to paint too sombre a picture of the country.

The military operations in which Judah and Israel became involved with their neighbours must now be briefly considered. Between the death of Solomon and the downfall of the Northern Kingdom in 721 Egypt made only one appearance in Canaan. Pharaoh Shishak took advantage of the confusion prevailing among the tribes of Judah and Israel to plunder the countryside, and on his return to Egypt he had a list made in Karnak of the cities he had 'conquered.' As it does not include the names of any places in Judah, it is likely that he left the actual territory of the Southern Kingdom in peace when Rehoboam sent him the palace and Temple treasures. The author who reports this incident in the Bible does not want to say outright that the king had parted more or less voluntarily with the precious possessions of the Temple, so he writes: "He [Pharaoh] took away the treasures of the house of the Lord and the treasures of the king's house; he took away everything. He also took away shields of gold which Solomon had made." (1 Kings 14:26) In fact, the Pharaoh had probably not even set foot in Jerusalem, but had been satisfied to let the king of Judah, albeit under pressure from the advancing Egyptian army, surrender his treasures without a battle.

To judge by the list of cities conquered by the Pharaoh it was Israel that suffered more than any other nation from his invasion. Jeroboam was obliged to abandon Shechem, his capital, and flee across the Jordan. Yet this military exploit was little more than a predatory raid on the Pharaoh's part. Egypt was not in a position at this time to undertake a more full-scale operation, although in the centuries that followed it was to play a leading role in world politics.

The Philistines had been beaten by David once and for all, and thereafter they never made any further attempt to conquer the highlands of Canaan. They were still strong enough, however, to hold their own in the coastal plain and engage in border warfare with the Israelites from time to time. We know only of two such incidents from the Bible (1 Kings 15:27 and 16:15), but as these are mentioned only because they happened to coincide with a change of power in Israel, it is likely that there were more frequent clashes between the two peoples.

Moab and Edom had been enemies of the Israelites for centuries, but David had defeated them and annexed their territories. After Solomon's death Edom remained under the rule of Judah, and Moab was annexed to Israel. As mentioned earlier, Edom represented a valuable addition to Judah. Its rich mineral deposits, the caravan routes passing through its territory, and the link it provided with the Gulf of Elath were very important for the prosperity of the Southern Kingdom. According to the Biblical writers Edom continued to be subject to Judah until the middle of the ninth century, when in spite of King Joram's efforts it succeeded in breaking away. The Biblical account concludes with the following words: "So Edom revolted from the rule of Judah to this day." (2 Kings 8:22) Later rulers of Judah tried to win back the lost territory. Thus we read that King Amaziah defeated the Edomites in the Valley of Salt, south of the Dead Sea, and captured Sela, a place as celebrated as it is unknown (2 Kings 14:7). His son, Uzziah (781–740), even succeeded in re-occupying Elath, in the south. But these successes must have been only temporary.

Relations with Moab followed very much the same pattern. By adopting harsh measures King Omri of Israel (885–874) was able to hold this territory for the Northern Kingdom, but when his son Ahab (874–853) fell in battle against the Arameans, Mesha, the king of Moab, seized the opportunity to make himself independent of Israel. Ahab's son, Joram (852–841), with the help of Judah and Edom, tried to reconquer Moab, but although he managed to invade it and surround King Mesha in his capital, Kir-hareseth, he failed to win the final victory. The Bible attributes a curious ending to this war: "Then he [Mesha] took his eldest son who was to reign in his stead, and offered him for a burnt offering upon the wall. And there came great wrath upon Israel; and they withdrew from him and returned to their own land." (2 Kings 3:27)

The puzzle presented by this text was only partly solved when during the last century there was discovered among the ruins of the trans-Jordanian city of Dibon, about forty miles south of the modern 'Amman, a stone slab on which King Mesha had set down his account of this conflict. From this it appears that for some reason the fortunes of war must have turned, enabling Mesha to extend his territory as far as the northernmost point of the Dead Sea. The Biblical author viewed the event primarily from a religious standpoint, which is probably why he ascribed the defeat of Israel to the 'great wrath' of the god of Moab, who was propitiated by the sacrifice of Mesha's son and again took over his territory. After this victory, Moab remained permanently independent of Israel.

The most dangerous enemy in the immediate vicinity of Is-

Plan and reconstruction of the 'Houses of Tell el-Fa'rah'

Tell el-Far'ah lies 7 miles north-east of the present Nablus. Since 1946 this mound has been under investigation by archaeologists. The results suggest that the site may be identified with the Biblical Tirzah, capital of the Northern Kingdom before Samaria. Below is a plan of two houses of the sort discovered in layer III, which must date from the period between 1000 and 890 B.C. The plan of both houses is more or less the same. From the forecourt one reached the inner courtyard by a single entrance. The first half of the inner court was divided by two rows of three or four columns into three areas at different levels, of which the two outermost were probably covered in. The remaining half of the inner courtyard was flanked by two apartments. It terminated in a lengthy room with a door in the centre, or else in two rooms, each with its own entrance. Below again is a reconstruction. The elevation is, of course, hypothetical; and the same applies to the windows (apertures for light and air). However, all in all it gives a fair impression of the kind of house commonly built in the East around an interior space.

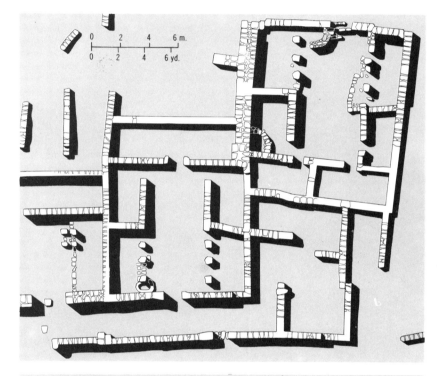

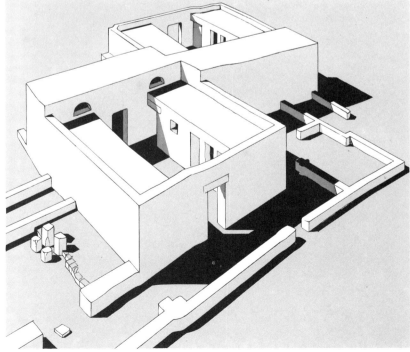

rael was the Aramean state which had formed around the city of Damascus. The rulers of this kingdom were continually trying to extend their territory to the west and to the south. They were attracted by the fertile soil and the caravan routes in these areas. Several times they managed to push right through to the walls of Samaria itself. To help it withstand this constant pressure from Aram, Israel turned especially to the powerful sea towns of Phoenicia. From time to time Israel gained the ascendancy, and on one occasion the king of Aram was even obliged to seek a humiliating peace: " 'The cities which my father took from your father I will restore; and you may establish bazaars for yourself in Damascus, as my father did in Samaria.' And Ahab said, 'I will let you go on these terms.' " (1 Kings 20:34) But the peace had more the character of a temporary armistice, and after a short time hostilities broke out again. So peace and war succeeded each other by turns. Only when the threat presented by the major power of Assyria in northern Syria became an acute menace did Samaria and Damascus combine their forces to meet the common foe.

2. THE RELIGIOUS SITUATION IN JUDAH AND ISRAEL

When the kingdom of David and Solomon split up about 930 B.C., the effects of the political rupture were felt in the religious

Campaigns of Pharaoh Shishak, ca. 925 B.C.

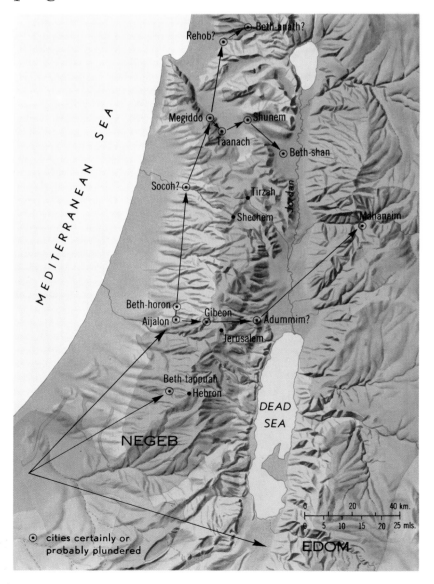

⊙ cities certainly or probably plundered

sphere also, for with Jerusalem both the royal residence and the central sanctuary had fallen to Judah. Temple and palace were in those days regarded as a single entity, and the modern distinction between Church and State did not exist. It was therefore inevitable that the conflict between Judah and Israel concerning the question of the kingship in particular and political authority in general should have extended into the sphere of religious life and practice. The concern for the right forms of religious practice and observance was in fact central to most ancient religions. In those days people were far less concerned with the abstract truths and tenets of religious belief than with the cultic activities which embodied them. The cultic activity was, in a very real sense, a concrete expression of their belief, and it was therefore this which appeared to matter most. Since this cult of Yahweh had in Solomon's time found its highest expression in the cult of the Temple at Jerusalem, the northern tribes had either to accept the authority of the Jerusalem Temple or set up a new cultic centre in opposition to it. The latter choice was the inevitable one, because they had already claimed their independence from the country in which the city of David was situated.

King Jeroboam (926–907) tried to remedy the situation for the Northern Kingdom by elevating the ancient cultic centres of Dan and Bethel to royal sanctuaries. He installed his own priests in these places and set up cultic images. Of this the Bible says: "So the king took counsel, and made two calves of gold. And he said to the people, 'You have gone up to Jerusalem long enough. Behold your gods, O Israel, who brought you up out of the land of Egypt.' " (1 Kings 12:28) This action is often referred to in the Bible as 'the sin of Jeroboam.' Nevertheless, it is difficult to determine the actual significance of the two calves.

If we take the Biblical text at its face value, we might think that the king had introduced a form of idol-worship into the Northern Kingdom. But this would be to forget that the Biblical account is more a religious testimony than a precise record of what actually took place. Moreover, it is almost unthinkable that the northern tribes would have cut themselves off from the tradition of Yahwism after the split with Judah. Shechem, Bethel, and Dan were traditional sanctuaries, and the recognition of their importance in the Northern Kingdom speaks for itself. Also, the 'creed' of Jeroboam quoted above refers to the Exodus from Egypt, the great saving event for Israel. Among other peoples of the ancient East the deity was often depicted with a bull or a lion beneath his feet, and Jeroboam may have intended the images of the bulls to be understood simply as the visible footstool for the invisible Yahweh. This seems quite likely, because the Temple in Jerusalem itself contained images of cherubim—winged beings, half-animal and half-human—above which Yahweh was conceived as invisibly enthroned. The most probable explanation is that Jeroboam was trying to combine in some way the religion of Yahweh with the Canaanite cult of Baal, especially as Canaanites formed a large part of the population of his kingdom.

Although Jeroboam probably did not actually intend to depict Yahweh, an identification of the image with him was bound to occur. The leaders of the Chosen People held more or less to the idea that Yahweh could not be portrayed, but for the simple Israelite there was a mysterious yet very real link between an

Wars in Palestine from 930 to 730 B.C.

1. Ca. 925 Pharaoh Shishak invaded Canaan; he seized the treasure from the Temple at Jerusalem and plundered many cities of the Northern Kingdom.
2. 909 Baasha murdered King Nadab of Israel while the latter was besieging the Philistine town of Gibbethon.
3. Ca. 900 Benhadad of Damascus invaded north-eastern Israel at the request of Asa of Judah.
4. 885 The Commander, Zimri, murdered King Elah at Tirzah, while the latter's troops were besieging Gibbethon.
5. 860 Benhadad II of Damascus invested Samaria unsuccessfully.
6. 859 Expedition from Damascus directed against Israel; Benhadad was taken prisoner at Aphek and was released.
7. 853 Judah and Israel joined forces to recapture Ramoth from Damascus.
8. Ca. 850 Together with Judah and Edom, Joram of Israel organized a punitive expedition against rebellious Moab. The allies were forced to retreat; and Moab seized the territory north of the Arnon as far as the northern end of the Dead Sea.
9. Ca. 845 Judah's punitive expedition against an insurgent Edom miscarried.
10. 841 Battle between Israel and Aram for Ramoth.
11. Ca. 830 Damascus conquered the whole area east of the Jordan.
12. Ca. 820 Damascus took Gath and threatened Jerusalem; Judah bought off the enemy with the Temple treasure.
13. Ca. 810 Damascus held the Northern Kingdom down for some years.
14. Ca. 795 Israel shook off a Damascus weakened by the attacks of Assyria.
15. Ca. 790 Amaziah of Judah conquered Sela.
16. Ca. 770 Jeroboam II expelled Aram from Israel once for all.
17. Ca. 750 Azariah of Judah defeated the Philistines and Edom.
18. Ca. 734 Damascus and Samaria threatened Jerusalem; Ahaz of Judah appealed to the Assyrians, who soon afterwards over-ran Damascus.

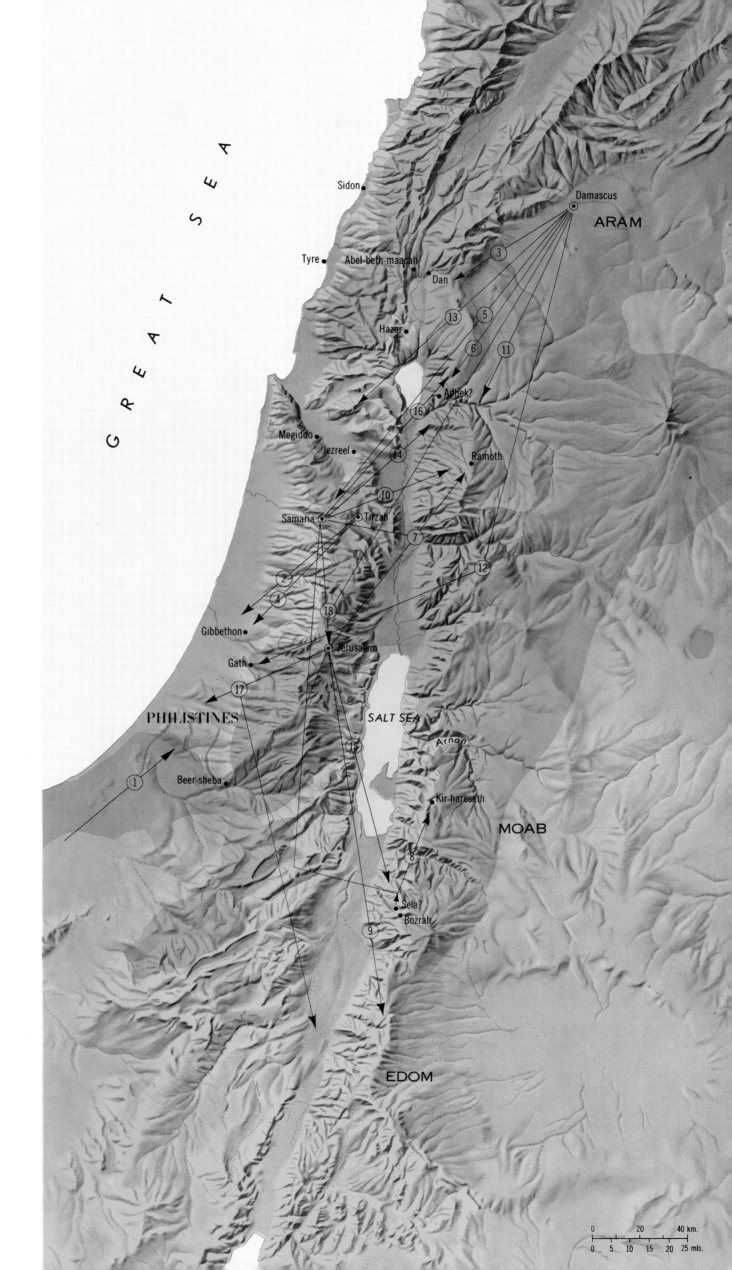

image and the reality that it represented. It must also be borne in mind that the ninth and eighth centuries B.C. were a time of great tension and insecurity for Israel, and it would be understandable if a large part of the population had fallen away from the original form of the religion of Yahweh and looked for salvation to a god whose presence was visibly verifiable.

In the unquiet and difficult times that Judah and Israel were now experiencing, foreign influence and pressure in the spheres of politics and religion were increasing all the time. Religious life was affected particularly by the close contacts between Israel and the sea ports of Tyre and Sidon. During Omri's dynasty (885–841) the friendly relations with these Phoenician cities continued and was cemented by intermarriage between the royal houses. Ahab, Omri's son, married Jezebel, the daughter of King Ethbaal of Tyre. According to popular tradition, which has influenced the Biblical account, the persecution of all worshippers of Yahweh was carried on at her instigation. This persecution is not to be compared, however, with the action taken against the early Christians or the persecution of the Jews in the recent past. The fact that the children of Ahab and Jezebel had Yahwistic names like Ahaziah, Jehoram, and Athaliah, speaks for itself, although we should not overrate this official lip-service to Yahweh. The king built a temple in Samaria in honour of the Tyrian Baal, which was later to be destroyed by Jehu (1 Kings 16:32; 2 Kings 10:21), and did everything to advance the cult of Baal in the country.

This certainly won him considerable sympathy among the Canaanite section of the population, but at the same time he alienated those Israelites who, like the prophet Elijah, held firmly to the Yahwistic faith of their fathers. Ahab's son and successor, Ahaziah (853–852 B.C.), was the first to experience their hate. When, after a fall from a window of his palace, he took counsel of Baalzebub, the idol of the Philistine city of Ekron, Elijah challenged him angrily and prophesied in the name of Yahweh his imminent death (2 Kings 1:1–16). Finally, the long pent-up fury against the house of Ahab led to an open rebellion during the reign of Joram of Israel (852–841).

The revolt of Jehu, commander of the Israel army, took place at the direct instigation of the prophet Elisha who enjoyed great prestige among those Israelites who had remained faithful to Yahweh (2 Kings 9:1–10). Only Athaliah escaped the subsequent bloodbath carried out against Ahab's descendants. She had been married by her father to the ruler of Judah, and for a time it looked as if the house of Ahab would at least rule on the throne of the Southern Kingdom. When she learned that even her son, King Ahaziah of Judah, had been murdered during a visit to the Northern Kingdom, she immediately seized power in Jerusalem and officially introduced the cult of Baal in the south as well. Five years later, however, the opposing party of the Yahwist believers rose against her. She was overthrown on the instructions of the High Priest Jehoiada, and Jehoash, Ahaziah's seven-year-old son, was installed on the throne of his father. With Athaliah, the temple and the priests of Baal also disappeared from Jerusalem (2 Kings 11). This put an end to the official recognition of the cult, but its attraction persisted for many years and revived later when Israel was threatened by Assyria.

The growing power of Assyria made a deep impression on Israel and Judah. Since their settlement in Canaan, almost their

The Wadi el-Hesa is often—and probably rightly—identified with the Biblical Zered (Num. 21:12 and Deut. 2:13-14). It runs from the highlands of trans-Jordan to the southern extremity of the Dead Sea. Although the Bible makes only a few passing references to the Zered, it is generally considered that this valley formed the natural frontier between the people of Moab on the north and the tribes of Edom in the south. In prehistoric times the whole region was volcanic, so that black hills are to be seen towering up here and there. In the middle of the Wadi el-Hesa stands one of these grim looking summits, which the Arabs call 'the mountain of evil.' The Nabateans, too, appear to have found this eminence awe-inspiring. About the beginning of the Christian era they built a temple on a hill, just to the west of the black mountain. The ruins of this temple are known as Khirbet et-Tannur.

The spring at Jericho plays a major role in one of the legendary stories about the prophet Elisha (2 Kings 2 : 19-22). That is not very surprising. The town of Jericho was totally dependent on this water. During the summer months the valley becomes oppressively hot, and everything is dried up. The country around Jericho is as much as 1,000 feet below sea level. The original spring has not so far been traced: people lived so close to it that it soon became buried beneath the rubble of prehistoric, Canaanite, and Israelite Jericho (Tell es-Sultan). The water now appears out of the mound, whence a number of small channels convey it to the oasis of modern Jericho.

sole direct contacts had been with the minor principalities around them. In the ninth and eighth centuries, however, Israel's horizon became much wider. It gradually became aware that it was part of history on a world scale. The centre of events was no longer Jerusalem. Judah and Israel were small parts of a mighty whole, carried along on the current of world affairs. This experience shook the traditional faith of many Israelites. The Bible tells us of an action by King Ahaz of Judah which offers an excellent illustration of this crisis of faith.

About 734 B.C. Aram and Israel were threatening Judah. Despite the urgent warning of the prophet Isaiah to depend solely on Yahweh's help in this situation (Isaiah 7), Ahaz thought he could ward off these attacks by sending presents to Tiglath-pileser of Assyria and asking for his assistance. This was graciously accorded him, but at a high price. Ahaz was summoned to Damascus, where he had to acknowledge the Assyrian potentate as his liege lord and do homage to the Assyrian gods. He subsequently had a new bronze altar erected in Jerusalem similar to the one he had seen in Damascus (2 Kings 16). He may have been forced to do this by Tiglath-pileser, but it nevertheless meant that the King was publicly asserting that the Assyrian gods were more powerful than Yahweh.

The time of this crisis of faith was also the age of the classical prophets. For centuries now the ancient East had been producing prophets of one god or another, as, for example, the one who appeared in the town of Mari on the Euphrates about 1700 B.C. The account of Wen-Amon's journey in the eleventh century, which was mentioned earlier, also tells of a young man from Byblos who had prophetic gifts. A great deal is known about the group of prophets who surrounded Saul after Samuel anointed him king (1 Sam. 10:1–12), and there is constant mention of prophetic figures in Israel such as Samuel, Nathan, and Gad. Prophets continued their activities even after the Solomonic kingdom split up. Ahijah of Shiloh played a leading role in the establishment of the Northern Kingdom (1 Kings 11:29–39). Shemaiah prevented immediate hostilities from breaking out between Judah and Israel (1 Kings 12:21–24). Micaiah opposed King Ahab when he was fighting the Arameans in league with Judah. Besides this there are constant references to unnamed prophets, as for example in 1 Kings 13:1, 11; 16:7; 20:13, 35. The prominent figures in this period, however, were the prophets Elijah and Elisha. They fired the imagination of the people in such a way that supernatural powers were ascribed to them, and these popular traditions subsequently found their way into the record of the religious history of Israel (1 Kings 17ff and 2 Kings 2ff).

It is not easy from the sources available to us to reconstruct the development of the prophet's office, nor is it possible to state clearly what the activity of the prophet consisted of. Some slight indication is given in 1 Samuel 9:9, where we are informed that "he who is now called a prophet was formerly called a seer." This suggests that the original emphasis lay in the ability to express a feeling of ecstasy. Men of religious sensibility, under the stimulus of music and the dance, experienced a visionary awareness, and in this state of rapture they uttered their oracles. But as the years passed, this developed into a profession that one could learn to practise. Prophets organized themselves into groups and began to wear special clothing and other marks of their office (1 Kings 20:38 and Zech. 13:4). Since the business of prophesying had now become their means of livelihood, they spoke such oracles as were called for by the personal interest of the client or by the pride of the nation. The king and the whole people received pronouncements in the belief that the word would become reality.

Under the pressure of the threat from Assyria there was a strong reaction against this professional prophesying. Men appeared who understood what was happening in the world and who had the courage to speak the truth about it. Usually these

The nomadic life of the Hebrew tribes in the wilderness was so idealized that in the time of the monarchy one group in Israel repudiated city culture on principle. They lived just like this shepherd with his sheep, refusing to occupy houses or to work in field and vineyard. They were known as the Rechabites, after their putative progenitor, Rechab. In 2 Kings 10 : 15, 23 their leader, Jehonadab, appears as a zealous champion of Yahweh; and in Jeremiah 35 : 6-11 there is a succinct description of their outlook on life.

prophets took an individual stand, and their actions were independent. Religious ecstasy informed only a part of their vision. Their demeanour was, in general, sober, and suggested a full awareness of this world's realities. They possessed in addition, however, an intense religious conviction, and out of this they delivered their message to rulers and people alike, in words that were often pithy and poetic. The greatness and prosperity of Israel and Judah could not, they said, survive the Assyrian menace, unless the people were devoted to the worship of Yahweh and respected their fellow-countrymen. This is strikingly expressed in Hosea 6:6: "I [Yahweh] desire steadfast love and not sacrifice, the knowledge of God, rather than burnt offerings." In Micah 6:8 the thought is put even more clearly: "He has showed you, O man, what is good; and what does the Lord require of you but to do justice, and to love kindness, and to walk humbly with your God?"

Many of these prophets have left us their sayings and their discourses. These often give the impression that the entire nation had fallen away from Yahweh, but fortunately this was not the case. The prophets had friends, followers, and sometimes even pupils. The latter, in particular, would repeat, expound, preserve, and collect the utterances of their masters. In this way the books of the various 'writing prophets' gradually came into being. It is often difficult, however, to separate the actual words of the prophets from the many additions and explanatory comments of a later period.

These writing prophets can be roughly divided into four groups. As will be seen later on, the first group made its appearance in the second half of the eighth century, when the Northern Kingdom collapsed under the pressure from Assyria. There were Amos and Hosea in Israel, and Isaiah and Micah in Judah. The second group came about a hundred years later, just before the Exile of Judah, and comprised Jeremiah, Zephaniah, Nahum, and probably Habakkuk as well. A third group ministered to the exiles in Babylon between 598 and 538 B.C. It included Ezekiel and a nameless prophet who, because his sayings are found in the Book of Isaiah (chs. 40–55), is known as Deutero-Isaiah. Finally, after the Exile there came a fourth group, Haggai, Trito-Isaiah (Is. 56–66), Malachi, Zechariah, and probably also Joel, Deutero-

Zechariah (Zech. 9–14), and Obadiah. The form of prophecy practised by this last group already shows signs of decline when compared with the classical prophets. The prophet now either becomes the seer of the last times, whose visions foretell the future of his people, and of the whole world, or else his mode of writing suggests the wise man who seeks to refute his opponents by the techniques of disputation.

This brief survey of the course of Israelite prophecy has already gone beyond the framework of the present chapter, and it is now necessary to return to the religious literature of the two states of Judah and Israel in the period from the tenth to the eighth centuries.

3. THE FURTHER ESTABLISHMENT OF A BIBLICAL TRADITION

In the last chapter some account was given of the religious tradition established by the Yahwist school of thought. Curiously enough, some considerable time afterwards a second collection was made of the ancient traditions of the people and was worked into a unified whole. As with most of the writings in the Old Testament the name of its author has not been handed down. Whereas the first tradition used the name 'Yahweh' for God, the second called him 'Elohim,' and is therefore known as the Elohist school. The difference may appear to be insignificant, but a deeper issue is involved. For the ancient Semites a name was something of far greater significance than it is for us today. The name was identical with reality. It was through the name that the person was encountered, and the person was thought to reveal himself in his name. When the name of a deity was used in worship, contact was made with that deity. Then a man could be confident that he was being heard by the god. The naming of God was therefore a very serious matter and explains why the two schools would have considered themselves quite distinct from one another.

Despite this, however, there are resemblances. Both the Yawhist and the Elohist writings were based on oral and written traditions that had been preserved, interpreted, and handed down over many centuries. The part played by the various sanctuaries, such as Bethel, Gilgal, Hebron, Shiloh, Shechem, and Dan, in the final stage of this process should not be underestimated. These were the places where the people came together to meet with the God who had shown himself mighty in the past and so was able to influence the present. On these occasions men were constantly re-inspired by the old traditions, which they first elaborated into narratives, and then into narrative cycles. These lay ready to hand when the Yahwist and Elohist authors began to collect the ancient traditions of the people and give them a deeper religious significance.

It is generally considered today that the Yahwist texts were written in the south in the tenth century. It is more difficult to state when and where the second set, the Elohist texts, came into being. Some parts seem older, others more recent than the parallel traditions in the Yawhist documents. It is possible that the Elohist texts were written down over a fairly long period, but they were probably completed by the first half of the eighth century, when Judah and Israel were enjoying relative prosperity. As the Yahwists worked in the south, it was thought at one time that the Elohist writings must have originated in the Northern Kingdom, but there are no decisive arguments to support this view. Nor is there any evidence to support the case that one school collected the traditions of the southern tribes, and the other those of the tribes of central Palestine and Galilee. It is clear from the overall intention of both, that they saw and described Israel as a whole and conceived of it as one people. Since, however, it is unlikely that both works were written at the same time and in the same place, it is, perhaps, reasonable to assume a northern provenance for the Elohist texts.

Of course there are divergences of style in both sets of texts. For example, the language of the Yahwist is often simple, though evocative and arresting. The famous paradise narrative in Genesis 2–3 is a vivid instance of this. The Elohist, on the other hand, is usually down-to-earth and matter-of-fact, and sometimes more long-winded. We need only read the dream narratives in the Joseph story (Gen. 40–42) or the story of the Golden Calf (Ex. 32), which are both ascribed to the Elohist school, to see this. In addition, there are differences in the choice of words. We have already mentioned the two different names for God, Yahweh and Elohim. The Yahwist generally refers to the in-habitants of Canaan as Canaanites and to the holy mountain in the desert as Sinai, while the Elohist sometimes uses the names Amorites and Horeb for these.

In view of the similarities already mentioned between the two schools, these last differences in usage are remarkable. How was it possible for the holy mountain, which held a central place in the religious traditions of Israel, to have two different names among one and the same people? Does this mean that by the tenth century it was no longer possible to state precisely where this mountain was situated? Or are two different mountains involved? Whatever the answer, the location of Sinai-Horeb is still an unsolved problem. It is generally said to be in the south of the region traditionally known as the Sinai Peninsula or the Desert of Sinai, but this location is by no means certain. It depends for support only on the tradition of the Eastern Church, which goes back no farther than the fourth century A.D. We know that there was a place of pilgrimage here, from the numerous inscriptions that Nabatean pilgrims made on the rock walls of Jebel Serbal in the second and third centuries A.D.

But can we automatically identify this sacred spot with Sinai-Horeb? There are many passages in the Scriptures which suggest that Sinai was much closer to Palestine, as, for example, Deuteronomy 33:2: "The Lord came from Sinai, and dawned from Seir upon us; he shone forth from Mount Paran." These places take us into the region between the Dead Sea and the Gulf of 'Aqaba, but it is impossible to give them a more precise location.

There are further important differences in outlook and style between the Yahwist and the Elohist writings. Like the Yahwist, the Elohist interprets the growth of Israel from a religious standpoint, but unlike him he does not deal with the earliest stages of the nation's history. He starts neither with the Creation

Up to some time in the 9th century B.C. Moab regarded the Arnon (Wadi el-Mujib) as marking its northern border (cf. plate on page 60). Until then the district north of this wadi came under the authority of Israel; and Moab itself was obliged to pay tribute to the king of the Northern Kingdom. At about 850, however, Moab rebelled. The punitive expedition which Israel then conducted in company with Judah and Edom miscarried. Moab made a decisive crossing of the Arnon and conquered the whole area east of the Dead Sea. From then on, Israel called the region east of the Jordan by the Dead Sea 'the country of Moab' (Ruth 1 : 1 *et al*; cf. Deut. 1 : 5).

story, nor with the Flood, but with Abraham, the father of the people of Israel. Hence the Elohist tradition lacks the universal and dramatic setting that is characteristic of the Yahwist school. This suggests that the Elohist was more nationalistically minded and that he more or less excluded other peoples from salvation. It is true, however, that the Yahwist's enthusiasm for the kingdom of David and Solomon probably prevented him from seeing any problem here: national greatness and religious salvation seemed to coincide.

In this respect the Elohist texts are more sensitive, possibly as a result of the discouraging experiences that followed the split in the Solomonic kingdom. For the Elohist, salvation and peace lay primarily in the fact that Israel belonged to God. A passage like Exodus 19:5-6, which probably stems from the Elohist tradition, illustrates this well: "Now therefore, if you will obey my voice and keep my covenant, you shall be my own possession among all peoples; for all the earth is mine, and you shall be to me a kingdom of priests and a holy nation."

It is true that these words do not directly allow salvation to all peoples, but at least the good fortune of Israel is not seen in primarily material terms. The explicit reference to God's power over the whole earth is also striking. If this passage is authentic, then this Elohist declaration of faith has been influenced by the prophets. This is suggested by various other passages. For instance, even Abraham was described as a prophet (Gen. 20:7).

Moses, especially, was highly esteemed by the Elohists. He was considered to be the prophet above all others, and something more besides. For with prophets God spoke in dreams, but "not so with my servant Moses; he is entrusted with all my house.

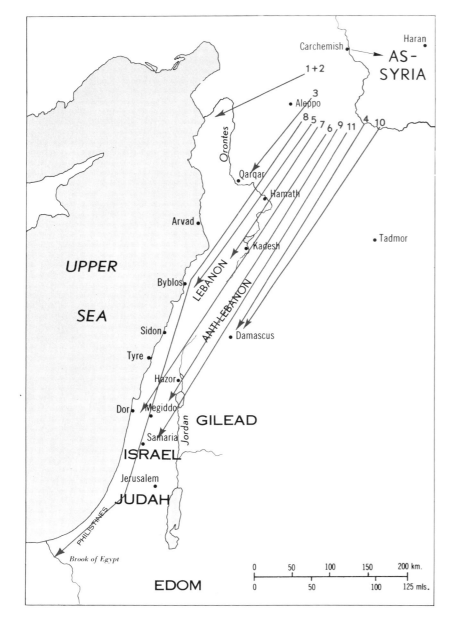

Assyrian invasions of Canaan

1. Ashurnazirpal II (883-859) crossed the Euphrates at *Carchemish* and pushed on to the Mediterranean (Upper Sea). He received tribute from, among other places, *Tyre*, *Sidon*, *Byblos*, and *Arvad*.
2. Shalmaneser III (858-824), in the first year of his reign, likewise thrust as far as the *Upper Sea*. Every state in northern Syria was obliged to pay him tribute.
3. Led by *Hamath* and *Damascus*, the small states of greater Canaan united to resist the danger threatening from Assyria. When in 853 Shalmaneser again marched westward, he found himself confronted at Qarqar by the coalition of twelve kings from Canaan, including Hadadezer of *Damascus* and Ahab of *Israel*. The Assyrians failed to force a decision.
4. In 841 Shalmaneser marched westward for the sixteenth time. He laid siege, ineffectually, to *Damascus*. To judge from various pictorial representations and the text on 'the black obelisk,' *Tyre*, *Sidon*, and Jehu of *Israel* paid him tribute.
5. In 837 Shalmaneser made his twenty-first (and final) incursion into the west. He received tribute from *Damascus*, *Tyre*, *Sidon*, and *Byblos*. In the years that followed, the Assyrian forces were obliged to give their whole attention to the eastern and northern frontiers, which were constantly being invaded by savage mountain-tribes. Damascus then found itself free to oppress Israel and Judah.
6. Adad-nirari III (811-783) also led various expeditions to the west. He received tribute from *Tyre*, *Sidon*, *Damascus*, *Israel*, *Edom*, and the *Philistines*. In 802 he very largely destroyed the power of Damascus; but not long afterwards Assyrian power was itself temporarily broken. Israel and Judah then prospered for a period.
7. Under Tiglath-pileser III (744-727) Assyria recovered its strength. In 743 Tiglath-pileser made his first incursion westward, as far as the mountains of Lebanon. *Judah* became involved in the international political scene for the first time; and King Azariah of Judah paid him tribute. From this time on, Tiglath-pileser conducted a campaign in the west annually. He no longer contented himself with receiving tribute but more and more adopted a policy of transporting the élite of the conquered peoples to other parts of his empire.
8. In 734 Tiglath-pileser's campaign took him as far west as *'the Brook of Egypt.'*
9. In 733 Tiglath-pileser decimated *Israel*. Megiddo and Hazor were laid waste; the territory beyond the Jordan, Galilee, and the sea-coast were confiscated and turned into the Assyrian provinces of Gal'aza (Gilead), Magidu (Megiddo), and Du'ru (Dor).
10. One year later, at the request of Ahaz of Judah, Tiglath-pileser attacked *Damascus*. That city was conquered and destroyed, the cream of the population carried off, and the country divided up to form four Assyrian provinces. Samaria was spared this fate, because the people put their rebellious king, Pekah, to death, thereby disposing the Assyrian ruler in their favour.
11. In 724, Shalmaneser V (727-722) took the field against the rebellious king of Israel, Hoshea. Hoshea was captured; and the siege of the capital city, *Samaria*, began. In 721 the Northern Kingdom was obliterated. Sargon II (722-705) took the city of Samaria and deported the cream of the population.

The celebrated monastery of St. Catherine in the Sinai mountains, where about a hundred years ago von Tischendorf discovered the Codex Sinaiticus, a manuscript of the 4th century A.D. This institution, which dates from the beginning of the Byzantine period, is intended to commemorate, *in situ*, the events which took place on Sinai (Ex. 19ff). But whether the identification of Sinai with this place is correct is a major question. It was not until the Christian period that Sinai-Horeb came to be located in this wilderness of rock and mountain. The relevant Old Testament passages are far from clear or even unanimous. They place this mountain either in Edom (Judg. 5 : 4-5 and Deut. 33 : 2), west of the Arabah (Deut. 33 : 2 and Hab. 3 : 3), at Teman (Hab. 3 : 3), or south of Beer-sheba (1 Kings 19 : 8).

With him I speak mouth to mouth, clearly, and not in dark speech."(Num. 12:7-8) The exceptional position accorded to Moses, which was to become even greater in the succeeding centuries, is all the more remarkable, since the Elohist tradition was generally far more conscious of God's transcendence than was the Yahwist. It represented contact between God and man as taking place only indirectly. Indeed, God did not speak in a human fashion—he was far too holy for that, and man was too weak. Therefore God had to speak through his emissaries or in dreams. The prophetic strain is also recognizable in such passages as Exodus 32:34, where the Elohist makes God say to Moses: "But now go, lead the people to the place of which I have spoken to you; behold, my angel shall go before you. Nevertheless, in the day when I visit, I will visit their sin upon them." The prophets spoke almost constantly of a future purification of the nation.

The work of the Elohist school had now increased the number of Biblical writings, and the Yahwist epic was already to hand. The earliest psalms were being sung in the Temple court

In the middle of the mound at Megiddo is a pit over 20 feet deep. It is some 35 feet across at the top, and at the base 23 feet. Round the edge run two flights of steps, leading to the bottom. The pit is not hewn out of the rock like the well at el-Jib, but has been dug out of the rubble of earlier centuries. The face has been reinforced with a wall of stones. Everything points to the pit having been used as a grain silo. It dates from the 8th century B.C.

and at the other sanctuaries, and people had begun to commit the utterances of the prophets to writing. Moreover, collections were probably already being made of the sayings of wise men such as Solomon. Unfortunately, however, we no longer have the original Elohist texts, and it is impossible to reconstruct them completely. There came a time, probably after the collapse of the Northern Kingdom, when the Yahwist and Elohist traditions were woven together in Judah. Fortunately, they were not completely merged into one, and it is still possible to discern at various points of the narrative a break in the text or dual traditions, running parallel. The Yahwist traditions evidently enjoyed far greater prestige, and it is probably for this reason that the Elohist texts have been only partially preserved.

4. THE DOWNFALL OF THE NORTHERN KINGDOM

Excavations carried out in the northern parts of the Tigris and Euphrates valleys have yielded large numbers of clay tablets inscribed with texts in cuneiform script. Many of these have preserved for us the accounts left by Assyrian kings of their campaigns. As a result, it is not difficult to reconstruct, in broad outline, the course of events during the Assyrian expansion westwards, which brought about the collapse of the Northern Kingdom.

It was in the ninth century that at long last kings of real stature appeared once more as rulers in the land of Ashur. And because no other state was in a position at that time to claim dominion of the known world, nothing stood in the way of Assyrian expansion. Ashurnazirpal II (883–859 B.C.) had already penetrated as far as the Mediterranean coast in the neighbourhood of Tyre and Sidon, the small Hittite-Aramean states in Syria having apparently been no match for the mighty Assyrian army. His successor, Shalmaneser III (859–824 B.C.) subsequently organized a number of campaigns against central and southern

The mound at Megiddo, seen from the east. The plateau covers a surface area of 13½ acres and is approximately 65 feet high. The broad cut in the centre is where the tell has been excavated down to the lowest level of habitation. In the foreground can be seen a small part of the plain of Jezreel. Its situation on the edge of this plain was one of the natural factors that made Megiddo the important place it was. Caravans from north and east alike had to pass near Megiddo through what is now the Wadi 'Ara in order to reach the coastal plains of Palestine.

Syria, and this continuing threat made the small Syrian states forget for a time their private quarrels.

Thus in the year 853 B.C., according to the Assyrian annals, Shalmaneser found himself facing a coalition of twelve minor princes. Among these was Ahab of Israel. The latter is said to have had at his command 2,000 chariots of war and 10,000 foot-soldiers, which made him one of the most powerful men in the coalition. The Assyrian report informs us that the allied kings were defeated near Qarqar, to the north of Kadesh. The Assyrian victory, however, should not be rated too high, for according to the Assyrian records only a small number of the coalition army were killed, and Shalmaneser preferred to return to his own country rather than push farther southwards. A few years later there was another clash, but again the Assyrians were unable to win the day. The same thing was repeated a number of times.

It was not until his sixteenth expedition to the west that Shalmaneser was able to get as far as the walls of Damascus, the centre of resistance to Assyrian expansion. On this occasion Jehu of Israel had to pay tribute. An account and a depiction of this event is to be found on the famous black obelisk of Shalmaneser. The king of Israel is given a strange title in the text. He is called 'Ia-u-a mâr Hu-um-ri,' which means 'Jehu, son of Omri'. Considering that it was Jehu who exterminated Omri's entire family, the Assyrians do not seem to have been very well-informed about the domestic situation of Israel, in spite of the fact that Omri's dynasty had created a memorable impression on the surrounding countries. Fortunately for Damascus and Samaria, the expansion of Assyria was checked soon after this episode. Internal upheavals and attacks by predatory bands

from the region of the Caucasus prevented further expansion for the time being.

About a century later, however, there was a revival under Tiglath-pileser III (744–727). As early as 740 B.C. he and his troops marched into Syria, and on this occasion large stretches of territory were permanently added to the Assyrian kingdom. Most of the Canaanite states hastened to pay him the tribute he demanded. According to both the Bible (2 Kings 15:19-20) and the Assyrian chronicles, Menahem of Israel was among them. By adopting these submissive tactics the Northern Kingdom was able to remain in existence for a few years longer.

Shortly afterwards, Pekah of Israel and the ruler of Damascus tried to raise a rebellion against Assyria. They attempted to force Judah on to their side, but this proved to be a disastrous move, for as we have seen King Ahaz asked the king of Assyria for help (against the advice of the prophet Isaiah (Is. 7–8)). Tiglath-pileser responded promptly (2 Kings 16) by conquering Damascus and dividing up its territory into several provinces.

Israel, too, had to pay for taking part in the rebellion. The land east of the Jordan, the whole of Galilee, and the coast south of Mount Carmel were taken from the Northern Kingdom and made into the Assyrian provinces of Gal'aza, Magidu and Du'ru. This was not without its repercussions on the internal politics of Israel. King Pekah was assassinated, and his murderer, Hoshea, was able to reign for eight years over the rump state on the mountains of Ephraim, with the approval of the Assyrian king. After the latter's death, he stopped paying tribute money to Assyria and turned for support to Saïs, then the capital of Egypt (2 Kings 17:1ff). The new king of Assyria, Shalmaneser V (727–722), captured Hoshea outside the town of Samaria in 724 B.C. Thus the last king of Israel came to an ignominious end.

Samaria, the capital, continued the struggle for more than a year. Perhaps the early death of Shalmaneser strengthened the inhabitants in their resistance. But his successor, Sargon II (722–705), soon put an end to any hopes they might have had. He conquered the town in the first year of his reign, and in that same year the Northern Kingdom finally ceased to exist. The area that had remained under the dominion of the last king of Israel now became the Assyrian province of Samerina. The ruling classes were carried off into exile, disappearing from history altogether, and the Israelites who remained behind found themselves living side by side with foreign settlers who had been transported from other parts of the Assyrian empire (2 Kings 17:24ff). The two groups gradually intermingled, and from this fusion there later arose the Samaritans, a people who have managed to preserve a separate identity right up to the present day.

The religious traditions of the Northern Kingdom, however, were not obliterated. We have no written evidence that the Israelites fled to the Southern Kingdom when the Assyrian threat could no longer be averted, but we can assume that many devout people escaped from the Northern Kingdom into Judah. These refugees probably helped with the task of combining the Yahwist and Elohist traditions, a process that was carried out in Judah probably about 700 B.C. It is also fairly safe to assume that this group played an important part in the Deuteronomist movement, which began in Jerusalem during the reign of King Josiah (640–609). This will be dealt with in the following chapter.

VI. CONTINUED GROWTH OF THE BIBLE

Further growth of the Bible against the background of the Exile in Babylon: 7th and 6th centuries B.C.

1. JUDAH PRIOR TO THE FALL OF JERUSALEM

Judah's position was seriously weakened by the destruction of Samaria. For the first time in its history the country shared a frontier with its mighty neighbour Assyria. Fortunately, there was little about this mountainous and barren region to attract Sargon II and his successors, and the Southern Kingdom enjoyed relative peace so long as it paid the annual tribute demanded by the Assyrian rulers and fell in with their political aspirations. On the borders of Judah there were other and larger territories which invited more attention from the Assyrian overlords, and besides this, a constant watch needed to be kept on those that had already been incorporated within the empire.

Assyria's apparent indifference sometimes caused the people of Judah to think that the despot's power was declining and that they could regard themselves as once more independent. In 705 B.C. Sargon II, the conqueror of Samaria, died, and the leaders of many satellite states took this as a signal for open rebellion. Among them was King Hezekiah (716–687 B.C.) of Judah, who withheld the annual tribute and broke off political and religious relations with Assyria.

He may have been influenced in this decision by the example of the Babylonians. There is a report in the Bible that one day a mission from distant Babylon came to visit Hezekiah in Jerusalem and brought him presents and a letter from their king, Merodach-baladan (2 Kings 20:12ff). The exact wording of this letter is unknown, but the Babylonian ruler undoubtedly called upon the king of Judah to join Babylon in rebelling against Assyria: his own position would be greatly strengthened if there were to be a revolution on the western border of the Assyrian empire. Nor was Egypt sitting quietly by, as can be seen from the account left by Sennacherib, Sargon's successor, of his campaign there. There is also the evidence of 2 Kings 18:21, where the Assyrians scoff at the trust Judah places in Egypt, and Isaiah 31:1-3, where the prophet condemns this trust "in chariots because they are many."

The rebellion was joined by the minor princes of Ammon, Moab, and Edom, and some of the Philistine towns followed the general example. When Padi, the ruler of Ekron, refused to break with Assyria, the angry inhabitants deposed him and sent him in chains to Hezekiah. This suggests that the latter was the leader of the rebellion in the whole area around Jerusalem, and

In 1956, near the small Arab village of el-Jib, about 6 miles north of Jerusalem archaeologists discovered a large well. The rubble inside it contained, among other things, nearly thirty pitcher-handles on which was inscribed in ancient Hebrew the name 'Gibeon' —consequently this place is presently considered to be the site of that town. This well is something quite unique. It has been hacked out of the solid rock and has a diameter of 35 feet and a depth of 32 feet. Set in the face of the rock are steps, 5 feet in width, with a hand-rail; and these spiral down to the bottom, where they continue through into a tunnel, 48 feet in length, ending in a cave. Here at one time people drew the water which had collected underground. In the 8th century this water-system, which may date from the 11th century B.C., evidently proved inadequate. The well was closed off, and a few yards further on a tunnel was cut to give access to the spring at the foot of the hill. This photograph of the steps going down gives some impression of the scale of the construction.

would explain why Sennacherib visited his rage on Judah and Jerusalem in particular.

In 701 B.C. this ruler began his campaign against Syria and Palestine to put down the rebellion in the countries in the western part of his empire. It was not until he had defeated the Egyptians and the Philistines, Moab, Ammon, and Edom, that he turned to attack Judah. He captured one fortified town after another and, according to his own account, took more than 200,000 prisoners. Hezekiah hastened to release his prisoner Padi and sent many gifts to the Assyrian ruler. This did not satisfy Sennacherib, however, and his army shut Hezekiah up in Jerusalem 'like a bird in a cage.' The holy city looked like being conquered within a matter of days, when something

unexpected happened. The Assyrians raised the siege and returned to their own country. The Bible says that this was due to the intervention of 'the angel of Yahweh,' who is reported to have caused great destruction in Sennacherib's army (2 Kings 19:35). This passage, which gives a religious explanation of what happened, may refer to some calamity that befell the Assyrian forces, an infectious disease or food poisoning. But it may also be that unrest at home called Sennacherib back to his own country, especially as there is evidence that he was not popular in Assyria. He was murdered in 681 B.C., as 2 Kings 19:37 and various Assyrian texts bear witness.

During this period a tunnel was built at Jerusalem that still survives. It winds through the rock under the Ophel in the shape of an S for 550 yards. It is roughly two feet wide, and its height varies from eighteen inches to nine feet. This achievement is mentioned with some pride in 2 Kings 20:20, 2 Chronicles 32:20, and Ecclesiasticus 48:17. The latter text reads: "Hezekiah fortified his city, and brought water into the midst of it; he tunnelled the sheer rock with iron and built pools for water." Now this narrow aqueduct, which brought water from the spring of Gihon into the city, was not, in itself, unique.In several other towns in Palestine similar constructions have been found, e.g. at Megiddo, Gezer, Gibeon, Etham, Ibleam, and, some years ago, at Tell es-Sa'idiyeh (which J. B. Pritchard has identified with Zarethan).

It is not difficult to guess the reason for these tunnels. Nearly all the larger settlements of that time were built on hills for defence. Until people had sufficiently mastered the art of catching and storing rain-water in cisterns, it was necessary to draw water from springs or wells that lay at the foot of the hill. As siege warfare developed, however, such supplies could not be relied on, for the first thing the enemy occupied was the base of the hill. As early as the Canaanite period this problem had been solved by cutting a tunnel. Thus a safe and secret access to the spring was guaranteed, or else the water was conducted through the tunnel into the town, with the spring itself concealed from the enemy's view by a wall or mound.

The course of the tunnel and the manner of its construction were determined by the particular circumstances of each place. It could be quite straight, as at Megiddo, or with a number of bends in it, as at Jerusalem. It could be cut through the rock (Jerusalem and Megiddo) or else provided with a cover for all of the way (Tell es-Sa'idiyeh) or for part of it (Gibeon).

Even before the time of Hezekiah Jerusalem had something

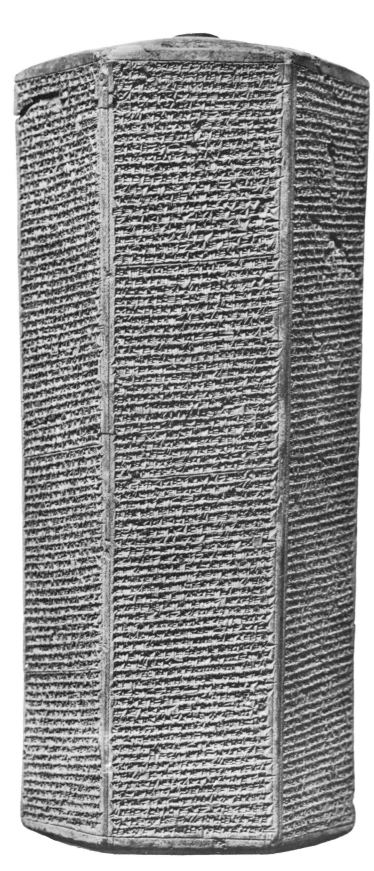

The famous Prism of King Sennacherib, on which is inscribed a record of his principal campaigns and victories. The king had this hexagonal clay column prepared as a commemorative monument for a new palace in his capital city of Nineveh, completed in 689 B.C. In 1952 a duplicate of this prism was discovered, bearing more or less the same text. After a brief prologue in which the king introduces himself comes an account of eight campaigns: to Babylonia in 702, against the Kassites in 702, to the country of Hatti (in those days northern Syria) and to Judah in 701, to southern Babylonia in 700, to Armenia in 696, to some undecipherable country in 694, to Elam in 693, and finally to Babylonia again in 691. The third part of the inscription is concerned with the building of the palace; and here Sennacherib describes the situation prior to his initiative and what he has been able to accomplish. Finally come the customary blessings and anathemas and the date.

The shaft of the water tunnel in Megiddo. To the right of the modern iron steps are traces of the ancient steps. When the inhabitants introduced the system at the end of the 12th century B.C., they had to work their way through more than 30 feet of rubble, then a layer of rock extending downwards for another 50 feet. After that they cut a tunnel almost 200 feet long, which ran practically straight except for a bend just by the spring. The calculations behind this plan and its execution evidence a high degree of skill both theoretical and practical on the part of the Canaanite engineers.

This impression of a water tunnel is diagrammatic: the point of it is to illustrate the system. Point 1 represents the spot where the water would normally have come out of the rock. This hole was closed off by a wall or a heap of stones. Figure 2 indicates the actual spring. From this point a tunnel was cut in the direction of the city and carried beneath the city walls. If, as in Jerusalem, there was no low point inside the city itself, then a shaft with a flight of steps had to be hewn out, so that a passage could then be made to the tunnel near the spring.

of this kind, for the Canaanites had already cut a shaft through the rock. The water from the spring was brought to the foot of the shaft, and so a well was created with a permanent supply of fresh water. It seems that this system proved unsatisfactory, and finally, after a number of other experiments, Hezekiah's canal was constructed. The inscription on the rock face at the city end of the tunnel was discovered only last century, and it can be seen today in the Istanbul Museum of Archaeology.

The resistance offered by Jerusalem could not prevent the Southern Kingdom from again becoming a vassal state of Assyria, with consequences in the field of politics and religion that are familiar enough. Under Hezekiah's successors, Manasseh (687–642 B.C.) and Amon (642–640 B.C.), syncretism, as we learn from the Bible (2 Kings 21), became very extensive. Yahwism became interfused with Canaanite and Assyrian idol-worship. The reaction to this came as soon as the political situation made it possible.

Meanwhile, another ruler, Ashurbanipal (668–629 B.C.?), had come to the throne in Assyria. In the first years of his reign he was warlike, and King Manasseh of Judah lost no time in paying tribute when Ashurbanipal marched to do battle with Egypt. But the Assyrian ruler subsequently transferred his attention to quite different matters. Under his supervision a large library was founded in the capital city of Nineveh. A great many ancient texts dating from the civilization of Sumeria and from the earlier periods of Egyptian and Babylonian history were collected and

transcribed. Thanks to the fact that after its destruction in 612 B.C. Nineveh was never rebuilt, modern archaeologists have been able to extract the enormous collection of clay tablets from the rubble.

In 640 B.C. Josiah became king of Judah. As the Assyrian empire met with increasing difficulties after the death of Ashurbanipal, he seized the opportunity to assert his independence against Assyria and gradually incorporate parts of the former Northern Kingdom into his own territory. It was a favourable moment, since there was no rival power in Palestine at the time. Consequently, Josiah was soon able to extend his influence over the whole district to the west of the Jordan. Hand in hand with this national reawakening there went a programme of religious reform which sought to free the worship of Yahweh from all pagan accretions. The climax of this process is marked by an event which probably took place about the year 620 B.C. From 2 Kings 22 we learn that during restoration work on the Temple a 'Book of the Law,' known also as the 'Book of the Covenant,' was discovered. When it was read to the king, he was so affected that he immediately set about putting its directives into execution, for, as will be seen, some of them involved a complete reform of the worship of Yahweh.

This national and religious revival was brought to a sudden end when Judah again lost her independence. The Assyrian empire had been shrinking steadily, and on every side the conquered peoples were throwing off the Assyrian yoke. Assyr-

(W) = WATER TUNNEL

Judah prior to the fall of Jerusalem

When Samaria had fallen, the situation looked black indeed for Judah. The Southern Kingdom now found itself sharing a frontier with the mighty state of Assyria, which had set up various *provinces* in Palestine: Samerina, Asdudu, Du'ru, Magidu, and Gal'aza. Besides Judah itself, the *minor states* of Ammon, Moab, and Edom preserved a degree of independence. Just occasionally, a king of Judah would take some action within the former Northern Kingdom. According to 2 Chronicles 30 : 6-11 King Hezekiah (716-687) sent emissaries to Zebulun, that is, into what is now Galilee. This was only a passing attempt to win over the remaining Israelites. The danger from Assyria was far too great for anything else.

Against this threat King Hezekiah caused the celebrated *water-tunnel* to be cut through the rock beneath Jerusalem. In this he was following the example set by the towns of Megiddo, Gezer, Gibeon, Ibleam, and Zarethan, where tunnels of this sort had already been in existence for a longer or shorter period. Rather less than a century later, King Josiah (640-609) interested himself in the territory north of Judah. As Assyria was just then enfeebled, he was able to exert some control over the area, even though his kingdom proper ran only from Geba to Beer-sheba (2 Kings 23 : 8). Full of enthusiasm for the Deuteronomic reformation, he crossed over to Bethel and laid waste that ancient sanctuary of the Northern Kingdom (2 Kings 23 : 15). He then passed through Samaria, treating in the same fashion every site of cultic practices (2 Kings 23 : 19). Typically, he met his death in 609 at Megiddo, trying to bar the passage of Egyptian forces to the north (2 Kings 23 : 29).

ia's most dangerous enemy lived in the southern part of Mesopotamia. Here, in ancient Babylonia, the Chaldeans, who were a people from the Persian Gulf, had long been settled. Together with the Medes, who inhabited the region to the east of Assyria, they advanced upon that country. In 612 B.C. they overran the hated capital of Nineveh. Its fall must have sent a shock through the whole of the Near East, because for over two hundred years the rulers of that city had decided the destinies of all the neighbouring countries. This is well illustrated by the prophetic book of Nahum, which presents the fall of Nineveh as a judgment of God on the oppressors of Israel.

The Pharaoh of Egypt, Neco, foresaw what would be the consequence of Assyria's downfall. If no-one intervened, Babylon would quickly take the place of the former oppressor. He therefore assembled his troops and hurried northward to the help of the Assyrians, who were concentrated around the ancient town of Haran. Failing to understand Egypt's policy, and fearing that

Neco was attempting to gain dominion over Syria and Palestine, Josiah heroically confronted him, intending to halt the foreign troops with his tiny army at the mountain pass of Megiddo. But "Pharaoh Neco slew him at Megiddo, when he saw him." (2 Kings 23:29)

It is not altogether clear from this sentence whether there was a battle, or whether the king of Judah fell into Pharaoh's hands in some other way. Whatever happened, the unexpected and humiliating death of so good and courageous a king was a blow from which his country was unable to recover. His son Jehoahaz, who succeeded him, did not continue the policies of his father and syncretism seems to have flourished once more. But he also seems to have been unsatisfactory from the Egyptian point of view, for after three months he was taken prisoner by Neco, who put another of Josiah's sons, Eliakim, on the throne, in the hope that he would be more loyal to him. At Pharaoh's command, he had to change his name to Jehoiakim, as a token of Egypt's overlordship.

Judah was once more a vassal state, but Neco's policy of maintaining a balance of power in the Near East miscarried. He

The mound of Tell es-Sa'idiyeh lies about 28 miles north of Jericho in the eastern valley of the Jordan. The tell has a surface area of about 20 acres, a clear indication that this was a settlement of some importance. What has so far been established is that the site was inhabited during the period of the Israelite monarchy. On the north side of this hill have been discovered the remains of a water tunnel constructed on quite unusual lines (centre, in the photo). In the flank of the hill and clean through the rubble of preceding centuries the inhabitants quarried a deep groove, the sides of which were lined with a wall of stone. At the base of the wall they used boulders to make a long flight of steps; and down the middle they built a brick wall. All this they roofed over to make a tunnel with two channels, which apparently passed under the city wall and emerged at the spring (in the foreground).

was unable to prevent the fall of Assyria and the further advance of the Babylonians. In 605 B.C. they drove Neco out of Syria and Palestine. Judah then acquired a new overlord. It is true that King Jehoiakim did try after a time to throw off the Babylonian yoke, but the Babylonian ruler Nebuchadnezzar crushed this rebellion in 598 B.C. Jehoiachin, the son and successor of the deceased Jehoiakim, was carried into exile with a number of other important Israelites. In his place, Josiah's third son, Mattaniah, was put on the throne and had his name changed to Zedekiah.

This was the king who finally brought destruction to Judah and Jerusalem. In the ninth year of his reign Egypt incited him to open rebellion against Nebuchadnezzar, with the result that the Babylonian forces again invaded Judah. One town after another was forced to surrender. Only the cities of Lachish, Azekah, and Jerusalem were strong enough to put up any sort of resistance (Jer. 34:7). Jerusalem withstood the Babylonian siege for two years, but in 587 B.C. the city was finally taken. All the buildings, including the Temple and palace, were put to the torch, and the city walls were razed to the ground. Nebuchadnezzar had the

(Opposite) About 11 miles north of Lachish, near the modern Kefar Zechariah, lies the mound known as Tell Zakariyeh. This has been provisionally identified with the Biblical Azekah. At about the turn of the century a British expedition carried out limited excavation. Azekah is known chiefly from two literary sources. In Jeremiah 34 : 7 it says that, together with Jerusalem and Lachish, Azekah held out longest against the Babylonians. The well-known ostraca of Lachish appear to corroborate this. The reverse side of no. 4 says: ''. . . he lets it be known that we are on the look-out for the lights of Lachish, according to the directions that my lord has given, for Azekah we do not see." The commander wanted to contact Lachish by fire signals, as signals from Azekah had ceased.

King Sennacherib decorated his palace at Nineveh with a large number of reliefs. This is a section of one depicting the conquest of the town of Lachish in Judah. It is probably based on an episode in the year 701 B.C., when Sennacherib conquered almost every city in Judah and encircled Jerusalem. The relief shows two men of Judah walking barefoot and in long garments in front of an Assyrian. With their hands they are making the sign of surrender. The Assyrian with his plaited beard and heavy armour keeps a close eye on them from the rear. Behind the soldier is to be seen part of another scene: two men of Judah are being flung naked into a river.

king, courtiers, and everyone of any consequence led away to captivity in Babylon, leaving only the simplest and poorest people behind in Judah. This was the end of the Southern Kingdom.

2. THE DEUTERONOMIC REFORMATION

In the years of religious revival under King Josiah there appeared a second group of prophets. Their names are known to us from certain books of the Bible: Jeremiah, Zephaniah, Nahum, and Habakkuk. There were others also. In Jeremiah 26:20–23, for instance, there is a passing reference to a prophet Uriah, who was put to death by King Jehoiakim. We know, too, of the prophetess Huldah, whose advice Josiah sought (2 Kings 22:14–20). To judge from their writings, however, it appears that these prophets held aloof from what is called the Deuteronomic reformation. Jeremiah probably supported the movement to begin with, but he was soon repelled by the narrowness of its nationalistic zeal. Hence there are few optimistic passages in the prophetic writings of this period. Again and again one encounters prophecies of woe, the aim of which is to bring a 'stiff-necked' and obdurate people to repentance. The predominant note of these books is disappointment at the failure of reform and apprehension at the threat of destruction hanging over Jerusalem.

It is almost universally accepted today that this programme of reform is embodied in the Book of Deuteronomy, which in its essentials was probably the Book of the Law found in the Temple in 622 B.C. and read aloud to King Josiah. Of course the book we have today is not identical in every respect with the book that was found at that time. Thus, for example, chapters 1–3 and 31–34 were undoubtedly added later, and we might ask whether the introductory and concluding sections, chapters 4–11 and 27–30, were not originally somewhat briefer. But these qualifications do not affect the kernel of the book, chapters 12–26, which contain the actual prescription of the law and were probably essentially the same as we have them today.

This collection of laws, however, is not homogeneous in character. Many of the prescriptions seem to come from a time when there were no kings, while others clearly presuppose the conditions of a later age. The latter is the case, for example, with the law concerning the king, 17:14-20. In verse 15 it states: "You may indeed set as king over you him whom the Lord your God will choose. One from among your brethren you shall set as king over you; you may not put a foreigner over you, who is not your brother." Why did the 'law-giver' say this? In the whole course of the Southern Kingdom's existence, there was never a foreigner on the throne of David. Such a possibility, however, cannot be ruled out for the north. It is likely that, for instance, King Omri was not an Israelite. This and other considerations suggest that the origins of Deuteronomy are to be sought in the north.

It is still not known today how Deuteronomy reached

Campaigns in Palestine from 721 to 587

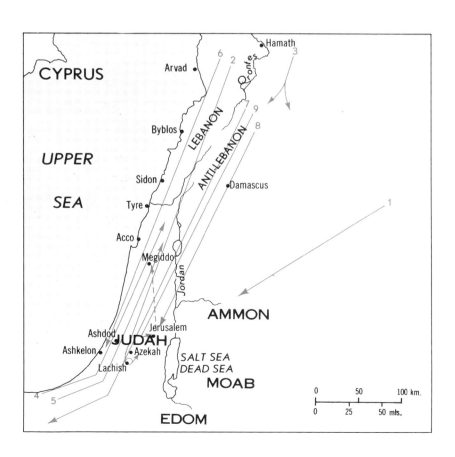

1. Ca. 703 B.C. a mission from Merodach-baladan of *Babylon* arrived in *Jerusalem* to incite Judah against Assyria.
2. In 701 Sennacherib (705-681) of *Assyria* marched against the insurgent peoples of Canaan: namely, *Sidon, Acco, Arvad, Byblos, Ashdod, Ammon, Moab, Edom, Ashkelon,* and *Judah.* He subjugated them and defeated the Egyptian auxiliary forces in the coastal plain. His army appeared at *Jerusalem* but had to return prematurely to Assyria. In his palace at Nineveh Sennacherib had the conquest of *Lachish* depicted in relief. His successor, Esarhaddon (680-669), preserved the frontiers of the empire by—for example—pushing back the Egyptians on several occasions as far as the Delta.
3. In the early part of his reign King Ashurbanipal (668-629) broke the power of *Egypt* and of certain *Arabian* tribes. Later he neglected military affairs, and Assyrian power declined.
4. In 616 *Egyptian* troops moved through Canaan to support the *Assyrians* against attack by an insurgent *Babylonia.*
5. In 609 Pharaoh Neco II again advanced to the Euphrates in an attempt to support an enfeebled *Assyria* against insistent pressure from the *Babylonians* and *Medes.* King Josiah of *Judah* tried to halt the *Egyptian* forces at *Megiddo.* He was killed in the first encounter. Palestine and Syria remained under Egyptian domination until 605.
6. One year after his victory over the Egyptians at Carchemish in 605 Nebuchadnezzar of *Babylon* advanced into the coastal plain of Palestine and took *Ashkelon. Judah* became a vassal state.
7. In 601 there was an indecisive battle between *Pharaoh Neco* and *King Nebuchadnezzar* on the Egyptian frontier. Jehoiakim of *Judah* thereupon sought to align himself with Egypt.
8. In 598 Nebuchadnezzar again advanced westward. *Jerusalem* lacking the support expected from Egypt, was forced to surrender. Part of the ruling class was carried off to Babylonia (first deportation). Some years later representatives of *Edom, Moab, Ammon, Tyre,* and *Sidon* came to *Jerusalem* to plan an uprising against Babylon.
9. In 588 Nebuchadnezzar marched on the rebellious cities of *Tyre* and *Jerusalem;* the siege of Jerusalem began. In the summer of 587 the Babylonians forced their way into the city and set it on fire. Again, the leading families were deported (second deportation).

(Left) In the Palestinian landscape trees are often a conspicuous and striking feature. There are not many woods; but in a deserted and barren area a solitary tree may suddenly greet the eye. In times past this was a real symbol of fertility and life; and so it was that the tree came to play an important role in Biblical stories. One has only to think of the tree of life (Gen. 2 : 9, 3 : 22, 24; Rev. 22 : 2), the oak at Shechem (Gen. 12 : 6; 35 : 4), the palm of Deborah between Ramah and Bethel (Judges 4 : 5), and the 'Diviners' Oak' (Judges 9 : 37). The tamarisk pictured here (in the northern Negeb) makes the point extremely well. Of course, a tree of this sort was then, as it is today, a reliable landmark for travellers (Gen. 12 : 6; 13 : 18), and moreover its shade offered a welcome resting-place (1 Sam. 14 : 2, 1 Kings 13 : 14).

(Left, below) The almond tree is already in bloom before its green leaves have opened. In the spring its whitish-pink blossom is first to herald the arrival of the new season. Its name in Hebrew is 'shaqed.' This name, and the fact of its early flowering, prompted the prophet Jeremiah to see in it a living symbol of Yahweh's watchfulness. The verb for 'keeping watch' in Hebrew has the same consonants, which is why in speaking of God's approaching judgment Jeremiah could say: "And the word of the Lord came to me, saying, 'Jeremiah, what do you see?' And I said, 'I see a rod of almond.' Then the Lord said to me, 'You have seen well, for I am watching (shoqed) over my word to perform it.'" (Jer. 1 : 11-12).

(Opposite) A tower could assume a variety of forms, depending on its function. At a gate in a city wall or on an acropolis the tower was the strongest point; and in this form it became a symbol of strength and security (Ps. 61 : 4; Prov. 18 : 10). But 'towers' were also built in the countryside. Here a few poles, some branches, and some leaves were all that was needed. The purpose of these small huts was to give the man who protected the crops shelter from the fierce sun by day and the demoralizing cold of the night-time. After the harvest, the little cabin, abandoned to its fate, would very quickly collapse. This particular form of 'tower' was a symbol of frailty and transience (Is. 1 : 8; Job 27 : 18). The little 'houses' of the Feast of Tabernacles must have been very similar. The one pictured here stood in 1963 on the edge of the broad and fertile wadi that runs from Kerek (right, on the sky-line) to the Dead Sea.

Jerusalem, but it is reasonable to assume that after the fall of Samaria those Israelites who were particularly nationally or religiously minded fled to Judah, and that among them there were some who brought with them the work in its original form. As mentioned earlier, this would have constituted chapters 12–26 of the present book. The tradition they represent probably derives from the covenant with Yahweh made at Shechem under Joshua's leadership (Josh. 24).

After their arrival in Jerusalem these refugees may have attempted to institute a religious reform, for the situation under King Ahaz would have accorded ill with their traditional beliefs and attitudes. It is also likely, however, that the atmosphere during his reign was unsuited to a revival of pure Yahwism, and that as newcomers the fugitives were not immediately assimilated into the community at Jerusalem. The book they brought with them was then possibly put aside or forgotten, until it was brought to light again a century later through the activities of King Josiah and his followers.

The Deuteronomic writers used this work to give their views enhanced authority, for Josiah's reforming zeal, which aimed at changes never proposed before, undoubtedly met with opponents. One of the main aims of the reform was to enforce the centralization of all religious activities. In order to understand this it must be remembered that from earliest times there

had been sanctuaries all over the country. The Israelites took them over from the indigenous population, and with them they also took over the pagan practices which had become part of the traditional ritual at these places. At one time paganism threatened to overwhelm the worship of Yahweh even in Judah. What was more natural, therefore, than to attempt to concentrate the orthodox cult in Jerusalem? By abandoning the centres of worship in the mountains it was also possible to do away with the practices associated with them.

There was probably no longer any need to campaign against 'the sin of Jeroboam,' the bull-cult at Bethel and Dan. For all practical purposes this was a thing of the past. On the other hand, the number of local sanctuaries had actually multiplied over the years, and the increasing localization of the cult had produced all kinds of aberrations, some of which may have been encouraged by the memory of earlier pagan practices. The new movement aimed at purging religion of this idolatrous element by concentrating the performance of all sacrifices in the Temple at Jerusalem, for it was at Jerusalem that the Ark of Yahweh, the main Hebrew sacred object ever since the time of the tribes, had been set up in the reign of David. The reformers based their claim for centralization on the law concerning the altar which is contained in chapter 12 of Deuteronomy, where it is required that all the altars in the land should be destroyed and all sacri-

fices made only at the 'place that the Lord will choose.' It was scarcely possible to interpret this as meaning any other place than Jerusalem.

It was probably in the Southern Kingdom that the book of Deuteronomy was expanded and received its characteristic shape by the addition of the introductory and concluding sections mentioned earlier. These additions consist of a varied collection of statements that can easily be imagined as coming from the mouth of a priest. Expressions such as 'do not follow other gods,' 'love Yahweh and serve him with your whole heart and your whole soul,' 'that you may have long life and that it may go well with you' recur constantly. In this tradition the holy mountain in the desert is not called Sinai, but Horeb, as in the Elohist parts of the Old Testament.

A further peculiarity of these discourses is that they are all put into the mouth of Moses. By adding them as an introduction and conclusion to the Deuteronomic law, the latter is presented as the spiritual testament of the great prophet. This literary fiction served to show contemporary Israelites that they were the recipients of these divine promises and precepts. The book is not so much a reminder of the past as something that attempts to make the past present in the here and now. The introduction to the Decalogue states quite justifiably, therefore, that: "The Lord our God made a covenant with us in Horeb. Not with our

fathers did the Lord make this covenant, but with us, who are all of us here alive this day." (Deut. 5:2–3) The atmosphere and tone of this book are in harmony with the most ancient traditions of Israel, and for this reason it is called 'the second law.'

Deuteronomy may thus be seen to have had a long and chequered history behind it before it was rediscovered more or less by accident. The king decided to make it solemnly binding on his people, and it became valid law. All the altars throughout the country were immediately destroyed (2 Kings 23), in an attempt to lead the nation to renew the covenant with Yahweh. Unfortunately it soon appeared that the population carried out the reforms only in a very superficial way. What was intended in Deuteronomy as a reminder of the covenant with Yahweh at Sinai was now seen as a confirmation of Judah's special place among the peoples. Also, the significance of the idea of centralizing worship was missed when it led to a false over-estimation of the position accorded to the Temple at Jerusalem. Apparently it was widely believed at this time that the divine goodwill would be guaranteed so long as Yahweh was overwhelmed with sacrifices. Social evils remained, in fact, the same after the reform as before.

This was probably the reason why such prophets as Jeremiah, who were able to see more clearly than their contemporaries, soon turned their backs on it in disappointment. In

The plain of Shechem, with in the background, left, Mount Gerizim and right, Mount Ebal. The small town of Shechem now Tell Balata, lay in between these two mountains, at the foot of Mount Ebal. Excavation has revealed that about 1600 B.C. Shechem was a strong fortress within a 'cyclopean' wall—that is, a wall of massive, uncut boulders. The east gate, the construction of which is still clearly to be seen on the ground dates from a somewhat later period. Shechem had its place in the very oldest traditions of Israel. One of the most important events to occur there was the concluding of the covenant under Joshua, an echo of which is to be found in Joshua 24. This event was the reason why Shechem continued to be a sacred locality for Israel until the Assyrian and Babylonian conquests and the centralization of the cult in Jerusalem brought its role to an end.

Jeremiah 7 we have a discourse in which the prophet condemns in strong language this false piety: "Do not trust in these deceptive words: 'This is the temple of the Lord, the temple of the Lord, the temple of the Lord.'... Go now to my place that was in Shiloh, where I made my name dwell at first, and see what I did to it for the wickedness of my people Israel. And now, because you have done all these things, says the Lord, and when I spoke to you persistently you did not listen, and when I called you, you did not answer, therefore I will do to the house that is called by my name... as I did with Shiloh. And I will cast you out of my sight, as I cast out all your kinsmen, all the offspring of Ephraim." (Jer. 7:4-5)

As with many before that time and many after, this warning too went unheeded. But it is notable that it was precisely these threats of disaster that enabled the devout minority amongst the people to find their faith again after the collapse of Judah and Jerusalem. It was not the gods of Babylon that had proved mighty, but Yahweh, who had prophesied the whole thing long before through the mouth of his prophets.

The Book of Deuteronomy was not the only work that this school produced. Some traces of their activity may be found in the Yahwist and Elohist texts already discussed. They were especially concerned with the traditions of the period from Joshua down to the last of the kings, set out in the books known as 'the Former Prophets' (see page 112), which, in the Hebrew tradition of the Old Testament, precede the books written by the great prophets. The reform welded these written and oral traditions into a single whole and gave them a particular emphasis. The whole body of writing is therefore described as 'the Deuteronomic history,' though it is by no means history in the modern sense of the word. There are large gaps in the narratives dealing with the kings of Judah and Israel, and the principal events retained are those that had some connection with the Temple at Jerusalem. For the rest we are referred to 'the chronicles of the kings of Judah and Israel,' of which unfortunately no trace remains.

A fixed pattern of apostasy and judgment, conversion and deliverance, occurs repeatedly in these works. Judges 3:5-11 affords a good illustration: the disobedient are punished and the righteous rewarded. The danger inherent in this excessively automatic scheme for the majority of the population soon became apparent. Apart from encouraging the people to treat religion as a merely outward observance and to offer sacrifices chiefly to ensure prosperity, as mentioned earlier, it had the effect of making them lose their faith when this prosperity vanished with Josiah's death in 609 B.C. and Judah was once more deprived of her independence.

All the leaders of the Deuteronomic reformation did not, however, suddenly vanish on the day the pious King Josiah died. It seems rather that the new king, Jehoahaz, simply did not give them his support, and that as a result it was impossible for them to extend their activity beyond a limited circle. In the ensuing years the movement of reform was gradually cleansed of its excessively nationalistic tendencies, and its representatives concentrated more and more on what was fundamental, a process accelerated by the Exile.

The Book of Deuteronomy, therefore, is not just a product of the Josian reformation. As with most Biblical writings, it was not brought out in a given year and thereafter copied without alteration. It remained a living force in the period of the Exile which followed, and was probably not worked into its final form until, during the Exile, it was merged with the already extant literature of the Yahwist and Elohist traditions.

The same is true of the writings known as the Deuteronomic history. Apart from anything else, it is clear that the account of events after the death of Josiah shows that this epic was not completed in the year of his death. The epilogue in 2 Kings 25:27-30 was in fact written years later. According to this passage, King Jehoiachin, who had gone into exile in 598 B.C., was pardoned in the thirty-seventh year of his captivity, which indicates that additions were still being made to the Deuteronomic history in or about 561 B.C.

3. THE EXILE

587 B.C. was a calamitous year for the Israelites of the Southern Kingdom. Archaeological evidence has confirmed that about that date almost every walled settlement in Judah proper was devastated by the Babylonians. Judah ceased to exist as an independent state, and the Davidic dynasty disappeared from history. It used sometimes to be thought that all the inhabitants of Judah were transported to Babylon, but this is only partly true. The unrest in the period after King Josiah had resulted in a considerable decrease in the population of the Southern Kingdom. Many were killed in battle, murdered, or simply died of starvation during the various sieges. Moreover, during these years various groups fled from Judah to the surrounding countries, such as Egypt (Jer. 42ff), and to the region beyond the Jordan (Jer. 40:11). This was, in fact, the beginning of the Diaspora, the spread of Israel beyond the borders of Palestine.

Judah, then, was already partly depopulated when Jerusalem was conquered. The deportation to Babylon simply made the situation worse. King Nebuchadnezzar's policy was to remove the influential members of the community from the population of the occupied territory. The number deported has been estimated at about 20,000, a figure based on a passage in Jeremiah (Jer. 52:28-30), which gives the numbers involved in three successive deportations. Added together, they make a total of 4,600 men, but allowing for the fact that such figures often refer only to the adult males, the number has to be multiplied by four or five to include the women and children. If the figures are correct, then quite a large number of people were still left behind in Judah.

Babylon had nothing to fear from them, however, for they were the weakest group, both economically and socially. Furthermore, Babylon employed different tactics from those adopted by Assyria a century earlier with regard to the Northern Kingdom. Groups of people from other parts of the Babylonian empire were not brought into Judah, and the country remained empty and forsaken. This proved to be of great importance to the exiles: the country was waiting, as it were, for their return. What is more, in Babylonia they were not scattered among the local population, but placed together in colonies. These two factors were eventually to make their return from Exile possible. If Nebuchadnezzar had pursued the same policy as Sargon of Assyria, Judah would have disappeared for ever, just as Israel had done after the fall of Samaria.

After the conquest of Jerusalem by Nebuchadnezzar the terms 'men of Judah' and 'Israelites' become meaningless, since they denote nationality and presuppose the existence of an independent state, to which the year 587 B.C. put an end. The remnant of Judah was composed of people who felt themselves bound together by religion and race. In later Biblical writings this group is still often referred to as Israel, but it is then primarily a religious term. In a secular context they came to be known as Jews, a word that was first used during the post-exilic period of Persian domination.

For the Jews the Exile was an experience that tore at the very roots of their religious existence. Almost everything they had taken for granted, everything on which for centuries past they had come to rely had now been lost. They found themselves in a hopeless situation, for the traditional unity between religion and the state had been shattered. The 'promised land' had always held a central place in the mind of every devout Israelite. That land was the necessary dwelling-place for the 'Chosen People,' by virtue of a succession of saving acts on the part of their God. This God had promised 'that the house of David' would occupy the throne for all time. The peace, prosperity, and happiness of this people was to be a blessing from which not only they, but all the nations of the earth would derive benefit. The heart and centre of this holy kingdom was Jerusalem, the city of David. Their God had chosen this city that he might cause his 'name' to dwell there for ever. There stood the Temple that Solomon had built, a place where heaven and earth met. In the Holy of Holies this mighty God was present in a very special way. In the court of the Temple, through sacrifice, through prayer and song, the nation came into contact with him. It was a contact indispensable to a life of prosperity and peace.

The Deuteronomic reformation had once again brought this vision of country, people, king, capital, and Temple sharply into focus and intensified it, when suddenly the belief on which it was founded was shattered. The destruction of Jerusalem and the deportation did away with all forms of security. It was as if the word of their God, that they had never known to be other than efficacious, had been rendered powerless by merely human forces and in an almost effortless fashion. The 'promised land' had been plundered and stripped bare, and part of its population banished to a strange land. For the first time since the days of David Jerusalem had been razed to the ground, and the house of David divested of all its power. The source of the deepest despair was that the Babylonians had plundered and set fire to the Temple, the house of Yahweh. The place where their God sat enthroned above the cherubim—the Holy of Holies—had been utterly destroyed, and the Ark, together with the stone tablets of the covenant, had vanished without trace.

The grief and despair of those days are reflected in the Book of Lamentations. It comprises texts that were probably written soon after the conquest of Jerusalem by those who remained behind. The following verses give an indication of its general tone:

> The joy of our hearts has ceased;
> our dancing has been turned to mourning.
> The crown has fallen from our head;
> woe to us, for we have sinned!
> For this our heart has become sick,
> for these things our eyes have grown dim,
> for Mount Zion which lies desolate;
> jackals prowl over it.
> But thou, O Lord, dost reign for ever;
> thy throne endures to all generations.
> Why dost thou forget us for ever,
> why dost thou so long forsake us?
> Restore us to thyself, O Lord, that we may be restored!
> Renew our days as of old!
> Or hast thou utterly rejected us?
> Art thou exceedingly angry with us?
> (Lam. 5:15–22)

The rocky southern tip of the Ophel, the city of David. When Jerusalem was destroyed by the Babylonians in 587 B.C., it meant the end of the Ophel as the residential centre of the old city. After David the arena of political and religious life was the northern hill, where Solomon had had the Temple and the palace built. Various exilic and post-exilic passages in the Bible bear witness to the total destruction of the city by the Babylonians, which meant that after the Exile the residential centre shifted gradually toward the north and west. In the post-exilic period, and even during the very early years of the Christian era, the Ophel still formed part of the city; but in the 2nd century A.D. the Romans left the hill of David outside the walls of the city to which they gave the name of Aelia Capitolina. The existing Turkish walls follow the same course, although for a few centuries during the Byzantine period the Ophel was once again incorporated within the city.

Psalm 137 also contains a clear echo of the melancholy of the exiles:

By the waters of Babylon, there we sat down and wept,
when we remembered Zion.
On the willows there
we hung up our lyres,
for there our captors
required of us songs,
and our tormentors, mirth, saying,
"Sing us one of the songs of Zion!"
How shall we sing the Lord's song
in a foreign land?
If I forget you, O Jerusalem,
let my right hand wither!
Let my tongue cleave to the roof of my mouth,
if I do not remember you,
if I do not set Jerusalem
above my highest joy! (Ps. 137:1-6)

This was the situation which was the main influence on the views of the later Deuteronomic writers. They depicted the whole history of Israel since the death of Joshua as a progressive falling away of the people, interrupted only occasionally by a brief period of return to faith. Thus it was not a wilful act on Yahweh's part but one of just retribution, if, when warnings and chastisements had been of no avail against the sins of his people, he had responded with total annihilation.

This interpretation was not, however, the only one which the Deuteronomists gave their contemporaries. At the end of the Second Book of Kings, for instance, it is pointed out that Nebuchadnezzar's successor, the Babylonian King Evil-merodach has released King Jehoiachin from prison. This has been seen rightly as a conclusion that allows the readers of the work to hope for God's grace. It is, nevertheless, a very subdued hope and a long way from that certainty of salvation with which Ezekiel and the so-called Deutero-Isaiah were to comfort the Jews in their Exile.

The crisis of faith affected both the Jews who went into exile and those who remained behind. The conflict was heightened for the exiles by the fact that it was the first time this comparatively unsophisticated people had come into contact with a cosmopolitan culture. In comparison with Babylon Jerusalem was a little provincial town. The deportees looked with amazement and admiration at the imposing palaces and temples, the splendid religious ritual, the broad, straight streets and the bustling crowds. They felt weak and powerless.

It would not have been surprising if, in these circumstances, they had given up their religion. Largely as a result of their experiences in the wilderness, the Israelites had advanced from the primitive Hebrew conception of a tribal god who reigned alongside a great number of other mysterious powers to what we now call mono-Yahwism. The idea that Yahweh was simply one among equals had been gradually excluded, but this process had taken centuries. The major prophets had declared categorically that these other 'powers' were in fact totally powerless, and Yahweh alone was mighty. This was the stage which had been reached just before the Exile. But now it appeared that the power might lie with the heathen gods after all. Nebuchadnezzar's armies had robbed Yahweh of his land, his people, his city and his Temple.

Despite everything, however, this seemingly unremarkable little group of exiles clung to their ancient traditions and remained loyal to Yahweh, an achievement which might almost be regarded as superhuman. A great part was played in this preservation of their faith by those men who were able to give comfort and hope to the exiles by virtue of their spiritual authority. Those were the priests, and above all the prophets Ezekiel and Deutero-Isaiah.

It might be thought that once the Temple in Jerusalem had been destroyed the priests would have lost their influence. It is true that the Deuteronomic reform had forbidden every sacrificial cult outside Jerusalem. Only in the Temple was it permitted to offer to Yahweh the fruits of the field and the first-born of the flocks and herds. As a consequence, any sacrifice in Babylon was out of the question. But besides their role as ministers of the sacrificial rites the priests had always had another quite different duty, which is clearly laid down in, for instance, Jeremiah 18:18: "For the law shall not perish from the priests, nor counsel from the wise, nor the word from the prophet."

This brief formula indicates the proper task of the priests, the wise men, and the prophets. The priests had to expound the law, i.e. give directives for the day-to-day practice of religion. In giving instruction to the people, they drew on the centuries-old traditions of the various sanctuaries. When the Exile made their cultic activities impossible, the priests turned their whole attention to this task, and with great success. Their influence and authority constantly increased, especially in the period after the Exile when, along with the monarchy, prophetism also gradually disappeared. The almost unassailable position they occupied in the post-exilic period had already begun to take shape during the Babylonian captivity.

They set before their fellow-countrymen their religious traditions, and the people adhered to them firmly. The priests concerned themselves in the first place with those which emanated from their own circle, especially from the Temple at Jerusalem. In this way a fourth strand with its own particular emphasis began to evolve, known as the 'priestly' tradition (alongside the Yahwist, Elohist, and Deuteronomic ones). Of course, this is not to say that the priests did not have a hand in shaping the texts already in existence since earlier times, but the traditions that began to take literary shape during the Exile have a stronger priestly character than the other collections of writings. The Book of Leviticus is a good example of this, with its many prescriptions concerning the practical details of regular religious practice in private and public. Also the familiar opening verses of the Bible, which describe how God created and populated heaven and earth in six days and rested on the seventh, belong to this stream of tradition. It found its final literary form in the fifth century, but its beginnings undoubtedly go back to the time of the Exile.

Not every religious practice, however, disappeared with the Temple sacrifices from the life of the Jews in exile. Circumcision and the observance of the sabbath continued to be important within the community, even more so than previously. The observance of the sabbath had been a distinctive mark of the religious practice of the Jews from the earliest times. The origin of the day of rest is still uncertain. No doubt the great emphasis which we elsewhere find placed on the number seven had something to do with it, as well as the custom found amongst many peoples of regarding certain days as taboo. But the combination

The inner gate of Lachish, from outside. Lachish stood about 28 miles south-west of Jerusalem, where the mountains of Judah descend to the coastal plain. This circumstance gave the town its considerable strategic importance, and explains why in 701 B.C. Sennacherib personally directed its siege and capture before attacking Jerusalem. In 588 B.C. Nebuchadnezzar also concentrated first on Lachish, before he took Jerusalem a year later. Excavation in the thirties uncovered a number of ostraca which date from Judah's final years. Eighteen items were found in a guardroom between the outer and inner gates (see p. 68; in the photo, right, in front of the wall) and three items near the palace on the acropolis. They are chiefly short messages dispatched by an officer at a military post to his commander in Lachish.

of the two, a day of rest and on the seventh day in particular, has not so far been found in any other ancient community in the Near East. During the Exile the sabbath became almost automatically an essential characteristic of the Jewish religion. The first creation story, mentioned above, expresses the esteem felt for it.

The special place accorded to circumcision is not exclusive to the Jews. Most people in Canaan practised circumcision. The Philistines were the only exception, which is why they are constantly referred to in the Old Testament as the uncircumcised. However its use as a widespread custom declined, and Israel came more and more into contact with people who did not practise it. During the Exile this contact was intensified, and as a result circumcision also began to develop into a special mark of the Chosen People, a sign of the covenant with God.

It is likely that this was also the period in which the synagogue had its origin. The Jews in Babylon probably came together regularly, especially on the sabbath, to sing, pray, and read from the sacred scrolls. There was no other religious activity that they could still engage in together. This does not mean that they now started to build special houses of prayer. Like the first Christians, they would meet in private houses. Only later did this practice become institutionalized by the erection of public buildings which were set aside for it. Such religious gatherings were of great importance for the development of the Jewish religion. They could be held anywhere without much difficulty, and this enabled the people to become more and more familiar with the writings in which the once oral traditions had been incorporated. Moreover, they strengthened the position of the laity in the life of the community, for no priest was necessary for these synagogue services. Thus the laity had the opportunity to limit the power of the priests, which had greatly increased during and immediately after the Exile. A way was now opened up for the Scribes and lay theologians of a later period.

One of the most important figures of the Exile was undoubtedly the prophet Ezekiel. He was one of the Jews who had gone into banishment in 598 B.C. with King Jehoiachin. He must already have been of some importance in Jerusalem, since it was only the élite of the people that were affected by this first deportation. However, it was not until the fifth year of his exile that he was called upon to be a prophet (Ezek. 1:2). In the course of more than twenty years' activity the content of his message changed greatly. Up to the final collapse of Jerusalem Ezekiel regarded his task as that of destroying the deceptive hopes of his fellow captives for an early return to their native land. In his view there was nothing that could stop the judgment of Yahweh on his city and his Temple.

After the fall of Jerusalem, however, Ezekiel worked to comfort the exiles in their despair and to strengthen their will to return. He found in Yahweh's jealousy for the honour of his name the guarantee that he would create a new people of God, who would one day return to Palestine and reconstruct the Temple, where Yahweh would once more reign supreme: "Thus says the Lord God: It is not for your sake, O house of Israel, that I am about to act, but for the sake of my holy name, which you have profaned amongst the nations to which you came... and the nations will know that I am the Lord, says the Lord God, when through you I vindicate my holiness before their eyes. For

I will take you from the nations... and bring you into your own land... I will take out of your flesh the heart of stone and give you a heart of flesh. And I will put my spirit within you, and cause you to walk in my statutes and be careful to observe my ordinances. You shall dwell in the land which I gave to your fathers; and you shall be my people, and I will be your God." (Ezek. 36:22–28)

Another leader, who probably appeared a little later, was the unnamed prophet now known as Deutero-Isaiah. He is designated thus because his sayings are found in the second part of the Book of Isaiah (chs. 40–55). He was without doubt one of the most profound thinkers of the Old Testament community. The fundamental idea contained in his writings is that because Yahweh alone is God, and all other so-called gods are totally powerless idols, he can and will redeem Israel. The past history of the nation proves that they are his Chosen People. Therefore, just as in earlier times he led them out of Egypt through the wilderness into the promised land, so now he will lead the exiles home to Jerusalem.

> But now thus says the Lord, he who created you, O Jacob,
> he who formed you, O Israel:
> "Fear not, for I have redeemed you;
> I have called you by name, you are mine.
> When you pass through the waters I will be with you;
> and through the rivers, they shall not overwhelm you;
> when you walk through the fire you shall not be burned,
> and the flame shall not consume you...
> Fear not, for I am with you;
> I will bring your offspring from the east,
> and from the west I will gather you;
> I will say to the north, Give up,
> and to the south, Do not withhold;
> bring my sons from afar
> and my daughters from the end of the earth,
> everyone who is called by my name,
> whom I created for my glory,
> whom I formed and made."
>
> (Is. 43:1-7)

Indeed, Yahweh holds the whole world in his hand. Even Cyrus, the mighty king of Persia, is his servant. He will therefore cause Cyrus to rise up against Babylon and destroy it. Then will come Israel's redemption. Deutero-Isaiah always bases his message of consolation on this idea of God's saving activity in Israel's past and on his creative power. For him it is certain that Yahweh, the God who grants salvation to Israel, is at the same time Yahweh, the God who calls everything and everyone into existence.

From what has been said it should be clear that the Exile proved to be a turning-point in the history of Israel. Out of the lowest depths of despair the people attained a rock-like trust in God. After the Exile, however, it soon became apparent that even this trust relied too much on human insight. The people evidently could not fully grasp the message of Deutero-Isaiah, otherwise the period after the Exile might have been expected to mark a high point in the religion of Israel. Instead, it was not long before narrowness and rigidity once more set in.

VII. THE OLD TESTAMENT NEARS COMPLETION

Judah as a theocracy. Final stages in the growth of the Old Testament: 5th to 3rd centuries B.C.

1. JUDAH AS PART OF THE PERSIAN EMPIRE

Ever since its foundation the neo-Babylonian empire, which had put an end to the independence of Judah under the house of David, had been faced with a powerful rival. When the Babylonians had captured and destroyed the Assyrian capital of Nineveh in 612 B.C. they had been aided by the Medes, who lived to the east of Assyria in the mountainous parts of what is now Iran. Since neither one of these people was strong enough by itself to claim dominion over the whole of the Assyrian empire they set about dividing its territories between them. Step by step the Babylonians sought to establish control over the Syro-Palestinian area, while the Medes extended their power over the northern parts of the defeated empire.

A way was thus opened up for the Medes to expand in a westerly direction, and it was not long before Armenia and the central area of Asia Minor came under their control. During the brief period of its existence, therefore, the Babylonian empire had never extended beyond the countries lying to the south-west of Media, and not even all these states were effectively mastered. Egypt, for example, held her own during all these years. In fact, the Chaldean empire looked more powerful than it really was and depended for the maintenance of its position on a number of talented kings, the most remarkable of whom was undoubtedly Nebuchadnezzar, the one responsible for the destruction of Jerusalem. After his death in 562 B.C. the inherent weaknesses in the structure of the empire soon became evident.

Meanwhile an important change was taking place in the empire of the Medes. One of their vassal states was Persia, a region to the east of Babylon, and about 550 B.C. the vassal Cyrus led a rebellion against the ruling house of Media and captured Ecbatana, the capital city, thereby becoming at one stroke master of the whole empire.

The general expectation was that Cyrus would now immediately launch an attack against Babylon, on account of both its greatness and its proximity to the Persian homeland. That the Jews in exile nurtured the same expectation, is evinced by the words of the prophet, Deutero-Isaiah: "Thus says the Lord to his anointed, to Cyrus… 'I will go before you and level the mountains…' " (Is. 45:1-2). Many years were to pass, however,

before these expectations were fulfilled. Cyrus realized that the strength of Babylonia was more apparent than real, and this led him to adopt a different course. First of all he directed his attention to Asia Minor. This area had long remained politically weak after the downfall of the Hittite empire, but by the sixth century B.C. there had come into being the powerful state of Lydia, which was ruled over by Croesus, legendary for his riches. In the mid-winter of the year 546 B.C. Cyrus crossed the Halys, a river that flowed along the eastern border of Lydia, took Croesus completely by surprise and captured the capital city of Sardis. The Persian

The cylinder of Cyrus on which he describes how he entered Babylon 'as a friend' and how in matters of religion he honoured the wishes of the peoples whom he had conquered. This policy was not simply the outcome of personal inclination. Various texts of Cambyses and Darius I make it clear that these successors to Cyrus behaved similarly. Their religion evidently allowed scope for the religions of all peoples.

empire now stretched as far as the Aegean Sea. Never before had an oriental power thrust so far to the west. A favourable situation was thus created for the fusion of the eastern and western worlds, which was to be undertaken two centuries later by Alexander the Great.

With these successes behind him Cyrus turned eastward, and after some time spent in subduing the regions known today as Pakistan and Afghanistan, he marched on Babylon, where Nabonidus (555–539 B.C.) was then the reigning monarch.

There are many and varied opinions concerning this ruler. Recent discoveries which have come to light during excavations in upper Mesopotamia suggest that in the early part of his reign at least he possessed sufficient energy and determination to steer his country through the many internal and external dangers which threatened it. Not until it became clear that he was failing in his attempt to subjugate the desert tribes of Arabia—a protracted struggle which had lasted ten years—did the hostility of the Babylonian priests constitute a serious threat to his power.

When he finally gave up his attempt to subjugate the desert tribes he had achieved nothing but to force them on to the side of Cyrus.

The king's enemies now took advantage of his weakened position to overthrow him, and a year later they invited Cyrus to invade the realm. Cyrus encountered little opposition. After a brief engagement in the north his troops succeeded in 539 B.C. in taking the capital without a blow being struck in its defence. As the inhabitants of Babylon welcomed Cyrus as a liberator and deliverer, the rest of the empire, including the insignificant district of Palestine, soon fell into his hands.

The Persian empire owed its amazingly rapid expansion very largely to the exceptional political skill of Cyrus and his successors. A splendid illustration of this is afforded by the record of events contained on the famous Cylinder of Cyrus, where Cyrus states that it is thanks to the god Marduk that he has been able to establish a world empire. From this it appears that he too saw history in a primarily religious light. Some passages in the text

The Persian Empire

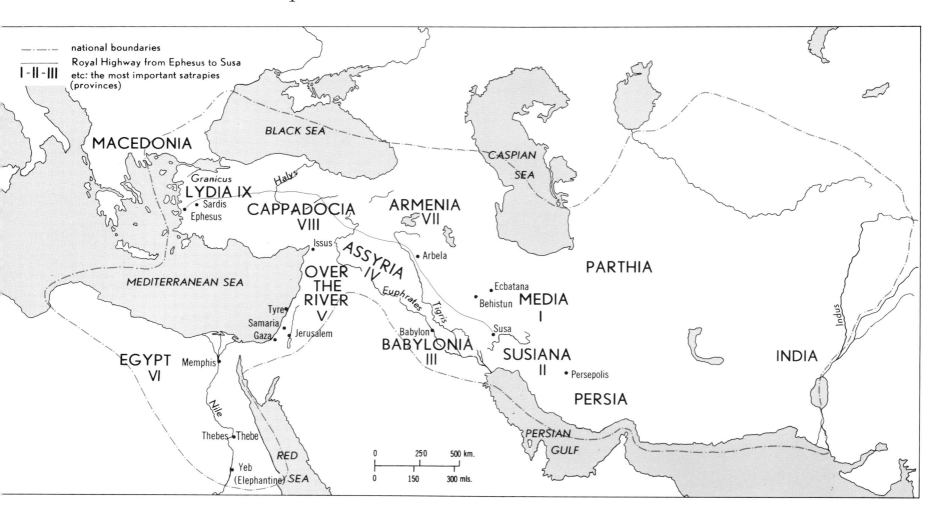

Principal political events: 550: From his base at Persepolis Cyrus of Persia made himself master of the country of the Medes. He advanced into Lydia and reached the west coast of Asia Minor. He then turned east and pushed on as far as India. **539:** Cyrus took Babylon; and as a result Syria and Palestine (= Beyond-the-River) fell into his hands as well. Bands of Jews returned to Judah. **525:** Cambyses (529-522) Cyrus's successor, subjugated Egypt. Among other things he established a military colony of Jews at Yeb (Elephantine). **522:** Darius I (522-486) enlarged the empire to the east and the west. With the royal residences of Susa, Persepolis, and Ecbatana as his centres, he divided the empire into some twenty districts (satrapies). Palestine and Syria became the fifth satrapy. **490-450:** Repulsed by the Greeks, the Persians were obliged to withdraw from Europe and from the sea-ports of Asia Minor. **333:** After a preliminary encounter at the Granicus (334), Alexander the Great defeated the Persian army in a major battle in the plain of Issus, and overran the western part of the empire (Syria, Palestine, and Egypt). **331:** The battle at Arbela. The Persian Empire ceased to exist.

even contain thoughts similar to those found in Deutero-Isaiah. The following is an example:

> …Then he [Marduk] uttered the name of Cyrus, the king of Anshan; he uttered his name that he might become ruler over the whole world…
>
> Without a struggle of any kind he [Marduk] permitted him to enter his city of Babylon, thus saving Babylon from all disaster. He handed over to him Nabonidus, the king who did not venerate him [Marduk]. All the inhabitants of Babylon, the whole land of Sumer and Accad with the princes and governors bowed down before him [Cyrus] and kissed his feet… With joy they hailed him as their lord, by whose help they had been restored from death to life… When I [Cyrus] entered Babylon as a friend and amid jubilation and rejoicing took my seat upon the throne of the rulers in the royal palace, then Marduk, the mighty lord, caused the magnanimous inhabitants of Babylon to take me to their hearts. And I daily bestirred myself to do him worship… The kings of the whole world, from the Upper [Mediterranean] Sea to the Lower Sea [Persian Gulf], they who have their seats in throne-rooms, they who live in other buildings, and the kings of the west who dwell in tents, they all brought me a rich tribute and kissed my feet in Babylon… To the sacred cities on the other side of the Tigris, to the holy places which had long been in ruins, I caused to be returned the images that belonged to them, and I had permanent sanctuaries built for them. I also gathered together all the inhabitants and had them return to their dwelling-places…

This clay cylinder of Cyrus shows that the Persian ruler did not drive the conquered peoples out of their homelands, but on the contrary gave such exiles as there were the chance of returning to the countries of their birth. At the same time—and this is even more remarkable—he respected the local and regional religions. He actually worshipped gods of other peoples, such as Marduk. It was a distinctive feeling for religion—which the renowned Zoroaster was later on to develop further still—that encouraged this attitude in the Persian kings.

In their view all local deities were representatives, so to speak, of their own god, Ahura-Mazda, the wise lord, the god of light. Opposed to him was Ahriman, the author of evil. This dualistic view led to their adopting a tolerant policy in religious matters, so that most peoples welcomed Cyrus with open arms. The Bible itself has nothing bad to say about him. Whereas Assyria and Babylonia were often threatened with the vengeance of God, Cyrus, according to the prophet Deutero-Isaiah, is God's servant. Through his activity the Chosen People are to experience a new exodus, and God's dominion is to be established over the whole world. Later on, the author of the Book of Daniel was to set the Persian empire in a different light, but in so doing he had a particular literary and religious purpose in view.

Cyrus's liberal policies, however, did not extend to allowing any nation to regain its independence. The Persian rulers exercised a better control over every part of the empire than even the Assyrian and Babylonian potentates had done. In this respect the work of King Darius (522–486 B.C.) was especially important. The empire was divided up into twenty satrapies, each

Judah and neighbouring provinces of the Persian Empire

538: A first batch of exiles returned, led by Sheshbazzar. They had to remain near Jerusalem as the southern part of former Judah (Idumea) appears to have been settled by Edomites.

Ca. 530: Under the leadership of Zerubbabel and Joshua (Jeshua) a second batch of exiles returned. The rebuilding of the Temple and the walls of Jerusalem was hindered by the authorities in Samaria.

515: The consecration of the second Temple in Jerusalem.

445: Nehemiah, a prominent Jewish member of the royal court at Susa, came to Jerusalem to make Judah a province in its own right, separate from Samaria. The walls of Jerusalem were speedily rebuilt. Twelve years later Nehemiah returned to Susa.

Ca. 430: Nehemiah came a second time to look after the interests of the Jews in Jerusalem and Judah.

398 (or 428 or 458): The priest Ezra came to Jerusalem to set religious affairs in order. The 'Law of Moses' was proclaimed and accepted as authoritative for the Jewish community. The Samaritans became a separate religious group alongside the Jews.

It was from Lachish that during the Persian period a governor administered the province of Edom, which came to be called Idumea. On the acropolis of the mound known as Tell ed-Duweir some of the walls of the government building still stand. Relations between Judah and Idumea were strained. Judah resented the Idumeans because during the Exile they had occupied a part of the former Southern Kingdom—among other places, the sacred city of Hebron. Idumea was afraid that Judah intended to extend her domination to the south.

of which again comprised a number of provinces. Furthermore, a system of regular postal services was developed, so that the Persian king in his capital could easily receive prompt information about the situation in even the most distant parts of his realm. For example, there was an imperial highway running from Susa in Persia as far as Ephesus in Asia Minor, a distance of some 1500 miles.

Judah and the exiles in Babylon were among those who benefited from the new political situation. Ezra 6:3-5 preserves in an Aramaic version the text of one of Cyrus's decrees, which is generally acknowledged as authentic. The text runs as follows:

A record. In the first year of Cyrus the king, Cyrus the king issued a decree: Concerning the house of God at Jerusalem, let the house be rebuilt, the place where sacrifices are offered and burnt offerings are brought; its height shall be sixty cubits and its breadth sixty cubits, with three courses of great stones and one course of timber; let the cost be paid from the royal treasury. And also let the gold and silver vessels of the house of God, which Nebuchadnezzar took out of the temple that is in Jerusalem and brought to Babylon, be restored and brought back to the temple which is in Jerusalem, each to its place; you shall put them in the house of God.

The Jews in Exile probably overestimated the significance of this decree. It sometimes looks as though they thought that Cyrus was here acknowledging Yahweh as the only God, and

that as worshippers of Yahweh they enjoyed a privileged position. Full of enthusiasm, a group of exiles set out on the journey to distant Judah. Their leader was a certain Sheshbazzar, who was probably a lineal descendant of David. On their arrival in Palestine, they found themselves confronted with a depressing situation. Judah was still an impoverished and backward country with a deficient economy. On the hilltops lay the ruins of what had formerly been cities, and amid these remains there lived a few villagers, who were practically strangers.

These simple Jews who had been left behind at the time of the deportation were now the new owners of the land, and as such they were not immediately willing to recognize the rights of the returning exiles (Ezek. 33:13-25). Some districts in the south had even been taken over by Edomites, who had been obliged to abandon their own territory to make room for intruding Arabian tribes. The resulting social tensions and the economic distress caused by a bad harvest scarcely left the returning exiles time and energy enough to attend to the rebuilding of the Temple (Hag. 2:15-17). Although under Sheshbazzar an immediate start was made on the laying of the foundations, work soon came to a standstill, and was not resumed for many years (Ezra 5:16).

The new impetus arrived with a second group of exiles who probably returned to Jerusalem during the reign of the Persian king, Cambyses (529–522 B.C.). They were led by two particularly energetic men: Zerubbabel, nephew to Sheshbazzar, and Jeshua, who later became High Priest. The joy with which this group was welcomed was soon fanned into an hysterical expectancy by political events. When Cambyses, the conqueror of Egypt, died in 522 B.C., unrest and rebellion began to spread through many parts of the now enormous empire, and to many Jews it seemed as though Yahweh was at last about to establish his dominion over the entire world. This new note of optimism was struck especially by the prophet Haggai. He said that Yahweh would overthrow all kingdoms, that the Temple in Jerusalem would soon become the hub and centre of the world, and that David's descendant, Zerubbabel, would then reign as the chosen servant of God. Ideas of this kind are to be found in Haggai 2:6-9, 20-23, and in the works of another prophet, Zechariah, whose words are on the whole more moderate in tone.

The actual course of events, however, was quite different from what had been predicted and soon had a sobering effect. The new king, Darius I, quickly suppressed all rebellious tendencies, so that the Persian empire seemed, if anything, stronger than ever. Nevertheless, urged on by the prophets Haggai and Zechariah the Jews continued with the building of the Temple. In the year 515 B.C., about twenty years after Cyrus had first issued his decree, the ceremony of consecration was at last performed. The Jews once more possessed a centre for their activities, and a holy place from which Yahweh could proceed to exercise his dominion. No doubt many were disappointed when they found that it was only for them—the tiny group of Jews settled around Jerusalem—that this holy place had any significance, while the world at large was either ignorant of it or indifferent towards it.

The hope that the Davidic dynasty might be restored gradually faded. Descendants of David certainly continued to be known for another century, as is shown by the list in I Chronicles

3:10-24, but the prospect of establishing a great kingdom under a member of David's line vanished with the death of Zerubbabel. From then on the High Priests became more and more the authoritative leaders of the nation. One after another, Jeshua, Joiakim, and Eliashib fulfilled this function. They held the nation together through a period of about half a century, of which little is known. The feeling dominant in the Jewish community at this time was probably one of impotence and resignation. Only the appearance of two men of remarkable insight and energy, Nehemiah and Ezra, was able to save the nation from the disintegration which threatened it.

It is difficult to give an account of events from the middle of the fifth century onwards and the precise role played by these two men, because we do not know whether they were both active at the same time or whether one of them preceded the other. Our information, whether from the Bible or from other sources, offers no conclusive solution. In the account that follows, it is assumed that Nehemiah made his appearance before Ezra, but this is not to be taken as a final judgment on the question.

In the year 445 B.C., almost a hundred years after the fall of Babylon, a small party of Jews from Palestine reached the Persian court at Susa, where Nehemiah, a brother of one of the travellers, held high office. They described the tragic situation in Jerusalem, where the Temple was unprotected because the city walls still lay in ruins, and the people were living in a state of uncertainty and dejection under the supervision of the regents in Samaria. The book of the prophet Malachi, which in all probability deals with this period, helps to fill in the picture. According to this, the duties attaching to ceremonies of the cult were being neglected, and various social evils were rampant, including marital infidelity and a contempt for justice. On hearing these reports Nehemiah asked leave of the Persian ruler to spend a number of years in Jerusalem in order to reorganize the Jewish community. His request was granted, and he was appointed governor of Judah, which was detached from Samaria to become a separate province of the fifth satrapy.

When, invested with his authority, Nehemiah arrived in Jerusalem, it was the city walls that first commanded his attention. In the middle of the night he went out alone to take stock of the situation (Neh. 2:11-15). He managed to prevail upon the leaders and the people of Jerusalem to undertake the rebuilding of the walls immediately and on a massive scale. Indeed, it was necessary to carry out the work with all speed, because the Jews in Jerusalem were surrounded by enemies who could easily represent this activity to the Persian king in a false light. If Nehemiah's motives were to be made to appear suspect, his position and even his life would be in great danger. One of these enemies was Sanballat, the governor of Samaria, who became related to the high-priestly family in Jerusalem and would naturally have been glad to see his authority restored over the province of Judah. He was supported by Tobiah, the governor of the province of Ammon, and Geshem, the governor of Edom and southern Judah. In spite of the intimidating behaviour of these opponents, or perhaps because of it, the Jews completed the city wall in record time, thus ensuring security from external enemies.

Nehemiah next turned his attention to social conditions within the community. Here, the situation was deplorable. The land, as well as all other possessions, were in the hands of the

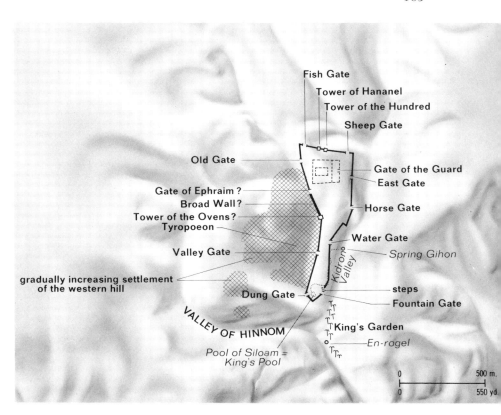

Jerusalem after the Exile

The destruction of 587 left very little of Jerusalem. The rubble filled the valleys around the hill of David (Neh. 2 : 14). About 150 years later Nehemiah initiated the rebuilding of the walls; and in that connection one finds names given to various points in the city wall. Obviously, these names have more to do with the situation known to the author of the Book of Nehemiah in the 4th century than with traditions from pre-exilic times. It is possible, therefore, that the names of various gates had changed. Here are the details provided by the Chronicler on the occasions of a nocturnal walk (Neh. 2 :12-15), of the rebuilding (Neh. 3 : 1-32), and of the feast celebrating the completion of the work (Neh. 12 : 30-39), arranged on an anti-clockwise circuit from the north-east.

Walk	Rebuilding	Dedication
	Sheep Gate	Sheep Gate
	Tower of the Hundred	Tower of the Hundred
	Tower of Hananel	Tower of Hananel (Temple fortress?)
	Fish Gate	Fish Gate
	Old Gate	Old Gate
		Gate of Ephraim
	Broad Wall	Broad Wall
	Tower of the Ovens	Tower of the Ovens
Valley Gate	Valley Gate	
Dragons' Spring		
Dung Gate	Dung Gate	Dung Gate
Fountain Gate	Fountain Gate	Fountain Gate
King's Pool	Wall of the Pool of Shelah	
	King's Garden	
	Steps to the city of David	Steps to the city of David
	Water Gate	Water Gate
	Horse Gate	
	East Gate	
	Gate of the Guard	Gate of the Guard

If this evidence is taken in conjunction with other post-exilic texts, what is presented here is an acceptable reconstruction. The area covered by the city in the 4th and 5th centuries B.C. would certainly not have been any bigger than during the period of the monarchy. There can be no doubt, however, that the central function of the Temple exercised a powerful attraction on the Jewish nation; singers built permanent residences around Jerusalem (Neh. 12 : 29), and migration to the city was encouraged (Neh. 11 : 2).

In the middle of modern Hebron stand the lofty walls that protect the tomb of Abraham and some of his immediate family. There are six empty mausoleums—those of Abraham and Sarah, Isaac and Rebekah, Jacob and Leah. Beneath the floor of the mosque is a cave, which is supposed to be the actual burial-place. No doubt this veneration is based on ancient and hallowed traditions; but only when a scientific excavation has been carried out will it be possible to say anything about the factual basis.

few, while the majority were virtually slaves. At Nehemiah's instigation all debts were cancelled, so that the economically weaker could breathe more freely and trade could once more revive. He set an example himself by waiving his claim to the revenue which the people had to provide for him by virtue of his office (Neh. 5:14-19).

His leave of absence having expired after twelve years, he returned to the Persian court, but a short time later he was allowed to go to Jerusalem again. During this second period he seems to have concentrated primarily on laying down regulations concerning religious observance. He forbade all profane activities in the Temple, and the whole of Judah had to undertake to hand over one tenth of its entire produce for the priests and the other Temple ministers. Henceforward no business of any kind was to be transacted on the sabbath day. Finally, he expelled from Jerusalem a son of the High Priest Joiada, who was married to a daughter of Sanballat. This action was part of his campaign against mixed marriages. Nehemiah describes in the strongest terms the measures he adopted to combat these unions: "And I contended with them and cursed them and beat some of them and pulled out their hair; and I made them take oath in the name of God, saying, 'You shall not give your daughters to their [non-Jewish] sons, or take their daughters for your sons or for yourselves.'" (Neh. 13:25)

These last-named measures enforced by Nehemiah were possibly connected in some way with the role played by Ezra. Un-

fortunately, the accounts which have come down to us concerning the activities of this post-exilic reformer are anything but clear. It is true that Ezra chs. 7–10 and Nehemiah chs. 8–9 contain between them a detailed narrative written in the first person, but unlike the record of Nehemiah its value as source material is still disputed. The only account which has so far been proved reliable is the Aramaic version contained in Ezra 7:12-26, according to which the Persian king Artaxerxes (?Artaxerxes I, 464–424 B.C.) invested Ezra with authority to go to 'the province Beyond the River' and there implement 'the law of the God of Heaven.' This wording is so vague, however, that it is difficult to say with any certainty what it meant, though it may possibly refer to one or more of the minor statutes which have come down to us in Leviticus chs. 1–7, 11–15, or 17–26. Whatever the case may be, Ezra's 'law' seems to have aimed at giving the Jewish community at Jerusalem the inner spiritual direction for which Nehemiah had provided the outer framework. During the week of the Feast of Tabernacles Ezra read aloud daily from the Book of the Law, and his assistants expounded the difficult passages to the people (Neh. chs. 8–10).

Once the Jews had become convinced of the significance of the ancient law it began to have a profound effect on their daily conduct, and the resulting revolution in the life and thought of the community was to be of crucial importance to the future history of the whole people. Ezra was especially successful in one particular respect. From the time of the Exile Judah had ceased to exist as an independent state, but this fact was not easy to accept. Again and again the hope was revived that it would regain its independence. What Ezra did was to enable the people to take a positive attitude to the realities of the new situation. They were encouraged to regard themselves not so much as a nation as a religious community, whose special identity consisted in its being 'the people of the law.' From now on neither nationality, participation in the Temple cult, nor even ancestry was to be the prime consideration in determining whether or not a man was a Jew. More important than all these was his acceptance of, and obedience to, 'the law of Moses.'

Little is known about the fortunes of the Jewish community in the period after Nehemiah and Ezra. It seems to have been like an island, cut off from the rest of the world by its religious temperament. Not until about two hundred years later did it emerge from its retreat to face the challenge of Hellenism. This encounter was to put an end to its spiritual isolation and have far-reaching consequences for its faith.

2. THE OLD TESTAMENT NEARS COMPLETION

During the fifth, fourth, and third centuries B.C. the Old Testament gradually assumed the appearance which it presents today. This development was favoured by the fact that the Jewish people were primarily a religious community. However, since relatively little is known of the events which befell Judah in this period of its history, it is impossible to ascertain with any degree of accuracy how the Old Testament came to receive its final shape. For the most part only general conclusions are possible.

One factor which has so far not been mentioned contributed significantly to the literary formation of the ancient traditions. The Persian rulers not only made full allowance for national consciousness and local religious cults: they also respected the native languages of the peoples they had conquered. This explains why so many Persian texts were set down in parallel versions, in old Persian, Babylonian, and Elamite, the three main languages spoken by the peoples living in the central part of the empire. The best known of these trilingual texts is the famous inscription on the rock-face of Behistun. High up on its surface King Darius is depicted in relief with a number of defeated enemies, and surrounding this relief a text, written in the cuneiform script of these three languages, describes the enemies Darius had to subdue in order to restore peace within the empire. One may well wonder which was the greater achievement, that of the Englishman Rawlinson, who in the last century scaled the rock-face with rope ladders in order to examine and transcribe the text, or that of the people who managed to put it there as long ago as 500 B.C.

In the south-western part of the empire, from Babylonia to Egypt, the official language was Aramaic. It owed its pre-eminence to a long process of development which had been well under way three centuries earlier. It appears from one passage in the Old Testament that both the leaders in Jerusalem and Sennacherib's officers were required to know Aramaic (2 Kings 18:26). One of the main reasons for its importance was that the Aramean states in Syria were largely in control of international trade. As a result, their relatively simple language and alpha-

When the Pentateuch was given its final form at about 400 B.C., only a few Jews were still living like these Bedouin women with their donkeys. The authors of the Biblical documents were well aware, it is true, that according to ancient tradition Israel's ancestors had been nomads; but the customs and the whole mode of life associated with this wandering existence were quite foreign to them. It is not surprising, therefore, that on such details the 'history of salvation' which they recorded is faulty and far from comprehensive.

betic script spread through every country in the Near East. The process was further accelerated in Palestine by the immigration of Aramaic-speaking groups after the collapse of the Northern Kingdom, and by the fact that the Judean exiles came into contact with the language while they were in Babylonia.

After the Exile the feeble Jewish community was unable to maintain its native Hebrew in this Aramean environment. Hebrew did, of course, continue to be employed for cultic purposes, but since its use was here confined to the fixed formulae which accompanied the celebration of the religious mysteries, it ceased to develop as a spoken language. It is perhaps permissible to assume, therefore, that Ezra's assistants explained to the people in Aramaic what their leader had read out in Hebrew, "so that the people understood the reading" (Neh. 8:7-8).

In some such way, at any rate, Aramaic versions of the entire Old Testament gradually came into existence. Even the Hebrew texts of the Old Testament are interspersed with passages in Aramaic. In Genesis 31:47, for example, the heap of stones

The relief and inscription which Darius I (522-486) had carved on a wall of rock near what is now Behistun. The carving is on the almost perpendicular face of a bare wall of rock some 300 feet above the ancient caravan route from Babylon to Ecbatana. In three languages, Old Persian, Elamite, and Accadian, the king describes how he put down every rebellious movement in his empire. The relief depicts the conquered rebels before the throne of Darius. Over it stands a figure representing the god, Ahura-Mazda. The relief as a whole is executed in an Assyrian style, but the solar disc supporting the figure is more of an Egyptian symbol. In his hand the god holds a ring as a token of the authority delegated to Darius.

which Laban and Jacob erected in token of a covenant bore the Aramaic name, 'heap of witness.' And in Jeremiah 10:11 there suddenly appears the Aramaic sentence: "The gods who did not make the heavens and the earth shall perish from the earth and from under the heavens." Besides these two brief fragments there are also the considerable Aramaic sections in the books of Ezra and Daniel. Finds of coins, seal-marks, and non-Biblical texts—such as the Elephantine papyri, for instance—confirm this ascendancy of Aramaic in the western part of the Persian empire. Nehemiah was already expressing disapproval of compatriots who were no longer conversant with the Hebrew tongue (Neh. 13:24), but this decline of the ancient mother tongue undoubtedly helped to accelerate the process by which the Hebrew traditions came to be cast in a definitive written form.

Naturally enough, the most important traditions were the first to be recorded in writing. The collections of the Yahwist and Elohist schools, as also the Deuteronomic history and the teachings of the priests, had been available in written form for some time already. During and after the Exile these various traditions merged. The unifying process was probably completed between 500 and 400 B.C., and it was during this time that the Pentateuch, traditionally known as the Law of Moses, was put together and given its final form.

The history of the Samaritan Pentateuch illustrates what happened in the case of the first group of Old Testament texts. From the time of the return from Exile there was tension between the Jews and the Samaritans. Political as well as religious factors played a part in this. Judah at first came under the administration of the governor of Samaria. Those who had returned from Exile filled with dreams of a magnificent future for their country found this political subordination very hard to bear. At the same time their strictness in matters of religion clashed with the more syncretistic approach of the Samaritans. The conflict was brought to a head by the actions of Nehemiah and Ezra. The former secured Judah's independence of Samaria, and it is

understandable that the governor Sanballat and his successors should have tried to oppose this reduction of their power. Ezra's action had the effect of prescribing for the Yahwist Samaritans how they should live. About 400 B.C. the Samaritans reacted by building a sanctuary of their own. In this they were supported by some of the high priestly family in Jerusalem who were hostile to Nehemiah and Ezra.

In a sense it was a repetition of what had occurred after the death of Solomon. In order to give expression to their political independence the people in the north chose a cultic centre of their own. So far as they were concerned the Temple at Jerusalem had served its turn. The division did not mean, however, that the Samaritans were rejecting their ancient traditions. They built their temple, for example, not in the relatively modern city of Samaria, but on the sacred mountain of Gerizim, near the traditional sanctuary of Shechem. They also retained their sacred scrolls, that is, the Pentateuch. They did not (and still do not) recognize other Old Testament writings as sacred, which suggests that prior to the Samaritan schism all who worshipped Yahweh had accepted the five Books of Moses as canonical. When the split occurred the Samaritans simply held on to what they had. The prophetic books and other Old Testament writings, therefore, must have acquired their form and general recognition *after* this break. When the Jewish community subsequently accepted these other books as holy writ, the Samaritans did not take over these Jewish innovations.

The second group of Old Testament texts consists of the prophetic books. The Former Prophets, as they are called, are Joshua, Judges, 1 and 2 Samuel, 1 and 2 Kings. They must have received their final written form some time after the Pentateuch was put together, but it is difficult to be more precise. It is even more difficult in the case of what are known as the Latter Prophets, i.e. Isaiah, Jeremiah, Ezekiel, and the twelve Minor Prophets. It is beyond doubt, for example, that the sayings of several prophets have been brought together in the Book of Isa-

work suggest that it assumed its final shape some time during the fourth century.

However, Jonah was not the last of the prophetic books to be written. There is reason to suppose that Deutero-Zechariah (Zech. 9–14) dates from as late as the beginning of the Hellenistic period, about 300 B.C. If this is so, then it is possible that changes and additions were made to all the books of the Latter Prophets right up to that time. The final redaction of the four books (Isaiah, Jeremiah, Ezekiel, and the Twelve) would in that case have been carried out some time in the third century B.C.

The third and last group of Old Testament texts comprises what were known as the 'Writings,' a collective term for a number of books belonging to various genres. They were given their final form at different times, and exact dating is difficult in the case of almost every one of them. What is fairly certain, however, is that the majority received their final shape in the third century B.C.

The Book of Psalms undoubtedly has a long history behind it. Various collections gradually emerged with the growth and spread of the religious cult, and from a combination of these the book as we know it eventually took shape. But when? One of the Qumran scrolls contains Biblical psalms among a number of hitherto unknown religious lyrics. This suggests that no very sharp distinction was made between psalms from the Bible and from elsewhere. Alongside this must be set the fact that collections such as the *Psalms of Solomon* and the *Hymns of Thanksgiving* from Qumran, dating from the first century B.C., were not incorporated in the sacred Writings. Since, however, various ancient manuscripts from Qumran do in fact preserve the content and sequence found in the Book of Psalms, it seems justifiable to maintain that the latter acquired its final form not later than the end of the Persian period.

iah, but this does not make it any easier to give a definite date to the final redaction.

A possible clue is provided by the Book of Jonah. Its place among the twelve minor prophets is a distinctive one, for unlike the other works ascribed to the 'writing prophets' it comprises not a number of sayings but a story and a psalm. The story is obviously a fable, intended as an attack on the exclusiveness of the Jews. According to the author God means his salvation to apply not to the Jews only, but to all peoples, including even that epitome of wickedness, Nineveh, the now devastated capital city of the ferocious Assyrians. The form and content of this

△
(Above) On the site of modern 'Amman there once stood the capital city of the Ammonites, Rabbath-ammon. After Alexander the Great this oriental city was transformed into a Hellenistic metropolis, with the Greek name of Philadelphia. The Romans incorporated it into the Decapolis. Modern occupation of the site has for the most part obliterated the remains of antiquity; but in the valley east of the acropolis lie the ruins of the theatre, built to accommodate about 4000 people. The 'box' for the city council is still to be seen in the centre block of seats.

(Right) Jerash lies almost 40 miles north of ▷ 'Amman. Although occupied in pre-Hellenistic times, it was not until after Alexander the Great that the town really came into its own. Its other name, Antioch on the Chrysorrhoas, sufficiently indicates its Hellenistic character. After a brief spell under the Hasmoneans, Gerasa passed to the Romans, who annexed it to the Decapolis. From this period date the magnificent ruins. The photo shows, in the foreground, a number of columns of the forum, itself well known for its rare elliptical shape. In the background are the remains of the temple of Artemis (2nd century A.D.).

The final stages in the shaping of the Book of Job do not present quite so much of a problem. Its author seized upon an existing tradition about an heroic figure of the remote past in order to open up for discussion the problem of suffering. The middle of the fifth century would seem to be a likely date for this book. Other books which may well have been cast in their final form during this period of Persian dominion include almost certainly the Song of Solomon, and perhaps also the Book of Proverbs, although some of its worldly wisdom must have been formulated prior to the Exile. The Book of Ruth could have been written before or after the Exile; the Book of Esther, on the other hand, in spite of its dealing with an event which takes place in the Persian capital of Susa, was probably not written before the third century. We can be rather more certain about the Books of Tobit, Judith, and Baruch. The fact that these short works failed to win a permanent place in the list of sacred writings points to a late origin. The Book of Baruch, which is named after the prophet Jeremiah's assistant, may even belong to the first century b.c.

The history of the First and Second Books of Chronicles and the Books of Nehemiah and Ezra, is known in somewhat greater detail. Originally, these four books constituted a single compilation written by someone who must have lived later than Nehemiah and Ezra. His purpose was to provide his contemporaries with an outline of something like the whole of history. For the period from Adam to David he contented himself with a number of genealogies. From the time of David up to the Exile he goes into much more detail, so that his narrative then runs parallel to the Deuteronomic history. If these two corresponding traditions are set side by side, certain peculiar features stand out immediately.

It becomes instantly noticeable that the Chronicler has fairly often taken over word for word—but without any mention of his source—certain passages from the Books of Samuel and Kings. Nowadays we would regard this as plagiarism, but in those days it was an accepted part of an author's business. Sometimes, for particular reasons, he introduces certain changes. A good illustration of this is the account of how David numbered the people. In the eyes of the pious Israelite this numbering of the people was an irreligious act, because David gave the appearance, at least, of having become powerful owing to the number of his able-bodied men rather than through the help of Yahweh. 2 Samuel 24:1 tells us that Yahweh himself, because his anger was kindled against the Israelites, induced David to commit this misguided action. The later Chronicler's view of God could not accommodate an idea of this kind. According to him (1 Chron. 21:1) Satan had prompted David to do it.

The chief differences between the two parallel texts, however, spring from the peculiar situation of the Jewish community after the Exile. It was this which prompted the Chronicler to omit some traditions, to add others, and to interpret others again from a new angle. The fact is that the Chronicler was living in a small religious community and not in a prosperous and independent secular state. This 'ecclesiastical' situation conditions the tone of his whole work, and in a sense, therefore, it might be described as an 'ecclesiastical history.' To the patriarchs and even to Moses he pays little attention, whereas David's religious activities and the importance of the Temple cult are over-emphasized. The purpose behind these modifications was to show that the Jewish congregation was the continuation of the Davidic-Israelite community, and they may even be intended in part as a polemical attack on the Samaritans and the sanctuary of Mount Gerizim.

The Chronicler's work soon seems to have been divided up into two parts. In the list of sacred books those of Ezra and Nehemiah were placed before 1 and 2 Chronicles. The reason is probably that the Books of Ezra and Nehemiah were felt to be a sequel to the Deuteronomic history and to add something entirely new to the existing texts. As a result a higher value was set upon them more quickly than on the Chronicles, which simply appeared to contain a number of as yet unrecorded traditions from the period of the monarchy. The Greek translation, indeed, gave these books the title of *paraleipomena*, 'fragments left over' from the original collection of sacred writings.

The Book of Ecclesiastes dates from the end of the third century, though it was subsequently copied and appeared in many versions. According to the introductory verse it comprised "the words of the Preacher, the son of David, king in Jerusalem," that is, Solomon. Such a claim must, however, be understood within the current of tradition, which tended more and more to attribute the laws to Moses, the psalms to David, and the wisdom literature to Solomon. In fact, the author clearly lived at a time when the old values were beginning to crumble beneath the influx of Hellenistic ideas. He gave his opinion regarding the relative character of all that happens in this world in the familiar text which asserts that all is vanity (Eccles. 1:2-11).

Finally, it remains to mention one more book that can be dated with a fair degree of accuracy. In fact it was translated into Greek by the author's grandson in the year 132 b.c. The author himself was by his own account (Ecclesiasticus 50:27) a son of Sirach, in Hebrew, Ben Sira. This is why the book is sometimes called 'Sirach,' after the Greek form of the name. Although this work failed to gain a permanent place among the sacred books of the Jews, it provides illuminating evidence concerning the final shaping of the Old Testament. In a hymn of praise to the forefathers of Israel (Ecclesiasticus 44–50), which incidentally reveals how a Jew of this time regarded the traditions of the past, the author uses words and expressions which are virtually quotations from other Old Testament texts. These must therefore have already been extant in his day. The book also contains a brief reference to the twelve prophets: "May the bones of the twelve prophets revive from where they lie, for they comforted the people of Jacob and delivered them with confident hope." (Ecclesiasticus 49:10) The fact that these twelve men are referred to collectively suggests that their sayings had already been combined, and this in turn permits us to conclude that all the prophetic books had reached a state of completion by about 180 b.c., forty to sixty years before the Greek translation of Sirach was completed.

All this goes to show that the events of the fifth, fourth, and third centuries were of major importance for the development and completion of the Old Testament. In the two centuries which followed little more was added. This period saw the rise of that current of Hellenistic thought which later made such deep inroads into the life of the Jewish community. Some brief description of it is therefore essential.

In Old Testament times Tyre was one of the most powerful cities of Phoenicia. The influence of its rulers extended to Jerusalem (2 Sam. 5 : 11 and 1 Kings 5 : 15-26) and to Samaria (1 Kings 16 : 31). Its favourable island site enabled Tyre to preserve its independence during the periods of Assyrian and Babylonian expansion. In 322 B.C. Alexander the Great invested the town for seven months and was able to take it only when he had built a causeway from the mainland. This changed the situation of the town completely. Tyre became an ordinary port on the mainland; and it was then easy for Hellenistic culture to make headway in the town. The photo shows the remains of a colonnaded street, over 30 feet wide, in the town's southern quarter. Archaeologists have opened up one level which is Byzantine (4th century A.D.) and one belonging to the Roman period (1st century A.D.); but the plan itself certainly dates from the Hellenistic period.

3. THE RISE OF HELLENISM

From the time of Nehemiah onwards the province of Judah had been permitted to order its own religious affairs. Internal administration, too, was very largely in the hands of the Jewish community. Despite this relatively independent position all kinds of cultural and religious trends emanating from the Persian world empire began to affect Jewish life and thought. The immediate result of this was a broadening of the Jewish outlook in many spheres. The list of peoples in Genesis 10, which comes mainly from the priestly tradition, offers an example. Following a genealogical scheme, the list divides the nations according to their various historical and geographical connections. The whole of mankind is seen as having sprung from Noah and his three sons. The progeny of Japheth inhabit Asia Minor and the coastal areas of the Mediterranean Sea. Among the descendants of Ham are included the Egyptians, the Ethiopians, the Arabs, and the Canaanites; whilst the Elamites, the Assyrians, the Arameans, and the Hebrews are described as deriving from the family of Shem. An attempt is therefore made to account for the origins of the whole human race, even though Israel is still accorded pride of place among the nations as the Chosen People of God.

The Jews of the Diaspora were especially affected by this broader outlook, but it also had repercussions in the smaller world of the theocratic state of Judah. For instance, various

books in the Bible that date from this period contain ideas which owe a great deal to the religious genius of the Persians. The history of religious thought in Israel reveals a growing conviction that Yahweh is the prime cause of all things, but after the Exile an element of dualism begins to appear. This is manifested in the idea that there is a continuous struggle between good and evil, light and darkness, truth and falsehood. At first it assumes the form of a contrast or conflict between God and Satan with their respective emissaries. In a later period the idea was further elaborated, particularly in the Book of Daniel, where the struggle takes on cosmic dimensions.

The main stimulus which produced a change of outlook came not from Persia, however, but from the west. At first the wars waged by the Persian rulers against the Greeks prevented the ties which had existed for many centuries between Greece and the eastern shores of the Mediterranean Sea from being tightened. But the westward advance of the Persian armies was stopped. In the end the Persians were obliged to relinquish the western sea-ports of Asia Minor to the Greeks. From that time on, elements of Greek culture made their way, under steadily mounting pressure, along the trade routes and through the ports into the eastern world. The familiarity and concern with the Near East that one finds in the fifth-century Greek historian Herodotus strikingly exemplify the importance of these contacts.

In the second half of the fourth century the period of Persian dominion came to an abrupt end. The age of Hellenism was about to dawn, and a great wave of enthusiasm for the new Greek ideals was to sweep over the countries of the Near East. In 336 B.C., at the age of twenty, Alexander the Great became king of Macedonia. Inspired by the philosopher Aristotle, he set out quite deliberately to create a world empire that would have a single unified culture: Macedonians, Greeks, and all the peoples of the east were to be united under the rule of one man, so that they might form the civilized population of a new world.

But such an ideal first called for a military operation. The conquest of a divided Greece presented few difficulties. With the Greek ports on the west coast of Asia Minor behind him Alexander advanced against the Persians. His celebrated phalanx quickly carried the day. In this new strategy the heavily armed soldiery formed a series of closely packed squares. The Persian armies dashed themselves to pieces against it in the plain of Issus, east of Tarsus. So in the year 333 B.C. the entire western part of the Persian empire fell into Alexander's hands. By way of Tyre, Samaria, and Gaza he advanced towards Egypt. That country, which for two hundred years had been forced to accept the overlordship of Persia, welcomed him as a liberator. And Alexander behaved like one. He made his way to the oasis of Siwa, a notable sanctuary in the western desert, where the Egyptian priests venerated him as a new pharaoh, or god. After this he pushed forward to the very heart of the Persian empire and deep into what is now India. Although he survived this gruelling campaign he shortly afterwards fell ill and died in Babylon in 323 B.C., when he was scarcely thirty-three years old.

After Alexander's death his immense empire immediately fell apart. There ensued a number of wars between various generals, but two powerful factions gradually emerged: one in the north-east, which embraced Mesopotamia, Syria, and a great part of Asia Minor; and one in the south-west, which had control over Egypt and Palestine. The familiar situation in the Near East appeared to have been restored: one state with its centre of gravity in Babylonia and Assyria, and another with Egypt as its centre. This was so in appearance only, however, for new cultural centres were created by the foundation of new cities. Rulers and monarchs did not take up residence in already famous places such as Babylon, Ashur, Nineveh, Memphis, or Thebes. Seleucus and his successors who ruled the north-east resided sometimes in Seleucia, the new city on the Tigris, but more frequently in Syrian Antioch. The Ptolemaic family, which had obtained control over Egypt and Palestine, chose as its seat of government Alexandria, a city founded by Alexander himself in 331 B.C.

These new capitals were the symbols and outward manifestations of a revolutionary change. Everywhere along the route taken by Alexander's army new cities had sprung up and these instilled new life also into old centres of habitation. All these new places, peopled with a mixture of Macedonians, Greeks, and Orientals, encouraged the spread of Hellenistic culture. The agora, a rectangular open space bounded on each side by arcades, became the focal point of public life. It was here that civic matters were discussed, where business was transacted, and justice administered. A city of this kind possessed a number of straight, intersecting streets which gave easy access to temple, theatre, and gymnasium.

The latter building in particular played a leading part in the dissemination of Hellenistic culture, which set a high value on the physical aspects of man's nature. Bodily health was encouraged by the pursuit of such sports as wrestling, foot-racing, boxing, and throwing the discus. There were also facilities for bathing and for being massaged with oil. All these activities were usually performed in a state of nudity, the word 'gymnasium' itself deriving from the Greek *gumnos*, 'naked.' The gymnasium also served as a rendezvous for all who were bent on propagating the new culture.

Furthermore, on the model of the Greek 'polis,' towns of this sort had municipal councils, elected by the citizens themselves and possessing a fair degree of autonomy. Consequently, to be a citizen of such a town was a fiercely sought-after privilege among the higher classes of people in the east.

A factor which helped to spread and establish the new culture was the *koinē* or common language, a simplified form of Greek. From the time of Alexander until well into the Christian era this language made it possible to move around with ease and transact business of every kind anywhere in the Near East. The place it held is more or less comparable with that of English in the world of today. Common Greek was used in politics, administration, trade, education, and cultural life. It also gradually came to play a part in the religion of Israel. Even the Jews of the Diaspora settled in foreign countries soon ceased to be able to understand the Hebrew texts of their sacred scrolls, with the result that Greek translations were made of them. Tradition has given to these the collective title of the 'Septuagint.' In this way Judaism acquired a powerful influence in its turn. In this Greek translation its religious ideas were disseminated throughout the Hellenistic world. However, the oriental languages did still manage to hold their own among the local population and in the countryside. Aramaic, for instance, was still generally spoken in Palestine up to the first century A.D., though its use as an inter-

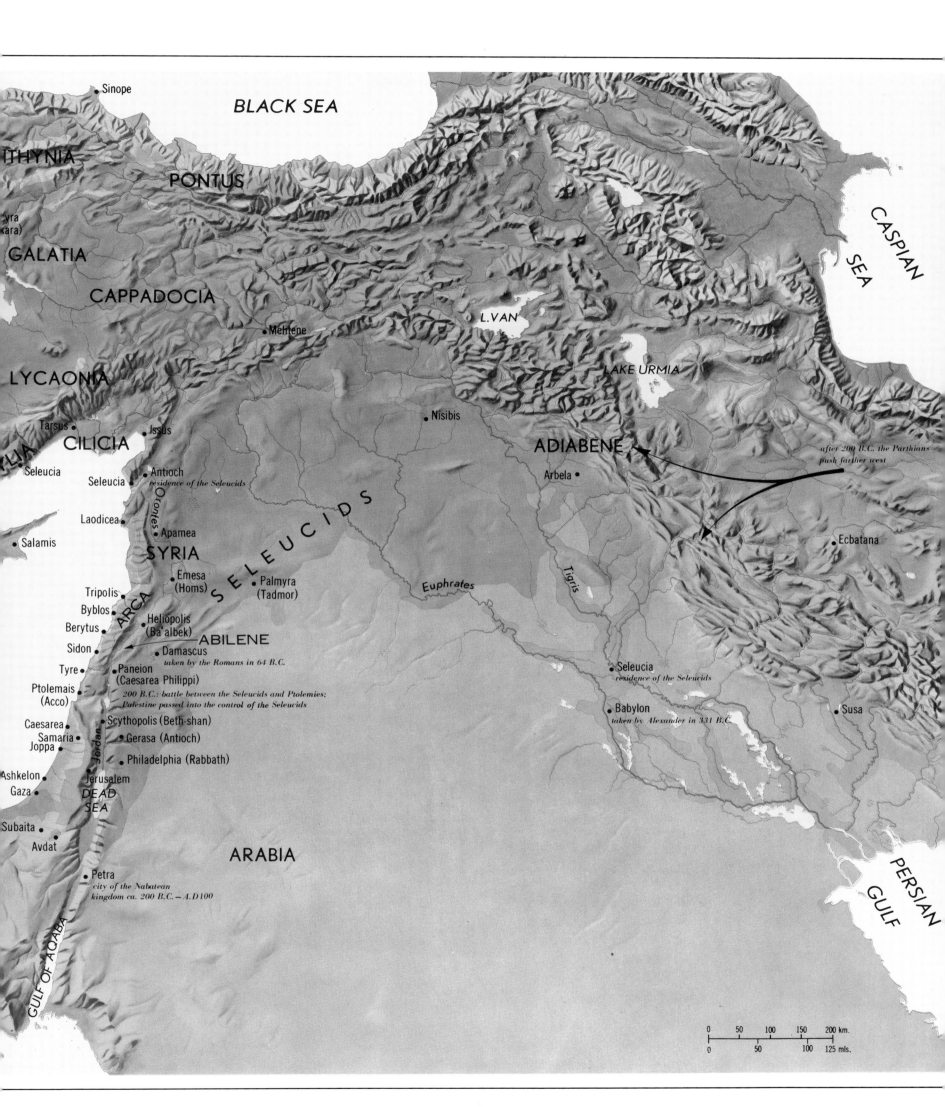

BLACK SEA

ITHYNIA

PONTUS

GALATIA

CAPPADOCIA

LYCAONIA

CILICIA

Tarsus
Issus
Seleucia
Seleucia
Antioch
residence of the Seleucids
Orontes
Laodicea
Apamea
SYRIA
Salamis
SELEUCIDS
Emesa
(Homs)
Palmyra
(Tadmor)
Tripolis
Byblos
ARCA
Berytus
Heliópolis
(Ba'albek)
ABILENE
Sidon
Damascus
taken by the Romans in 64 B.C.
Tyre
Paneion
(Caesarea Philippi)
Ptolemais
(Acco)
200 B.C.: battle between the Seleucids and Ptolemies;
Palestine passed into the control of the Seleucids
Caesarea
Scythopolis (Beth-shan)
Samaria
Gerasa (Antioch)
Joppa
Philadelphia (Rabbath)
Ashkelon
Jerusalem
Gaza
DEAD SEA
Jordan

Subaita
Avdat
ARABIA
Petra
city of the Nabatean
kingdom ca. 200 B.C. – A.D 100

GULF OF AQABA

Sinope

Mehtene

L. VAN

LAKE URMIA

CASPIAN SEA

Nisibis

ADIABENE

Arbela

after 200 B.C. the Parthians
push farther west

Ecbatana

Tigris

Euphrates

Seleucia
residence of the Seleucids

Babylon
taken by Alexander in 331 B.C.

Susa

PERSIAN GULF

0   50   100   150   200 km.
0   50   100   125 mls.

The Near East after Alexander the Great

national language, or as a language for official purposes, must have declined considerably by this time.

The initial period of Hellenism might well be defined as a time of accelerated growth and radical, even revolutionary change. The accepted traditions of the past were disappearing all too quickly, and the new ideas had not yet acquired any settled form. All kinds of political, social, and religious institutions were undergoing far-reaching transformations. The ideal of world citizenship engendered a strong current of cosmopolitan feeling that broke through traditional boundaries, and parallel with this there came into being a revolutionary way of regarding the individual. There was a growing conviction that what determined a man's worth was not so much race, class, or lineage, as his character and personal qualities. However, since the old ideas and customs were being too hastily thrust aside, there was a general loss of depth and substance in the spheres of culture and religion. Small communities which for centuries past had been able to maintain their own beliefs and traditions suddenly found themselves exposed and defenceless amid the ebullient life of the new age. Artistic fashions in the fields of sculpture, architecture, and literature were conveyed along the trade routes to the far corners of the kingdom, where they were often adopted all too unquestioningly. The lifeless imitations to which this gave rise became the common property of every nation. The same applied to basic viewpoints about man, society, and the gods.

On an ethical level this loss of traditional values threw the old problem of the nature of good and evil into sharper relief. These troubled and unstable conditions gave rise to many private philosophies and religions. Three different sorts of answers to the new doubts in particular gained currency. In educated circles the philosophies of Stoicism and Epicureanism were developed, and among simpler people the mystery religions became spectacularly and indeed alarmingly popular.

Stoics saw in the universe a single divine principle of reason and justice which was also to be found within man. It was the

task of every man to live in accordance with this divine spark, to heed the prompting of reason and deny the impulses of passion. Indifference to material and bodily things and the duty owed to divine reason led to an austere moral outlook. Epicureans believed that man should concentrate his intellect and energies on living a good life in terms of the world he knew; and the best life was that which yielded the highest pleasure. This could have been made to lead to excesses, but in fact the early Epicureans' idea of a life of pleasure was refined and almost puritanical.

Ordinary men, however, needed something more. This they found in astrology, in magic, and in particular in the mysteries, as they were called. These sacral rites and ceremonies centred in the main on the oriental deities, Cybele, Isis, Mithras, and Dionysus. The rites and formulas were kept secret from outsiders. Only initiates knew the words and actions by which, as they believed, it was possible to be delivered from suffering and calamity in this life and in the hereafter. Belief in magic and the supernatural was rife, and the mysteries led to deplorable excesses.

One answer to this longing for assurance and security was provided by the cult of the ruler. In Hellenistic practice the reigning prince or potentate was worshipped as a manifestation or incarnation of a deity. Alexander the Great had already accepted this kind of veneration in Egypt and in Persia. Those who succeeded him, the Ptolemies and the Seleucids, did the same. That is evident, for example, from the additional names which they adopted. One called himself *soter*, 'saviour' or 'deliverer'; another appended to his name the title of *epiphanes*, the 'appearing (god).' They caused temples to be built in their own honour, and had images of themselves erected, before which sacrifices were offered. In particular, the days on which the monarch had been born, ascended the throne, or made his entry into a city or province, were occasions of amnesty. Even in the Roman period this religious practice survived in the cult of the Caesar.

In the early stages the Jews living in Judah were able to stand aside from the increasing confusion of ideas which these practices encouraged. Strategically and economically, the little community in the mountainous district around Jerusalem mattered hardly at all to the Ptolemies of Egypt. Those liberal-minded potentates demanded nothing more than an annual payment of taxes. Under the High Priest's direction the Jewish community was allowed to manage its internal affairs for itself. With the territories around Judah, however, the situation was very different. The coastal region and the trans-Jordanian plateau meant more to Egypt, because through them ran the great trade routes. Strongly hellenized cities were to be found there too, such places as Ptolemais (the old Acco), Gaza, the Nabatean capital of Petra, and the trans-Jordanian Philadelphia, formerly known as Rabbath-ammon (the present-day 'Amman). The new culture undoubtedly infiltrated from these towns into the tiny state of Judah, as the Book of Ecclesiastes reveals. But in general the Jewish religion and way of life succeeded in holding their own.

This peaceful situation came to an end when Egyptian power could no longer be maintained in Palestine and domination by Syria took its place. The rulers of that state had special reason, where Judah was concerned, for carrying out a hellenizing and therefore anti-Jewish policy. Jewish resistance gave rise to the wars of the Maccabees, and it was out of this conflict that the last books of the Old Testament emerged.

The high esteem in which the body and man's physical nature were held during the Hellenistic period is well illustrated by this relief on the base of a statue in Athens. Six completely naked men are playing something that resembles a game of hockey. At the sides are four players watching two others in the centre contending for possession of a 'ball.' Not unnaturally, such a cult of the body injected great confusion into prevailing attitudes in the Near East, where matters of sex were treated with some degree of reticence.

VIII. COMPLETION OF THE OLD TESTAMENT

Confrontation with Hellenism. The Maccabean Revolt. The political situation prior to the New Testament: 2nd and 1st centuries B.C.

1. THE MACCABEAN STRUGGLE

It has been seen that from the time of the Exile in the sixth century B.C., first the Persians and then the Ptolemies of Egypt, exercised control over Palestine. Under these rulers the Jews had enjoyed a broad measure of religious freedom. Peaceful conditions in the spheres of both politics and religion created an atmosphere congenial to literary activity, and as a result many of the Old Testament books reached the final stage of their development during this period. The year 200 B.C. brought about a reversal of this situation. Judah was now forced to relinquish its sheltered position and play a part once more in the mainstream of events. The immediate cause was the victory of Antiochus III (223–187 B.C.) over the Egyptians at Paneion, later to be known as Caesarea Philippi. As a result of this victory Palestine was annexed to the empire of the Seleucids, and the Jewish community found itself under a new ruler with very different views from the Ptolemies in matters of religion.

The conflict between Syria and Egypt had not come about by chance. Antiochus III was inspired by the ideal of restoring the empire of Alexander the Great, and to this end he was bent on gaining mastery over the whole of the civilized world. His earliest campaigns took him deep into the then unknown land of India, but he felt himself constantly threatened in the rear by Egypt. The battle of Paneion removed this threat. His next aim was to add Asia Minor—and in particular Macedonia, Alexander's country of origin—to his empire. However, his campaigning in the west brought him up against a new world power. This power was Rome.

Antiochus's activities invited the Romans to turn their attention towards the east. His claim to Macedonia clashed with their view that it fell within their sphere of influence. What is more, Antiochus was foolish enough to extend hospitality to Rome's arch-enemy, Hannibal of Carthage. It was a gesture that cost him dear. Rome reacted immediately. In 190 B.C. Antiochus suffered a crushing defeat at Magnesia in the west of Asia Minor. The peace-terms were extremely severe. For the next twelve years the Syrian ruler had to pay a heavy tribute. It was a crippling obligation which he could not evade, because the Romans had carried off a number of Syrians as hostages, including one of the king's sons, who later became Antiochus IV

(1 Macc. 1:10). Antiochus III thus found himself seriously short of money and was scarcely able to pay his army of mercenaries. Necessity drove him to plundering the temples, which had long been the repositories of considerable wealth. Three years after his defeat, he was assassinated while trying to appropriate the treasures of a temple in Elam.

His son and successor, Seleucus IV (187–175 B.C.) had no option but to act likewise. Under him the first attempt was made to claim the treasures of the Temple in Jerusalem as the property

This painting well illustrates the comment in 2 Maccabees 4 : 12: "for with alacrity he [the high priest Jason] founded a gymnasium right under the citadel, and he induced the noblest of the young men to wear the Greek hat" (the *petasos*, a broad-brimmed felt hat). This means that these young men had adopted Hellenistic culture and frequented the gymnasium. Along with the *petasos* went the *chlamys*, the short cloak which left much of the legs uncovered. Originally, this costume had been worn in Greece especially by travellers. Hermes, the god of travellers, was depicted in it. When Hermes became the god of the gymnasium, the broad hat and short cloak became the symbol of the new culture in Jerusalem. This portrait adorns the inner surface of a drinking vessel of ca. 500 B.C.

The wilderness of Judah lies between a line from Jerusalem to Hebron and the Dead Sea. Although it is called a wilderness, the landscape of this region is very varied. The Hebrew word *midbar*, usually translated as 'wilderness,' 'desert,' has a much wider meaning, therefore. It was a name given to a larger or smaller area in which people had no settled abode and where sowing and harvesting were impossible; one simply passed through it. Whether there were sandy plains, steep and craggy rock formations, or bare hills was neither here nor there. The wilderness of Judah in fact had all these types of landscape. The terrain was a favourite haunt, therefore, of rebels and bandits. David roamed it for several years (1 Sam. 22ff), and the Maccabees used it (1 Macc. 2 : 29) as a base for their forays against the Syrian troops.

of the state. According to the legendary account in 2 Maccabees 3:1-40, however, the enterprise failed, and he too was assassinated. Seleucus was succeeded by his brother, Antiochus IV (175–164 B.C.), who had just been released by the Romans. This ruler acted so foolishly that the conflict between Hellenism and Jewry now exploded with full force.

A variety of political and religious factors determined the origin and course of the ensuing struggle. The Seleucid ideal of a world empire could no longer be realized by expansion in a westerly direction. Through his enforced stay in Rome Antiochus was too well acquainted with the power of that state even to attempt to move in the direction of Greece again. His aspirations were therefore of necessity directed towards gaining control of Egypt. In such a policy Palestine was of great strategic importance, for if that territory were not firmly under Antiochus's control, any assault on Egypt would be risky in the extreme. In addition, the fabulous wealth of the Temple at Jerusalem could help considerably in financing his military and cultural enterprises. The principal motive for his actions, however, was the Hellenistic ideal he had inherited from his father. He considered himself a god in human guise, and as a consequence

adopted the name of 'Epiphanes.' This explains why he fastened his attention on such a tiny place as Judah. It was a Jewish island, so to speak, in an ocean of Hellenism, a black spot on the white vesture of the new culture and civilization.

Despite his superior strength, Antiochus's policy for Judah miscarried completely. This was due just as much to the religious convictions of the Jews who resisted him as to the military skill of the men who led these Jews. But there were also other factors. The Romans in the west and the Parthians in the east remained persistent threats to the Syrian empire, so that Syria's main fighting force was usually committed somewhere in Mesopotamia. The clashes with the Jewish rebels in the mountains of Judah were merely local incidents. Moreover, in its final stages Syria had no stable government. Revolutions repeatedly broke out, making any effective action against Judah all but impossible.

When Antiochus IV first came to power he probably thought that the task of hellenizing Judah would present little or no difficulty. Among the Jews themselves there were in fact quite a large number in favour of this. Thus, in 174 B.C., he was able to depose the conservative High Priest, Onias, and replace him with one of Onias's brothers, who had promised him large sums of money. The fact that this man bore the Greek name of Jason shows where his sympathies lay (2 Macc. 4:7-14). The new High Priest at once set about building a gymnasium (of which, however, no trace has so far been discovered), and the extent to which the individualistic temper of Hellenism had already found acceptance in Jerusalem soon became apparent. People immediately proceeded to adopt the new style of dress, and many of the younger ones took to wearing the *petasos*, a broad-brimmed hat familiar as the headgear of Hermes, the tutelary god of the gymnasium. To the indignation of the conservatives the long robe customary in the orient was discarded in favour of the short Greek tunic, which left the legs bare.

The new conception of the dignity of the human body and the emphasis on the physical side of man's nature was popularized in the very streets of Jerusalem. Old and young alike seem to have been infected with enthusiasm for these new ideas, according to the author of 2 Maccabees, who writes: "There was such an extreme of hellenization and increase in the adoption of foreign ways because of the surpassing wickedness of Jason, who was ungodly and no High Priest, that the priests were no longer intent upon their service at the altar. Despising the sanctuary and neglecting the sacrifices, they hastened to take part in the unlawful proceedings in the wrestling arena after the call to the discus." (2 Macc. 4:13-14)

The changes introduced by Jason went no further, however. He confined his activities to purely cultural matters, and was

The mound known as Tell Abil, which conceals the ruins of the ancient Abel-beth-maacah (2 Sam. 20 : 14-22; 1 Kings 15 : 20, 2 Kings 15 : 29), lies 4½ miles north-west of Tell el-Qadi, site of the Biblical Dan. Both towns stood at the foot of Mount Hermon, in the valley where lie the sources of the Jordan. A place somewhat further east, near the Syrian Baniyas, has been identified as Paneion, the sanctuary of the god Pan. Near here in 200 B.C. there took place the decisive engagement between the Ptolemaic ruler and the Seleucid king which resulted in the tiny country of Judah being caught up in the tidal wave of Hellenism. Tell Abil has still not been excavated.

only a lukewarm supporter of Syrian foreign policy. For Antiochus IV this was reason enough for deposing him and bestowing the office on a certain Menelaus, who was probably not even descended from the priestly stock of Aaron, but who had offered him still larger sums of money. There were now three High Priests—Onias, Jason, and Menelaus—each claiming a legitimate right to the office and each supported by mutually antagonistic parties of followers. The unrest caused by these internal dissensions did not, however, flare up into open rebellion until some time later, so that Antiochus was able to proceed for the time being with his plans of aggrandizement.

In 174 B.C., with Menelaus as his ally in Judah, he marched into Egypt. At first the tide of battle flowed in his favour, but when in 168 B.C. the Roman fleet appeared unexpectedly at the mouth of the Nile (Dan. 11:30), Antiochus retired without so much as offering a fight. After this loss of prestige the Syrian ruler had to re-direct his attention to Judah. Even before the failure of the Egyptian campaign Menelaus had been deposed by Jason, and Antiochus had been obliged to re-instate his protégé forcibly. But he had also taken advantage of the situation to rob the Temple of its treasures, and it was probably this action more than any other which led to the first outbreaks of rebellion in Judah. In order to quell these and to obtain a firm hold on Jerusalem Antiochus ordered his troops to occupy the Temple fortress. They remained there throughout the years of the uprising which was to follow. It was not, in fact, until 141 B.C. that Judah was able to recapture the fortress and could cease to regard it as a symbol of its subservience.

Antiochus's next move was to enforce the state cult of Hellenism. The Temple at Jerusalem was consecrated to the Greek god, Olympian Zeus, and the Samaritan sanctuary on Mount Gerizim was given over to the worship of Zeus, the Friend of Strangers (1 Macc. 1:54; 2 Macc. 6:2). As the king held

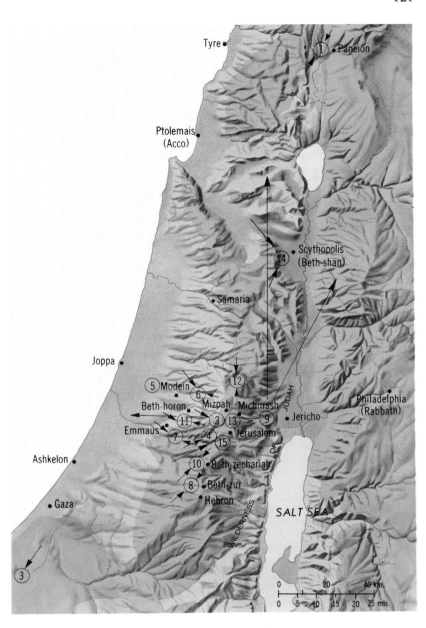

The course of the Maccabean Revolt

1. 200: The Seleucids overthrew the military power of Egypt at Paneion. Palestine and Jerusalem came under Syrian domination.
2. 174: The Syrian king appointed the Hellenist, Menelaus, High Priest in Jerusalem.
3. 174-168: Antiochus IV waged a successful war with Egypt; but the Romans prevented his further advance.
4. 168: Syrian troops occupied the Temple fortress. The Hellenistic state religion was introduced.
5. 167: Mattathias and his sons started a revolt at Modein.
6. 166: Judas defeated a division of the Syrian army near Beth-horon.
7. 165: In two stages Judas defeated at Emmaus the Syrian troops despatched to put down the insurgents.
8. 164: Indecisive battle between the rebels and a Syrian army at Beth-zur. Judas purified the Temple.
9. 163: The Maccabees made a number of raids into Galilee, trans-Jordan, and the coastal plain, in order to protect the Jews living there.
10. 162: The insurgents failed to check the Syrian army at Beth-zechariah and withdrew into Jerusalem.
11. 160: Judas defeated Nicanor and his army at Beth-horon.
12. 160: Judas fell in battle, north of Jerusalem. The insurgents very soon united under Jonathan, who settled in at Michmash.
13. 153: Jonathan ensconced himself in Jerusalem.
14. 145: Jonathan attempted to halt the advancing Syrians at Beth-shan. He agreed to peace negotiations and was made prisoner at Ptolemais.
15. 143: A Syrian army tried to take Jerusalem; but bad weather conditions prevented it. Simon became High Priest, commander-in-chief, and leader of the Jewish nation.

himself to be an incarnation of Zeus, this act amounted to imposing upon the Jews the cult of the ruler, which in their eyes was an abominable sacrilege. At the same time festivals in honour of Dionysus and the Dionysiac mysteries were probably introduced, with all the orgiastic behaviour associated with the cult of this god (2 Macc. 6:6).

The king further promulgated a number of inhibitive laws. The sabbath and other Jewish feasts were abolished (1 Macc. 1:45; 2 Macc. 6:6), the dietary laws were annulled, and the Jews were compelled to eat the flesh of pigs consumed at pagan sacrificial meals (1 Macc. 1:47; 2 Macc. 6–7). Circumcision, the token of the covenant with God, was also forbidden (1 Macc. 1:48; 2 Macc. 6–7). The passing of yet another law, which made it a punishable offence to possess sacred scrolls suggests that the dissemination of sacred texts had already taken place on such a scale that the Syrians saw it as a real threat to the hellenizing of Judah. It may fairly be assumed that in the course of this religious war certain textual traditions were permanently obliterated, but it probably also encouraged the establishment of an authoritative corpus of writings.

Revolt was inevitable. Since the occupation forces were stationed chiefly in the towns, the rebellion broke out in the countryside.

It began in the small village of Modein, now thought to have stood about 19 miles north-west of Jerusalem. A Syrian official and a Jew, about to offer sacrifice on a pagan altar, were killed by a priest called Mattathias and his five sons. This was the signal for a general uprising. As this particular village had an exposed situation on the edge of the coastal plain, the rebels could not remain there with safety. Like David, centuries before them, they fled into the wilderness of Judah, where the fantastic rock formations, twisting wadis, and hidden caves offered an excellent hiding-place.

Mattathias and his family were joined by a number of zealous Jews, who took their women and children with them. A more or less official seal was set on the rebellion when it was joined by a group calling themselves 'Chasidim' (Hasideans), or 'the pious ones.' Unfortunately, we know little more about them than their name, which is said to derive from the fact that they drew strength for their faith from the accounts of those of their forbears who had put their trust solely in God. However, there is also some reason for thinking that their hopes and expectations were coloured by the apocalyptic views which we first encounter in the Book of Daniel, written during this period.

The first clash between the Syrian soldiery and the rebels turned out badly for the latter. Prompted perhaps by Jews who were favourably disposed towards Hellenism, the Syrians employed the strategem of waiting for the sabbath before they attacked. The uncompromising devotees of the law then simply allowed themselves to be killed off (1 Macc. 2:31ff). This tragic event required that a major step be taken to accommodate the law to the harsh facts of life. From then on, people used force in self-defence, even on the sabbath.

Mattathias died in 166 B.C., and his son Judas took his place as leader. As he was not the eldest son, he must have possessed exceptional gifts as a fighter. Judas's followers gave him the nickname of 'the Maccabee.' Its meaning is uncertain, but it may be connected with the Hebrew word for a hammer. At all events Judas's personality made such an impression that his name came to be traditionally attached to the whole family of Mattathias, and the revolt which he now led came to be known as the Maccabean revolt.

Judas led the rebellion for only six years, yet he crowded the events of a lifetime into that short period. The author of 1 Maccabees ends his account of Judas's career thus: "Now the rest of the acts of Judas, and his wars and the brave deeds that he did, and his greatness, have not been recorded, for they were very many." (1 Macc. 9:22) Although such an editorial comment is a customary form of ending—witness also the conclusion to the Fourth Gospel (John 21:25)—it contains a core of truth.

In the year 166 B.C. the situation did not look at all favourable for Judah. As a result of the rebellion, hellenization was being forced on the Jewish people with considerable brutality. The only possibility open to the tiny band of rebels, poorly armed as they were, was to try to undermine the military strength of the occupying power by guerilla action. So long as Judas's men could avoid an open encounter with the Syrians in the plain, they had the advantage. They had at their disposal people who knew how to find a way through the mountain country, even by night. Successful actions in the vicinity of Beth-horon and of Mizpah, followed by an inconclusive engagement at Beth-zur left the way open for Judas to occupy Jerusalem.

He marched on the city and purged the Temple by putting an end to all idolatrous practices. The event was subsequently commemorated annually by the Feast of the Dedication of the Temple. The religious nature of the struggle is evinced by the fact that Judas did not expel the Syrian occupiers of the Temple fortress. The Jews were apparently too accustomed to centuries of subservience to consider the immediate possibility of political autonomy. Circumstances were only gradually to change what was a religious movement into a political action.

The growing power of the rebels caused disquiet among the Hellenists in the surrounding districts. In trans-Jordan, Galilee, and the coastal areas, in fact everywhere where Jews were living, they became the victims of oppression. The Maccabees hastened to the assistance of their co-religionists. They carried out a number of successful raids into these territories, rescuing the persecuted Jews and bringing them back to Judah. These successes added greatly to the popularity of the cause. As a result, the number of fighting men available was continually on the increase, and the frequent calls for help meant that the army had to be kept in a constant state of readiness.

When in 164 B.C. Antiochus IV perished in the struggle with the Parthians, Judas ventured to lay siege to the Temple fortress. The new king, Antiochus V (164–162 B.C.), realized that this was the final step toward independence. He entered Judah at the head of his army from a south-westerly direction. Against such superior strength the rebels failed to hold their own at Beth-zechariah, and were forced to seek shelter within the walls of Jerusalem. The Syrians then invested the city, and the end of the rebellion seemed to be near. However, the matter was settled by the outbreak of a rebellion in Syria itself. The king made a hasty settlement with the Jews. He gave them official permission to live 'after the Jewish fashion,' and withdrew his army.

But the peace did not last long. The man responsible for stirring up fresh trouble was a certain Alcimus, leader of the

The town of Beth-shan lay 16 miles south of the Sea of Galilee. The mound, known nowadays as Tell el-Hosn, stands about 130 feet high, and shows that the town had a long history behind it. Excavation has revealed that people have been living there since the Chalcolithic Age. In the Hellenistic period the place was called Scythopolis, 'city of the Scythians'; and it was the principal town of the Decapolis. Many eastern cities which were hellenized had no room on their acropolis for public buildings such as a gymnasium, theatre, and stadium; and that is why the theatre in this instance lies to the south-east of the mound itself.

Hellenistic party among the Jews. When a new ruler, Demetrius I (162–150 B.C.), had come to the throne, Alcimus betook himself to Antioch and devised with the king a scheme for hellenizing Judah. Having then been appointed High Priest, he returned to Jerusalem to put his claims into practice. It was not long before the resistance of the orthodox party flared up into open rebellion. The Syrian king then dispatched a certain Nicanor to Jerusalem with an army. After several minor engagements the decisive encounter took place at Beth-horon. Luck was with the rebels, and Nicanor was killed during their first assault. The Syrian forces panicked and fled.

It might have been expected that such a victory would put new heart into the insurgents, but oddly enough the opposite was the case. More and more of his soldiers left Judas, probably because they realized that complete victory over Syria was after all an impossibility. Moreover, Judas's men were not mercenaries like the Syrian soldiery. They were volunteers, ordinary fathers of families, who had already spent many years trekking through the mountains. These people longed to return to their homes and families and look after their possessions. Thus Judas's army became smaller and smaller. In the year 160 B.C. the end came. In a final engagement the Syrians' superior strength proved to be too great, and Judas fought until he was killed. His followers scattered in all directions.

Those who supported the Maccabees suffered great hardship. All power was now in the hands of the High Priest, Alcimus, and he persecuted them whenever and wherever he could. In this way he hoped to remove all opposition to the Hellenistic reform once and for all. But their misery simply induced the orthodox Jews to close ranks once more, this time under the leadership of Judas's brother Jonathan (160–143 B.C.). Jonathan avoided as much as possible encountering the Syrian troops in the open and contented himself with making raids from his base in the wilderness of Judah. Through a combination of his own wiliness and a series of favourable circumstances he soon found himself in a strong position. In 159 B.C. Alcimus died, and as a result the Hellenistic party lost much of its influence. Moreover, the Syrian ruler was in no position to concern himself overmuch with Judah, since other parts of his empire were just then demanding his attention. Thus for a time the Jews were left unmolested. The author of 1 Maccabees writes of this period: "Thus the sword ceased from Israel. And Jonathan dwelt in Michmash. And Jonathan began to judge the people, and he destroyed the ungodly out of Israel." (1 Macc. 9:73)

Jonathan found himself in an even more favourable position when in 153 B.C. two factions in Syria began contending for power. Since both claimants to the throne tried to win Jonathan's support, they both acknowledged him as leader of all the Jews

124

The landscape in the vicinity of Beth-horon. The easiest line of advance toward Jerusalem from the coastal plain passes through Beth-horon and Emmaus. The country there changes quite gradually from level plain to mountainous terrain; and one can soon reach the table-land north of Jerusalem. From there the way to the capital lies open. It is not surprising, therefore, that the Syrian troops several times attempted to approach Jerusalem by this route. As the Maccabeans realized that they would not be able to contain the Syrian army on the plateau north of Jerusalem, they launched their counter-attack in the hills around Beth-horon and Emmaus, before chariots and cavalry were in any position to play a decisive role in the battle.

and appointed him as High Priest. Jonathan thereupon took up residence in Jerusalem and fortified the city, and the Jews now appeared to have a considerable measure of independence. Jonathan had backed the stronger side in the Syrian quarrel, and was thus able to maintain power and preserve peace in Judah up to 145 B.C. In this year, however, a new ruler arose in Syria, who was hostile to Jonathan and his government. With his army he marched as far as Beth-shan, south of the Sea of Galilee, where he encountered Jonathan and pretended to make him an offer of peace. Jonathan accepted it and went with a small retinue to Ptolemais to celebrate the agreement. Once he was in their hands, however, the Syrians made him a prisoner.

Jonathan's elder brother, Simon, immediately took charge in Jerusalem (143–134 B.C.). He was probably only too eager to assume the leadership. For years he had been obliged to take second place under his younger brothers Judas and Jonathan. Now his time had come at last. When the Syrians approached Jerusalem with Jonathan as a hostage, Simon did not greatly exert himself to rescue his brother. He did attempt to block the enemy's approach to Jerusalem, but in this he was only partly successful. Finally, unusual weather conditions came to Simon's assistance. According to the account in 1 Maccabees 13:20-23 it snowed so heavily during one particular night that the enemy cavalry were unable to make any further advance. The Syrian

commander thereupon ceased to give battle. He had Jonathan put to death and made his way back to Antioch. This gave Simon time and opportunity to consolidate his power. He fortified several towns and built a number of forts. In the end weakness obliged Syria to yield to Judah's demand for independence. This is reflected in the words of the author of 1 Maccabees: "...the people began to write in their documents and contracts, 'In the first year of Simon the great high priest and commander and leader of the Jews.'" (13:42) After four and a half centuries Judah had, for a brief period, regained her autonomy.

2. THE KINGDOM OF THE HASMONEANS

Simon first directed his attention to the Temple fortress. This building, at the north-west angle of the Temple courtyard, was still held by an occupying force of Syrians–a symbol of the military power of the north. Now that Judah had become more or less independent, the presence of these foreign troops was no longer tolerated. The king of Syria could not come to their aid, because more serious matters demanded his attention. The warlike Parthians were attacking from the east, and there were disturbances at home. The Jews therefore had very little difficulty in expelling the garrison, which for some time past had been left to fend for itself. Once this had been accomplished, the city was firmly in Simon's hands.

The fight for religious freedom having now been won, the Jews became more and more concerned with consolidating their political power. Simon began by restoring the links with Rome and Sparta which had already been established by his predecessors. The Romans welcomed his advances, for this strengthened their influence in the Near East. It was a policy that to begin with protected Judah from Syria, but the Romans were not content simply to remain on good terms indefinitely. Less than a hundred years later Judah, too, was to fall victim to this western power and its lust for conquest. As a result, however, a situation was created which was to be highly favourable to the spread of Christianity and the formation of the New Testament.

For the time being, Simon was able to extend his sphere of influence. He captured and permanently occupied Joppa. This action indicates that the Maccabeans were at last strong enough to leave the shelter of the mountains and move into the coastal plain, in contrast to the time when according to 1 Maccabees, King Demetrius II had accused Jonathan of being afraid to engage in an open fight: "Why do you assume authority against us in the hill country? If you now have confidence in your forces, come down to the plain to meet us, and let us match strength with each other there." (1 Macc. 10:70-71) With the conquest of Joppa, Judah acquired a sallyport which gave it access to the eastern end of the Mediterranean Sea. As a result, its contact with the culture of this region was intensified, and at the same time closer ties were formed with the Jews of the Diaspora. It is characteristic of the new situation that Simon conquered the area with troops consisting chiefly of mercenaries. The army of enthusiastic volunteers drawn from the people, which under Judas and Jonathan had fought for the right to practise their own religion, was becoming smaller and smaller.

When Judah had once more established its right to certain territories, the question naturally arose as to who should govern the country when the elderly Simon, the last of the Maccabees, died. It was probably Simon himself who saw to it that the necessary arrangements were made, although tradition suggests that he neglected to deal with the matter. According to 1 Maccabees 14:25-49, the people acted to safeguard the future by 'spontaneously' recognizing the position held by Simon as a right in perpetuity. Thus the principle of hereditary succession was once again accepted in Israel, and it was possible for a new dynasty to emerge. The rulers who sprang from this line later came to be known as the Hasmoneans, because, according to the Jewish historian Flavius Josephus (ca. A.D. 37–100), Simon's grandfather had borne the name of Hasmon.

Even Simon died a violent death. Urged on by the Syrian king, the commander in charge of the fortress of Dok, near Jericho, who was a son-in-law of Simon's, aimed at taking over power. The opportunity to do so occurred when Simon and two of his sons were visiting the fortress .The visitors were murdered while eating. Even so, the rebellion miscarried. Simon's third son, John Hyrcanus (134–104 B.C.), happened to be in the town of Gezer, west of Jerusalem, at the moment when the outrage was committed. When he heard the news of the murder, he proceeded immediately to Jerusalem, where he was straightway acknowledged to be the lawful successor. At that moment the

Syrians arrived to give active aid to his brother-in-law. As John had not been able to organize the country's defence in time, he had no alternative but to withdraw behind the walls of Jerusalem. The Syrians laid siege to the city, and the newly founded Hasmonean dynasty would have come to a sudden and untimely end, if the Romans had not intervened. Their power in the Near East had already increased to such an extent that a word from them was sufficient to induce the Syrians to raise the siege.

The power therefore remained in John's hands. As a soldier he had undoubted talents and was able to establish his authority throughout the country. During his long reign he even managed to enlarge the kingdom to a considerable extent. In trans-Jordan

Palestine under the Hasmoneans

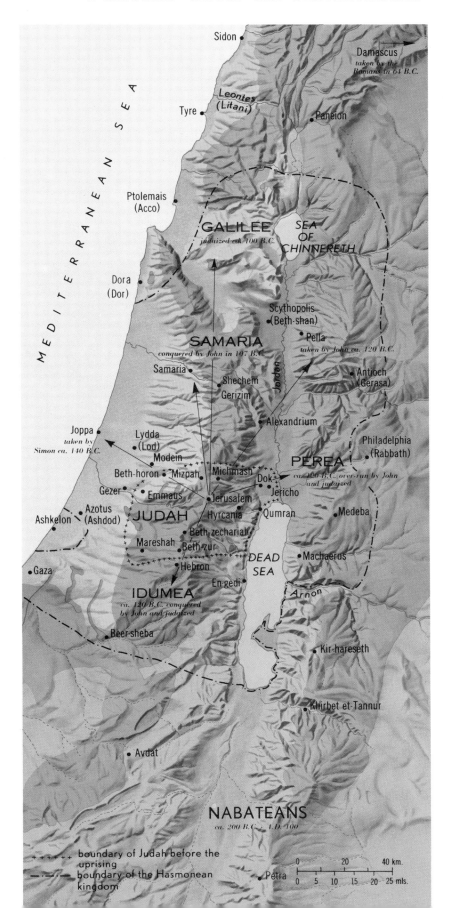

he subdued the district north of the Arnon, capturing, among other places, the town of Medeba. To the south he annexed Idumea to his kingdom. The inhabitants of this region, descendants of the earlier Edomites, were obliged to accept and observe the Jewish law and were forcibly circumcised. This had important consequences for later developments in the New Testament period, for it enabled an eminent family from Idumea to acquire a position of importance in the Jewish state. Less than a hundred years later a descendant of this family was to become, with the approval of the Romans, king of Judah, and to be known to history as Herod the Great.

John's troops also pressed northward. About 125 B.C. he conquered Shechem and destroyed the Samaritan sanctuary on Mount Gerizim. In 107 B.C. he even succeeded after a protracted siege in capturing the city of Samaria itself. When he died in 104 B.C., he was succeeded by his son, Aristobulus. The dynasty now seemed to be so firmly established that he was able to adopt the title of king. It was during the brief reign of Aristobulus that the process of assimilating the population of Galilee to Judaism was begun. In earlier times Simon the Maccabee had had to fetch a number of Jews from Galilee to Judah, because they were a minority in the north and could not be given sufficient protection (1 Macc. 5:16-23). Now that the Hasmoneans were much stronger and Syria had hardly any authority left in Galilee, the judaization of this district presented little or no difficulty. Numerous synagogues were built, itinerant Pharisees instructed the people, and Galilee, which at one time had been known as the land of the heathen, rapidly became a place where the Jewish religion and way of life were taken almost more seriously than in Judah itself. At a later period this helped to make it a fertile breeding-ground for Christianity and a centre of fanatical resistance during the Jewish uprisings against the Romans.

Aristobulus died after a reign lasting only a year, and was succeeded by his brother, Alexander Janneus (103–76 B.C.). Unfortunately, the conduct of this ruler served to widen the breach which had for some time past been growing between the Hasmonean royal house and the orthodox party, a group now known as the Pharisees. The conflict had probably begun back in the days of the last Maccabees, and John Hyrcanus had almost certainly helped to increase the feeling of hostility. The mere fact that he gave his sons Greek names suggests that he had a certain sympathy for Hellenistic culture. For the Pharisees, with their wholehearted devotion to the Law, the power and prestige of the Hasmoneans must have seemed intolerable. They had dared to call themselves kings, although they had no connection at all with the family of David. Even their high priesthood was considered unlawful. Their ancestor Mattathias had belonged to a priestly family, it is true, but he was not of the lineage of Aaron.

The Pharisees might perhaps have accepted this untoward situation as a necessary but temporary evil, had they not been provoked by Alexander's style of living. To their mind his behaviour was scandalous. It no longer conformed in any way with the aims of the Maccabean rebellion. Despite his high priestly office and the dignity it conferred on him Alexander did not observe a single requirement of the law. Open resistance to him, however, was hardly possible, since he had an army of mercenaries at his disposal. He also dealt severely with rebels and is said to have put hundreds of Pharisees to death on one occa-

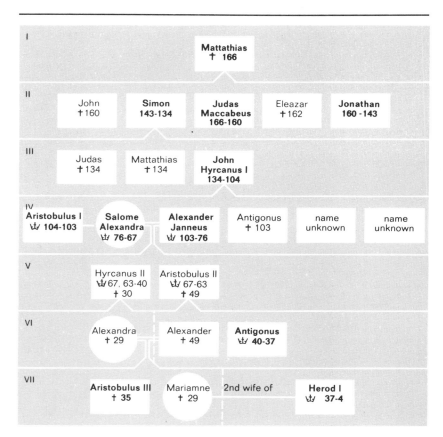

The house of Maccabees and Hasmoneans. The rectangles enclose males and the circles females.

Mattathias and his five sons are classed as Maccabees. Mattathias, Judas, Jonathan, and Simon were successively the leaders of the insurrectionist movement.

Beginning with Simon's son, John Hyrcanus I, the family are known as the Hasmoneans. There ruled over the Jews, in succession, John Hyrcanus I, Aristobulus I, Alexander Janneus, Alexandra, Hyrcanus II, and Aristobulus II. With the arrival of the Romans, Hyrcanus II was permitted to act once more as High Priest. During the Parthian invasion (40-37) Antigonus acquired the status of king. With help from the Romans Herod the Great succeeded in expelling this last Hasmonean ruler. Aristobulus III was allowed to discharge his role as High Priest for a further year; then Herod had him assassinated too.

sion. Besides the army the Hasmonean family also possessed a number of forts which they had had built at strategic points. Jerusalem was secured by a ring of these strongholds. The main bulwarks were Machaerus, Hyrcania, Dok, Alexandrium, Bethzur, and Gezer. As beacons formed a communication-system between all these forts, the Hasmoneans, and later on Herod the Great, were able to keep the reins of power firmly in their grasp.

Realizing that latent opposition among the people constituted a considerable danger to his successor, Alexander advised his consort Alexandra (76–67 B.C.), to come to terms with the Pharisees after his death. Acting upon his advice she sidetracked her energetic son, Aristobulus II, and appointed her other son, Hyrcanus II, to the office of High Priest. In this way she won the support of the opposing party. Hyrcanus was a feeble personality and the Pharisees were now able to have a greater say in the conduct of religious matters. It was a position which they never again surrendered. For those who were opposed to the orthodox party this reversal of fortune was hard to bear, for it meant that they had lost their own position of influence. As long as the queen remained in control, however, the country was quiet.

After the death of Alexandra the conflict broke out afresh, and this time it was eventually to lead to the downfall of the whole Jewish state. First of all, Aristobulus II made a successful bid for power. He established himself as both king and High Priest, as his father had done before him. He took his brother Hyrcanus prisoner, and refused to release him until the latter had sworn to submit to his authority. This might have been the end of the matter, if a certain Idumean called Antipater had not also had pretensions to power. Some time earlier, when the district was being forcibly converted to Judaism, Alexander Janneus had made this man's father governor of Idumea. Seeing his own chances of self-aggrandizement threatened by the energetic Aristobulus, Antipater supported the deposed Hyrcanus in secret, and one day escaped with him to the Nabatean capital of Petra. The Nabateans had been trying for some time to extend their power to the north-west, in order to gain control of the trade routes in this area. Antipater had little difficulty, therefore, in persuading the ruler of the country to march with Hyrcanus and himself against Jerusalem. Because Aristobulus had not as yet sufficiently consolidated his strength, he could not check the enemy's advance and was forced to take refuge behind the city walls.

This turn of events caused havoc in the internal affairs of the Jewish state. There were now three contending parties. Within the city, Aristobulus was entrenched with his following of priests and most of the leading Jewish families. Outside, Hyrcanus and Antipater were joined together with the Nabateans. The third party consisted of the Pharisees and their followers, who would have preferred to see the defeat of both these Hasmoneans. Aristobulus was well aware that without outside help he would not be able to withstand a siege for very long. For this reason he betook himself to Damascus, which had just been occupied by a Roman army under the command of Pompey.

The other two parties also sought help from the Roman general, however. The Pharisees asked him to abolish the kingship in Judah and re-establish the kind of theocratic constitution which had existed in the time of Ezra and the Maccabees. They hoped that in this way the Law would regain its former dignity and prestige. Pompey finally decided to grant them their wish, but the result was very different from what they had expected. First he sent a messenger to the Nabatean king ordering him to vacate Judah. Next, he moved in with his own army, took the dangerous Aristobulus captive, and sent him to Rome. The weak and pliable Hyrcanus was then once more permitted to act as High Priest, albeit with certain stipulations.

The territory he governed was severely reduced in size, and only those districts that were preponderantly Jewish came under his administration, Judah with Idumea, Perea beyond the Jordan, and Galilee were all that remained of the Hasmonean kingdom, and even these districts came under the supreme authority of Rome. Since Palestine was of great strategic value to the Romans in maintaining their position in the Near East, the whole area was counted as part of the province of Syria. Only in matters of religion did the Jews continue to have any degree of autonomy, and even this was undermined by the weakness of Hyrcanus as High Priest, which simply reinforced the position of the stronger man, the Idumean Antipater, and created a situation which later enabled his son, Herod the Great, to rise to power.

3. THE LITERATURE OF THE MACCABEAN AND HASMONEAN PERIODS

During the period of the Maccabean war a remarkable book was written which might be described as the typical literary product of a resistance movement. It came to be known as the Book of Daniel, not because a prophet of this name wrote it, but because he is its principal character. It must have appeared some time between the years 167 and 164 B.C., for the writer speaks of the war with the Syrians as being still in progress and of Antiochus IV as still being alive. This is evident, for example, from the passages in which he mentions "the abomination that makes desolate" (Dan. 11:31; 12:11; cf. 8:13; 9:27). The reference here is to the pagan cult in honour of Olympian Zeus, which Antiochus IV introduced and Judas terminated prior to the death of Antiochus.

Although the actual writing of the Book of Daniel can be dated fairly precisely, its contents raise a considerable number of problems. The first six chapters contain various stories about what happens to Daniel and his three friends in Babylon. They are persecuted by the heathen for their loyalty to God and, more

The fortress of Dok, where Simon the Maccabee was murdered by his son-in-law in 134, must have been located in the vicinity of Jericho. The mountain peak which dominates the whole area to the west of the town is the most likely spot. On the summit are the remains of an ancient church, partly restored some years ago by the monks of a monastery built against the mountain-side. In the foreground is part of the Tell es-Sultan, the mound formed by the rubble of ancient Jericho. A considerable part of the remains of the archaeological work carried out between 1952 and 1958 has already been washed away by the winter rains.

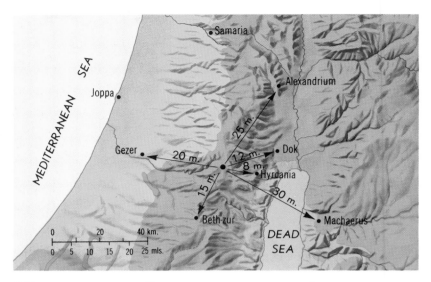

Hasmonean fortresses around Jerusalem

Dok: The fortress must have been situated a little to the west of Jericho, quite possibly on the top of the slope against which there now stands a Greek Orthodox monastery. It was here that the Maccabee Simon was murdered with two of his sons in 134 B.C.

Alexandrium: Alexander Janneus (103-76) built this fortress on a summit overlooking the spot where the Wadi Far'ah (a route through the hills) joins the Jordan valley.

Hyrcania: John Hyrcanus (134-105) built this fortress in the northern part of the Wilderness of Judah so that it would, with that at Dok, protect the eastern approaches to Jerusalem. Herod the Great used this fort as a prison.

Machaerus: Alexander Janneus constructed this fort on a mountain-top on the eastern shore of the Dead Sea to provide a defence against the Nabateans pressing up from the south. Tradition identifies this as the place where John the Baptist was beheaded.

Gezer: This town was heavily fortified as early as the Amarna period (ca. 1400 B.C.). It stood on a strategic eminence at the western edge of the central highlands and thus commanded the coastal plain.

Beth-zur: The name signifies 'house of rock.' There was a strong fortress at this place even in the Hyksos period (ca. 1600 B.C.). It commanded the southern approaches to Jerusalem.

particularly, their strict observance of the Jewish dietary laws, but God rewards them for their faithfulness by intervening at the crucial moment and saving them by a miracle. The subject-matter of the next six chapters is quite different, and is concerned with Daniel's interpretation of a series of enigmatic visions. He sees the whole course of world events as strongly influenced by the powers of evil. The culmination comes with the desecration of the Temple by Antiochus IV. After such an act only God's personal intervention can bring about the establishment of a kingdom of righteousness and peace.

In spite of the allusions to Antiochus and the war with Syria, everything that happens in the Book of Daniel is described as taking place in Babylon during the reigns of Nebuchadnezzar, Belshazzar, Darius the Mede, and Cyrus of Persia. As a result the authorship of this book was attributed by the Christian Church for many centuries to a prophet called Daniel, who was supposed to have foretold the course of history during and immediately after the Exile. He thus came to be known as one of the four major prophets, and the book which bears his name was placed after Isaiah, Jeremiah, and Ezekiel. Jewish tradition, however, placed it among the 'Writings,' in other words, works which were not regarded as being primarily historical.

A good deal of what it presents as history is indeed improbable. It may be questioned, for instance, whether King Nebuchadnezzar ever acknowledged the God of the Jews as the sole power in heaven and on earth (Dan. 2:47; 3:29; 4:28ff). Nor is there any known fact to support the idea that Nebuchadnezzar suffered from fits of madness (Dan. 4:30ff). In all probability this story reflects the popular view of the peculiar behaviour of King Nabonidus in switching his residence from Babylon to the oasis of Teima. Again, Belshazzar was not the son of Nebuchadnezzar (Dan. 5:2) but of Nabonidus, and furthermore, he was never king. As crown prince and governor he administered the kingdom for his father, but King Nabonidus had already resumed the reins of government before the fall of Babylon. Lastly, King Darius was no Mede but a Persian, and it was not he but Cyrus who conquered Babylon (Dan. 5:30). Such crass inaccuracies cannot be laid at the door of an educated Jew living in the first half of the sixth century, even though there are some things in this book which point to a reasonable degree of familiarity with the period round about the year 500 B.C.

Apart from the contents of the book the language in which it is written offers some peculiarities. The author starts in Hebrew, switches at Daniel 2:4 to Aramaic, and then from Daniel 8:1 onwards uses Hebrew again. If the narrative section (chs. 1–6) had been in Aramaic and the visions (chs. 7–12) in Hebrew, there would be an obvious explanation for the change. As this is not the case, we are faced with something of a puzzle. The solution offered by many Biblical scholars nowadays is as follows. During the Persian period there arose a number of Aramaic folk-tales in which a popular religious figure called Daniel was the leading character. In the course of the third century most of these legends were collected and combined to form a single narrative.

Later on, in the early stages of the struggle with Hellenism, an unknown author composed several visionary accounts of the eventual destruction of evil, woven around this same figure. Because the revival of nationalism had to some extent restored the popularity of Hebrew, these visions, with the exception of the first, were written in the language of Israel. Later on again, in the course of the Maccabean rebellion, another writer reworked this material, expanding it and putting the whole emphasis on the struggle with Antiochus IV. He began to translate the original collection of stories into Hebrew, but gave up because time was pressing and he regarded his message as of more consequence than the language in which it was written.

Whether or not this is an accurate reconstruction of its composition, the Book of Daniel is the first that can properly be called apocalyptic, and its effect on the Jewish community was very considerable. According to modern ideas the method pursued by the apocalyptic writers was a curious one. They set their message within an artificial framework. We are asked to believe that some well-known religious leader of an earlier period (Enoch, Abraham, Moses, Isaiah, Ezra, Daniel, and others) had made a record of disclosures about the future, which God had given him in the form of visions, and that the book in question had then been lost or hidden away for many years. In fact, the apocalyptic books do not contain any detailed predictions: they are 'emblematic' accounts of the past. With this background as their starting-point these writers made prognostications of the imminent future in enigmatic visions which foreshadowed the decisive battle between good and evil.

It was the desperate situation of the Jewish people in the final centuries of its existence that obliged the apocalyptists to adopt this manner of writing. They had a precedent for it in the prophets (for example, Amos, Ezekiel, and Deutero-Zechariah) who had expressed their message partly in visions. At the time when Jewish life and thought was in danger of being swamped by Hellenistic culture and the power of Rome there no longer were any prophets; and yet there was now a greater need than ever for authoritative utterances that would affirm the old, consoling doctrine that God was the lord of history, that in the end the hostile powers would lose the battle, and that the pious Jews would find deliverance.

This was the aim and purpose of the Book of Daniel too. It was intended to encourage the resistance-fighters. Daniel and his three friends were a heartening example to the orthodox Jews who kept the food laws and refused to worship the Hellenistic gods. The visions served to reinforce their belief in the approaching victory. In the persecution practised by Antiochus IV the power of evil in this world was exerting its last ounce of strength. With God's help the zealous Jews would annihilate the aggressor. The man who fell in this struggle had no need to despair: he too would obtain a place of honour in the kingdom of God, for he would awake out of the sleep of death to 'everlasting' life (Dan. 12:2-3).

In spite of their great popularity most of the apocalyptic works failed to gain a place in the list of sacred books. Both the Pharisees and the Sadducees, generally speaking, had reservations about these visions, with their grotesque symbols and obscure allusions to the future. In this they were followed by the early Christian Church. Only the Book of Daniel and the apocalyptic Revelation to John were eventually able to keep their place as sacred books.

About 100 B.C. the Jews experienced a brief period of prosperity. The Hasmoneans were in control of an area that had more or less the same frontiers as the former kingdom of David. But internally the state was weak and disunited. The Hasmo-

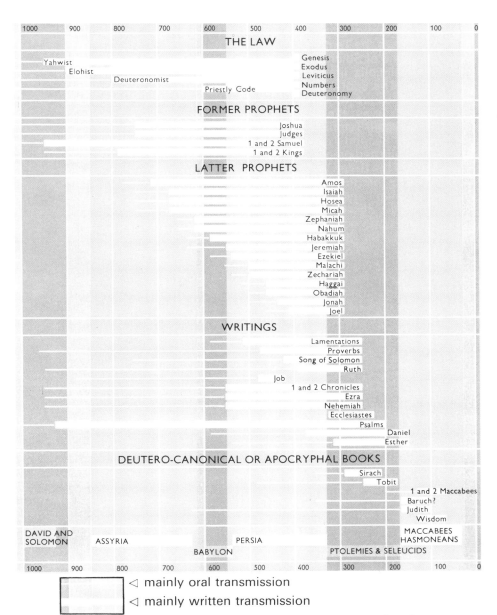

1000	900	800	700	600	500	400	300	200	100	0

THE LAW

Yahwist
Elohist
Deuteronomist
Priestly Code

Genesis
Exodus
Leviticus
Numbers
Deuteronomy

FORMER PROPHETS

Joshua
Judges
1 and 2 Samuel
1 and 2 Kings

LATTER PROPHETS

Amos
Isaiah
Hosea
Micah
Zephaniah
Nahum
Habakkuk
Jeremiah
Ezekiel
Malachi
Zechariah
Haggai
Obadiah
Jonah
Joel

WRITINGS

Lamentations
Proverbs
Song of Solomon
Ruth
Job
1 and 2 Chronicles
Ezra
Nehemiah
Ecclesiastes
Psalms
Daniel
Esther

DEUTERO-CANONICAL OR APOCRYPHAL BOOKS

Sirach
Tobit
1 and 2 Maccabees
Baruch?
Judith
Wisdom

DAVID AND SOLOMON | ASSYRIA | BABYLON | PERSIA | PTOLEMIES & SELEUCIDS | MACCABEES HASMONEANS

1000	900	800	700	600	500	400	300	200	100	0

◁ mainly oral transmission
◁ mainly written transmission

Origin, growth, and revision of the Old Testament books
Any schematic description of an historical process must deal in generalities. So, this outline can give only a generalized account of the process by which over ten centuries the books of the Old Testament evolved to acquire their eventual form.

neans did not have the profound religious vision of David's time, and they had even lost sight of the ideal that had originally inspired the Maccabean warriors. Admittedly, there was a con-

According to 2 Maccabees 6 : 2, Antiochus IV instituted the worship of Olympian Zeus in Jerusalem and of Zeus Xenios on Mount Gerizim. The Book of Daniel (9 : 27 et al.) calls this pagan worship in Jerusalem 'the abomination in the sanctuary.' The veneration of Zeus under many names made considerable strides during the Hellenistic period. Originally lord of the sky and clouds, from the tops of mountains he ruled over wind, rain, and thunder, and was the overlord of the other gods. He was thus readily identified with leading Semitic gods such as Baal. In many places Zeus was venerated for one of his several activities, distinguished by special titles such as Alexikakos (shelterer from calamity), Gamelios (patron of weddings), and Agoraios (protector of assemblies). His shrine on Mount Gerizim emphasized his protection of guests and visitors (*xenios*, 'guest'). Under the name of Olympian Zeus, the god presided over all gods and men from his seat on Mount Olympus in Greece. Zeus was customarily depicted as a man in the prime of life with a luxuriant head of hair and a well-tended, curly beard.

130

The eastern edge of Jerusalem stretches the Temple terrace, from the time of Solomon the centre of the religious life of Israelite and Jew. The spot now occupied by the Mosque of Omar (the large dome) was the actual site of Solomon's Temple and of the so-called Second Temple, built after the Exile and greatly elaborated by Herod the Great. With the destruction by the Romans in the year 70 of town and Temple, Jewish religious observance on this spot came to an end. Later, in the 7th century, the Muslims accepted the place as holy. They restored Herod's periphery wall and raised the Mosques of Omar and (at the left end of the terrace) of el-Aqsa.

siderable measure of religious freedom, but there was little else. Almost all those who had taken part in the rebellion against the Syrians were now dead, and with them the true enthusiasm for re-establishing and upholding the Jewish Law seems to have vanished as well. The new generation followed the fashions of the day and accommodated itself to the changed circumstances. Only a few small groups looked back nostalgically to a time when all the inhabitants of Judah had risked their lives for their faith.

Such was the climate in which two men, one of them in Judah and the other probably in Alexandria, began to write narrative accounts of the Maccabean struggle. When they started work, tradition had long since idealized and simplified the facts of the illustrious past. Fortunately, a certain Jason of Cyrene had already written an extensive work about this period (2 Macc. 2:23), and they were able to make use of it.

Yet for these authors the historical events were not of primary importance. They were first and foremost preachers and instructors, not historians. They wanted to make clear to their fellow-Jews that it was God alone who had once again preserved his Chosen People, and that their salvation had not been brought about by their own efforts. They illustrated their message with stories of the Maccabean conflict. The rebel force was presented as an insignificant little band, whereas the Syrian forces were built up into a mighty army. It was therefore only with God's help that the Maccabees had been able to defeat their enemy. The authors put the same message into the mouths of the Maccabean leaders, who make long speeches about the littleness of Israel and the almightiness of God. Well-known instances of this may be found in 1 Maccabees 3:16-22 and 2 Maccabees 8:18-20.

The method of these two authors was not, therefore, to record every known detail of history, but to make a selection from the material that was available and work it over to suit their own viewpoint. There are, however, differences in style and content between the two books. The first was originally written in Hebrew although it has come down to us only in a Greek translation. It is characterized by a sober and factual presenta-

tion, which makes little use of rhetorical effects. The second, which is not a sequel to the first but deals exclusively with the initial phase of the conflict, was written in Greek by its Alexandrian author, and its style has been influenced by the narrative art of Hellenistic literature. The writer is fond of using folk-tales which contain an element of the unexpected or extraordinary. A well-known example is the story of the seven Maccabean martyrs (2 Macc. 7).

These two books on the Maccabean struggle were not accepted as Holy Writ by the leaders of the Jewish community in Palestine. It is true that the authors had implicitly criticized the conduct of the Hasmoneans by making a special point of the religiousness of their forefathers, but for the Pharisees this evidently did not go far enough. Some of the fame and glory of the Maccabees might still accrue to the Hasmoneans, and the Pharisees did not wish this to happen. In fact, it seems as if the Jewish leaders regarded the list of sacred books as being closed. Not a single one of the many religious works dating from the first century B.C. was elevated to the position already accorded to the Law, the Prophets, and the remainder of the Writings. From the point of view of form and content, some of them would certainly have been eligible for consideration, particularly a collection of eighteen hymns known as the 'Psalms of Solomon.'

Various allusions in these texts to historical events show that they originated not long after the Romans had arrived in Palestine. Despite the tone of hostility toward the occupying power they exhibit a genuine religious feeling. Their authors believed, for example, in the resurrection of the faithful (3:12; 13:11; 14:9-10), and from time to time they give quite clear indications of a messianic expectation, as in 17:21-31:

Take heed, O Lord, and raise up for them their king, the son of David,
At the time when you, O God, choose to rule over Israel, your servant,
Gird him with strength to cast down the unlawful rulers,
to wrest Jerusalem from the nations who wish to plunge her into ruin,

to banish the offenders from their portion of the inheritance with righteous wisdom,

to dash the pride of the sinner in pieces like the potter's handiwork,

to break them utterly with a rod of iron,

to destroy the nations without the law by the word of his mouth,

to drive the nations out of his presence with threats,

to accuse the offenders with their own words.

Yea, he will gather the holy people together to lead them into righteousness,

he will pick out the tribes of the nation sanctified by the Lord, his God.

He will not suffer unrighteousness to continue any longer in their midst;

no longer shall any man who purposes evil dwell with them,

for he shall declare to them that they are all sons of their God.

He will apportion them according to their tribes throughout the land

and no stranger or foreigner shall dwell any more with them.

He shall judge all nations with justice and wisdom.

Yea, he will compel all nations to serve him and to receive his yoke;

he will glorify the Lord at the best place in all the land

and he will purify and sanctify Jerusalem as in the former days.

Then the nations shall come to behold his glory upon the summit of the land;

they shall bring gifts for her needy sons

and they shall see the glory of the Lord, wherewith God has arrayed her [Jerusalem].

Even this nationalistic messianism, which came close to expressing the ideals and aims of the Pharisees, could not gain for the collection of hymns as a whole a place among the sacred books. The Psalms of Solomon, therefore, fell into oblivion, until in the seventeenth century they were recovered in a number of Greek manuscripts. The original Hebrew text, however, is still missing.

From the very beginning of its existence the city of Alexandria was a centre of Hellenistic culture and considerable literary activity. The Greek version of the Old Testament—the Septuagint, as it is called—bears witness to the fact that the Jewish community living there was likewise productive in this field. Another work which emanated from this same quarter in the first century B.C. served to show that the spirit and outlook of Hellenism had already made deep inroads into Jewish life and thought. The book was given the typical Jewish title of 'The Wisdom of Solomon,' because the author wished to give added authority to his teachings (7:1-5; 9:7-12). Everything in it, however, is strongly coloured by a Hellenistic outlook. Especially striking is the attitude it reflects towards the corporeal world. It has a clear message regarding the continued existence of the soul after death. Moreover, the dualism here sounds an emphatic note of pessimism. The body is envisaged as the soul's prison. The things of this world are of little worth, and life after death is more or less the only legitimate goal. Ideas of this sort suit ill with the traditional beliefs of the Old Testament, but the Jews, like the early

Christians, were evidently unable to avoid being influenced by them. Unlike the Jewish leaders in Palestine, the early Christians even included this work in their list of sacred books.

4. POLITICAL PARTIES OF THE JEWS AND SCHOOLS OF RELIGIOUS THOUGHT

The religious outlook of the Jewish nation in Palestine was much affected during the last two centuries before Christ by the Maccabean movement, the activities of the Hasmoneans, and the Roman occupation. These caused divergences of thought which resulted in the emergence of a number of parties with differing aims and attitudes. In the last analysis all Jews held fast to the Torah, the law that according to tradition had been revealed by God to Moses. But it was possible to interpret the Torah and the other sacred books in a variety of ways: on a nationalistic or a world-wide basis, from an apocalyptic or a purely matter-of-fact viewpoint, profanely or piously, messianically or non-messianically.

These differing interpretations did not give rise to parties in the modern sense of the term, but rather to schools of religious thought, whose ideas tended in various directions and were often difficult to define. It is possible, however, to distinguish fairly clearly between three main groups: the Pharisees, the Essenes, and the Sadducees. This is not to say that every Jew in Palestine was an adherent of one or other of these parties. The majority of the people in fact were probably content to live according to the traditional interpretation of the precepts of the Law, rather than become involved in what must have appeared to them to be purely theoretical contentions.

The best known of these groups is undoubtedly the party of

A view of Qumran and its environs from the limestone rocks west of the ruins. In the right foreground is the level bed of the Wadi Qumran. Behind it are spurs of the marl plateau, with Caves 4 and 5 and the ruins of the community-house. The northern tip of the Dead Sea is just visible. Towering up on the horizon are the mountains of trans-Jordan. To the left, the town of Jericho lies concealed on the horizon, about 7½ miles to the north.

The situation of Qumran

Despite its proximity to Jerusalem and Jericho, Qumran is an isolated spot. To the east the Dead Sea forms a barrier; and to the west rises a protective line of hills. The hills meet the Dead Sea south of the spring known as 'Ain Feshkha, thus forming a kind of cul-de-sac, in which the inhabitants of Qumran could feel safe.

The shore of the Dead Sea is not very congenial to permanent habitation, as various wadis, which shift their beds each winter, erode the surface. From the shore the terrain slopes up gradually until a narrow but elongated plateau of marl rises sharply above the low-lying strand. On this plateau were the central building of the Essenes (the ruins) and a number of caves containing writings, including Caves 4, 5, 7, 8, 9, 10. (The caves with writings have been numbered in the order in which they were discovered.) A little further west rise craggy limestone cliffs; and tucked away in these slopes also are numerous caves. In some of them (1, 2, 3, 6, 11) writings have been discovered; but the majority—about thirty—served as living quarters for the members of the community. Near the spring, some kind of industry was carried on.

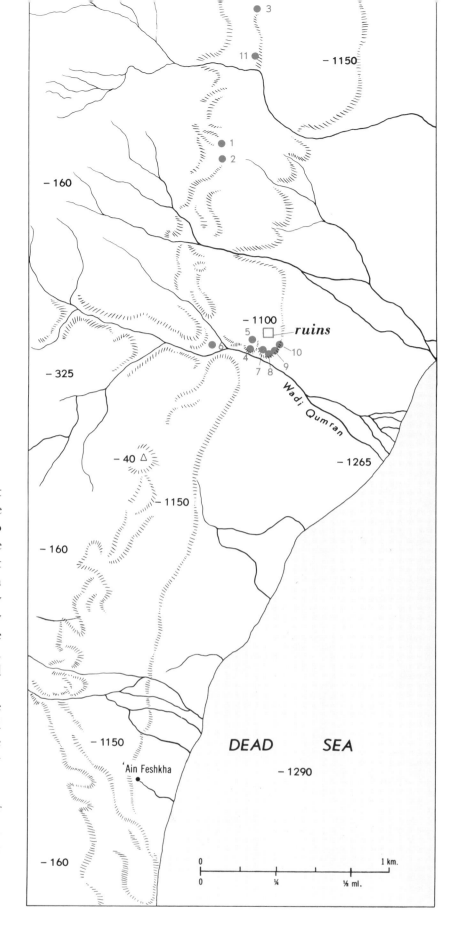

the Pharisees. It is no longer possible to say with certainty what their name signified. It may have had something to do with the Hebrew word meaning 'to separate,' and have been used to describe a group of people which had dissociated itself from some larger group with a differing line of thought and action. In fact the Pharisaic party may have had its origins in that group which detached itself from the Maccabean movement after the early successes of Judas, when the aims of the rebellion were already becoming predominantly political. Later on, they would have openly opposed the policies of the individual Hasmonean rulers, who from their point of view were betraying the most sacred traditions of the Chosen People.

This would also explain the line they pursued with the Roman Pompey, when he had captured Damascus. They asked him to do away with the kingship, so that they could effect the banishment of the Hasmoneans from Palestine. They probably saw in the actions of the Romans the avenging hand of God. But it soon became clear that they were mistaken. The Romans, too, had little respect for the Torah, and their yoke was, if possible, even heavier to bear than that of the Hasmoneans. This turn of events made the Pharisees more narrowly nationalistic than ever, and it was their overwrought messianic expectations which eventually led to armed insurrection against the Romans and the downfall of the Jewish nation in Palestine.

Initially, the Pharisaic party had taken little interest in politics. For them God was the only lord and master. He had already made his will known in the sacred writings of the Torah, which therefore constituted the sole norm for living. By providing commentaries on, and interpretations of, this Law their leaders had amplified it into something which could be applied to every aspect of daily life. Certain ideas, however, about which the Torah had nothing to say, were also accepted by them—as, for instance, personal immortality, judgment after death, and the resurrection of the body. Yet they did not in the first place constitute a school of theology. What they thought to be far more important was the religious conduct of every Jew.

Their interpretations of the teaching of the Torah were therefore concerned with its practical application. Many Pharisees, indeed, were also legal experts. The ordinary people would come to them with questions as to how they should act or behave in a given situation. Since the Pharisees on the one hand overstressed the absolute character of the Law and on the other felt themselves obliged to lay down all kinds of minute regulations, their teaching became bogged down in formalistic casuistry. In spite of this, however, they wielded great authority among the people, because they were the only religious leaders. The prophets who had formerly interpreted God's will were now no longer in evidence. There were still priests, of course, but these were concentrated in and around Jerusalem, where they could direct the liturgical ceremonies. Moreover, as a group they included only a few experts in the Law. Most of them could have answered only with some difficulty such questions as the people might have wished to ask them. The Pharisees on the other hand went to the people. Accompanied by a few disciples, many of them would travel around as rabbis, visiting the towns and villages throughout the land.

Another group were the Essenes, who are mentioned in several ancient documents. To judge from these texts they must have been fairly important, but up to a short time ago very little detailed knowledge about them was available. The discoveries made at Qumran from 1947 onwards, however, have revealed that from about 120 B.C. to A.D. 68 there lived on the shore of the Dead Sea a group of Jews who can be described as Essenes. It is even likely that this community formed the central core of the Essene movement. From the scrolls which they left behind they

would seem to have been a sect rather than a party of any kind. They were not a sect in the sense of a group with heretical beliefs, however. Along with all other Jews they held fast to the Torah and the Prophets. It was simply that they did not wish to identify themselves with the representatives of official Judaism.

The origin of the Essenes, like that of the Pharisees, is probably to be sought in the Chasidic movement. Their name also points in this direction, for it is thought to come from an Aramaic word which, like the Hebrew *chasid*, has the meaning of 'pious.' As a separatist group the Essenes may well have arisen in the following way. The resistance of the Chasidim to the hereditary high priesthood of Simon (143–134 B.C.) and of his son John (134–104) developed in two divergent directions. The movement as a whole withdrew its support from the ruling house of the Hasmoneans, but most of its members retained their place in Jewish society. These were the Pharisees. There were probably other members, however, who formed a separate group. These were probably markedly apocalyptic and would take their belief

The ruins of Qumran from the south-west. In the foreground the Wadi Qumran and the marl rocks, with Caves 5 and 4 (far right). Behind that, the plateau on which the Essenes constructed their community-house. Top left stands the great tower. It was there as early as the period of the monarchy; and it still stands 13 feet high. It is thought that the reference in such passages as Joshua 15 : 62 and 2 Chronicles 26 : 10 is to this tower. Between the tower and the plateau edge lie the remains of workshops and some wells. The ruins of the principal rooms—the refectory, assembly room, and scriptorium, for example—are to the right of the tower.

to the ultimate conclusion: John's position as High Priest was a contravention of the Law. As they conceived it, the entire cult in Jerusalem was thereby rendered unclean, necessitating a complete break with it. If this was what happened, then the main instigator was probably a man descended from Aaron, making his own claim to the high priesthood.

Other factors, however, may have contributed to bringing about this secession. It is clear from their documents that the community at Qumran had a different calendar from the official one. The year was divided exactly into 52 complete weeks, so that every feast fell on the same day of the week each year. This represented a departure from the liturgical year as observed in Jerusalem. As the Jewish religion was above all a matter of observance, their calendar made it impossible for them to participate in the official cult practised in the Temple. Furthermore, they had a special view of marriage. The texts are not always

Right beside the ruins at Qumran (page 133) runs a narrow spur. Set in the side of this are Caves 4 and 5, discovered in 1952. Cave 4 is well known because thousands of bits and pieces of text were found there—tiny fragments of possibly as many as four hundred scrolls. Cave 5 (shown above) lies immediately to the north of Cave 4; it contained only a few relics of the Essenes.

A ground-plan of the ruins at Qumran, showing the complex as it was during the latest period (ca. A.D. 2-68). The lay-out of the main features is as follows:

1. Main entrance.
2. Entrance for the Essenes living in the caves and tents.
3. Eight open courtyards.
4. Four water conduits.
5. Eight cisterns.
6. Apartment where three jars containing more than 550 coins lay concealed in the floor, before habitation was resumed about the beginning of the Christian era.
7. Inner gate.
8. Tower
9. Steps leading to the ground floor.
10. Probably the small assembly room.
11. Spot where the stone writing-tables belonging to the upper storey were discovered.
12. Probably a kitchen.
13. Toilet.
14. The laundry.
15. Two potteries.
16. Refectory, with a stone dais for the reader.
17. Store-room for pots and dishes.
18. A still visible crack in the walls and floors, caused by the earth-quake in 31 B.C. which ended the first period at Qumran.

N

0   10   20 m.
0   11   22 yd.

Looking south from the tower of Qumran one sees the walls of the chamber (No. 11 on the ground-plan) in which the archaeologists came across the broken pieces of the writing-tables. It is no longer possible to tell what the function of the room itself was. The layer of rubble on the floor suggests that there must have been an upper storey, containing the writing-room where most of the Qumran scrolls are likely to have originated. In the distance can be seen the area of green around the spring, called nowadays 'Ain Feshkha. Just to the south of it a spur of limestone rock juts out into the Dead Sea, making extremely difficult any approach to Qumran from the south.

equally clear, but it is certain that the majority of members of the Qumran community were celibate.

This probably sprang from their excessive concern with ritual purity. But another factor, which is connected with it, is not to be overlooked. Like the first Christians, the Essenes lived in a state of unduly tense expectation, for they not only believed that the world was an evil place, but that for this reason its end was at hand. Marriage in such a context made little or no sense. One had to be ready for the decisive moment at which God would set up his kingdom. They therefore looked for a solitary place not polluted by unlawful practices, where they could live the ascetic life that conformed with their ideals.

They found it on the marl plateau overlooking the north-west corner of the Dead Sea, where they settled down in the numerous caves in the limestone cliffs or in tents. They supplied themselves with food by cattle-breeding, cultivating fruit-trees, and also, perhaps, by a certain amount of horticulture near the spring known today as 'Ain Feshkha. In case of dire necessity food could always be obtained in Jericho, which was about 7½ miles to the north.

The centre of their communal life was the house which they built on the remains of a fort dating from the period of the monarchy. There they had, among other things, a pottery, a laundry, a kitchen, an assembly room, a writing-room, a refec-

This scroll from Qumran shows the condition in which many of the Essenes' manuscripts were found. In most cases the outside, that is, the opening part, and the underneath side (right in the photo) had been very much damaged by damp and vermin. Specimens like this were discovered in Caves 1, 3, and 11, which nestle in the face of the dry limestone cliffs. Cave 4 lies in the lower and damper marl. Of the several hundred scrolls stored in it, mostly only tiny fragments bearing a few words or letters remain.

tory, and a number of cisterns to catch the rainwater which during the winter ran off the limestone rocks. The existence of a writing-room is of particular interest because it sheds further light on the situation as regards the Bible in those days. In the caves nearby, fragments have been found of all the books of the Hebrew Bible with the exception of Esther. Some of the manuscripts date from about 200 B.C. Apparently, the Essenes carried with them into the desert sacred scrolls, which were afterwards systematically copied.

During the reign of the godless Alexander Janneus (103–76 B.C.) a great many new members came to swell the numbers of the community. The central building was then substantially enlarged. The arrival of the Romans in 63 B.C. did little to change the situation for Qumran. It simply meant that as far as the community was concerned the enemies of God had appeared in another guise. They continued to live quietly in the desert, until in the year 31 B.C. an earthquake seriously damaged the central building, and the community was obliged to evacuate the area. Where they went has not so far been discovered. At all events the spot remained deserted for about thirty years. However, at the beginning of our era a group of Essenes returned to Qumran and continued to live there until the first Jewish rebellion broke out in A.D. 66, soon after which the Romans drove them away. It is of course strange that the New Testament documents nowhere mention the Essenes as a group: only their ideas and their language find an echo there from time to time. It seems that they maintained no contact at all as a living community with official Judaism, out of which the Christian Church was eventually to arise.

The members of the Qumran community did not confine

themselves to copying out manuscripts of the Bible. They created their own literature too—and that mainly in Hebrew, the language which since the Maccabean rebellion the Jews in Palestine had learned to respect and value once more. They wrote topical commentaries on Biblical texts *(Commentary on Habakkuk)*, lengthy instructions on the life and activities of the community *(Rule of the Community)*, combative works dealing with 'the eschatological event' *(Rule of War)*, a number of psalms, and many texts of an apocalyptic nature. It remains an intriguing question whether this last group of texts originated in their own circle or were simply transcribed. In the third cave a curious document was found: a copper scroll listing the places in Palestine, where, it was claimed, valuable objects lay hidden. Many scholars believe that this record is not based on fact, but no-one has so far been able to explain why, in that case, the author took the trouble to engrave his text on such durable material.

From all these texts, although they are mostly mere fragments, it is to some extent possible to draw conclusions as to the world of thought in which the Essenes moved. Their leader was probably the man who is several times referred to as the 'Teacher of Righteousness.' In the *Commentary on Habakkuk* it says:

> God gave Habakkuk the task of writing down what was to befall the last generation. But the final consummation He did not reveal to him. Whenever it says "so that the passer-by may read it," the reference is to the Teacher of Righteousness to whom God has made known all the secrets contained in the sayings of His servants, the prophets. (1 QpHab. VII: 1-5)

◁ *(Opposite)* Columns 3, 4, and 5 of the Habakkuk scroll from Cave 1 at Qumran. The last three or four lines of each column have rotted away over the centuries. The scroll was probably written about 50 B.C.; but it is possible that what we have here is a copy. In that case the origin of the text itself must be assigned to a still earlier date. The content is typical of the Qumran community. Habakkuk chs. 1–2 are reproduced and commented on verse by verse; but the exposition is not objective. Each sentence of the prophetic book is applied to the Community and to the situation in which it found itself. Thus the author avers that in his view God's judgment had already begun and would soon be consummated. The scroll is designated 1QpHab, that is, Cave 1 at Qumran, pesher (commentary) on Habakkuk.

(Right) The copper scroll was found in 1952 in Cave 3 at Qumran. ▷ To read the text it was necessary, in a delicate operation, to saw the copper into a number of strips, now preserved in the museum at 'Amman. That copper instead of leather or papyrus was used shows that great value was attached to the contents. In the twelve columns mention is made of about sixty hoards of gold, silver, or other valuables supposed to be hidden away in various places within Palestine. The scroll dates from the 1st century A.D. There is some doubt, however, as to what the document is all about. Did someone bring together popular traditions about hidden treasures from the Temple of Herod, after the destruction of Jerusalem; and did the scroll end up in Cave 3 at Qumran by accident? Or did a member of the Qumran community, prior to the year A.D. 68, commit to writing certain ancient traditions concerning hidden treasures belonging to the pillaged Temple of Solomon; and was the scroll stowed away in Cave 3 at the start of the Jewish rebellion? The scroll is referred to as 3Q15.

The contrast is made repeatedly between this Teacher of Righteousness and 'the godless priest.' This probably refers to the 'illegitimate' High Priest Simon or his son John in Jerusalem.

When the number of members increased, a rule of life was drawn up on the basis of already established practices. The rule shows, among other things, that there was common ownership of property:

> All who present themselves for God's truth must bring their knowledge, their strength and their goods into the community of God in order thus to purify their knowledge by the truth of God's laws, to organize their strength according to

the perfection of his ways and all their goods according to his righteous decree. (1 QS I:11-13)

Membership was not something that could be obtained overnight. A trial period of at least two years had to be gone through. If after that time the candidate was judged worthy by the community, he became a fully accredited member:

When the decision has been taken that he be allowed to join the community, then he shall be registered according to his position among his brothers for the law, for justice, purity, and the common possessions. And his counsel and judgment are at the service of the community. (1 QS VI: 21-23)

The day-to-day administration was vested in a group of twelve men and (or including) three priests. Their chairman was a priest who bore the title of 'overseer.'

Reading the documents from Qumran, one cannot but be struck by the community's fanatical enthusiasm. They seem to have been obsessed with expectations of an apocalyptic and messianic nature. The crucial moment, they believed, was upon them, and it demanded a thorough preparation for, and a total commitment to, all that was pure and righteous. They saw the whole world as torn by two conflicting forces. 'The sons of light,' led by 'the spirit of truth,' had to do battle with 'the sons of darkness,' led by 'the spirit of evil.' This dualism was still in conformity with the Old Testament tradition in so far as it was explicitly asserted that God had created both the spirit of truth and the spirit of darkness. It was felt that the conflict would soon enter upon its crucial stage. Then the Essenes would be led in their struggle by certain messianic figures, known variously as 'the Messiah of Aaron,' 'the prophet,' and 'the Messiah of Israel.' The messianic task was shared, therefore, by a priestly, a prophetic, and a military figure. By mighty acts God would then finally establish his kingdom of righteousness.

A third important group were the Sadducees. They stood for little of real substance at the religious level, but they might be described as a group representing their own interests. Their origins, too, are somewhat obscure, but their name has been connected with Zadok, the man who under Solomon became High Priest in place of Abiathar. Like the Pharisees they are said to have been opposed, at first, to the high priesthood of the Maccabees and the Hasmoneans. The Pharisees' motives for this were religious ones, but the Sadducees were really contending only for their social and political position within the nation. Their party consisted mainly of priests and members of wealthy families. They insisted that the high priesthood—and the political power belonging to it—should go to one of their group. Their basic opportunism therefore made them quick to react to developments on the political and social level. When they had built up a strong position for themselves in the Hasmonean kingdom, they soon became supporters of the establishment. They remained loyal to the precepts of the Torah, but they showed little enthusiasm for the traditional teachings of the fathers, to which the Pharisees attached such great importance. Thus in matters of religion they were rather conservative and refused to accept new ideas, particularly that of personal immortality (Matt. 22:23; Acts 23:6).

This group also ceased to exist after the Romans had crushed

Jerusalem after its expansion under the Hasmoneans

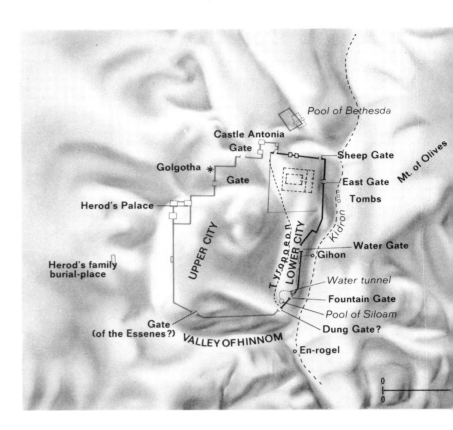

In view of the economic and political climate under the Hasmoneans, we may suppose that Jerusalem underwent considerable expansion during that period. This map, however, is based chiefly on literary and historical evidence and on the physical features of the site itself. Archaeological evidence is both vague and scanty; and the modern residential quarter makes any more extensive investigation almost impossible. The Hasmonean rulers probably built walls around the western hill, a great part of which was a residential area in their time, thus making it an integral part of the city. Over the years the Tyropoeon Valley had to a substantial degree been filled in, and it was natural for the earlier city of David to expand westwards. When this wide and lofty eminence was annexed, the defences were made to follow the contour of the hill-side to give maximum strength to the walls and towers. The wall of old Jerusalem, running along the Tyropoeon Valley (indicated here by a dotted line), then lost its importance and slowly disappeared. The lower and the upper city were soon welded into one by a system of small streets rather like staircases. Little is known about the gates in the new walls. We may assume, however, that at least one gate was built in the north, another in the west, and another in the south. The most likely spots are those shown. A century later the city was embellished and strengthened by Herod the Great. He enlarged the Temple court and built the castle of Antonia and his own palace on the western hill. To the north of the city the pool of Bethesda with its five colonnades and west of the city the burial site also probably date from the time of Herod, as do the three monumental tombs on the eastern side of the Kidron valley. The map also shows the traditional site of Golgotha, to the north-west of the city. Whether the rock on which the execution of Jesus of Nazareth took place was at this precise spot cannot be a matter of absolute certainty. What is certain is that during the first century A.D. this hill was used as a burial place.

the first Jewish rebellion. As a result of the downfall of Jerusalem and the destruction of the Temple, the priests lost their position, and the wealthy families lost their property. The role of the Sadducees in the Jewish community was then played out.

IX. THE TRANSITION FROM THE OLD TO THE NEW TESTAMENT

A sketch of the historical situation in the time of Jesus of Nazareth.

1. THE SITUATION IN THE ROMAN EMPIRE

When the Romans took Jerusalem in 63 B.C., the political situation within the empire had already been critical for some time. The Roman state had for centuries past been a republic governed by delegates drawn from the aristocracy. But with the conquest of new territories, the expansion of trade, and developments on the cultural front, the demand for a more democratic form of government became increasingly urgent. The leading classes in other cities, together with wealthy merchants, and the intellectuals amongst the ordinary citizens, wanted their share of power. The first clashes occurred as early as 133 B.C., but the situation remained in a constant state of flux until 49 B.C., when Julius Caesar, fresh from his military triumphs in Gaul, took advantage of the unsettled conditions to gain personal control of the empire.

To consolidate his position Caesar had to undertake a number of military campaigns. His chief opponent was Pompey, who had captured Jerusalem. The two rivals eventually landed in Egypt, which was just then attempting to extricate itself from the Roman sphere of influence. The Egyptians murdered Pompey the moment he set foot on their territory, and they shut up Julïus Caesar with his army in Alexandria. At this juncture Antipater, the father of Herod the Great, gave further proof of his political acumen. He dispatched his troops to Egypt to relieve Caesar, calling on the Alexandrian Jews to side with the Romans. Thanks to this support, Caesar was able to break through the encircling Egyptian forces.

In the 2nd and 3rd centuries A.D. it looked as if nothing could check the advance of the god Mithras in the Roman empire. In Rome alone he had upwards of a hundred sanctuaries at that time; and there were similar 'Mithraea' in Britain, France, Spain, Yugoslavia, Romania, Germany, Austria, and Turkey. Mithras was worshipped as the god of light; and his birthday was celebrated on December 25th. He was the invincible god who maintained justice and truth and was the giver of life. Central to this religion was the saving act performed by Mithras, the slaying of the primeval bull. The illustration reproduced here is concerned with that event. It is the kind of image that with greater or smaller variations was installed in the niche of every temple of Mithras. With his left hand the god pulls the head of the bull backwards; in his right hand (now missing) he grasped the dagger for the decisive thrust. On his head he wears the Phrygian cap, with a hole into which could be fitted a solar disc. The cloak billowing out behind him gives a natural liveliness to the whole. He supports himself on his right foot, while with his left knee he holds the bull firmly under control. Beneath the bull is a lion, symbol of the element of fire. The vessel at its side probably signifies the life-giving water. Near the hind legs a scorpion clutches the bull's testicles: is this a symbol of evil threatening to destroy the seed of life? To the left and right stand two figures, quietly looking on. Like Mithras himself, these figures wear Persian dress. Each carries a torch, one raised, the other held low: they symbolize the rising and the setting sun, light and darkness, life and death. Enclosing this scene are representations of various aspects and events connected with the cult of this religious fellowship and with the legendary life of Mithras. Top left, for example, is depicted the sun-chariot which conveys Mithras back into the heavens. Most of the text along the base has been obliterated.

The consequences for the Jews were far-reaching, for Caesar openly acknowledged his gratitude and gave practical demonstrations of it. For example, among other things he appointed the High Priest Hyrcanus ethnarch. This title gave Hyrcanus no great political authority, it is true, but it meant that his position in the Roman empire was universally recognized. Antipater himself obtained Roman citizenship and was made procurator of all the Jewish territories, an appointment which put civil and military power officially into his hands. To establish and maintain this state of affairs Antipater advanced his sons to positions of power. Phasael became governor in Judea and Herod in Galilee. Caesar's benevolence, moreover, was not without its advantages for the Jewish people as a whole. The tax, which every part of the empire had to pay, was substantially reduced in their case, and the obligation to provide auxiliary troops for the imperial army was rescinded. The effect of this gratitude on Caesar's part was felt throughout the empire. Many Roman officials and administrators, not venturing to lag behind their ruler, followed his example.

Thus the Jews in many Hellenistic cities and even in Rome itself found themselves in a favoured position. They were allowed, on a limited scale, to exercise their own jurisdiction in their synagogues. All this was advantageous to their life as a community, both internally and externally. To be Jewish became something of a privilege, and quite a number of Romans and Greeks who had acquired a knowledge of Jewish traditions through the Septuagint, the Greek version of the Old Testament, either showed their sympathy with Judaism as 'God-fearers' or identified themselves with it as 'proselytes.'

In the year 44 B.C. Caesar was assassinated. This made little difference to the position of the Jews, for they continued, on the whole, to enjoy the privileges obtained under Caesar up to the

(Top) Like every Hellenistic city, Petra had a number of public buildings; but in the course of time they have either been destroyed or have collapsed. Only the great theatre in the valley, foreground is still clearly recognizable. The 34 tiers cut into the rock are still largely intact. The stage has been partly restored.

(Centre) In the rock walls of the valley the Nabateans hewed out a large number of tombs. The decoration of the facades developed between 200 B.C. and A.D. 100 from simple rectilinear motifs in low and high relief to zigzag lines, curves, and elaborate symbols of various kinds. These tombs belong, therefore, to the earliest period.

(Bottom) In the cleft that gives access to Petra there nestles in the rock face a façade which illustrates how the Nabateans carved their monuments out of the virgin rock. The frontage has two richly ornamented storeys. The Corinthian columns, the other decorations, and the religious symbols (not visible in the photo) show that the monument belongs to the late period (ca. A.D. 100).

(Opposite) The peculiar character of the rock at Petra makes the city a sight worth seeing even today; for this rock exhibits surprising textures and colours and, because of its softness, is at the same time easy to work. The Nabateans turned these properties to good account. Traces of their activity are to be found along the mountains-sides of the entire valley; but wind and weather have had such an effect on the fabric of this dead city over the centuries that it is no longer always possible to say whether the rock formations are the product of nature or the work of human hands.

time of their first rebellion in A.D. 66. Caesar's violent death did, however, cause chaos within the Roman Empire, a situation from which Octavian and Antony emerged as the new joint wielders of power. When, soon afterwards they quarrelled, Octavian, the adoptive son of Caesar, carried the day triumphantly over the erratic Antony and became the new emperor and sole ruler.

So in the year 31 B.C. the freedoms represented by the Roman republic were decisively lost. The process that had started a century before had reached its culmination. Though Octavian was prudent enough at first to behave in Rome as though he were ruling on instructions from the senate, in the eastern parts of the empire he allowed himself to be honoured as a god. In Rome itself, he only permitted himself to be called 'augustus,' a term usually applied to temples and cultic objects and meaning something like 'possessing sacred power.' Its application to himself at once set him above other mortals and stressed the dignity of his office. Nor indeed did he bear the title of emperor. He did of course call himself Caesar, but in using his family name his intention was to indicate that he was the adoptive son of the great general. It was only under his successors that the names of 'Imperator,' 'Princeps,' 'Augustus,' and 'Caesar' were raised to the dignity of imperial titles.

Under Octavian the Roman empire entered upon a period of order and tranquillity, which in spite of a few wars in the border territories and minor insurrections in the provinces was to last for many years. The celebrated *pax Romana*, the Roman peace, was a fact. Anyone could now travel in safety through the whole of the enormous empire, on foot, on horseback, and even by ship across the Mediterranean Sea, which the Romans rather proudly referred to as *mare nostrum* or 'our sea.' From the Atlantic Ocean in the west to the Euphrates in the east a network of roads provided a means of communication between all parts of the empire. These highways, of which large sections still exist, were in the first place constructed for the army and for the government's intelligence service, but merchants and other people made frequent use of them as well. As a result of this intensive intercommunication, *koinē* or common Greek became the *lingua franca* for large parts of the empire, and was quite extensively spoken and written even in Rome and North Africa.

Where Christianity and the New Testament are concerned, a factor of much greater importance was the increasing interchange in matters of religion. In the east the cult of the ruler, which had become a generally accepted practice since the time of Alexander the Great, was given a new impetus by the elevation of the Roman ruler to the status of a god. There is clear evidence of this in the names given to temples and the images appearing on coins. Octavian's successors behaved more and more like oriental despots, so that the cult of Caesar made its way into the very capital itself. This form of religion found a forceful champion in the emperor Caligula (A.D. 37–41). He made it an absolute requirement that every subject should worship him as a god. However, this did not prevent his assassination after a brief period of power.

The oriental mystery religions also penetrated further and further westwards, and with growing effect. In the hearts of many there was evidently a deep longing for deliverance and salvation, which may partly explain the astonishing popularity of Mithraism. By A.D. 100 this originally Persian cult had obtained a firm footing in Rome, and about a century later there were already temples of Mithras in Spain, Germany, and even in Britain. The wide and rapid spread of Mithraism was brought about chiefly by the Roman army. It was a martial religion, designed exclusively for men, but apart from this very little is known about it. We do, however, know that the god Mithras was a saviour-figure, and that he was usually depicted as a bull-slayer. This was the means by which he was supposed to have brought new life into being, in which his disciples were able to participate.

It is easy to understand why so many oriental ideas and practices found their way into the west, when one considers the extent of the Roman empire at this period. From the third century onwards the Parthians had constituted an independent power to the south-east of the Caspian Sea, and like most peoples living on the borders of the civilized world they coveted the rich territories in Mesopotamia and those bounded by the Mediterranean Sea. It will be remembered that it was partly to them that the Maccabees owed the success of their rebellion, for the activities of the Parthians demanded the constant attention of the Syrian armies. When the Romans had taken the place of the Syrians the situation on the eastern frontier did not change. The Parthians took advantage of the chaotic state of affairs after the death of Julius Caesar to penetrate as far as Palestine, where they managed to establish themselves for a brief period. Their independent state on the eastern frontier continued to exist right into the third century A.D., and for the whole of this period they were a constant threat to the Romans. Naturally enough, traders and the wandering preachers of various religious cults generally steered clear of this dangerous area and made instead for the west.

Palestine, too, fell within this border territory, for the Romans had not yet ventured very far into the Arabian desert which lay beyond it. Hence, the Nabateans, who occupied this desert region, were able to maintain their independence up to about A.D. 100, when their kingdom was also incorporated into the Roman empire as the province of Arabia. The origins of these people and the course of their development as a nation are still fairly obscure. What is known, however, is that from the sixth century B.C. onwards the Edomites gradually began to move in a north-westerly direction and eventually settled in the southern part of Judah, where later on, in the prevailing Greek environment, they came to be called Idumeans and their country Idumea. Arabian tribes then moved into what had formerly been the land of the Edomites, and it was probably from these that the Nabateans originated. It seems that by 200 B.C., or thereabouts, they had developed into a powerful nation. Petra, their capital city, stood some 55 miles due south of the Dead Sea, and today its picturesque ruins are famous. It stood in a basin-like valley, protected on all sides by steep and rocky mountains. The only level means of access is still a dark and winding cleft, which over centuries in the distant past the water has worn through the rock.

The power of the Nabateans was not confined to Petra and its environs, but extended over the caravan routes to the east and south of Palestine. Thus they controlled the entire trade

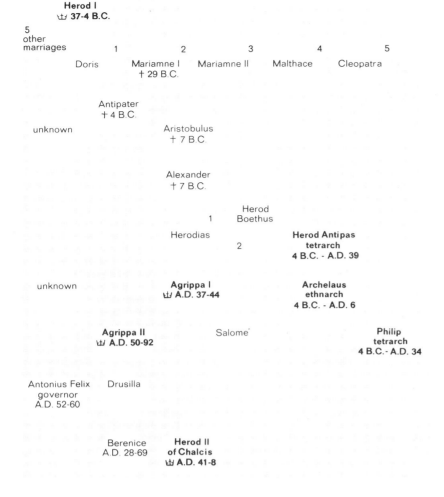

The genealogical tree of Herod's family: the rectangles indicate males, the circles females. The fact that Herod the Great married ten times makes a plan of his descendants a very complicated affair. Herodias, a granddaughter of Herod and Mariamne I, married Herod Boethus, a son of Herod I's third marriage, and later Herod Antipas, a son of the fourth marriage. Salome, a daughter of Herodias and Herod Boethus—and therefore both a granddaughter and a great-granddaughter of Herod I—married Philip, a son of the fifth marriage.

between Arabia and Egypt, and prospered greatly as a result. There is one striking instance of the extent of their influence. Over 300 miles to the south of Petra stands the present-day Meda'in-Salih, earlier known as Hejra, where beside the customary ornamented tombs, numerous Nabatean inscriptions have been discovered. These texts have their own alphabet, but the language is Aramaic. The names of persons and tribes show, however, that the Nabateans were of Arabian descent.

About 25 miles east of what is now 'Aqaba there was yet another settlement. The district is inhospitable, presenting a quite different prospect from the wilderness of Judah. Out of an enormous sandy plain, polished smooth by the winter rains and hardened by the sun, precipitous crags thrust up in every direction. One such peak is called er-Ram, 'the lofty (one).' At the foot of this eminence stand the remains of a Nabatean temple, built about 100 B.C. Other traces of Nabatean occupation may be found about 40 miles north of Petra, where on a hill-top at the southern edge of the Wadi el-Hesa—the Biblical Zered—there stand some ruins known as Khirbet et-Tannur. These are the remains of a temple that was in use from about 25 B.C. to A.D. 125. On a hill somewhat further to the south-east is a similar ruin, which has not yet been investigated.

Like other ancient Semitic peoples, the Nabateans apparently preferred to worship their gods on mountain peaks. Their main sanctuary at Petra, which goes by the name of 'the hill of sacrifice,' is likewise hewn out of a flat-topped precipitous rock. At Khirbet et-Tannur a stone image was discovered still occupying its original position. It probably represents not the Nabatean god, Dushara, but the Syrian Zeus-Hadad, whom the Nabateans venerated as 'the lord of heaven.' The image, which is in the museum at 'Amman, is a bearded male figure. Its right hand has disappeared, but in its left it holds a stylized representation of a thunderbolt, and it is flanked by two small lions or bulls. This image—and indeed the other decorations in the temple as well—show once more what rapid headway syncretism had made during the Hellenistic and Roman periods.

The merging of ideas and practices of various kinds also finds expression on the façades of the tombs at Petra. The Persians had already honoured their foremost kings with such sepulchral monuments, but the Nabateans had their own distinctive ways of decorating these façades. The earliest ones were kept simple enough, with a few horizontal lines in relief. At a subsequent stage zig-zag motifs were introduced, and this eventually culminated in all the profusion and excess of Hellenistic ornamentation, with diagonal lines, pillars, images, and urns appearing on the façades. The distinctive Nabatean style was thus lost. The Nabateans were also impelled by the climate of syncretism to adopt the cult of the ruler. In Petra there stands the small temple of en-Nmeir, hewn out of the rock in honour of King Obodas, who lived about 90 B.C. From the extant half of an inscription on the rock face over the niche intended for the image it would appear that this apotheosis took place during the reign of Aretas IV, at the beginning of our era.

The Nabatean influence also extended far into the west. On a lofty hill in the middle of the Negeb desert stand the ruined walls of the city of Avdat. From this fortified position the Nabateans were able to control the passing caravan trade. Their city was destroyed in A.D. 106 by the Romans. In the Byzantine period Avdat enjoyed a new prosperity, but the Arab invasion in the seventh century A.D. finally put an end to the urban culture which had developed there. However, since the Byzantine builders used the ruins of the pagan temple for the construction of their church, Nabatean inscriptions may be found among the remains of the Christian building.

The Bible makes surprisingly few references to the Nabateans. In 2 Maccabees 5:8 it states that when the Hellenistically inclined High Priest Jason had fled from Jerusalem, he was captured by the Arab ruler Aretas. This had already taken place before the Maccabean struggle broke out. According to 1 Maccabees 5:25 and 9:35 the Nabateans were sympathetic towards the Maccabean uprising. This is understandable enough when one considers that once the Jews had succeeded in gaining their independence, their territory would serve as a buffer state between the Nabatean kingdom and the mighty Syrian empire.

The power and influence of the Nabateans may be inferred from a number of passages in the New Testament. Antipas, the son of Herod the Great, was married to a daughter of Aretas IV, but he divorced her in order to marry Herodias, his brother's wife. John the Baptist fell victim to this circumstance, when he upbraided the Jewish ruler for the iniquity of this action (Matt. 14:3ff). The Nabatean king took affront at this treatment of his daughter and marched with his army into Antipas's territory.

Antipas suffered a crushing defeat, and the Romans were obliged to hurry to his assistance. Not long afterwards the governor of King Aretas in Damascus was taking action against Paul, when the latter first appeared in public to proclaim the Christian faith. Paul himself wrote, "At Damascus, the governor under King Aretas guarded the city of Damascus in order to seize me." (2 Cor. 11:32) From this it would appear that the power of the Nabatean ruler at this time stretched as far as Damascus, and that the Roman emperor Caligula had ceded rights in this territory to Aretas IV.

These examples of Parthian and Nabatean power on the borders of Roman-occupied territory all go to show how much the westward movement of Christianity was bound up with the circumstances of history. The situation may perhaps be summed up in this way. In the east and south those who preached the Christian faith found their way blocked by hostile powers, whereas they could move with comparative freedom inside the territories of the empire, whose centre at Rome naturally exerted a pull towards the north-west. Moreover, the west in general displayed a lively interest in currents of thought emanating from the east, so that after a tentative beginning the message proclaimed was readily accepted in many quarters.

2. THE SITUATION IN PALESTINE

In the year following the assassination of Julius Caesar Antipater was poisoned. Herod the Great, his son, at once set about extending his authority from Galilee to cover all the Jewish territories, and thanks to his exceptional gifts as a politician he succeeded. As Caesar's assassins held the reins of power in the east just then, he at first co-operated with them. When they had been defeated, however, and Antony had assumed control, Herod was quick to support the new ruler. It was to this that he owed his appointment as tetrarch of the Jewish territories.

But he could not maintain his authority for long. The Parthians, the sworn enemies of the Romans, invaded Syria and

When Herod the Great founded the port of Caesarea, he also equipped the town with the necessary public buildings, such as an amphitheatre, a temple, an aqueduct, and a theatre. The photo shows the northern part of the theatre, which the Israelis have restored. In the background is the Mediterranean with, right, a few scanty remains of the south pier of the ancient harbour.

drove Antony westwards. The invaders gave their support to the Hasmonean Antigonus, the son of Aristobulus II, whom Pompey had deposed in 63 B.C. With their help Antigonus became king in Jerusalem for a short time, and Herod had to flee to Rome. Because Octavian and Antony regarded him as an ally against the Parthians, he was formally appointed king of Judea—although far from his homeland—in the year 40 B.C. Whilst the Romans were fighting the Parthians, Herod had to deal with Antigonus. After three years he was finally victorious and entered Jerusalem in solemn triumph. He had already taken to wife Mariamne, granddaughter to both Hyrcanus II and Aristobulus II, a step which made him a member of the Hasmonean royal family. In this way he hoped that many Jewish people would be prepared to accept him as their ruler.

When the struggle between Octavian and Antony broke out, he was obliged, of course, to side with the later, for the eastern part of the empire was in Antony's hands. But Herod gave his support with a certain amount of reserve, evidently because he had more confidence in Octavian. When, therefore, in 31 B.C. the latter defeated Antony and became sole ruler of the Empire, Herod was able to retain his position. It was indeed one of Herod's greatest accomplishments that he succeeded in winning and retaining the trust of the Roman rulers at every turn in his career. He seems to have achieved this partly by insisting on the necessity of a personal meeting. During his

exile in Rome he had called upon Octavian and Antony. In 31 B.C. he went to the island of Rhodes to plead his cause there with Octavian. He also accompanied Octavian on his journey to Egypt and to Antioch in Syria.

Herod is notorious for his cruelty. He knew, apparently, that despite his positive achievements he was disliked and that he could maintain his position only by intimidation. The many sons with which his ten wives presented him he regarded more as rivals for the throne than as successors to it. He therefore had a number of them put to death. The high priestly family also suffered at his hands, and suspicion drove him to such lengths that he even had his favourite wife, Mariamne, murdered. The massacre of the innocents in Bethlehem, as recorded in the Gospel of St. Matthew, seems to accord with Herod's reputation as a tyrant.

It would be wrong, however, to attribute only acts of cruelty to this king. As befitted a ruler who was also a true Hellenist, he made it his business to promote many of the cultural and economic ventures of his times. He had not himself enjoyed the benefits of a 'higher education,' but he saw to it that his sons were instructed at court by philosophers. Two of them were even permitted to pursue their studies in Rome. It was on building projects of various kinds, however, that most of Herod's energies were expended. He built so thoroughly and on so extensive a scale that many imposing remains can still be seen, even today. The ancient city of Samaria, once the capital of the Northern Kingdom was considerably enlarged and strengthened by Herod. On the acropolis, where formerly had stood the palace of King Ahab, he erected a temple dedicated to Octavian. Besides this, Herod also built a forum, a theatre, a stadium, colonnaded streets, and new city walls. Traces of this activity are to be seen at every turn. In honour of the Roman ruler Herod also had the name of the new city changed to Sebaste, the Greek equivalent of Augustus. The name still survives in that of the tiny village of Sebastiyeh, nestling against the eastern slope of the hill.

There was no point on the coast south of Mount Carmel at which ships could anchor safely. Herod had two piers built out into the sea to form a man-made harbour. He also provided this place, which he named Caesarea in honour of Octavian, with the public buildings which every Hellenistic town possessed at this time. Because of its favourable position Caesarea quickly became the chief port of Palestine and the gateway to the Greek and Roman world. At a later period the Roman governors chose this town as their place of residence.

Herod did not confine his activities to Palestine. He seems to have been anxious to acquire fame abroad, and provided many towns with substantial subsidies for the building of great monuments. Among those which benefited from this largesse were Damascus, Antioch in Syria, Byblos, Berytus, Tripolis, Tyre, Sidon, Athens, Sparta, and the islands of Rhodes and Chios. One result of these activities was that Herod unknowingly prepared the way for the spread of Christianity. Indeed, as a result of these benefactions and of his good relations with Octavian the standing of the Jews in the Diaspora was notably improved, and the number of God-fearers and proselytes perpetually on the increase. For those who were later to proclaim the message of Christianity this formed a favourable basis on which to build.

All these activities did not lead Herod to neglect his home territory. His Hellenistic bent prompted him to carry out various building projects in Judea as well. He even turned his attention to places of importance specifically to Jewry. According to tradition the caves where Abraham and his immediate family were supposed to lie buried were situated on the edge of Hebron. In order to protect this sacred spot from profanation Herod had it enclosed within an immense wall which is still mostly intact. Just north of Hebron, at the site alleged to be that of the oaks of Mamre (Gen. 13:18), he did the same.

His great achievement, however, was the Temple at Jerusalem. The sanctuary which had been built after the Exile had long since ceased to bear comparison with the Hellenistic temples of neighbouring countries. In the year 20 B.C. a start was made with this ambitious project, and after only nine years it was

◁ *(Opposite)* The desert north-east of 'Aqaba is quite different in character from the Judean desert. Here the main feature is a sandy plain. Trading caravans could cross it without difficulty: they were able to take their bearings from the rock outcrops, some big and some small, which rise on every hand.

The town of Ashkelon always managed to avoid any direct control by Israelite or Jew. Even Herod the Great was unable to annex to his kingdom this port on the Mediterranean Sea. In New Testament times Ashkelon was a free city, set under the authority of the Roman consul in the province of Syria. During the Crusades this ancient Philistine city was an important military base; vestiges of a fort of that period still stand by the sea shore.

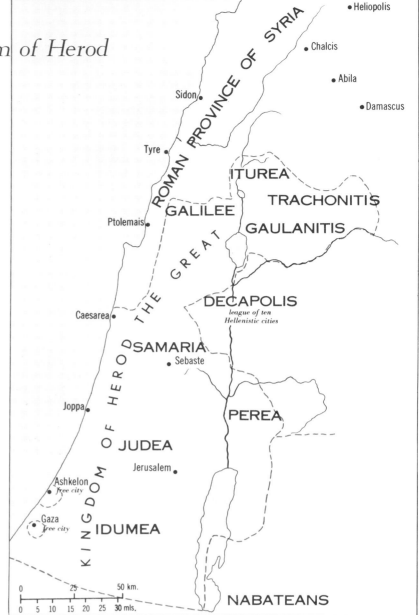

possible to consecrate the new building for use. But this did not mean that the work on it was completed. In the case of Semitic sanctuaries the temple proper was usually only the central part of a larger whole. Around 'the house of God' the courtyard with its additional buildings, colonnades, water-basins, altars, and so forth had to be constructed, and the whole complex had then still to be enclosed by the Temple wall with its gates. In Jerusalem the courtyard was made exceptionally large. To give added emphasis to the sacred character of the place four forecourts were built around the Temple itself—areas assigned respectively to the priests, to Jewish men, to Jewish women, and to Gentiles of both sexes. This last group were strictly forbidden to set foot in the other courts. By a stroke of fortune the stone plaque on which this prohibition was displayed has been recovered. The text, in Greek of course, reads, "No alien is allowed to enter the enclosed area and the forecourt around the temple; anyone who does so is guilty, and will be punished with death."

The new design meant that the old Temple area had to be extended. The lie of the terrain gave rise to special difficulties, however, for the ground fell away fairly sharply toward the south-east. To bring this section up to a level with the rest it could have been filled in with rubble, but Herod's architects decided on another, very modern approach. They put about a hundred sturdy columns across the incline and made the southern part of the Temple court rest upon them. This created the Temple terrace and the enormous subterranean area known nowadays, quite wrongly, as 'Solomon's stables.' The space was to provide a second way of access to the Temple for the inhab-

An inscription, on stone, from the Herodian Temple. It was found during restoration work in the court of the Mosque and is now preserved in the museum at Istanbul. The text is inscribed not in Hebrew or Aramaic, but in Greek. It was intended, therefore, as a warning to non-Jews. Gentiles were permitted to set foot only in the outermost forecourt of the Temple; and for them the rest was forbidden territory. Originally, the stone was probably set in the wall at the entrance to the Women's Court.

itants of the low-lying Ophel. By passing beneath this part of the courtyard and up two flights of steps they were able to reach the Court of the Gentiles.

Herod saw to it that Jerusalem was also provided with buildings that would help to secure his own power and authority. At the north-west angle of the Temple court, just on the edge of the city, there had already stood for several centuries the strong tower of Acra. During the Maccabean rebellion it had housed a Syrian garrison, who had held it for twenty-six years. On this spot Herod built a fortress to which he gave the name of Antonia. It was not only designed to strengthen the otherwise vulnerable north wall against potential invaders: it also afforded a good view of the whole Temple court. The soldiers could intervene quickly, if rioting should break out among the easily inflamed mob. A good illustration of this is provided by the incident mentioned in Acts 21:27ff (see page 178). Nothing now remains of this fortress. After its destruction the city began to expand in a northerly direction, and since the Temple court no longer had any of its former functions to fulfil, there was no reason for rebuilding it.

Herod never actually resided in this fortress. He preferred an equally advantageous but more spacious site on the western hill by the Valley of Hinnom. Since the time of the Maccabean wars this hill had seen the gradual development of an urban quarter, and it was on its highest point, which commanded a view of the whole city, that Herod chose to build his citadel. With characteristic exaggeration the Jewish author, Flavius Josephus (ca. A.D. 80), writes of this building: "There stood the tower of Hippicus and close by it yet two others which Herod the Great had put up alongside the ancient wall. Their beauty and strength were so extraordinary that nothing in the world was to be compared with them. Indeed, it was not only the outstanding greatness of this prince and his preference for Jerusalem that prompted him to execute this building. He wished also to express his inmost feelings by immortalizing with this work the names of the three persons most dear to him..." It seems that Herod named the three towers after his friend Hippicus, his brother Phasael, and his wife Mariamne. Of this building, too, little remains standing. Only the base of the Tower of David bears witness today to Herod the Great's achievements.

Herod also sought to assure the maintenance of his power outside Jerusalem by extending and strengthening various strongholds built by the Maccabees and the Hasmoneans, and on an eminence to the east of Bethlehem he had a new fortress built which he named Herodium, after himself, and in which he was later buried. His most notable achievement of this kind, however, was a fortified palace which stood on the western shore of the Dead Sea, about 9 miles south of En-gedi. Tradition has it that it occupied the site of a smaller building erected by Jonathan, the Maccabee, on an isolated outcrop of rock, and known by the name of Masada. It was to Jonathan's fortress, apparently, that Herod had conveyed his kinsfolk when he was obliged to flee to Rome because of the Parthians. At some subsequent time during his long reign he expanded this into a luxurious winter residence, embracing a whole complex of buildings. The most impressive of these was the royal palace with its three terraces, built against the northern slope of the mountain. Excavations carried out since 1963 have shown that Herod spared no pains to make his residence in this lonely and barren region as agreeable as it could possibly be. Archaeologists have discovered there the remains of mosaic floors, frescoes, colonnades, and rooms for hot and cold baths.

All these projects called for a great deal of money, which had to come mainly from the people in the form of taxes; but the country was evidently prosperous enough to carry the burden. Palestine, like other places, was enjoying the benefits of the *pax Romana*. Trade between the various nations was steadily improving, and thanks to the new port of Caesarea this contact now extended to Herod's territories. Within the country itself there were hardly any customs barriers, because Decapolis was the only region that did not come directly under Herod's authority.

Despite all this prosperity, and despite the king's skill as a politician and his building projects for the Jewish holy places, Herod was not popular with the people. They never ceased to regard him as an interloper, and this feeling was only reinforced by his friendship with the Romans and his sympathy with Hellenistic ideas. His tyrannical conduct aroused fear and hatred in the hearts of many. They were few indeed who could respond with affection toward a prince who, as he lay dying himself, could still have his own firstborn son put to death.

The Pharisees at first considered him their ally, in so far as he had broken the power of the Hasmoneans, but he gradually

Against the northern slope of the hill of Masada, on the western shore of the Dead Sea, Herod built a palace consisting of three terraces. The uppermost of these formed the actual living-quarters: four spacious apartments decorated with mosaics and frescoes. The middle terrace (in the photo) consisted of a circular pavilion with a gallery on the south side; here it was possible to relax, sheltered from the broiling sun and the hot desert wind. The bottom terrace contained a rectangular room and a bath. In the year 73 the Romans destroyed all Herod's buildings. In the photo are still to be seen in the valley below the outlines of a Roman military camp.

stifled their attempts to gain a measure of freedom in religious matters. Nor did he respect in any way their regard for the Law, and the fact that he had ten wives was obviously totally unacceptable to them. At the end of his life, therefore, they were his most vehement opponents. With the Sadducees, however, the exact opposite was the case. As supporters of the Hasmoneans they began by being against Herod, but he overcame their resistance by taking complete personal control of the appointment of the High Priest and of nominations to other prominent posts. To fill these he appointed Sadducees, whom he was able to influence. In the long run, therefore, this party learned to accommodate itself to the changed circumstances, and co-operated with Herod as well as it could.

It was perhaps also at this time that a new party emerged which was favourably disposed towards Herod. The New Testament does indeed refer to Herodians (Mark 3:6; 12:13), although by this time Herod had in fact already been dead for many years. At all events, they formed a group which supported his family. During the régime of the Roman governors they probably made it their aim to restore the single kingdom under one of Herod's descendants. The great mass of the people, however, would not have been filled with grief when early in the year 4 B.C. their king became seriously ill. To find a cure for his disease he had himself conveyed as far as the warm springs of Callirrhoë on the eastern shore of the Dead Sea. When he felt his end approaching, he returned to his winter residence in Jericho to arrange the matter of the succession. He hurriedly asked Octavian for permission to have his eldest son put to death and himself died a few days later, just before the time of the Passover.

Herod had specified in his will that the three of his sons who were still living should each administer a part of his kingdom. The Roman ruler consented to this in broad outline, but he did not allow any further use of the title of king when it was brought to his notice that the people, led by the Pharisees, were opposed to it. As a result, the arrangements made for the administration of Palestine during the New Testament period are not at all easy to grasp. Herod had ruled over Judea (including Idumea), Samaria, Galilee, Perea, and the district of trans-Jordan south of Damascus. To the south and east his territory was bordered by the Nabatean kingdom. Between Perea and the region to the south of Damascus there lay Decapolis, a league of ten or so Hellenistic cities which came directly under the authority of Rome. To the north the Roman province of Syria marked the limits of Herod's territory. The frontier ran from Damascus past Galilee to a point south of the Carmel hills.

Such was the Jewish kingdom that was now to be partitioned. Its central core comprised Judea and Samaria, and these areas were assigned to Archelaus. He was given the title of ethnarch, a status somewhat inferior to that of a king. A further part of Herod's kingdom comprised Galilee and Perea, an elongated strip of land on the east bank of the Jordan. These districts, which had no common frontier, were put under the control of Antipas, another of Herod's sons. Antipas was still in office during the ministries of John the Baptist and of Jesus of Nazareth. He was called tetrarch, a title usually explained as meaning 'ruler of a fourth (part).' In practice, the word implied a rank lower than that of either ethnarch or king. The third

The Palestine of the New Testament

part of Herod's kingdom embraced the districts south of Damascus, known as Gaulanitis and Trachonitis (Luke 3:1). These came under the control of Philip.

Where politics were concerned, Herod the Great's descendants possessed nothing of his skill. The way in which Archelaus governed Judea and Samaria made the people there so discontented that after his exile the Romans put in a governor instead. Roman procurators then continued to govern this province, in almost uninterrupted succession, until the outbreak of the first Jewish rebellion in A.D. 66. In Galilee and Perea, Antipas did somewhat better. On the Lake of Gennesaret he built a town which he named after the reigning emperor Tiberius (A.D. 14–37). The third brother, Philip, also attached his name to a city. On the site of the earlier Paneion, where the Jordan had its source, he built, also in honour of the emperor, the famous Caesarea Philippi. This was the place where Peter recognized that Jesus of Nazareth was the Messiah (Mark 8:27).

Agrippa I, a grandson of Herod, was, however, the most successful of that king's descendants. For a brief period, from A.D. 41 to 44, he restored the kingdom of his grandfather and even managed to regain the title of king. He also constructed the third wall on the north side of Jerusalem, thereby annexing to the city the hill of Bethesda and the neighbourhood surrounding the traditional site of Golgotha. This wall presumably followed the same course as the Turkish wall which still exists on both sides of the Damascus Gate.

Despite the presence of this Jewish ruler, it was the Roman governors, generally speaking, who wielded the greatest power in Palestine after the exile of Archelaus. Up to the year A.D. 66. fourteen Romans held that office, seven before and seven after

The heart of the small town of Bethlehem, where both King David and Jesus of Nazareth were born, was situated on the north-western hill. In New Testament times the traditional site of the Cave of the Nativity lay outside the town to the south-east. Christian devotion ensured that this south-eastern hill was soon covered with buildings. Nowadays one can identify the area by the large number of towers belonging to the churches and monasteries there.

◁ It was in Galilee, and especially along the shores of the lake in that district, that Jesus of Nazareth chose to do his work. The photo shows the flat and fertile country north-west of the lake. In the centre is a mound, known in Arabic as Tell el-'Oreimeh. It has been identified with the Canaanite town of Chinnereth, from which the lake at one time took its name (Num. 34 : 11; Josh. 12 : 3, and 13 : 27). In the background are some of the high tops of the Galilean hills.

the reign of Agrippa I. Pontius Pilate was the fifth in this line. He governed over a relatively long period, from A.D. 26 to 36. Only his immediate predecessor was in office for longer than that. Others whose names are known to us were Antonius Felix (A.D. 52–60) and Porcius Festus (A.D. 60–62). As will be seen later it was Felix who kept Paul in jail for two years at Caesarea, in order to gain favour with the Jews (Acts 24:27), and Festus who sent him to Rome, after Paul had appealed for justice to Caesar (Acts 25:12).

3. JESUS OF NAZARETH

It is extremely difficult to describe the atmosphere and mental outlook prevailing among the Jewish people in Palestine about the year A.D. 30. Without doubt there was a powerful current of nationalism. Owing to Pontius Pilate's tactless behaviour there was a steadily mounting feeling of hostility towards the authority of Rome. It was especially hard for most Jews to accept the fact that the holy city of Jerusalem, and along with it the Temple, came under the control of the Roman governor. Earlier on, there had been agitation against Herod the Great and in turn against his son, Archelaus, but it seemed subsequently that the situation under both those rulers had been preferable to the rule of the governors. It is true that the Roman emperor spared their religious sensibilities as much as was possible, but his officials were faced with the onerous daily task of maintaining the authority of Rome and at the same time governing a people whom they did not understand. The fanatical and puritanical attitude of the Jews to their faith was something quite uncommon in the Roman world at this time. Religious feeling was the basis of their desire for national greatness. For the Jews, therefore, the Romans were not simply political adversaries: first and foremost they were the enemies of the Jewish religion.

It was within this political and mental climate that Jesus of Nazareth fulfilled his mission. Details of his life, however, and the dates of his activities which would be of interest from a historical point of view as touching on the wider political issues of the day lie buried in obscurity. Even the year of his birth cannot be ascertained exactly. One of the reasons for this lack of information is that no pagan author of the period wrote anything about him. His activities were of interest only to the early Christians, and they were not primarily concerned with his appearance as a figure in world history.

From the few pointers contained in the Gospels it would appear that Jesus must have been born in the last years of the reign of Herod the Great, and therefore prior to the year 4 B.C. The Gospels record that his birth took place in Bethlehem, traditionally the city of David, but Jesus spent the early years of his life in Nazareth, a hamlet in the hills of Galilee, frequently mentioned in the Gospels. This is really all that can be said about his life before the beginning of his ministry. The earliest Christians were evidently little interested in the facts of his birth. When they did reflect upon it, what mainly concerned them were the religious consequences of the event and not the question of its precise date.

This becomes clear when we consider the events recorded in the infancy-narratives of Matthew and Luke. The information they contain about the early life of Jesus is clearly presented for doctrinal purposes, though this does not mean to say that it has no factual foundation. The catechetical intention would nevertheless have an influence in deciding what was to be included or stressed in the account of Jesus's life written for the instruction of the early generations of Christians.

The situation is slightly different in the case of Jesus's public ministry and the events leading up to his crucifixion. To begin with, these were bound, for a number of reasons, to have been better documented than the events of his early life. His sayings and actions as a teacher and preacher would have had many more witnesses, especially as he was constantly moving from place to place. Moreover, his clashes with the authorities would have brought him into public notice, though the fact that these authorities did not realise with whom they were dealing may account for there being barely any mention of him in official historical records, such as those of Josephus. For the early disciples and the Evangelists, however, everything which Jesus said and did during the period of his ministry, or was reported to have said and done, would have been valuable as a testimony to the faith he had come to preach. The task of his 'biographers' in this case was to select those events which in their opinion most clearly illustrated the nature of their man and his mission. Again, therefore, they would not have been concerned with factual detail for its own sake. Consequently, they were not particularly concerned with either the exact dating of the various events in Jesus's life, or with a strictly chronological presentation of them.

The beginning of Jesus's ministry, according to the Gospel of St. Luke, was in "the fifteenth year of the reign of Tiberius Caesar" (Luke 3:1). Tiberius reigned from A.D. 14 to 37. Jesus's earliest activities might therefore be assigned to the year 29.

Modern Nazareth, from the north. For centuries the little town lay tucked away among the southern slopes of the Galilean hills. It therefore lay to the left of the principal trade-routes; and there is not a single reference to it in the Old Testament. Between 1935 and 1955 there was opportunity to investigate more closely the spot associated with the story of Luke 1 : 26-37; and this served to shed a certain amount of light on Nazareth's history. The ridge to the west of the town (right, in the photo) has three spurs, thrusting out into the valley below. Nazareth sprang up, originally, along the centre spur. Such traces as survive in the rocky soil suggest that in the pre-exilic period it was no more than a hamlet. The necessary water was always drawn from the spring at the foot of the northern-most spur. That is what Nazareth was like when Jesus spent his youth there. It was not until the Byzantine period that the hamlet expanded and became a small town.

The map (left) shows:

Heliopolis

ROMAN PROVINCE OF SYRIA

Chalcia

ABILENE
Abila
tetrarchy under Lysanias

Sidon

Damascus

Tyre

Caesarea Philippi

ITUREA
tetrarchy under Philip
4 B.C. - A.D. 34

GALILEE
(+ PEREA)
tetrarchy under
Herod Antipas
4 B.C. - A.D. 39

TRACHONITIS

Ptolemais

GAULANITIS

Tiberias

Caesarea

DECAPOLIS

Sebaste

JUDEA + SAMARIA
ethnarchy under Archelaus
5 B.C. - A.D. 6;
administered by governors,
including Pontius Pilate A.D. 26-36

PEREA
(+ GALILEE)
tetrarchy under
Herod Antipas
4 B.C. - A.D. 39

Joppa

Jerusalem

Ashkelon

Machaerus

Gaza

0   25   50 km.
0 5 10 15 20 25 30 mls.

NABATEANS

too much inclined to equate the coming of the kingdom of God with an upsurge in the fortunes of the nation.

From Galilee Jesus went to Judea. In doing so, he avoided as far as possible the short route across Samaria. There were, in fact, few Jews living in this area. He preferred instead the more round-about way through Perea, the Jewish country of Antipas on the far side of the Jordan. In Jerusalem, the very centre of the Jewish religion, there was naturally a lively yearning for independence and national greatness. At the same time the city was a nest of various factions and interests. That Jesus should not gain adherents in such an atmosphere is hardly surprising. He disregarded all parties and groups who wielded power, and acted and spoke on his own authority. Such independent behaviour aroused the suspicion, jealousy, and hate of all those who moved in influential circles.

The Sadducees were concerned to maintain their social standing, and the ideas which Jesus was propagating might easily lead them into difficulties with the Roman authorities. The Pharisees, though they could not on the whole understand him, considered his free interpretation of the Law an attack on the very foundations of the Jewish religion. The leaders in Jerusalem had the power to intervene and check Jesus's activities because the Supreme Council was backed up by the Romans. The task of this college was to govern the nation without allowing themselves to lose sight of Rome's interests. They even possessed a certain degree of judicial authority, although it is doubtful whether they could pass and carry out sentence of death on their own initiative.

The direction of this body lay with the High Priest. For

But it may also have been earlier, for Luke's dating could be reckoning from the time when Tiberius was co-regent (A.D. 11/12). Reckoning from this date we arrive at the year A.D. 26/27.

At a first reading, the Synoptic Gospels (Matthew, Mark, and Luke) convey the impression that Jesus was active for one year only, first in Galilee and finally in Jerusalem. But from the information contained in the Gospel of St. John it is possible to make out a case for a ministry extending over at least two years. Again, what is fairly certain is that Jesus was active mostly in Galilee, where Herod Antipas had the governing authority. The region around the Lake of Gennesaret seems to have had a special appeal for him, but he also went to the adjoining districts, to Philip's country in the east, and the Roman province of Syria in the west. It was evidently possible to cross the frontiers of these territories without much difficulty. The Biblical texts have nothing to say about any activity on Jesus's part in such important cities as Tiberias, Sepphoris, Scythopolis, and Ptolemais. He seems to have had a preference for the lowlands and the smaller places. On the whole the Galileans listened attentively to what he had to say. They were well known for their religious zeal, which seems to have been more genuine and heartfelt than among people in some other districts. It was natural, therefore, that they should respond to Jesus's message. That they were nevertheless frequently mistaken as to his real meaning, is understandable, since on the whole the Jews were

Against the eastern slope of Jerusalem's western hill lie the ruins of a mill dating from New Testament times. Among the archaeologists' finds there, around 1900, were coins, some of the year A.D. 3, some from the time of Herod Agrippa (A.D. 41-44), and some from the last years of the emperor Nero. The actual mill was in the large cavity, top left, which is about 10 feet across. In the centre of this space a raised part is still visible on which the millstones were set. A donkey circled round and round this and, his day's work done, went to the stall with its feeding-trough, which stands beside the mill, hidden beneath the rock. The small circular hole to the right of the mill was the silo, itself hewn straight out of the rock. The absence of plaster on the wall and the fact that the opening is 3 feet in diameter make it almost certain that this was not a well to hold water. Most of the other remains and fittings were dismantled in the Byzantine period to make room for the foundations of a monastery and a church bearing the name of Sanctus Petrus in gallicantu: that is, St. Peter-at-the-Cockcrow.

many years the office had been discharged by a certain Annas. When he was deposed, he succeeded in ensuring that after a brief interval the post went to his son-in-law, Caiaphas. This man kept his position from A.D. 18 to 36, although Annas remained the power behind the scenes. Apart from the High Priest, the Council had a total of seventy members, drawn from three different strata of Jewish society. The first group were known as 'the high priests'; these were in fact priests and laymen who under the High Priest's direction were charged with the day-to-day administration of religious affairs. Then came 'the elders,' the heads of distinguished families. Their contribution gradually diminished, because they had no solution to advance to problems that were becoming ever more complicated. The third group, on the other hand, had a mounting influence. These were the Scribes, men who had studied and knew how to interpret the Law and apply it to the affairs of everyday life. In the Council the Sadducees and the Pharisees had about an equal number of supporters. Most of the Scribes were representatives of the Pharisaic school, whereas the majority among 'the high priests' and 'the elders' were connected with the Sadducees. The composition and the vested interests of the Supreme Council made it inevitable that Jesus would find neither sympathy for his ideas nor mercy for himself amongst its members.

He also had little to hope for from the governor, Pontius Pilate. Pilate understood nothing of the Jewish outlook or of the Jews' problems. What concerned him was the maintenance of the authority of Rome, and in this he was anything but tactful. When he first took up his post, for example, he allowed his troops to enter Jerusalem carrying insignia that displayed the emperor's image. Octavian had earlier promised the Jews that he would grant Jerusalem immunity from such manifestations of the cult of the ruler. But Pilate would meet the legitimate demands of the people only when their vehement protests threatened to end in violence. He showed the same lack of understanding when he laid hands on money from the Temple chest, to pay for a water-conduit which was to lead from the pools of Solomon to Jerusalem. This high-handed behaviour was eventually to be his downfall. In A.D. 36, when disturbances broke out in Samaria, he acted with such violence and brutality that the emperor had him recalled. Pilate, then, was not the kind of person who might have seen the accusations against Jesus for what they were. When it was alleged that he was putting himself forward as king of the Jews, one can guess Pilate's reaction: a person with such ambitions could endanger the position of the governor and undermine the authority of Rome.

The date of Jesus's death is a matter of uncertainty. The execution undoubtedly took place as the Gospels state on the occasion of a Passover festival. This would account for the governor's presence in Jerusalem. Normally he resided in Caesarea, but on occasions that might prove in any way dangerous, he moved to the holy city and made his quarters in the palace which King Herod had built on the western hill. It was also because of the Passover that Herod Antipas had come to Jerusalem from Galilee. Pilate sent Jesus to him, when it transpired that the accused man's place of origin was Nazareth. But Antipas was crafty enough to avoid getting mixed up in the affair (Luke 23:6–12).

The three oldest Gospels seem to be in agreement that Jesus and the disciples shared a special private meal on the first day of Passover Week, and that his trial and execution took place on the actual day of the feast. This must be unlikely, however, as it would have meant the Jewish leaders violating the rest that was obligatory on that day. The chronology in the Fourth Gospel is more likely: there the meal, the trial, and crucifixion are described as taking place on the day preceding the feast.

In this case the meal Jesus took with his disciples, though of tremendous significance to them, especially in retrospect, was not a Passover meal; but it is easy to see how it could later be described as such as the overwhelming meaning of the 'breaking of the bread' and Jesus's identification with the Pascal lamb became clear (John 1:29; 1 Cor. 5:7).

It seems likely, then, that Jesus of Nazareth met his death on the eve of the Passover, that is, on the 14th Nisan. Now the 14th Nisan fell on a Friday in the years 30 and 33. The latter year is the less likely of the two, for it would mean that Jesus's ministry lasted for at least five years, and there is nothing in the Gospels to support such a belief. A more justifiable choice is the year 30, when the 14th Nisan fell on April 7th of the modern calendar.

On many maps of Jerusalem in New Testament times there is a street of steps, running down from the top of the western hill to the pool of Siloam in the Tyropoeon Valley. Today the area lies to the south of the walled city; but in the New Testament period it certainly formed part of old Jerusalem. The steps themselves probably date from the time of Herod and Pilate. Excavation around 1900 indicated that the street had been partly built over with a number of Byzantine buildings. This means that the steps are pre-Byzantine and probably earlier than the year 135, when the Romans laid this section waste and made Jerusalem itself into Aelia Capitolina. Since in the majority of ancient cities in the East the line of a street, and certainly of a flight of steps, tended to persist unchanged, one can assume that the position, at any rate, and probably the steps themselves date from the time of Jesus of Nazareth.

X. THE SHAPING OF CHRISTIAN TRADITION

First phase of the New Testament. The gradual development of the Early Church in Palestine ca. A.D. 40.

1. THE POLITICAL AND RELIGIOUS SITUATION

The death of Jesus of Nazareth brought about no great changes in Palestine. Pontius Pilate remained in office despite the growing discontent of the Jewish people, and the Supreme Council continued to exercise its authority over internal affairs. It was not until A.D. 36, at least three, and probably six years after Jesus's execution, that an imperial decree brought about a change in the political situation. This decree ordered Roman officials to exercise tolerance and consideration when dealing with the demands of the Jews in the empire.

In Herod's citadel on the western hill of Jerusalem the governor had for years had hanging a number of golden shields, on which were engraved the names of the emperor and of other benefactors. From the point of view of the puritanical Pharisees this ran counter to the commandment prohibiting images, and so profaned the city. When the contents of the decree reached their ears, they demanded that Pilate remove the shields. Although he consented, he found it hard to stomach such humiliation. Not long afterwards a crowd had gathered together on Mount Gerizim to attend a religious ceremony. Pilate saw in this an incitement to rebellion and used violent means to disperse it. As a result, there was such an uproar throughout the Jewish territories that his position became untenable. Vitellius, the legate of the province of Syria, summoned him to give an account of himself at Antioch and then sent him on to Rome. After this Pontius Pilate disappears from the pages of history.

At about the same time something else happened which likewise served to improve the position of the Jews. The Parthians were once again causing disturbances on the eastern frontier of the empire, and since the attention of the Roman army was very much occupied with repelling hostile attacks on Mesopotamia, it was anxious to avoid trouble in other border territories. As a result, certain concessions were made to the Jews. Vitellius removed the unpopular Caiaphas from his post as High Priest and appointed Jonathan, a son of the elderly Annas, in his place. The Roman official residing in Caesarea as Vitellius's representative received strict orders not to meddle in Jewish matters. The High Priest and the other Jewish leaders were now free, as they had not been for a long time, to manage all internal affairs as they wished.

This freedom did not last for long, however. A year later the emperor Tiberius, who had always considered the Jews' interests, died, and Caligula ascended the throne in his place. The new ruler was more of a Hellenist than a Roman, and made it absolutely obligatory for all his subjects to worship him as a god. It was an attitude bound to lead to conflict with the Jews. One of his first acts as emperor was to install in Judea a governor who exercised a stricter supervision over Jewish activities. But a fortuitous circumstance prevented the worst from happening. Herod the Great's grandson, Agrippa, who had been living in Rome for some years, had been a strong supporter of Caligula's aspirations to the throne. Because of this the emperor Tiberius had clapped him in gaol for six months. After Caligula had ascended the throne he rewarded his friend by granting him the title of king and the district south of Damascus to rule over.

Fortune soon smiled on him. His uncle, Antipas, envious of the honour which had been accorded his nephew, asked the emperor to raise his tetrarchy to the status of a kingdom. But this request was viewed with extreme disfavour in Rome. Instead of the royal title Antipas received a command to go into exile in Gaul, the Siberia of the Roman empire. Agrippa profited by this turn of events, for in the year 40 his uncle's territories were added to those he already held.

Agrippa was not without sympathizers among the Jews, since his new kingship lent lustre to Jewry and his friendship with Caligula afforded some softening of the emperor's hellenizing policies. With Caligula's increasing madness, however, a clash was bound to come. Before this could happen, Caligula was assassinated in the year 41.

Agrippa was just in time to trim his sails to the wind. Before Caligula's death Agrippa was already on good terms with the next emperor, Claudius, who after his seizure of power gave him control of Judea and Samaria as well. Thus Agrippa had succeeded, partly by accident and partly by skill, in restoring the kingdom of Herod the Great. In fact, his authority extended somewhat farther, because he was also ruler of the unimportant districts of Abilene and Arca in the mountains of Lebanon.

As a politician Agrippa I took more or less the same line as his grandfather. In Judea, Perea, and Galilee he was to the point of exaggeration a Jew among Jews. He apparently realized the power of the Pharisees, for he accommodated himself as much

The winged goddess Victoria, the Roman counterpart of the Greek goddess Nike, was the symbol of the worldwide power of Rome. Images of 'the goddess of victory' have been recovered from every part of the empire, including Palestine. This photo shows the Nike found in the Roman layer of the free city of Ashkelon. The goddess stands triumphant upon the vault of heaven, which is supported by the Titan, Atlas. To symbolize her power she usually holds a palm-branch in her left hand, at hip level, and in her right hand, above her head, a flaming sword or something of that sort. This statue, however, has lost those appurtenances.

as possible to their wishes. Outwardly he conducted himself as a true man of the Law, and the Jewish historian Flavius Josephus classified him accordingly among the great rulers. But in areas where there were few or no Jews living he went to work in a different way. There he was the Hellenistic prince, upholding pagan culture and religion with much pomp and ceremony. One result of these activities was that the prestige of the Jews increased among many Hellenists. A striking example of this is the fact that the ruler of Adiabene, a minor kingdom in Mesopotamia, accepted the Jewish religion, along with his mother Helena. After her conversion Helena spent most of her time, with her royal household, in Jerusalem, and even made arrangements to be buried there. The complex of tombs which she caused to be hewn out of the rock to the north of the city is still very largely intact and is known today as the 'Tombs of the Kings.'

It might well have been wondered how long the Romans would continue to stand by Agrippa. His vanity impelled him more and more to make a show of power that was not rightly his. For example, he tried to arrange a meeting in Tiberias of all the regional rulers governing the eastern part of the empire, but was prevented from doing so by the legate in Syria, who suspected that he was planning to secede from Rome. Whatever his intentions may have been, they were cut short when he died at Caesarea in 44, after a short illness (Acts 12:19-23). The emperor had for some time been looking with suspicion at events in Palestine, and after Agrippa's death he appointed a governor to take charge in Judea, Samaria, and Galilee. The deceased monarch's son, Agrippa II, was later allowed to reign over a few unimportant districts outside Palestine, when he had come of age, but no Jew ever again reigned as king over his own nation.

2. THE CHRISTIAN COMMUNITY IN PALESTINE

From the accounts of Jesus's trial and execution given in the Gospels it would appear that many of those who had been inclined to accept him as the promised Messiah turned against him in anger and disappointment when they discovered that he had not come to restore the nation to its former political greatness. It is also probable that those who had a somewhat deeper insight into his real mission, and saw in him a great moral teacher and prospective leader of the nation, lost all hope in his cause once his crucifixion and death had put an end to the possibility of his continuing his work in person.

The tiny group which had been with him throughout his ministry, however, found it difficult to accept his death as final. The strange power of his personality, the miracles he had performed, and the illumination of his teaching had so completely changed their lives and left such a vivid impression on hearts and minds that the idea of his death must have seemed inconceivable. How could he die who had been the embodiment of life abundant and eternal? The personal anxiety they must have felt for him from the time of his arrest up to his crucifixion would no doubt have left them shattered in mind and body, but their grief at his death may well have been more the result of shock and dismay than of despair. Without his personal presence and guidance, how could they continue to find their way in the world? They had given up everything to follow him, and they knew that the path he had shown them was the only true one. Yet how could they follow it if he was not there to lead them?

We may imagine that they were still in this state of confusion when two days later they were overwhelmed once again, this time by the joyful discovery that he had triumphed over death and was still with them. One of the most striking and memorable impressions which the Gospel writers convey in their accounts of Christ's resurrection is the natural way in which his disciples accepted this event, once the first shock of surprise was over. It is as though it had simply confirmed their innermost convictions. The initial doubts of Thomas, who is the one exception in this respect, are soon forgotten amidst the feelings of joy and triumph which rapidly spread through the community as Christ presents himself to one disciple after another. A few weeks later, after the excitement had died down and the disciples had come to realize that even when the time came for Christ to make his final ascent into Heaven he would still be with them in spirit, his return from the grave is something they seem to have taken for granted. In the account which Luke gives at the beginning of Acts they no longer register surprise when he appears among them, but talk with him and ask him questions, as they had done in the days of his public ministry.

When Christ finally ascended into Heaven, and the gift of

The Kingdom of Agrippa I

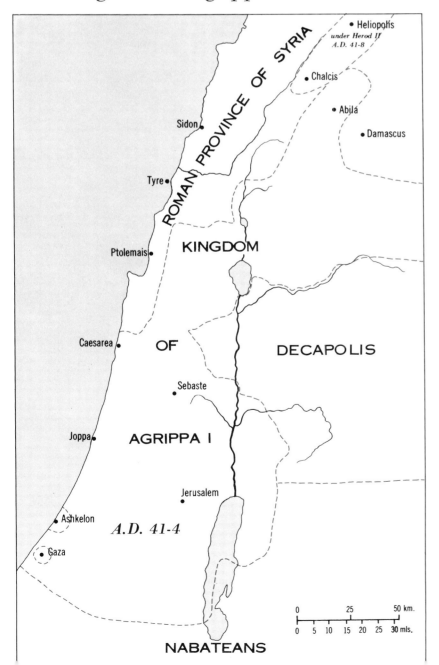

the Holy Spirit had been poured out on the disciples on the day of Pentecost, the work of conveying the Good News of the salvation of mankind began. This would eventually have to be carried to people who had never seen Jesus in the flesh and who knew nothing about him. They would have to be informed of the most essential and relevant facts concerning Jesus's life, and the significance of these would have to be explained to them. In particular, the meaning of Christ's passion and resurrection, as the means by which mankind had been saved, would have to be brought home to them.

To begin with, therefore, there was one important problem which had to be faced. The disciples had to understand and be agreed amongst themselves as to the meaning of Christ's coming. It was not enough simply to be convinced in their own minds of the truth of what they believed, for this conviction would eventually have to be made intelligible to others. There may have been no question at this early stage of the need for any public witness or testimony outside their own congregation, but since this congregation, according to Luke (Acts 1:15) already numbered about one hundred and twenty people, whose personal contact with Christ would have varied in degree from one member to another, a common expression for their general conviction would obviously have to be arrived at. One may imagine that by repeated reflection on what they had each individually experienced concerning Christ they were gradually able to reach a definition of their belief, which they formulated in the following way.

Jesus of Nazareth had not been sent to expel the Romans and restore the kingdom of David by force of arms. His mission was primarily in the spiritual realm. In him the promises recorded in the ancient holy books were eminently fulfilled, for through him God was to bring about the universal kingdom of love and peace. Although his death on the cross had the appearance of a defeat, it was in reality an act of redemption decreed by God to free the world from sin. Because Jesus accepted this death from the hand of God, he was invested with the power to make God's kingdom a reality. They further maintained that by certain mighty signs and tokens Jesus would soon triumph once and for all over evil, and, since the time of his second coming was close at hand, every man should hasten to make himself worthy to receive him.

The Easter faith which illumined this little group of adherents, and which they were only gradually able to put into meaningful words, gave a new colouring and a deeper resonance to the many sayings and actions of Jesus which they now began to recall to mind. They had kept alive in their own circle his exhortations concerning repentance, watchfulness, readiness, and poverty. The loving help he had given to everyone in need and distress was indelibly printed on their memories. Soon, they began to expand their message and to preach it to the people amongst whom they lived and moved.

At first, this did not imply any breach with official Judaism. They were still Jews amongst Jews, in spite of the fact that for them the Kingdom of Love, as exemplified in the life of Jesus, was greater than the Law. In fact, it was not until many years later that they renounced the Law completely. In the early years they quietly continued to frequent the Temple day by day (Acts 2:46), and since there was nothing revolutionary about their behaviour, the Pharisees were not overmuch concerned with them. Their attention was mainly taken up by the difficulties they were having with the governor, Pontius Pilate.

In this relatively peaceful atmosphere the followers of Jesus were gradually able to evolve, side by side with their religious practices as Jews, a religious life of their own. In this the lead and the example came, naturally enough, from a number of men who had known Jesus intimately during his lifetime. This is not to say that ideas and beliefs current among the Jews at this time had no effect on the little community of Jesus's followers. They were influenced especially by the apocalyptic traditions about the final coming of the kingdom of God, because there they found ideas and turns of phrase with which to express their belief that with Jesus the 'last days' had begun. This is why for them, as for the community at Qumran and for certain Gnostic schools of thought, marriage was unimportant. They even renounced for a time their right to personal ownership of property. In this way they were able to give concrete expression to their unity and their concern for the poor, but above all else this practice was inspired by the notion that worldly goods were of small importance in view of the imminence of the establishment of God's kingdom on earth.

This small community or congregation, which represented the beginnings of the Christian Church, would assemble in a private house and there they would share a meal in commemoration of the one Jesus had shared with his disciples on the evening before his death. On such occasions the leaders would bear witness to their Easter faith and formulate their beliefs for the benefit of the whole community. At first, the claim that Jesus of Nazareth was the promised Messiah produced difficulties for many members of the congregation. In Jewish tradition there was no place for a Messiah who suffered and died. In addition Jesus had died an ignominious death through the agency of the hated Roman authorities. These facts ran counter to the current notion of what a Messiah should be. The task confronting the leaders was to make their faith understandable both to themselves and to their followers.

As the books we now call the Old Testament were for them the sole word of God, it was there that the answers to these questions were sought. In seeking to evaluate these texts, which were disseminated among the Jews in a variety of versions, they applied, of course, their contemporary method of textual interpretation. They could command no scientific exegesis: their sole concern was to demonstrate the continuity of God's word. Their aim was to show that the Messiah had been bound to suffer all these things, so that he might enter into his glory (Luke 24:26). One of their earliest concerns, therefore, was to understand and interpret the events which had led up to the death of Jesus. In this way they revealed the meaning which lay behind his suffering and death, and showed how all the authorities and powers which had conspired against him, merely served to raise his dignity and status as a Messiah. Thus it was that the essential core of the later Passion narratives came into being. To this proclamation the leaders added their own profession of belief about the living Jesus. They bore testimony to their experiences after his death, relating their subsequent encounters with him as a

In the northern outskirts of Jerusalem, about half a mile from the Damascus Gate, is a complex hewn in the rock and known as the 'Tombs of the Kings.' A flight of twenty-six steps leads down to the portal. To the right of the steps are channels which catch the rain-water and discharge it into two large cisterns (photo). This water was used for the ritual ablutions which the Jewish religion required on the occasion of a burial. Through a door 10 feet in width one passes into a roomy courtyard, with walls of rock. On the south-west side stands the vestibule, with the entrance to the burial chambers. The large circular stone that sealed the chamber is still in its place beside the entrance.

In the Four Gospels the stone sealing off the tomb of Jesus of Nazareth is an item of some importance (Mark 16 : 3-4; Matt. 28 : 2; Luke 24 : 2; John 20 : 1). For the earliest Christians the fact that the stone was no longer in place helped to confirm, as a matter of physical observation, their belief in the resurrection of Jesus. The tombstone in this picture is in the hamlet on the eastern slope of the Mount of Olives, wrongly called Bethphage.

which recurs in many passages of the New Testament, undoubtedly represents an early form of speech in use amongst the first Christians.

Those Jews who accepted the message proclaimed by the disciples were baptized in the name of Jesus, and in this way they were incorporated into the Church. Subsequently they would be given further instruction with a markedly Christological emphasis. The essential point was always that Jesus was the Messiah. This confession of faith was made more intelligible by reporting the sayings and actions of Jesus which had been passed on within the Church community. Naturally enough, the same result was achieved by the reverse process: all traditions about the life of Jesus of Nazareth took their form of expression, or at any rate their particular emphasis, from the conviction that he was the Messiah. Thus the instruction came to include all sorts of brief biographical items to show how Jesus had lived and carried out his work. Hence there was no story about Jesus and no utterance of his which was not at the same time an affirmation of faith on the part of the first disciples.

In this instruction Jesus was presented as the great teacher and the point of any story told about him lay in bringing out the meaning of one of his sayings. One finds an illustration of this in, for example, Mark 2:23-27, where the passage leads up to the words, "The sabbath was made for man, not man for the sabbath." The role of Jesus as teacher was also illustrated by means of isolated sentences without any narrative context. Some sayings were held up to the new disciples for imitation, as for example the 'judge not' exhortations in Matthew 7:1-5. Other texts were intended to give the baptized a deeper insight into the nature and growth of the kingdom of God. The parables were very well suited to this purpose. Yet another group of sayings focused attention on the daily life of the congregation. People were taught how they should pray, fast, and give alms (Matt. 6:2-18), or were told why Simon Peter was their leader (Matt. 16:18-19).

Jesus was also proclaimed as a worker of miracles. There were descriptions—realistic and often very vivid—of how Jesus had power over the forces of nature or of evil. In these stories various events are related in detail, and in such cases these are of more importance than the sayings. We find an example of this in the story recorded in Mark 4:35-41, which ends with the rhetorical question: "Who then is this, that even wind and sea obey him?"

The acceptance of Jesus as Messiah, teacher, and miracle-worker posed the question as to where his authority and power came from. At first the answer was framed in terms of stories of the Resurrection. They enshrined the message that God had restored Jesus to life and had made him Lord over all. But later on it was affirmed that Jesus had possessed this status even during his earthly life. Such a view was a product of faith, and as

living person, and describing how they had seen him, and had spoken and eaten with him.

The little congregation gradually began to move out more into the open. What they had affirmed and experienced among themselves and their neighbours they now proclaimed and upheld in the Temple court and in the streets of Jerusalem. They addressed themselves to the city's inhabitants and to the many pilgrims who came to worship there. This activity attracted very little notice at first, mainly because Jerusalem was a meeting place for endless cross-currents of thought which the Jews of the Diaspora brought with them from all parts of the Roman empire.

At a later stage Luke wrote a book about the earliest activities of the Church, which came to be known as the 'Acts of the Apostles.' He presents Simon Peter delivering a number of speeches in Jerusalem (Acts 2:14-36; 3:12-26; 4:8-12), and on each occasion the pattern of these speeches is the same. The main point of his message is that Jesus of Nazareth, after his crucifixion and death, was brought back to life by God and so marked out as the Messiah. This claim is then substantiated with the help of one or more texts from the Law, the Prophets, or the Psalms: God's word as contained in the Scriptures confirms the status of Jesus and the testimony of the disciples. The speeches then finish with a call to repentance. Jesus must be accepted as Saviour, because only in and through him is forgiveness of sins possible. What we have here are not verbatim reports of what Peter actually said. The speeches are too meagre and schematic for that. But they show how the call to conversion was preached. Yet the scheme itself is certainly authentic, and the pattern, such went beyond the evidence of the senses. It could only be derived from personal knowledge of Jesus or from an authentic utterance of God. Such an utterance is to be found in the description of the Transfiguration (Mark 9:2-8), in which Jesus is identified as the Messiah with the words, "This is my beloved Son; listen to him"; and in the account of the baptism of Jesus in Mark 1:9-11, which ends with the words: "Thou art my beloved Son; with thee I am well pleased."

In the early years of the Christian community it was certainly the messianic status of Jesus to which most attention was paid, but later on people in the Church began to wonder how Jesus had behaved as an individual at particular moments in his life. They became more and more interested in minute details about the man himself. They very much wanted to know where and when he had been born, how he had spent his youth, whether he had not known temptation, whether he had not been afraid of suffering, and so forth. Passages such as Luke 2:41-52, in which Jesus is shown to have been no ordinary boy, even at twelve years of age, were written down in response to this interest.

To give shape and expression to all these recollections and beliefs was the work of many years. Contributions were made both by individuals and communities in Jerusalem, Judea, and even outside Palestine. The outward form in which these instructional materials were cast was determined by the religious convictions shared by all, but the actual situation that obtained in each congregation also left its mark on these stories and utterances. The proclamation of the message was not meant in fact to be primarily a recapitulation of the past. The first consideration was to get the message across to people living at a particular time in a particular place, beset by particular problems. When, at a later stage, those who had personally known Jesus were no longer living, the sayings and stories about him became crystallized, and assumed a fixed form. 'Standard' accounts developed and were committed to writing, giving rise to the first literary documents of the New Testament.

The more the Church moved outwards and set itself up alongside official Judaism, the stronger became the official resistance to it. The first serious clash occurred in the year 36, when Pontius Pilate had left Judea, and the legate, Vitellius, had put the High Priest, Jonathan, in administrative control. The Jewish leaders used this as an opportunity to take more forceful action against the followers of Jesus of Nazareth. Several leading members of the Church were arrested (Acts 5:17ff). But the proceedings taken against them came to nothing. No-one could point to any definite violation of the Law, for the only ground of complaint was that they considered Jesus of Nazareth to be the Messiah. And so on the initiative of Gamaliel, a man of great authority and an expert on the Law with liberal ideas, the prisoners were released. To avoid further trouble, however, they were forbidden to speak of Jesus again.

The conflict intensified when the Jewish leaders themselves came under attack. This was something that could hardly have arisen among the first disciples. They had been pious Jews who had continued to visit the Temple and had mostly deferred to authority. But the Church had now acquired new members. Particularly noteworthy had been its success among the Hellenistic Jews, who spoke Greek instead of Aramaic and were not so nationalistic in their outlook as the more orthodox Jews. Within a few years this group were demanding a say in the government of the Church, and this they were given. Seven men were appointed from among them—Stephen, Philip, Prochorus, Nicanor, Timon, Parmenas, and Nicolaus. Their names clearly indicate a Greek background. The last-mentioned, Luke tells us (Acts 6:5), was not even a Jew by birth, but a proselyte from Antioch. This would mean that he had been born a pagan and had as an adult accepted the Jewish faith.

Within this 'progressive' group Stephen evidently occupied a prominent position, and his activities gave an impetus to the spread of the new teaching. He spoke out with great eloquence about his convictions in the synagogues frequented by the Jews of the Diaspora, but some who heard him reacted violently against his views. He was seized and brought before the Supreme Council, where he was accused of denying that the Temple was the only centre of worship, and that the Law was the sole authority in religious matters. Luke comments that the accusation was false (Acts 6:13), but the speech which he puts into the mouth of Stephen certainly implies an equivocal attitude towards the supreme position accorded to the Temple.

This address (Acts 7:3-53) is not a word-for-word reconstruction of what Stephen might have said, but neither are these entirely the words of Luke. Here again we have a striking example of the use of the Biblical tradition for purposes of proclamation. A considerable part of the history of the Chosen People is given in summary form, linked with quotations from the Old Testament. The rest must come from the circle of those Pharisees who had joined the congregation of Jesus, for it is quite noticeable that various traditions referred to in the course of the address have no counterparts in our Biblical texts (cf., for example, Acts 7:3 and Gen. 12:4; Acts 7:16 and Gen. 33:19, Gen. 50:13, and Josh. 24:32).

These extra-Biblical ideas are probably part and parcel of the oral traditions which circulated among the Pharisees. Thus Stephen's speech illustrates quite admirably what the attitude was in those years with regard to many of the 'historical' data in the Old Testament. People accepted without question the discrepancies between the various traditions. They were concerned less with historical accuracy than the proclamation of a message in which they fervently believed. The same applies to several of the facts and events recorded in the Gospels.

Although Acts 7:3-53 is obviously not a verbatim report of Stephen's speech, it is probably a fairly faithful reflection of the attitude of the Church in the year 36. Very hesitantly, its members had begun to abandon the Temple cult and to disavow the Jewish claim to sole authority in religious belief. As a 'Hellenist,' Stephen was a step ahead of Jesus's first disciples along this path, and this was probably not easy for them to accept. On higher orders the Roman official in Caesarea was keeping out of Jewish affairs, so that the High Priest and his Council had a free hand in deciding Stephen's fate. This was why, on grounds of his alleged blasphemy, he was condemned to suffer the Biblical penalty of death by stoning (Deut. 17:2-7). It was when sentence was being carried out that there came into prominence for the first time a man who was soon to proclaim the name of Jesus in many a city of the Roman empire and was also to make a significant contribution to the New Testament writings. He was a young

On the eastern side of the Kidron valley stand several monumental tombs which in pious legend have been regarded as the final resting-places of the prophet Zechariah (cf. Matt. 23 : 35), of James the Younger, and of Absalom (cf. 2 Sam. 18 : 18). In fact these are Hellenistic tombs, dating probably from the Herodian period. On the right in the photograph is the 'nephesh' of the Tomb of Absalom. A sepulchral monument of this sort was supposed to keep alive the 'name' of the departed. Scattered about among the weeds are stones from modern Jewish graves; and in the background is the high wall protecting the court of the Mosque. This was for the most part built by the Muslims; but the base in many places belongs to the wall of the Temple terrace, in which up to the year 700 Jews and Christians together worshipped their God.

and fanatical Pharisee who went by the name of Saul. In all probability he attended the execution as the representative of the Supreme Council.

The summary action taken against Stephen was the signal for an attack on the whole congregation of Jesus. "Saul laid waste the Church, and entering house after house, he dragged off men and women and committed them to prison." (Acts 8:3) The members of the Church who had not declared themselves as openly as Stephen against specific Jewish beliefs found it possible to remain in Jerusalem, but the rest were obliged to flee from the city and take refuge in the countryside of Judea and Samaria. The positive aspect of this set-back was that the new faith was carried beyond the confines of Jerusalem on an extensive scale for the first time.

Several incidents in Acts reveal that the missionary activities of Jesus's followers outside Jerusalem were not unsuccessful. Philip, one of the seven 'Hellenists' who had numbered Stephen among their company, went to the city of Samaria. This seems strange, because Samaria was very much of a hellenized town. Would a missionary really have turned, at such an early stage,

to a place where hardly any Jews were living? Perhaps Acts 8:5 should be interpreted as saying that Philip went to a city of Samaria. It is possible that Philip hoped for converts among the Samaritans precisely because of the traditional enmity between them and the orthodox Jews. Whatever the case may have been, the outcome was so successful that two leaders from Jerusalem, Peter and John, went to Samaria to confirm the new disciples in their faith.

It would appear that from this time on Peter made regular journeys through Palestine. On one of them he came to the port of Joppa, where he took lodgings with a tanner. The fact that Peter would stay the night with a man of this occupation shows that even the original disciples of Jesus no longer considered themselves so strongly bound by the laws of official Judaism. In the eyes of the Pharisees the tanner's calling was unclean, probably because such a man came in contact with the skin of unclean animals. While Peter was staying there, a message reached him from a Roman officer called Cornelius, asking him to come to Caesarea. Peter went; and this action marks a critical turning-point in the ideas of the early Church.

The Roman in question was a pious God-fearing man, but he was not a proselyte, that is, he had not been circumcised. Yet Peter went openly into the Gentile's house, and after he had preached his message, he baptized every member of the household. The news of what he had done shocked the disciples in Jerusalem, who had always observed the requirements of the Law, and it was probably to give added justification for this action that Luke narrates twice over the substance of a dream in which God seems to be telling Peter how he should proceed in this matter (Acts 10:11-15 and 11:5-9). During the very early years of the Church this experience of Peter's was evidently the classic argument for baptizing Gentiles. It meant that, in principle, the recognition and observance of the Jewish Law was no longer necessary. One could be baptized in the name of Jesus without being circumcised, which implied that believing in Jesus was not just a continuation or extension of the Jewish religion. It was to be some years, however, before the final conclusion was drawn and the Law was no longer regarded as obligatory even for believers turning from Judaism to Christianity.

In A.D. 37 the emperor Caligula restricted the authority of the High Priests, and it once more became the Roman governor's duty to supervise all the affairs of Palestine. This put a temporary halt to the persecution of the followers of Jesus, and for the next few years the Church was able quietly to consolidate its unexpected growth. The situation changed again four years later, however, when Judea came under the royal authority of Agrippa I (41–44), who collaborated with the Pharisees to break the strength and influence of the young Church. The easiest way to reach this goal, it seemed, was to eliminate the leading members of the congregation. James, the brother of John (Acts 12:1-2), was put in prison, and without even the pretence of a trial was beheaded.

When Agrippa discovered that the band of disciples had done nothing to resist this action and that it had brought him a measure of popularity among a wide section of the Jewish community, he went a step further and had Peter, the most influential of the disciples, taken into custody. Whether Agrippa was planning to put him to death as well remains uncertain, for Peter managed to escape from prison. Since he could no longer remain in Jerusalem in safety Peter left the city and did not return for a number of years.

Apparently Agrippa and the Pharisees then considered their purpose achieved, for the other James, a relative of Jesus, now took the place of Peter in Jerusalem. This James had always insisted on the necessity of keeping the Jewish Law. Consequently, under his leadership the Jerusalem congregation lived in greater conformity with the requirements of Judaism. But the expansion of the Church outside Jerusalem, and particularly outside Palestine, had in the meantime reached such proportions, that in the long run the conservative group in Jerusalem were bound to yield to the more liberal ideas which the larger Church represented and developed.

Antioch in Syria (now Antakya in Turkey) stood on the left bank of the Orontes (in the middle distance) in a fertile valley. Politically, economically, and culturally, the city was of outstanding importance. It enjoyed excellent communications with the rest of the Roman empire. About 16 miles to the west lay the important seaport of Seleucia. From 64 B.C. Antioch, the former capital of the Seleucid Kingdom, was the seat of the Roman governor of the province of Syria. After Rome and Alexandria, it was the third city of the empire, with an estimated population of 500,000. Nowadays the area covered by the city and the number of its inhabitants are considerably smaller.

3. DAMASCUS AND ANTIOCH

The persecution that had broken out in Jerusalem as a result of Stephen's activities did not last for long. The desired outcome was quickly attained. Most followers of Jesus of Nazareth who shared Stephen's ideas left the city as rapidly as possible. They scattered as far as Cyprus and Phoenicia. Some even settled in Antioch on the Orontes. As they did so, they did not remain silent, but made their faith known to the Jews in those regions (Acts 11:19). Some of the fugitives probably sought refuge in Damascus. At all events it came to the ears of the Supreme Council that a group of Jews in that city were giving their support to the same dangerous opinions. The Jewish leaders were able to take action, because at this time the High Priest had been given a measure of control even over the Jews outside Palestine. So Saul was able to go to Damascus with a document authorizing him to carry out the same kind of purge among the Jews there as he had done in Jerusalem.

It is remarkable that by the years 36–37 a number of followers of Jesus of Nazareth were living in Damascus and that their activity attracted so much attention that the Jewish leaders in Jerusalem had to take the matter in hand. No doubt there was a large Jewish colony there, because even before the Exile the Israelites had established a trading quarter in this Aramean city. After its conquest by Alexander the Great the ancient town,

which is now being rediscovered in the south-east corner of the modern metropolis, was rapidly hellenized. Among much else a theatre and odeon were built. The broad, intersecting streets were lined with colonnades. One of them was the now famous 'street called Straight' (Acts 9:11), the main artery for east-west traffic.

As Saul was approaching Damascus with his entourage, he had a strange and overwhelming experience. Later on (Acts 9:3-9; 22:6-11; 26:13-18), Luke was to give no less than three accounts of the experience of Saul, better known as Paul. It is obvious that this author regarded what happened to Paul as of very great importance to the plan of his book. The three accounts are not consistent in matters of detail, and the differences show, once again, how such events were described in order to stress specific aspects. The point of the three stories lies in 'the words from heaven.' In this way Luke makes it clear that the living Jesus of Nazareth entered into contact with Paul and called him to appear as his witness.

Unlike many other Mediterranean trees, the fig-tree loses its leaves in November. Its pale bark then gives it every appearance of being dead. But early in spring the buds begin to swell; and in March the first leaves appear—a sign that summer is on its way (Matt. 24 : 32). The early figs appear first in June. The cursing of the barren fig-tree is therefore something of an enigma; for it was not the season of figs (Mark 11 : 12-14).

The Jordan had its place in the religious traditions of Israel, for this little river was regarded as the eastern border of the Promised Land: the Chosen People had to cross the Jordan in order to enter the Promised Land (Josh. 3). In the New Testament this theme was revitalized. Jesus of Nazareth started to preach the glad tidings after he had been baptized by John in the Jordan (Mark 1 : 9-11); and Christians received the new life by baptism (Rom. 6 : 1-11).

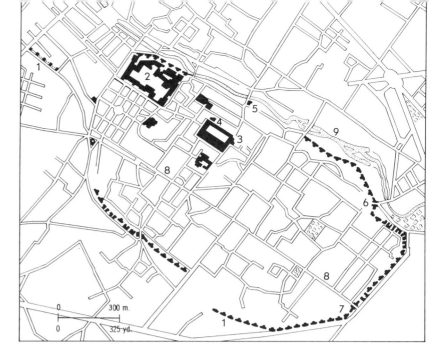

In the south-eastern corner of modern Damascus the Roman town can be traced. Unlike many eastern cities Damascus stood on fairly level ground. This circumstance made it easier to transform the city into a Hellenistic 'polis.' Colonnaded streets ran straight across the town. The famous street called Straight (Acts 9 : 11), now for the most part a narrow bazaar, was one of the main thoroughfares. Of the majority of public buildings, such as the theatre, the odeon, and the gymnasium, little or nothing remains today. Only the 'holy place' has been preserved. The existing mosque and its precincts, as is usually the case, occupy what was during the Byzantine period a site of Christian worship. It had been used for a similar purpose by the Hellenists of the Graeco-Roman period and by the Arameans. The mosque itself was built about 400 as a Christian church.
1: 12th-century city wall. 2: 13th-century citadel. 3: Mosque and precincts. 4: 12th-century mausoleum of Saladin. 5: North Gate (Bab el-Faradis). 6: Thomas Gate (Bab Tuma). 7: East Gate (Bab Sharqi). 8: Street called Straight. 9: River Barada.

162

Shocked and downcast, Saul entered Damascus. There he was received by Ananias, a Jew who was a follower of Jesus. It goes without saying that Paul could not manage a complete turn-about all at once. The transition from orthodox Pharisaism to the freedom of brotherhood was too great a step to be taken easily. According to a letter that he later wrote to the faithful in Galatia (Gal. 1:17) he went away for a certain time to Arabia, and by that he must have meant the extensive region ruled by the Nabateans. The reference is vague, but we must make do with it. In the year 38 he came out of his seclusion and returned to Damascus. Immediately afterwards he appeared in the synagogues, and set to work there with what from then on was to be his characteristic outspokenness.

He proclaimed with complete assurance that Jesus of Nazareth was the promised Messiah. This was startling enough; but as his later Letters show, Paul's ideas in general must have seemed to his fellow Jews alarmingly radical. It was no wonder there were vehement protests. At first this might seem to be no cause for concern. It was a time when the Jewish leaders in Jerusalem no longer had any authority over this Hellenistic city. The Roman emperor had placed new restrictions on the powers of the High Priests, and the control of Damascus was now entrusted to Aretas IV, king of the Nabateans, who had put a governor in charge of the city. It is hard to discover therefore what made the governor help Paul's opponents. Bearing in mind the traditional hostility between Romans and Jews, one could argue that Aretas wanted to be on a friendly footing with the Jews in order to consolidate his position vis-à-vis the Romans. In actual fact, Aretas was not in very firm control of Damascus, as the town was isolated from the rest of the Nabatean country by the district south of Damascus, governed by Agrippa I, and he may have feared Agrippa's intervention.

Whatever his motives, the Nabatean governor ordered his soldiers to arrest Paul. There then followed the celebrated escape which Paul later described in a letter to the Christians of Corinth. "At Damascus, the governor under King Aretas guarded the city of Damascus in order to seize me, but I was let down in a basket through a window in the wall, and escaped his hands." (2 Cor. 11:32-33) Luke also gave an account of this event (Acts 9:23-25). The escape was probably not in itself a very difficult feat. Damascus was situated not on a mountain but in a plain at the foot of the Anti-Lebanon, and the distance between the window in the city wall and ground level would only have been a matter of feet.

Paul's next move was to make for Jerusalem. Not unnaturally, his arrival caused unease and suspicion. The man who only two years previously had thrown so many of Jesus's disciples in Jerusalem into jail now appeared saying that he had been converted. The Church understandably held itself aloof. For some days Paul wandered aimlessly about, until a disciple from Cyprus, Barnabas, disturbed at the plight of the newcomer, introduced him to Simon Peter. After this, Paul immediately resumed his preaching activities. Like Stephen, he addressed himself first and foremost to the so-called Hellenistic Jews (Acts 9:29). When this section offered violence in return, the leaders of the Church stepped in. The persecution that had broken out as a result of Stephen's activities was still fresh in their memory. Gently but firmly they persuaded Paul to leave Jewish territory. They took

him to the harbour at Caesarea and put him on a ship bound for Tarsus.

This Palestinian episode, which occupied a fortnight, may possibly have been a disappointing or even embittering experience for Paul. He was to all appearances unwelcome everywhere. He never spoke subsequently of his stay in Tarsus. About fourteen years later, in his Letter to the Christians of Galatia, he wrote quite noncommittally, "Then I went into the regions of Syria and Cilicia." (Gal. 1:21) Not once in his letters did he mention his native town, even though it occupied an important place among the cities of the Roman empire.

Tarsus had originally been the capital of the Roman province of Cilicia, the coastal district south of the Taurus mountains. Because Syria and Cilicia formed a natural unit round the northeastern bay of the Mediterranean Sea, they were eventually joined together into a single province, and Antioch in Syria became the new capital. But this did nothing to detract from the importance of Tarsus. For centuries the town had played a significant role on the world scene. In the fourteenth century B.C. it had been an important base for the Hittites in their advance toward Syria. The Hellenistic period saw its development as a prominent cultural centre. The philosophers and poets of Tarsus were even more celebrated than those of Athens and Alexandria. Because of its strategic position, however, it had repeatedly been disputed by rival powers, and its history was punctuated by destruction. Its remains are not abundant.

Tarsus contained a large Jewish community at the time when Paul was born there to a family of the tribe of Benjamin. As a man of Tarsus he automatically acquired Roman citizenship, and this is why he was also given the name of Paul. Paul's family must also have set great store by the ancient traditions of Jewry, otherwise the young man would not have been sent to distant Jerusalem for his education. In the holy city he sat at the feet of Gamaliel, and his mind was formed according to the rigid notions embodied in the Law of his ancestors (Acts 22:3).

Gamaliel was one of the most influential Pharisees of the time. He had himself been a pupil, and was perhaps even a relative, of the Pharisee, Hillel, who is still remembered for his liberal ideas. Gamaliel, too, had a realistic outlook on life, as witness the action he took in the Supreme Council on behalf of Peter and John (Acts 5:34-39). Paul was a zealous pupil, and no doubt this training had a decisive influence on the formation of his character. He later wrote of himself: "... and I advanced in Judaism beyond many of my own age among my people, so extremely zealous was I for the traditions of my fathers." (Gal. 1:14) This total commitment to a cause became evident once more, when he took up his missionary role as a disciple of Jesus. In this work his training as a Pharisee helped him enormously. In his preaching he was able to handle the texts of the ancient sacred books wherever and however he needed to do so. His argumentation was so subtle at times that today we no longer find it easy to follow him.

But he had also benefited from Gamaliel's realism. On practical issues he was consistently liberal. This outlook remained with him, but this did not mean that the change in him from persecutor to preacher was anything less than radical. In his early years he had considered the Jewish Law as absolutely necessary to salvation, but once he had understood the true meaning of Jesus's message, he abandoned the Law altogether as the means of salvation. As he now saw things, only faith in Jesus as Lord could bring salvation. Because Paul spoke bluntly and very much to the point in propagating these radical ideas, he was spared neither protests nor active opposition. One of the early consequences of this was his lonely sojourn in his native city.

Meanwhile the new teaching continued to spread steadily. Antioch on the Orontes in particular became the scene of great activity by the disciples. This had such a marked effect that the population of that city gave them the name of 'Christians' (Acts 11:26), thereby identifying them as followers of the 'Christ,' the Greek word for the Messiah. From Antioch this name soon made its way throughout the Roman empire, for as the capital of the province of Syria and Cilicia the town enjoyed contacts with many other regions. It was an outstanding example of the new kind of city and had been founded as recently as about 300 B.C. in the fertile valley between the Orontes river in the north and the Casius mountain range in the south. The city had slowly expanded, and in Paul's time it ranked third after Rome and Alexandria. It must have contained something like half a million inhabitants, and possibly ten per cent of these were Jews. Even so, it was a typically Hellenistic city, with colonnaded streets, an amphitheatre, a theatre, temples, and aqueducts.

All this helps to explain why the disciples who were forced to flee from Jerusalem after the death of Stephen settled there. Their preaching aroused a remarkable degree of interest among the Greeks and Syrians in Antioch, and before long a large number of Gentiles had swelled the ranks of the disciples. These were not required to have themselves circumcised or to keep the Jewish Law, and, since all members of the Church now mixed freely, the idea gradually arose that the Jewish laws regarding 'cleanness' were no longer of importance. In Judea a Gentile had in fact already been accepted, almost incidentally, as a disciple of Jesus, but that had brought no changes in the life of the congregation. What was happening in Antioch, however, was taking place on a considerable scale. The early Christian Church was acquiring a distinctive form of its own.

When rumours of the events in Antioch reached Jerusalem, doubts arose among the disciples of longer standing. It was thought that the right person to go to Antioch as an emissary from Jerusalem was the Cypriot Barnabas. As a Jew of the Diaspora Barnabas possibly felt more at home there than in Jerusalem, and, perhaps for this reason, decided to remain. It is also possible that his decision was affected by the fact that Agrippa's persecution of the followers of Jesus was becoming more and more menacing. Whatever the reason, the danger of persecution in Jerusalem directed attention away from the changes that were taking place within the church in Antioch. Barnabas quickly

The city wall which now encloses Damascus in the south-eastern corner follows the line of the foundations of the Roman wall. The wall has been destroyed several times since Paul's day; but every time it was restored—including, according to ancient custom in the East (Josh. 2:15), the small houses standing on and against the city wall. Thus it is still possible, even today, to have a clear picture of how Paul escaped from Damascus (2 Cor. 11:32-33).

In the 19th century a monastery was built against a mountain-side west of Jericho as a tribute to the sacredness of the spot which ever since the 4th century had been identified as the 'wilderness' in which Jesus of Nazareth prepared himself for his ministry (Matt. 4 : 1-11). It was here that he was said to have been tempted by the devil to turn stones into bread. So convinced were pious people that this was the spot that they built a church on the very top of the mountain, but only a few vestiges remain today.

became the leader of the congregation there, and in that capacity he soon took a step which was to have a considerable effect on the spread of the Christian faith. He remembered from his time in Jerusalem the notable zeal of Paul, and decided that this was the right man for the growing church in a Hellenistic city like Antioch. He therefore went to Tarsus, and from there he brought Paul to Syria.

In Antioch the life of the Church followed a similar pattern to that in Jerusalem and in the other towns of Palestine. People assembled together in order to reflect upon the person and the life of Jesus of Nazareth and on what these signified. In doing so they relied on traditions handed on by the Jerusalem congregation. But in Antioch these traditions were no doubt given a different emphasis. It is quite clear that the 'Gentile' element in the Church was strongly represented. Furthermore, none of the leaders there belonged to the original company of disciples. Acts 13:1 specifically says: "Now in the church at Antioch there were prophets and teachers, Barnabas, Symeon who was called Niger, Lucius of Cyrene, Manaen a member of the court of Herod the tetrarch, and Saul." Whether for public worship, instruction, or preaching, therefore, the facts were only to be had at second hand in Antioch. As a result, the existing traditions could all the more readily evolve in response to developing beliefs and religious conviction.

In addition, the peculiar situation of the Antiochian congregation called for some adaptation of creed, catechesis, and proclamation. Every region, every race, and every religion inevitably has its own outlook and mode of expression. Changes in terminology and in the traditions were inevitable, therefore. Even content underwent some modification. For the benefit of converts from paganism certain specifically Jewish elements had necessarily to be toned down or interpreted. Above all, the gospel tidings were adapted to their outlook and sensibilities. In proclamation the emphasis was placed on the more universal aspects. Less attention was paid to the favoured position of the Chosen People, and preaching was more advisedly centred on the theme of salvation for all men. In this way certain traditions gradually took on new forms of expression, which then acquired an existence in their own right, side by side with their Palestinian originals. The evangelists subsequently drew upon this Antiochian material, when it had acquired a fixed and settled form.

The success of the Church in Antioch produced an astonishing burst of activity. It was resolved that the tidings of salvation must be proclaimed in other places, too. This was not done under the stress of persecution or on orders from Jerusalem. People acted quite spontaneously and on their own initiative. Once again, however, the direction in which Christianity was to spread was conditioned. There was too much danger in any move eastwards, because the Parthians were still constantly at war with Rome. To the south Palestine offered no scope for missionary activity, since the whole area fell within Jerusalem's sphere of influence. The choice lay between the north and the west. Barnabas, Paul, and Mark were the three chosen to be sent out on a preaching mission. They might have travelled northward, but Paul possibly felt little inclined to visit his native region. Whatever the reason, they moved west, to the island of Cyprus. They were to some extent already conversant with the place, as a number of the disciples in Antioch, including Barnabas himself, had originally come from this island (Acts 4:36; 11:20). This offered an advantage that more than outweighed the risk of the voyage.

The city of Samaria was considerably enlarged by Herod the Great and provided with numerous public buildings. But among the ruins as they are today relatively few date from the Herodian period—the town has had too turbulent a history for that. The steps in this picture belonged to the temple of Augustus, which Herod had built on the acropolis and which was restored about A.D. 200 under the emperor Septimius Severus.

XI. GROWTH OF THE NEW TESTAMENT

Paul's missionary work. The first New Testament texts ca. A.D. 50-60.

1. PAUL'S JOURNEY TO CYPRUS AND ASIA MINOR

It is not always possible to date Paul's activities with complete accuracy, and secular history provides only three helpful points of reference. First, we know that the Nabatean king, Aretas IV, died in the year A.D. 40 and that Paul's escape from Damascus antedated that event. Secondly, Gallio, the Roman mentioned in Acts 18:12, was proconsul of the province of Achaia, in A.D. 52, and this confirms that Paul was active at Corinth in that year, during his second missionary journey. Thirdly, Porcius Festus was governor of Judea, Samaria, and Galilee from 60 to 62, and it was early in his governorship that Festus sent Paul to Rome. These facts, supplemented with less certain pieces of evidence, offer a sufficient basis for assigning the journey made by Barnabas, Paul, and Mark to Cyprus and Asia Minor to the years 46-48.

Setting out from Antioch they proceeded by way of the Orontes valley to the Syrian coast, at Seleucia, some 19 miles distant. There they boarded a ship bound for Cyprus. They had a favourable crossing, and immediately upon disembarking at Salamis, the island's eastern harbour, they started to preach their message in the synagogues. They then travelled in a westerly direction as far as Paphos, where the Roman proconsul, Sergius Paulus had his residence. Among the latter's entourage was a Jew, Bar-Jesus, who became fanatically opposed to the preaching of Barnabas and Paul, probably because he was frightened of losing his own hold over the proconsul. The proconsul was, however, so

impressed with the way in which Paul dealt with this man, that he accepted the apostle's teaching. In mentioning this incident (Acts 13:6-12), Luke seems to be giving an intimation of the kind of success that Paul was to have later on amongst non-Jewish communities. Many Gentiles from the Greek and Roman world responded to his message, whereas most of the Jews rejected it. At all events, it is probably significant that the apostle from now on dropped his Jewish name of Saul in favour of his Roman name of Paul.

At this time, too, Barnabas stepped into second place and Paul took over the leadership. The man whose personal link with the disciples in Jerusalem had been almost non-existent was

There is a spot in Athens north-west of the Acropolis known as the Areopagus, or 'hill of (the god) Ares.' This is the place where Paul may have addressed the Athenians during his short stay in the city. At all events Paul's speech in Acts 17 : 22-31 has been inscribed there on the stone plaque pictured here. Whether this is word for word what Paul actually said is questionable, however. What is more, it seems likely that the word 'Areopagus' in Acts 17 : 19-22 denotes the Court of Justice, which in earlier centuries had indeed held its sessions on 'the hill of Ares,' but which in Paul's time, while retaining the name Areopagus, met in another part of the city.

henceforward largely to determine the way of life of the churches outside Palestine. Foreseeably enough, this was bound to cause a number of difficulties. The first clash came when, after their departure from Paphos, Paul, Barnabas, and Mark reached the mainland of Asia Minor. They went ashore at the port of Attalia and at once moved some 12 miles inland to Perga. There some difference of opinion must have arisen between Paul and Mark. Perhaps Mark felt disinclined to venture any further north. Or was he perhaps at odds in some way with Paul's method of working or with his preaching itself? Whatever the reason Mark returned, not, however, to Antioch in Syria as might have been expected, but to Jerusalem.

Through the valley of the Cestrus—the present Aksu—Paul and Barnabas journeyed on into the inhospitable interior. Their destination was Antioch in Pisidia, which lay 95 miles north of Perga. In choosing to visit this city Paul was following his usual plan. In all his itineraries he would make for those places which were centres of some importance, leaving the more out-of-the-way parts to others. Antioch in Pisidia was an obvious choice in

About 2½ miles west of the spot where the Jordan flows into the Lake of Galilee lie the remains of one of the oldest synagogues in Palestine. This is assumed to be the site of Capernaum, the place where Jesus chose to enact much of his ministry (Matt. 9 : 1). However, the ruins themselves do not date from the time of Jesus. In all probability the synagogue was originally built about the year 200. The photograph shows the ruins from the south-east. Since the turn of the century numerous interesting fragments have been excavated; and from these it is possible to deduce a good deal about the original appearance of the building.

The photograph above has been used as a basis for this reconstruction of the synagogue at Capernaum. The drawing gives only a general impression; many of the details are guesswork. The length (78 feet), the breadth (100 feet), and the lay-out of the building, however, are based on data which the site itself has provided. There is a strikingly Roman touch about the whole. It is, in fact, a true basilica with an atrium (forecourt). But the main entrance was on the terrace (left) and gave direct access to the actual synagogue. Two rows of columns divided the area within into a 'nave' with two side-aisles. Stone benches stood against the walls on either side; and on top was the gallery for the womenfolk. The walled courtyard had a colonnade running along the north, east, and south sides.

The ruins of the synagogue at Chorazin, almost 2 miles north of Capernaum, date from the 3rd or 4th century A.D. Among the numerous blocks of stone was this piece of basalt carved as a chair (22 by 29 by 22 inches). The four lines of the Aramaic inscription on the front read: 'In commemoration of the good work of Judas, the son of Ishmael,/ who made this portico [stoa]/and its steps. For his work may/he share the lot of the righteous.' As the plan of the ruin makes it clear that this relatively small synagogue had an interior colonnade only, the text must refer to those columns and to the stone seats ranged along the walls. The chair itself was probably ornamental, a symbolic seat for Moses and his successors, the Scribes.

this respect, since it was a junction for military and civil traffic. Moreover, important centres such as this usually contained a Jewish community of some considerable size, and Paul's normal practice, when visiting any new place, was first of all to try to gain adherents among the Jews.

Luke later gave a detailed account of Paul's activities in Antioch (Acts 13:14-52). This is a particularly valuable piece of information because of the light it sheds on Paul's methods. In these, the synagogue occupied a prominent place. It might therefore be useful at this point to describe this Jewish phenomenon in its general features.

In the absence of positive evidence, it is usual to set the origin of the synagogue in the period of the Exile. Since there was no possibility of visiting the Temple during the period of the Babylonian captivity, one may suppose that the Jews gathered together in private dwellings in order to call to mind their sacred traditions and to pray, though this cannot be known for certain. The earliest historical references date only from the third century B.C., when various authors refer to Jewish houses of prayer in Egypt. Synagogues were in general use among Jews of the Diaspora by the beginning of our era, and to judge from the Gospel narratives this was so in Palestine as well. In Mark 1:39 it says: "And he [Jesus] went throughout all Galilee, preaching in their synagogues and casting out demons."

Even in Jerusalem these houses of prayer were to be found right beside the Temple. In Acts 6:9 Luke mentions the Synagogue of the Freedmen. Some years ago a commemorative stone was discovered which describes the building of a synagogue in Jerusalem round about the beginning of our era. Whether this foundation stone is connected with the Synagogue of the Freedmen is difficult to ascertain. What the inscription does clearly indicate, however, is that the synagogue was a well-established institution: "Theodotus, son of Vettenus, priest and synagogue-ruler, son of a synagogue-ruler, grandson of a synagogue-ruler, built the synagogue for the reading of the Law and for the teach-ing of the Commandments, as likewise the guest-house, rooms, and water supplies for the lodging of needy strangers. His fathers, the elders, and the son of Simon laid the foundations." In Acts 15:21 Luke writes: "*For from early generations* Moses has had in every city those who preach him, for he is read every sabbath in the synagogues." This assertion doubtless broadly accorded with the facts.

The synagogue was usually a rectangular building, so constructed as to face toward Jerusalem. In the style of the period such a house of prayer, like many early Christian churches, took the form of a basilica, with a row of columns running along each of three sides of the interior. The seats would be ranged along the walls, the front rows for the men, the rear ones for the women. Sometimes the women had a separate gallery. Against one of the shorter walls stood the ark containing the sacred scrolls. Near the wall at the other end was a place for the 'pulpit' and lectern. The care of the building and the conduct of the ceremonies were the business of the 'ruler of the synagogue' (Mark 5:22), assisted by 'the attendant' (Luke 4:20).

The ceremony took more or less the following form. To begin with the congregation recited together a form of creed, called after its opening words 'Shema' Yisrael' (Hear, O Israel). This consisted of three important passages from the Bible, namely Deuteronomy 6:4-9, 11:13-21, and Numbers 15:37-41. The first sentences of this Jewish creed read as follows:

Hear, O Israel: The Lord our God is one Lord; and you shall love the Lord your God with all your heart, and with all your soul, and with all your might. And these words which I command you this day shall be upon your heart; and you shall teach them diligently to your children, and shall talk of them when you sit in your house, and when you walk by the way, and when you lie down, and when you rise...

After the Shema' the ruler singled out someone to be the prayer-leader. This man, wrapped in the striped mantle of prayer, would then take up his position by the ark in which the sacred scrolls were kept. Here he would intone 'the eighteen-fold prayer.' This consisted of eighteen invocations and petitions. The spirit of the prayer is well illustrated by the following supplication:

Hear our voice, O Lord, our God, spare and have mercy upon us, and accept in mercy and favour our prayer. For a God that hearest prayers and supplications art Thou. From before Thee, O our King, do not turn us away empty-handed. For Thou hearest the prayer of Thy people Israel in mercy. Blessed be Thou, O Lord, who hearest prayer.

When the eighteen-fold prayer had been said, the attendant would take a scroll of the Law out of the ark. A few men selected by the ruler would then read out in Hebrew those passages from the Law which were appointed for the particular day. The passages had always to be read. Quoting them from memory was forbidden, even though many of the Scribes would probably have found it easy enough to do. The obligation to read stemmed from the reverence they felt for the letter of the Law. At the reader's side stood the interpreter. This man would translate verse by verse into Aramaic or Greek, since very many Jews were no longer able to understand Hebrew. He was not permitted to use a written text, but had to produce his translation on the spur of the moment. Despite this precaution a number of translations which were current were soon written down.

The Septuagint, the Greek version of the Old Testament, which was well known in many cities of the Roman empire, was certainly influenced by these extempore translations made in the synagogue. This is even more true of the Aramaic translations which came into existence in Palestine and Babylonia. Understandably enough, these Aramaic and Greek texts were very often used for preaching and instruction in both Jewish and Christian circles. There was little point in quoting something in Hebrew, if the majority of the congregation could not understand that language. On some occasions it is probable that even the preacher himself had no command of it. This explains why so many Old Testament quotations in the writings of the New Testament exhibit variations from the Hebrew text.

If it were the sabbath or a feast-day the attendant would then bring out of the ark a scroll of the Prophets, and from this, too, a particular passage would be read and immediately translated.

After the readings came the sermon. Generally speaking, it expounded or applied the passages previously read, although it was also permissible to speak on some special subject or other. It was apparently open to every male Jew, if he so wished, to address the assembly by invitation of the ruler (Acts 13:15), but since preaching a homily required both skill in speaking and a thorough knowledge of the Law and the ancient traditions, it was nearly always the Scribes who presented themselves for this purpose. The preacher was allowed to sit during his address (Luke 4:20). It has sometimes been thought that the so-called 'seat of Moses,' on which according to Matthew 23:2 the Scribes and Pharisees delighted to sit, was used in this connection. A chair of this kind has been found among the remains of the third-century synagogue of Chorazin, a little to the north of Capernaum; but this block of basalt seems more likely to have been an ornament than a real seat. Perhaps this 'sitting in the seat of Moses' ought not to be taken too literally. In all probability it simply meant that the Scribes regarded themselves as Moses' successors and disciples.

Luke tells us (Acts 13:5,14; 14:1; 16:13; 17:1-3, 10; 18:4, 19; 19:8) that it was Paul's custom to start his missionary activities by preaching in the synagogue. After the recitation of the creed, the eighteen-fold prayer, and the readings from the Law and the Prophets, he would give the address. Luke uses the episode in Antioch of Pisidia in order to describe in detail how Paul usually set about delivering his message. (In the subsequent part of his narrative he usually contents himself with a summary account of this method.) He relates how on the sabbath Paul attended the synagogue service and, when invited to do so by the ruler, took the floor. Paul's address (Acts 13:15-41) is cast in the traditional pattern in which Peter's preaching in Jerusalem had also been constructed. The essential core was the affirmation that Jesus of Nazareth had been appointed by God to be the Saviour of all men. Passages of Scripture were then quoted, to show that this affirmation was corroborated by God's word in the sacred books. In order to be saved, therefore, one must believe in Jesus Christ.

This speech of Paul's also shows an affinity with Stephen's preaching (Acts 7). Paul, like Stephen, gives a brief survey of

A view in close-up of the remains of the synagogue at Capernaum (see illustration on p. 166). Against the far wall a few columns still remain intact. On the second column from the right appears the following ancient inscription: 'Herod of Monimos [or: Mokimos] and his son Joustos together with the children have caused this column to be placed here.' Against the wall (left) one can see a section of the stone benches.

Israel's past, beginning with the patriarchs and ending with David. As Stephen had minimized the status of the Temple, so Paul does the same with regard to the Law: "...by him every one that believes is freed from everything from which you could not be freed by the law of Moses." (Acts 13:38-39) To Jews true to the Law assertions of this kind came as a tremendous shock. Paul seemed to be undermining the very foundations of their life. It goes without saying that the initial reaction of most Jews to such a message was hostile, and the conflict was intensified when Paul proceeded to put this teaching into practice.

In the synagogue Paul also made contact with numerous proselytes and God-fearers from the Greek and Roman world. After his sermons these people would talk amongst themselves about the new message, with the result that they would sometimes bring along their Gentile friends to hear him speak. The apostle received these people as disciples of the Messiah without imposing on them as much as a single practical obligation of the Law.

Another ground of complaint was the fact that, albeit unintentionally, Paul was encroaching on the position of the local Jewish leaders, for he alone was able to offer any authoritative guidance as to how the new doctrine should be applied in practice. It is not really surprising, therefore, that in many towns a breach should open between Paul and the local Jewish leaders. When this happened, Paul was of necessity obliged to address himself to the Gentiles alone.

It was not long before a head-on clash occurred between Paul and certain of the Jews of Antioch. These latter managed to persuade the municipal council to forbid Paul and Barnabas to remain any longer in the city. The two travellers now had to choose whether to take the Roman highway to the west or to the east. They opted for the east, being unwilling, perhaps, to move too far from Antioch in Syria. After a journey of about 90 miles they reached Iconium, the modern Konya. In Roman times Iconium was the principal centre of the region of Lycaonia. It, too, contained a Jewish community with its own synagogue. Paul went to work in this town just as he had done in Antioch in Pisidia, apparently with a reasonable degree of success. Despite the antagonism of some Jews, Paul and Barnabas were able to remain there for quite a time, but when they learnt that with the

municipal council's approval their opponents meant to stone them, they left the city and journeyed south.

They now entered a less cultivated area, where Hellenism had not yet worked its way down through all classes of the population. There were not a great many Jews living in the district, either. About 25 miles from Iconium stood the town of Lystra. It had no synagogue, and Paul started at once to speak in the street. When a crippled man regained the use of his legs in consequence of Paul's ministry there, the people became enthusiastic. They called out to one another that the gods, Zeus and Hermes, had appeared among them in the guise of men. According to Luke (Acts 14:11), the language of these people was not the *koinē* Greek, but their own Lycaonian, yet they were evidently already hellenized enough to worship Greek gods. The incident provides an interesting illustration of the relationship between Paul and Barnabas. Barnabas stood by in silence, while Paul did the talking—which is why the former was taken by the onlookers for the chief god, Zeus, and the latter for his messenger, the god Hermes.

The example of Paul's preaching which Luke gives here (Acts 14:15-17) is different from his homily in the synagogue. The ideas are more or less parallel to those which, according to Luke, Paul expressed on a later occasion in Athens (Acts 17:22-31). The Jewish emphasis was much less pronounced, while the message was proclaimed against a monotheistic background and

(Left) Antioch of Pisidia was founded in the 3rd century B.C. by the Syrian king, Seleucus Nicator. The Romans beautified and fortified the city, because this spot in central Asia Minor was an important junction of imperial highways. About 5 miles north of the ruins of Antioch some scanty remains of a Roman aqueduct, which brought water from the surrounding hills to the acropolis, are still standing.

(Right) When Paul on his first journey set off from the city of Derbe (see Map, p. 170) and when on his second journey he approached that city he had to travel through the terrain shown in this picture. At a distance these western spurs of the Taurus range present a formidable appearance; but they do not, generally speaking, extend above the tree-line. That the region is not inhospitable is evidenced by the numerous remains of Christian churches. Just to the north of the modern town of Karaman there is a district which actually bears the name of 'the valley of a thousand and one churches.'

Paul's First Journey (approx. 1400 miles)

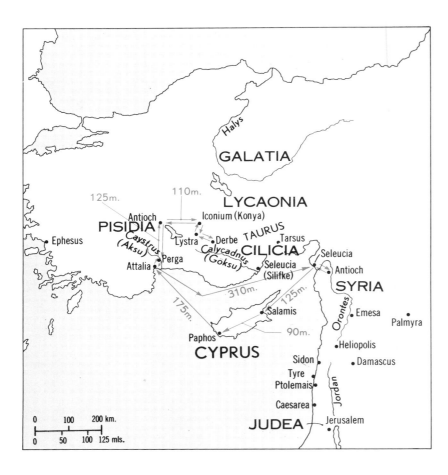

was supported by implicit or general references to passages in the Old Testament.

A short time later there came to Lystra Jews from Antioch in Pisidia and Iconium, whose arrival put an end to Paul's activities. The people, their passions aroused, pelted Paul with stones and dragged him out of the town. It would seem that his injuries were slight, for by the next day he and Barnabas were on their travels once more. They soon came to the town of Derbe, about 30 miles south-east of Lystra. Today Derbe is no more than a hamlet, but its position has been identified by means of an inscription dating from A.D. 157. Even in ancient times the town was not of very great importance, for it lay too far from any main highway. The travellers left it, therefore, after a brief but effective stay.

Paul and Barnabas might then have turned south through mountainous country to the valley of the Calycadnus, the modern Göksu. Along this valley they could easily have reached the town of Seleucia, the present-day Silifke, and the Mediterranean Sea. From Seleucia a level road ran along the coastal plain to Tarsus. Antioch in Syria was then no great distance away. But once again Paul avoided his birthplace. From Derbe they returned to Lystra, Iconium, Antioch in Pisidia, and Perga. His earlier hasty departures from these towns had evidently left Paul dissatisfied. On his later journeys he likewise seldom contented himself with just one visit to a city. He tried to leave behind him an organized congregation, and to that end he would appoint a number of people as *elders*—an office with which the Jewish communities were familiar. To these elders he would entrust the care of, and responsibility for, the neophyte Christians. Because the Christian congregation was something quite new, the elders did not derive their authority from already existing offices and traditions, as was the case with the Jews. They were appointed directly by the apostles—a fact which marked the beginnings of a new hierarchy.

In the harbour at Attalia the travellers boarded a ship bound for Seleucia in Syria, and after a fair journey they reached Antioch in Syria, whence they had originally set out.

2. THE JOURNEY TO GREECE

Some time after Paul and Barnabas had returned from their travels in Asia Minor, several disciples arrived in Antioch from Jerusalem. When they heard the accounts of how successful Paul and Barnabas had been, and especially when they saw how the Christian community at Antioch was conducting its affairs, they protested vehemently. They argued that every disciple of Jesus was bound to observe the Law of Moses if he were to be saved, and insisted that the Christian converts from paganism must be circumcised. But the Church leaders in Antioch would not agree. The dispute grew to such dimensions that the congregation sent Paul and Barnabas to Jerusalem to talk over the problem with the leaders there.

An account of this conference appears in Acts 15:6-29 and also in Galatians 2:1-10. The two versions are not entirely compatible, however, owing to the different standpoints of the two authors. In Acts Luke is mainly concerned with providing a schematic survey of the fortunes of the early Church, centred on the figures of Peter and Paul. Events therefore loom larger than points of controversy. Paul on the other hand, in his Letter to the Galatians, is more concerned with arguing out the principles of belief. He defends both his position as an apostle and the very essence of the message he was proclaiming. Both accounts agree on the crucial point at issue: that the Gentiles who were converted were under no obligation to have themselves circumcised.

According to Luke it was Simon Peter who appealed to his own experience and solved the difficulty (Acts 15:7-11). According to Paul he himself forced the decision by taking Titus, a Christian of Gentile origin, with him to Jerusalem. The acceptance of this uncircumcised disciple was to be the test case. But the major difference between the two versions emerges in what is known as the apostolic decree. In Luke's account (Acts 15:23-29), James succeeded in ensuring that the Christians of Gentile origin in Syria and Cilicia be required "to abstain from the pollutions of idols and from unchastity and from what is strangled and from blood." This meant, in effect, demanding of these people what the Law (Lev. 17–18) already laid upon non-Jewish people living among the Jews. Furthermore, the Gentile Christians had to pay due consideration to the degrees of kinship within which people were forbidden by Jewish law from contracting marriage.

In this way it was made possible for Christians of Jewish origin and those from the Gentile world to break bread together in fellowship. But Paul, for his part, said nothing in his letter to the Galatian Christians about this decree, nor did he ever mention it in his other letters. On the contrary, he entirely disregarded it. There are two possible explanations for this. Either the decree was meant simply for the Christians in Syria and Cilicia, so that Paul could ignore it in other areas, or else Luke, in order to preserve the plan of his book, transferred a rule applied to Syria and Cilicia at some later stage to an earlier point in time. After the meeting in Jerusalem there are indeed only incidental references in his book to Syria and Cilicia. Whatever explanation one accepts, in principle the question of circumcision was now resolved. Along with two other men, Judas and Silas, Paul and Barnabas were able to return to Antioch in Syria satisfied with the outcome of their visit to Jerusalem.

Not long after this, Paul prepared himself for another journey to Asia Minor. Barnabas proposed that Mark, who had separated from them at Perga during the first tour, should accompany them again. The background circumstances are obscure, but Paul refused, causing a rift between the two leaders. Barnabas took Mark with him and set off on a second visit to Cyprus. Paul found a new travelling companion in the person of Silas, also called Silvanus, who had recently been sent to Antioch by the leaders in Jerusalem. This man was probably another Jew of the Diaspora; like Paul, he was a Roman citizen (Acts 16:37-38).

The two men journeyed overland in a north-westerly direction. Having travelled round the bay of Issus they came to the region of Cilicia, where they visited various communities of Christians. It is a striking feature of Luke's narrative that it refers again and again to local churches whose founders are quite unknown to us. What is clear is that there were others beside Paul engaged in this missionary work.

Paul's Second Journey (approx. 2800 miles)

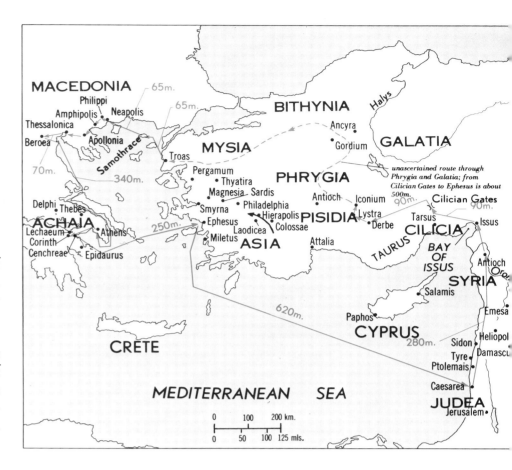

The northern approach to the Cilician Gates. From early times this pass, over 4000 feet above sea-level, was the natural link between the interior of Asia Minor and the district of Cilicia along the Mediterranean coast. The Hittites marched through here on their way to Syria, bent on extending their empire. Alexander the Great led his army through this pass with great skill and subsequently defeated the Persians at Issus. A stele, now illegible has been carved out of the rock-face (left, in the photograph). At some time or other a general must have put it there as a record of how his troops conquered the locality; and the apostle Paul, on his second and third journeys, must have travelled through this pass from south to north.

When the travellers had left the Taurus mountain-range behind them, they struck out to the west. They came first to Derbe and then to Lystra, towns which Paul had already visited on his first tour. In Lystra Paul and Silas were joined by Timothy. He was the son of a Greek and a Jewess and therefore uncircumcised, and in Timothy's case Paul insisted on the operation being performed. Such an action appeared to contravene Paul's principles, which is why Luke, in Acts 16:3, is at pains to supply an explanation: "He [Paul] took him and circumcised him because of the Jews that were in those places, for they all knew that his father was a Greek." The argument is an odd one. What probably lies behind it is that for Jewish Christians the obligation imposed by the Law still applied, in a limited sense, and Timothy was, after all, the son of a Jewess.

The three of them made their way to Iconium, but after this the exact course of their journey is unknown. Luke does not mention any other towns, only districts such as Phrygia, Galatia, Mysia, and Bithynia. It is possible that Paul was not sure where he intended to go. After much wandering, however, they finally ended up in Troas, on the north-west coast of Asia Minor. Then (Acts 16:10), and without offering to explain it in any way, Luke suddenly starts to write 'we' instead of 'they.' This first 'we-section' continues until the party is described as having arrived at the town of Philippi (Acts 16:16). Later on ,when the narrative reaches the point where Paul pays his second visit to Philippi, Luke again writes 'we' (Acts 20:5) and continues to do so to the end of the book. The usual explanation for these 'we-sections,' as they are called, is that although Luke never refers to himself he was in fact a member of Paul's party during both these periods. He compiled a record of their journey at the time, and later on made use of it in his book.

Luke tells us that at Troas Paul had a strange dream, in which a Macedonian asked him to visit his country. The dream signalized Paul's momentous decision to leave Asia and cross into Europe. It is also possible that Luke, who by his own account was very much at home in Macedonia, himself supported the decision. Its execution was facilitated by the fact that ships sailed regularly from Troas to Macedonia.

The ship brought the travellers first to the island of Samothrace and then to Neapolis, the modern Kavalla. They soon left the port behind them and travelled inland to Philippi, the ruins of which lie 8½ miles north-west of Kavalla. Philippi was a city founded in the fourth century B.C. by Philip, the father of Alexander the Great. The place had since become a military centre of some importance. In the Roman period the famous Via Egnatia, the road linking the western with the eastern part of northern Greece, ran right through the city. Yet there were only a few Jews living there, and they had no synagogue.

Outside the city gate stood a private house where there were regular meetings for prayer. There Paul and his two assistants met Lydia, a seller of purple goods from the city of Thyatira, in Asia Minor, who, though a pagan, had loosely attached herself to the Jewish community. She had herself baptized by Paul, together with her household, and invited the three missionaries to stay with her. This was a hopeful beginning, but after a few days they were told to leave the city. It is no longer possible to say exactly what took place. The impressive account in Acts 16:11-40 has features that suggest legend, but there may be a hard historical kernel in verses 19-23, in which we learn that a case was brought against the missionaries and that the magistrates ordered Paul and Silas to be beaten. This fits in with Paul's remark in 1 Thessalonians 2:1, where he says that he had "suffered and been shamefully treated at Philippi."

(Top) The remains of the western gate of Troas with the adjoining walls, dating from the third millennium B.C. In the background one can see the not very distinct vestiges of the megaron, the great hall of the palace belonging to the same period. It was in the neighbourhood of this that in the 19th century Schliemann discovered 'the treasures of Troy.' The town was still inhabited in Paul's day; layer 9 is in fact Roman. However, it can hardly have been the apostle's point of departure for Macedonia. Troas lies about 3 miles from the sea and has never been a port. Paul's harbour town should presumably be identified with the modern Eskistanbul; its site was formerly occupied by the little town of Alexandreia hē Troas.

(Centre) The Via Egnatia was one of the highways built for the army and for the postal and transport services of the Roman empire. These roads were so solidly constructed that large sections of them are still intact. The picture shows the road running through the town of Philippi. To the left of the road lay the lower town and to the right the acropolis. This highway traversed northern Greece and linked Byzantium (Istanbul) with the port of Apollonia on the Adriatic.

(Bottom) The street in Corinth called Lechaeum. It ran from the agora to the western harbour, from the direction of which we are looking. To left and right lie the remains of the Roman city. Visible in the background is the 1880-foot summit on which stood the citadel, Acrocorinthus. This hill dominates the whole surrounding district and served as a place of refuge in times of danger.

Paul, Silas, and Timothy then continued westward along the Via Egnatia. After some 100 miles they came by way of Amphipolis and Apollonia to the important city of Thessalonica, which owed its prosperity not only to its situation on the Via Egnatia, but also to the fact that it was the chief port for the northern inlets of the Aegean Sea. The Jews were so numerous here that they were able to maintain their own synagogue, and Paul adopted the same methods to convert them as he had used in other cities. Luke writes: "And Paul went in [to the synagogue], *as was his custom*, and for three weeks he argued with them from the scriptures, explaining and proving that it was necessary for the Christ to suffer and to rise from the dead, and saying 'This Jesus, whom I proclaim to you, is the Christ.'" (Acts 17:2-3)

Paul must in fact have stayed in Thessalonica much longer than three weeks. As we learn from his Letter to the Philippians, he was partly supported during this period by gifts of money from the Christians at Philippi (Phil. 4:16), and when we remember that the messengers would have had to travel over a hundred miles in each direction, and that the Christians at Philippi would not have been able to raise the money in a moment, it seems reasonable to estimate Paul's stay in Thessalonica at several months. The same is probably true in the case of Beroea, Paul's next stop, though he may not have stayed quite so long in this comparatively unimportant place.

According to Luke's account in Acts 17:1-15 Paul was forced to leave both Thessalonica and Beroea because of the hostility of the resident Jews. At all events, he seems to have moved on before the persecution of the young Church began in earnest, for Luke tells us that the persecutors sought Paul, but did not find him (Acts 17:5f).

From Beroea Paul proceeded alone to Athens, the very heart of Greek civilization. He spoke in the synagogue and the agora, the open space that was the hub of social life. There Paul caught the attention of a number of Athenian philosophers, who invited him to expound his philosophy to them on the Areopagus. Luke makes this the occasion to describe Paul's customary method of proclaiming his belief to Gentiles. The core of the message which he propounded was still that God had entrusted judgment to the man whom he had raised from the dead. This assertion was set within the context of a broad monotheism, supplemented not only with ideas from the Old Testament, but also with quotations from pagan authors. It would appear that despite this accommodation to his audience Paul's preaching was a complete failure. Only a handful of people took him seriously (Acts 17:34) and no proper church seems to have been founded. This would explain his statement in 1 Corinthians 2:3 that he had gone on to Corinth "in much fear and trembling." Nor would Paul have called the household of Stephanas "the first converts in Achaia" (1 Cor. 16:15) if he had baptized anyone in Athens.

The city of Corinth lay about 55 miles to the west of Athens and had been a place of some considerable importance for centuries. Situated on the narrow neck of land known as the Isthmus, the city controlled the flow of trade between the northern and central parts of Greece. From the ports of Lechaeum and Cenchreae, lying on either side of the Isthmus, the influence of Corinth extended eastward and westward across the sea. As early as the eighth century B.C. Corinthian colonizers had settled in Sicily and Corfu. It became the commercial rival of Athens, and it had been a flourishing city at the time when Hellenistic culture had reached its height. It had suffered a severe setback, however, when the Romans extended their power eastward. In 146 B.C. the city was completely devastated, so that among the present ruins there are relatively few remains older than the Roman period.

A hundred years later Julius Caesar founded a new city at this strategic point, and people from every part of the Roman empire were soon emigrating to this new capital of the province of Achaia. They consisted of Roman citizens and soldiers, Greeks from the north and south, orientals from Asia Minor, Syria, and Egypt, and also a large number of Jews. Corinth became a cosmopolitan city, where there were no traditions of any long standing, and where people were open to the influence of new ideas. There is even a Greek verb dating from this period, which can be translated as 'to Corinthize.' It meant 'to live without restraint, to lead an unfettered life.'

In Corinth Paul took lodgings with Aquila and Priscilla, a Jewish couple who had recently settled there as tentmakers. On weekdays Paul would assist with the work, but on the sabbath he would visit the synagogue and ask permission to speak. After a time, when he had been joined by Silas and Timothy from Macedonia, he gave up his manual work and devoted himself entirely to preaching. The good relations which at first existed between Paul and the Jewish community gradually deteriorated, however, and Paul transferred his activities to the home of a Godfearing man who lived next to the synagogue.

For some eighteen months—probably from the winter of the year 50 to the summer of 52—he continued to preach there with considerable success. Even the ruler of the synagogue, together with his whole family, took sides with Paul. The Jewish community as a whole, however, refused to tolerate the support given to Paul in a house adjoining their synagogue. They brought him before the proconsul, Gallio, whose custom was to administer justice in the immense square of the agora. His seat of judgment stood in the southern part of this busy open space, and anyone was at liberty to lodge a complaint with him there. Fortunately, Gallio had the philosophical temperament of his brother, Seneca. When he had heard the charge brought by the Jews, he gave his verdict without even calling on Paul to defend himself. Luke reports Gallio as saying: "If it were a matter of wrongdoing or vicious crime, I should have reason to bear with you, O Jews; but since it is a matter of questions about words and names and your own law, see to it yourselves; I refuse to be a judge of these things." (Acts 18:14–15)

After his acquittal Paul remained in Corinth for some time, and it was during this period that he wrote the first document which was eventually to be included in the collection of writings now known as the New Testament. It was occasioned by the arrival of Timothy, his fellow-missionary, with news of the Church in Thessalonica. The way in which the Thessalonians were conducting their lives was evidently satisfactory, but they were not clear on specific points of Christian belief, and were apparently asking how the dead would be able to partake in the kingdom of God, which Jesus was to establish at his second coming (1 Thess. 4:13-18). Paul answered their doubts with a letter, which was to be the first of a whole series written to various communities. These documents were not private letters, but neither are they comparable to works of literature intended primarily for publication. One might describe them as 'semi-public,' in that Paul addressed them to a particular group of people (1 Thess. 5:27), and in doing so employed a form common enough in his time.

He invariably began by saying for whom the letter was intended and added the names of the people who sent it. After an introductory statement of the theme came the main part of the letter, usually made up of a primarily dogmatic section followed by an exhortatory one. The closing section usually contained personal news, messages, and greetings. The collected New Testament writings include what we refer to as the First and Second Letters of Paul to the Thessalonians, but whether Paul actually wrote the second of these is disputed. There are in fact points of agreement but also of considerable difference between the two documents. If we assume that Paul is indeed the author of 2 Thessalonians, then the style and contents suggest that he must have written this second text soon after the first one. If, however, Paul is not the author, the second letter must have originated in the period subsequent to the year 70, when some Christian author, using 1 Thessalonians, recast Paul's message for his own day in a more apocalyptic form.

In the summer of 52, Paul made his way to Cenchreae, the eastern harbour of Corinth, and there took ship for Ephesus, on the west coast of Asia Minor. He made a short exploration of the city which was to be the centre of his activity during his third journey, and then boarded a vessel bound for Caesarea in Palestine. From there he continued overland to Antioch in Syria.

3. THE JOURNEY TO EPHESUS

While Paul was back in Antioch a brief but heated conflict arose. In a letter to the Christians of Galatia, written about a year later, he described it in these terms: "...when Cephas [Peter] came to Antioch I opposed him to his face, because he stood condemned. For before certain men came from James, he ate with the Gentiles; but when they came he drew back and separated himself, fearing the circumcision party. And with him the rest of the Jews acted insincerely, so that even Barnabas was carried away by their insincerity. But when I saw that they were not straightforward about the truth of the gospel, I said to Cephas before them all, 'If you, though a Jew, live like a Gentile and not like a Jew, how can you compel the Gentiles to live like Jews?'" (Gal. 2:11-14)

This report does not seem at all consistent with the decisions taken in Jerusalem in the year 45. But in the meantime the situation of the Jews had changed, and with it the position of those Christians who were converts from Judaism. By command of the emperor Claudius (41–54) the Roman governors in Palestine during the forties had adopted sterner and more rigid policies, and the Jews were in no position to rebel, being at that time faced with economic crisis and famine. In the year 50, however, the situation altered. The economy revived, and political unrest mounted. In Alexandria it led to a struggle between the Jews and the Hellenists, and in Rome the Jews' nationalistic claims became the cause of fierce rioting. The emperor Claudius had the offenders driven out of the capital. Aquila and Priscilla, the couple with whom Paul had taken lodgings in Corinth, were among the victims of this persecution.

In Palestine itself the party of the Zealots, impelled by a fanatical and nationalistic messianism, were growing more and more violent in their resistance to the Roman occupying power and to their compatriots who sympathized with Hellenism. Claudius temporarily changed his tactics, and by making certain concessions to the Jews, attempted to regain their goodwill. In Alexandria he took them under his protection and in Palestine he replaced the existing governor with Antonius Felix (52–60), who was favourably disposed towards Jewry, and had married the Jewish princess Drusilla, youngest daughter of Agrippa I. But all this served only to strengthen the Zealots' influence, and it put Christians of Jewish origin in a very difficult position. The majority were no doubt compelled to go along with the new movement, with its excessive emphasis on the importance of the Law and the Temple, and it is probable that some of them even gave active support to the Zealots.

It is understandable, therefore, that when a group of fanatical Jewish Christians arrived in Antioch from Jerusalem, Peter—and even Barnabas, who had evidently returned from his journey to Cyprus—ceased their practice of breaking bread with the Gentile Christians. It might be said that Peter was guilty of nothing more than an indiscretion, but his conduct had unfortunate consequences, because it appeared to make the Jewish Law binding on all Christians, whether or not they were Jews

Paul's Third Journey (approx. 2800 miles)

by birth. Paul, whose own experience and insight had convinced him that the Law was of only minimal importance for Christianity, quite properly took an opposing stand. Nowhere are we told explicitly what the outcome of this conflict was, but the tenor of the Letter to the Galatians suggests that Peter admitted being in the wrong. One possibility is that a practical solution was found in the apostolic decree, and that Luke, when writing the Acts of the Apostles, transferred this to the time of the Jerusalem meeting some years earlier.

Shortly afterwards, probably before the end of the year 55, Paul left Antioch, never to return. He again journeyed in a north-westerly direction through Cilicia and the Taurus mountains to Phrygia and Galatia, in order to give support and spiritual strength to the disciples in those parts. The exact route of his itinerary on this occasion has not been handed down to us, but we do know that he eventually reached Ephesus, on the west coast of Asia Minor. This city was to be the centre of his activity over the next three years.

For centuries Ephesus had been the meeting-point of various cultures, emanating from east and west. The city stood at the mouth of the river Caystrus, to which the hinterland owed its fertility. During the Hellenistic and Roman periods Ephesus was especially renowned for the cult of a goddess known to the Greeks as Artemis and to the Romans as Diana. Apart from her name, however, the goddess of Ephesus had few western characteristics. She was much more the type of the mother-goddess, who in Asia Minor went by the name of Cybele. Archaeological investigations have shown that as early as the seventh century B.C. a temple dedicated to this goddess stood at the foot of the acropolis. The sanctuary was devastated on several occasions, but each time it rose again more splendid than before. As a result, it had come to be regarded as one of the seven wonders of the world. In the third century B.C., a new city had been built across the river, south-west of the acropolis, because the harbour was silting up and Ephesus depended for its prosperity on its proximity to the sea. One result of the move was that the temple complex was left standing outside the town. This in no way detracted from the popularity of the sanctuary, which continued to attract both sight-seers and pilgrims. It was only

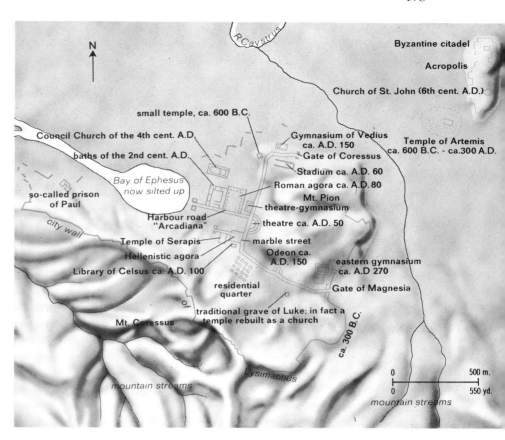

Ephesus in Hellenistic and Roman times

Originally, Ephesus was centred on the temple of Artemis and the acropolis; but by the end of the 4th century B.C. the harbour had become so silted up that the city had to move almost a mile and a half to the south-west to maintain contact with the sea. This meant that the sanctuary of Artemis now lay outside the town. A sacred road was built to connect the temple with Ephesus. In the 6th century A.D. the city was again shifted, for the silting up of the harbour had so increased that it was no longer sensible to remain down in the valley by the coast in a position which was difficult to defend. The city settled once more around the acropolis. Because Ephesus was moved in the 4th century B.C. and again in the 6th century A.D., one finds hardly any but Hellenistic and Roman remains.

(Left) For some years now the excavation of an entire residential area at the northern foot of Mount Coressus has been in progress. Notice the tiny figures of the workmen. The results show that despite its imposing buildings and its broad streets Ephesus had not wholly lost the character of an oriental city. Climbing the rising hillside are narrow streets of steps and a maze of houses. But the spacious and lofty rooms indicate that even in this district Hellenistic culture was a dominant influence.

to be expected, therefore, that sooner or later those who were proclaiming the Christian faith would clash with the devotees of this fertility cult, which was such a crucial factor in the economic, social, and religious life of the place.

Ephesus was not only an important religious centre. Merchants from the surrounding territories regularly visited the city. They came mounted or on foot from the interior of Asia Minor, or by ship from Greece and Macedonia. As the capital of the province of Asia, Ephesus was in close and constant contact with the other parts of the empire. For Paul's purposes the city was very conveniently situated. It was easy for news of the churches in Asia Minor and Greece to reach him there.

On one occasion, for example, he heard that trouble had arisen in the district of Galatia, which he had visited in his second

The Greek goddess, Artemis, known to the Romans as Diana, was the protectress of natural life and patroness of the hunt. She was usually depicted as a young girl in a brief tunic. The Artemis of Ephesus was a fertility goddess of a quite different character. She was portrayed as a mature woman with a large number of breasts and various fertility symbols. In 1956 a statue was found at Ephesus which is more or less a duplicate of the one reproduced here. Only the head-covering is appreciably different.

and third journeys. The people causing the upset probably belonged to the same faction as had been responsible for the conflict between Paul and Peter in Antioch. Here also, they were contending that even the Gentile Christians must keep the Jewish Law, if they were to be saved. To give added prestige to their own authority they questioned Paul's. His pronouncements concerning the Jewish Law were held to be invalid, because he was no apostle. The reports which Paul received at Ephesus indicated that the simple and unsophisticated Galatians were in a state of confusion on these issues.

Paul reacted by writing a letter in which he defended his mandate to be a missionary and emphasized once more the essence of the message he proclaimed. The impassioned tone of the letter is well illustrated by the following sentence, in which Paul attacks his antagonists: "I wish those who unsettle you would mutilate themselves!" (Gal. 5:12) These words contain a covert suggestion that the champions of circumcision were no better than the followers of the cult of Cybele, who insisted on ritual castration. Some scholars nowadays believe that Paul addressed this letter to the disciples in Pisidia and Lycaonia, whose acquaintance he had already made on his first journey. Those districts were indeed at one time or another part of the province of Galatia. If this is so, Paul might have written the letter while on his second visit to Corinth, and the Letter to the Galatians would then be Paul's earliest.

The letter of Paul to the Philippians probably dates from this period also. Until recently, it was attributed to a subsequent period, when Paul was imprisoned in Rome. This was natural enough, since he makes mention in it of his imprisonment and its approaching end (Phil. 1:7-13; 2:24). But the letter also reveals that there was a good deal of coming and going between Philippi and the place where Paul was living (Phil. 2:19-30). This certainly did not apply to Philippi and Rome, which were a considerable distance from each other. What is more, the style and content of this document have more in common with the letters written during his journey than with those written during his imprisonment in Rome. In view of this it has been suggested that Paul had also been in jail, for a short time, during the three years he spent in Ephesus. Ephesus was indeed at no great distance from Philippi. The letter would then have been written in the year 56 or 57, and not in 63. That Luke fails to mention this brief captivity in Ephesus can be explained by the fact that he gives only an outline of Paul's activities.

At Ephesus Paul also kept in contact with the Church in Greece, especially with Corinth. It is thought that he sent at least four, and possibly five, letters to that city, and that during his stay in Ephesus he actually visited Corinth on one occasion for a short period. This is inferred from the two letters to the Corinthian Christians which are to be found in the New Testament. It would appear from 1 Corinthians 5:9-13 that Paul had already written a letter dealing with the problem of moral laxity, which seems to have been rife among the inhabitants of Corinth. It is possible, however, that part of this original letter was incorporated in 1 Corinthians, which may therefore be made up of two letters, an earlier and a later one. In the spring of 57 he received a letter from Corinth asking for guidance on a number of questions regarding marriage, celibacy, the eating of meat offered in pagan sacrifices, various 'gifts of the Spirit' (*charismata*), the resurrection, and other matters. Paul answered in writing with what is now known as the First Letter to the Corinthians.

Before dealing with the questions raised, however, he discussed the division prevailing within the congregation. Various groups had formed, which Paul describes thus: "each one of you says 'I belong to Paul,' or 'I belong to Apollos,' or 'I belong to Cephas,' or 'I belong to Christ.'" (1 Cor. 1:12) Timothy was the bearer of this letter (1 Cor. 4:17). It appears that the situation among the Christians of Corinth had become strained, probably because some of them were no longer willing to recognize Paul's authority. Paul thought that he could resolve the difficulties by going personally to Corinth (2 Cor. 1:23; 2:1; 13:1-2), but the visit turned out to be a total failure. Back in Ephesus he then wrote a third letter, the 'epistle of tears,' as it is sometimes called (2 Cor. 2:1-11; 7:5-12). His assistant, Titus, was to deliver it. Again, the document in question does not appear to have been preserved, though there are those who consider that what remains of it is contained in chapters 10–13 of 2 Corinthians.

Meanwhile there was growing displeasure in Ephesus over the activities of Paul and his companions. Because of their success, the traders at the temple of Artemis were experiencing a decline in business, and this aroused the anger of the silversmith, Demetrius and his fellow artisans. They took their grievance to the market-place, and so worked on the feelings of the populace, that a furious crowd dragged Gaius and Aristarchus, two of Paul's assistants from Macedonia, into the theatre. Paul wanted to go as well, but his own followers and a number of friendly officials restrained him. Fortunately, Gaius and Aristarchus came to no harm, thanks to the forceful interven-

tion of the town clerk (Acts 19:35-40). This official pointed out to the mob the illegality of their conduct: if Gaius and Aristarchus were in fact guilty of an offence then a complaint should be lodged with the proconsul, but by this hotheaded behaviour they ran a great risk of being accused of sedition. With this the incident was concluded.

The atmosphere in Ephesus had now become so strained that there was little likelihood of Paul's achieving much more in this city. He had been thinking for some time of ending his work in Asia Minor and Greece, and two of his assistants, Timothy and Erastus, had in fact already been sent on ahead to Macedonia. Soon afterwards he himself departed from Ephesus with the intention of returning to Jerusalem via Macedonia and Achaia, and then undertaking a further journey, to Rome and the west (Acts 19:21). While he was visiting the communities in the north of Greece, Titus rejoined him with good news from Corinth. Nevertheless, he still could not face the prospect of an encounter with the disciples there, and so in the autumn of 57 he sent Titus on ahead with a fourth letter, traditionally identified with the present Second Letter to the Corinthians. In the closing chapters of this letter (2 Cor. 10–13) Paul launches a violent attack on his detractors. It has therefore been argued that this section is not of a piece with the earlier chapters, and that it must represent one of two separate letters which were later joined together. If this is in fact the case, Paul must have written five times in all to the Church at Corinth, though the argument for the existence of a fifth letter is not particularly convincing.

Towards the end of the year 57 Paul did finally go to Corinth, and according to Luke (Acts 20:3) he remained there for three months. Throughout the winter, however, he seems to have

In the New Testament period Miletus was still a port of some importance. The town stood on the south side of a bay on the west coast of Asia Minor. The ship which took Paul back to Jerusalem at the end of his third journey put in here for some time (Acts 20 : 15ff). It was on this occasion that the apostle summoned to Miletus the leaders of the church in Ephesus, which lay about 45 miles further north. Since the Middle Ages the bay has been completely silted up and the site abandoned. Everywhere the remains of a civilization that extended over many centuries are to be seen thrusting up out of the sand. The most impressive ruin is that of the theatre, which dates from about 200. The distance across it is 450 feet, and it seated 25,000 spectators.

been thinking about his next move, and contemplating the possibility of a visit to Rome and the western part of the empire (Rom. 15:23-24). In the early part of the year 58 he wrote a letter from Corinth to the Christians in Rome. His many contacts had no doubt given Paul some acquaintance with a number of Christians in the capital, but with the community as such he was unfamiliar. Unlike his other letters, therefore, this one was not written to deal with specific questions or problems that had been raised by the community itself, but was simply meant to give the disciples in Rome a clear picture of how he himself saw the Christian faith. The result was a letter profound in content but quiet in tone, which focused attention on the basic principles of Christ's message.

Paul's intention was to board a ship at Corinth which would take him to Syria. He would then be able to reach Jerusalem before the Passover Feast. However, he had to abandon this plan, because, as Luke tells us (Acts 20:3), certain Jews laid a plot against him. It seems that the fanatical Zealot party had acquired an influence which extended over a wide area in the west. Paul was therefore obliged to travel by way of Macedonia, and to celebrate the Passover in Philippi. It was probably in this city that Luke rejoined Paul's company, for from Acts 20:6 onwards he again writes 'we' instead of 'they.'

After the feast Paul crossed over to Troas, where he stayed for some days. From Troas he travelled overland to Assos, about 25 miles further south. His companions made the same journey by ship. In Assos Paul rejoined his companions, and they all took ship again. By way of Mitylene, on the island of Lesbos, past the islands of Chios and Samos, they sailed to the town of Miletus, where the ship dropped anchor for several days. Paul took advantage of the opportunity thus offered to summon the 'elders' of Ephesus to Miletus for some final words of exhortation. The ship then carried them by the islands of Cos and Rhodes to Patara, on the south coast of Asia Minor. There they had to wait for a ship going to Syria. They went ashore at Tyre, where a Christian community had already been founded. After spending a few days here Paul and his companions took ship to Ptolemais, where there was also a Christian community. They then journeyed overland to Caesarea, where Paul took lodgings with Philip. Some time before, Philip and Stephen and five others had been appointed as the leaders of the Hellenistic Christians (Acts 6:1–6).

Since leaving Corinth, Paul had been warned by various persons that if he went to Jerusalem he would certainly be imprisoned by fanatical Jews. But Paul was not to be put off. He wanted to call on the leaders in Jerusalem and to hand over personally the money which he had collected in the course of his travels for the poverty-stricken community in the holy city. In Jerusalem he went to stay, not with one of the leaders of the local church, but with a certain Mnason from Cyprus, a Jew of the Diaspora.

4. PAUL'S IMPRISONMENT AND SUBSEQUENT JOURNEYS

In Jerusalem Paul was received with mixed feelings. Even James and the other leaders were not altogether happy about his arrival. The reason for this was the mounting hostility on the part of the fanatical element amongst the Jews. Luke intimates that the Christian community itself was being affected by the attitude of these people, when he reports James as saying to Paul, "You see, brother, how many thousands there are among the Jews of those who have believed; *they are all zealous for the law.*" (Acts 21:20) Paul's reaction was to compromise. He conformed to the requirements of the Law and allowed himself to be purified in the Temple along with four others, even defraying on their behalf the cost of the sacrifice. When the time of purification was complete, certain Jews from Asia Minor who had come to Jerusalem for the Feast of Pentecost saw Paul in the Temple courtyard. They stirred up other Jews against him, and he was dragged out of 'the forecourt of Israel.'

From his vantage-point in the castle Antonia the Roman commandant noticed the scuffle. He sent down soldiers to take Paul into custody. From the castle steps Paul tried in vain to plead his cause before the excited crowd. Then the Roman commandant decided to have Paul flogged—the usual method of loosening the tongue of an accused person. However, when the apostle appealed on the ground of his Roman citizenship, this penalty could not be inflicted. The commandant found himself none the wiser when on the next day he brought Paul before the Supreme Council. The accused exploited the quarrel which already existed between the Pharisees and the Sadducees. One party acknowledged the resurrection of the dead, and the other did not; and so, as Luke tells us, he argued himself out of the situation by claiming, "I am a Pharisee, a son of Pharisees; with respect to the hope and the resurrection of the dead I am on

Alexander the Great had been dead for just ten years when the Romans constructed their first major road. This was the Via Appia, completed in 312 B.C. The road took its name from the Roman statesman, Appius Claudius, who initiated the enterprise. The Via Appia ran southwards from Rome by way of Capua (near Naples) and Tarentum as far as Brundisium (Brindisi), a port on the Adriatic Sea. According to Acts 28:15, Paul, on the last stage of his journey to Rome, travelled up the Via Appia, which, after the custom of the time, was flanked by a great number of sepulchral monuments.

Paul goes as a prisoner to Rome (approx. 2200 miles)

trial." (Acts 23:6) In this way he was able to put his accusers in the wrong. The ensuing tumult prompted the commandant to take Paul back to the castle. When he learned that a band of Jews were planning to kill his prisoner before any verdict had been passed, he evaded responsibility for the matter by having Paul conveyed to Caesarea under armed guard by night.

Some days later, Felix, the governor in Caesarea, heard both the charge brought by the Jews against Paul and also Paul's defence. He well knew the inflammatory nature of the problem he had to deal with, and avoided the necessity of having to pass an immediate verdict by promising to look further into the matter. He then adopted delaying tactics, and kept Paul under arrest for two whole years. During this time, however, he was allowed regular visits from his friends. In the year 60, Felix was succeeded by Porcius Festus, who took immediate action. He wanted Paul's case to be settled in Jerusalem, but the prisoner refused, and as a Roman citizen appealed to Caesar. Festus could do no other than comply with this request.

Paul was put aboard a ship from Adramyttium, a port on the west coast of Asia Minor, known today as Edremit. He was accompanied by Aristarchus of Thessalonica and probably by Luke as well. Along with them went a Roman officer called Julius and a number of soldiers to guard the prisoner. The ship brought them via Sidon and along the coast of Cilicia and Pamphylia to Myra in Lycia. There the whole party boarded a ship from Alexandria which was bound for Italy. Because of contrary winds it was only with some difficulty that the ship was able to make the south-western tip of Asia Minor. The captain therefore altered course and sailed to the port of Lasea

on the southern coast of Crete. Since this, however, seemed an unsuitable place to winter in, he decided to sail on.

Once they were on the open sea a violent storm sprang up. For fourteen days the ship was at the mercy of the winds, and was driven completely off course. Eventually it ran aground on the coast of Malta, and the entire company was obliged to pass the winter on this island. In the spring of 61, Julius put his prisoner aboard another ship from Alexandria which was going to Italy. From then on the journey went well. After a brief stop at Syracuse in Sicily and at Rhegium on the southern tip of Italy they reached the port of Puteoli, a little west of where Naples stands today. There they went ashore. Paul obtained leave to visit the Christians, who, remarkably enough, had already formed a community even in this town. The company then made their way northward up the famous Via Appia. At the places known as the Forum of Appius and the Three Taverns, 40 and 24 miles respectively from Rome, Christians from the capital had come out to welcome Paul, which must have put him in good heart.

Paul's imprisonment in Rome was rather like being put under house arrest today. He was allowed to set up house for himself, and a soldier lodged with him as his warder. He was also permitted to receive visitors, Jews as well as Romans. Luke describes Paul's life in Rome in the following way: "He lived there two whole years at his own expense, and welcomed all who came to him, preaching the kingdom of God and teaching about the Lord Jesus Christ quite openly and unhindered." (Acts 28:30-31)

Because of the restrictions placed on his freedom in Caesarea and Rome, Paul had had ample time in which to ponder on the faith he had now been proclaiming for so long. One of the results of this enforced leisure may have been the letters which he is thought to have written while in Rome—the 'epistles of captivity,' as they are called.

To this group belongs in the first place the letter addressed to the Christians of the city of Colossae, which lay about 110 miles east of Ephesus. The church there had not been founded by Paul himself, though he had probably sent Epaphras to the Colossians some time during the three years he had spent in Ephesus (Col. 1:7; 4:12-13). When on a visit to Rome, Epaphras had possibly sought Paul's advice about certain ideas current among the Christians at Colossae. The main problem concerned the position of Jesus as sole mediator and redeemer. Affected as they were by the religious and philosophical climate of Hellenism, some Christians at Colossae had adopted a negative attitude towards the material world, regarding the human body and man's physical nature with contempt. According to their view of man, Jesus of Nazareth could not have brought about by his death on the cross the total reconciliation of the world with God. The distance between God and the world was too great, and could be bridged only by the mediation of purely supernatural powers. These beings together constituted the fullness of the Godhead, and only through them was it possible for man to be reconciled and united with God.

Briefly stated, Paul's reply to these mistaken notions, was as follows: Jesus Christ is the sole mediator, "for in him all the fullness of God was pleased to dwell." This answer was given in writing to Tychicus and Onesimus (Col. 4:7-9). The authenticity of this letter, as of others traditionally believed to have been written by Paul while he was in Rome, is disputed by some scholars. They regard it as the work of one of his disciples, who may have written it at a later date, about 70. The main reason for this supposition is that the tone of the letter has a theological and scholastic quality all its own. Since, however, it quite clearly reflects the spirit of Paul's teaching, the question of authorship is perhaps of only secondary importance.

Before his departure for Asia Minor Tychicus was given charge of yet another letter (Eph. 6:21-22). As soon as Paul had dictated the Letter to the Colossians (Col. 4:18), if it was, indeed, from his hand, he wrote a second letter, known nowadays as the Letter to the Ephesians. The appellation is not accurate, for this document was probably intended for Laodicea and for other churches in the neighbourhood of Colossae (Col. 4:16). It is quite likely that Paul took the precaution of writing to these Christians more or less on the same lines as to the church in Colossae. If the letter was in fact addressed to several communities unknown to Paul personally, its character is more readily accounted for, for apart from himself and Tychicus, who carried the letter, Paul mentions no-one by name. Moreover, the errors and mistaken notions which it discusses are criticized from a more detached viewpoint than in the other letters. The doctrine is that of the Letter to the Colossians, though it is here expounded more calmly and in a more positive spirit.

Even on this hypothesis, however, the relationship between the two letters remains problematical. On the one hand the differences in vocabulary and in the development of the argument are considerable, whereas on the other, a remarkable

number of turns of phrase are the same in both. Paul was not the man simply to take over wholesale passages from one letter and use them in another. Some scholars have therefore proposed the following solution. After Paul's death, a pupil of his may have made a summary of the apostle's doctrine, using for that purpose the Letter to the Colossians, and calling it the Letter to the Ephesians. It could also be argued, however, that during his imprisonment in Rome Paul himself may have commissioned one of his pupils to do this.

It was also from Rome that Paul wrote his shortest letter (though some scholars hold that it was written during his stay in Ephesus). This was addressed to a certain Philemon, who on Paul's testimony had embraced the Christian faith. It appears from the letter that a slave of Philemon's, called Onesimus, had run away and had later met Paul in Rome. After Onesimus had been converted to Christianity, Paul succeeded in persuading him to return to his master. He gave him a letter, begging Philemon to welcome back in a spirit of love the runaway slave.

What befell Paul after his two years' imprisonment in Rome it is no longer possible to discover. Did he carry out his long-cherished plan to visit Spain (Rom. 15:23-24)? The only possible sources of information regarding Paul's further activities are 'the Pastoral Letters,' so called because their author's main concern is with the manner in which the 'shepherds' (pastors) of certain Christian congregations conducted their affairs. Included in this group are the First and Second Letters to Timothy and the Letter to Titus. If these were written by Paul, then his stay in Rome was followed by visits to Crete, Macedonia, Ephesus, Troas, and Nicopolis. The First Letter to Timothy and that to Titus would in this case belong to the years 64-65, when Paul was in Macedonia. He would have written the Second Letter to Timothy from Rome, just before his death in 67.

But serious doubt has been thrown on the authenticity of these letters. In style and vocabulary they differ markedly from Paul's other works. In content, too, they hardly reflect the mind and outlook of the apostle, for in his earlier letters he had shown much less concern with dogmatic issues and good works. Furthermore, there was already a tendency for the churches associated with Timothy and Titus to be organized on the basis of an ecclesiastical hierarchy, and this points to a stage subsequent to the apostolic period. For these reasons, therefore, many scholars have felt inclined to explain this anomaly by postulating that though written in the style of Paul, these three letters are the work of one or more Christian authors of the second generation.

Apart from the Pastoral Letters with their doubtful authenticity, we possess no account of Paul's activity after his imprisonment in Rome. How then did his life end? Luke himself is silent on the matter. If Paul had been released in Rome, it is unlikely that he would have withheld this knowledge from his readers. On a number of occasions he seems in fact to be preparing them for an account of Paul's martyrdom (cf. especially Acts 20:25, 38), and in the absence of any more precise information, we must accept these allusions for what they are worth.

Apart from Paul's letters, there appeared in the period between 60 and 70 a number of other documents that were later to find a place among the New Testament writings. These are briefly discussed in the next chapter (pp. 185 ff).

XII. COMPLETION OF THE NEW TESTAMENT

The second generation of Christians. The last New Testament books. The 'Holy Books' become one Book: ca. A.D. 70 and later.

1. THE END OF THE JEWISH THEOCRACY

The ever-widening breach between Christianity and official Judaism, which resulted in a complete split after the first Jewish uprising in the year A.D. 70 had begun to manifest itself some considerable time before. Paul's claim, tentatively supported by the other Christian leaders, that only faith in Jesus afforded salvation, and that both Law and Temple were unnecessary to that end, meant that the Jews could no longer regard themselves alone as the Chosen People. All their rights and privileges had devolved upon the disciples of Jesus, who were now seen as the new people of God.

This doctrine was affirmed with particular clarity in the Letter to the Hebrews. The author proclaimed quite explicitly that the dignity of Jesus Christ as 'heavenly man' set him not only above the angels but as prophet and leader above Moses and Joshua also, and as priest even above Aaron and his successors. The author presumably intended his letter for a group of Jewish Christians who in one way or another were intimately connected with the Temple cult and had a good knowledge of Greek. In view of the excellent Greek in which it is written, no-one nowadays supposes Paul to have been the author, although the closing passage (Heb. 13:1-25) may possibly have been added by him as a personal exhortation. One must suppose,

in view of the contents of the letter, that its recipients had asked what position they should now adopt regarding the Jewish manner of public worship. Perhaps they were aware of the advancing shadow of the first Jewish rebellion, or the signal for it may even already have been given. If so, the letter may have appeared at some time between A.D. 64 and 67.

Open hostility between the Jews and the Romans flared up in A.D. 66. The main causes of this were threefold: the Hellenistic policies of the emperor Nero, the harsh and corrupt administration of the most recent governors, and the persistent trouble-making of the Zealots. The signal for revolt came when by command of the emperor the governor Gessius Florus (64–66) demanded a large sum of money from the Temple treasury. The Jews refused, and immediately stopped offering the customary daily sacrifice for the emperor. This was tantamount to declaring that they no longer acknowledged him as the supreme authority in Jewish affairs.

The Romans at first under-estimated the strength of the rebels and their movement, and the revolt spread to Judea, Perea, and Galilee. On the Jewish side Josephus was the leader in Galilee, but many of the insurgents were more extreme than he, and neither he nor the Syrian legate succeeded in bringing the situation under control. Eventually, in the December of 66, Nero charged one of his generals, Vespasian, with the task of restoring

It is often hard to date accurately stone structures unearthed in Palestine. That applies to this water reservoir, discovered on the eastern slope of Jerusalem's western hill. It is not a normal cistern. These were usually hewn out of the rock in the form of a vat or tun and were covered over to prevent the water from being polluted and from evaporating. The uneven steps (right) remind one of the water reservoirs at Qumran; they made it easier to reach the water at varying levels. The supply-channel (left) is strange; and its course beyond this point has not so far been investigated. The cistern was probably part of the Jewish mill-complex somewhat further to the south (p. 151). It may even have been used as a bath by the Roman soldiers of the tenth legion, who from the year 70 onwards occupied a camp on the south-western hill.

◁ Fort Machaerus was situated on the eastern shore
of the Dead Sea. The Hasmonean Alexander
Janneus (103-76 B.C.) built the fort on this spot
to secure Perea against the Nabateans. According
to Josephus, Herod Antipas murdered John the
Baptist in this stronghold (Mark 6 : 17-29); it is a
fact that Perea was under his authority at the time.
After the Romans had taken Jerusalem in A.D. 70
the Jews continued to hold out here for some time.
Today the fort is a deserted tell; all that one can
see on the top are the scanty remains of walls. In
the photograph, at the foot of the eminence, to left
and right, part of the Dead Sea is visible; and behind
that lie the mountains of the wilderness of Judah.

(Opposite) Caves in the Wadi Murabba'at, which ▷
were used as hiding-places during the last Jewish
rebellion. To the left is the gloomy aperture of
Cave 1 and, right, the lofty entrance to Cave 2.
Notice the people at the entrance to Cave 1 and
on the right of Cave 2. Cave 3 lies a little further to
the left, that is, more to the west; and Cave 4 is a
short distance away in an easterly direction. Beside
the remnants of a leather scroll of the Twelve
Prophets, a number of papyrus fragments of
Biblical texts and some letters of Simon ben
Kosebah were found there and a number of
tephillin, prayer-thongs worn by the faithful Jew
on head and arms (Matt. 23 : 5).

the authority of Rome. Vespasian acted more circumspectly
than his predecessors and with more success. That winter he
assembled his troops in Syria, and then sent his son Titus to
bring reinforcements from Egypt. It was not until the spring of
67 that he advanced into Galilee.

The bands of rebels were unable to resist his army of 60,000
fully armed and well-trained soldiers for any length of time.
In a few months the whole of Galilee was in Roman hands. The
Jewish commander, Josephus, turned over to join Vespasian. As
a reward for his help and loyalty he was permitted to bear the
family name of the Roman general, Flavius. He later wrote an
account of the campaign in which he had taken part and so has
come to be known as the Jewish historian, Flavius Josephus.
After the Galilean campaign Vespasian sent his legions to
winter at Caesarea and Scythopolis, thus keeping Galilee cut
off from the districts in which the rebellion had not been quelled.

In the spring of 68, Vespasian advanced again. He restored
order first in Perea, and then in the west of Judea and Idumea.
This enabled him to encircle the remaining rebels and shut them
up within the area around Jerusalem and in a number of forts
surrounding the Dead Sea. At this juncture an unexpected lull in
the fighting occurred. On the 9th of June, the day after he had
been deposed by the senate, the emperor Nero committed
suicide. This sparked off a new struggle for political power.
Within the space of one-and-a-half years three emperors succeeded one another. None, however, was able to obtain the full
support of the whole empire. Vespasian kept himself apart from
these internal squabbles. Away in the east, he quietly bided his
time. Finally, in the summer of 69, the armies in the eastern
parts of the empire proclaimed him emperor, and when, some
six months later, the west also accepted him as their ruler,

Palestine prior to the Jewish Revolt

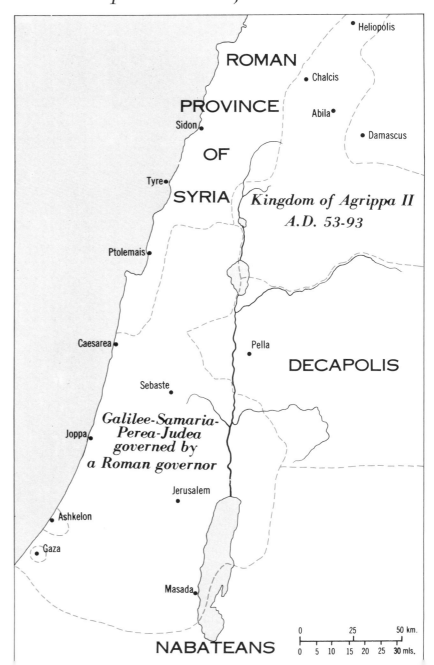

city, thus isolating the rebels from the outside world. He then concentrated his attack on the northern side, where the city was not protected by a valley, and where his battering-rams would therefore be most effective. It was in this northerly direction that the city had always expanded. From time to time a suburb with a new wall had been annexed to it, which is why in the year 70 Jerusalem possessed a first, second, and third wall on its northern side.

About twenty years previously King Agrippa I had started building the latest one, though he had been unable to carry the work to completion. The rebels now hastily completed this wall, but it was unable to withstand the battering-rams and the other up-to-date military equipment of the Roman army. Titus now advanced to the Temple court and the acropolis on the south-western hill, both of which had their own fortifications. Soon the castle Antonia was in Roman hands, leaving the way open to the Temple courtyard. Resistance around the sanctuary, however, was so fierce that only fire could drive the rebels out. Thus it was that in the August of 70 the magnificent Temple of Herod the Great perished in flames. Within a month the Romans had occupied the entire city. The two leaders, Simon bar Giora and John of Gischala, were taken prisoner. Along with many other Jews, as well as the booty and the Temple treasures, they formed part of Titus's triumphal procession in 71 at Rome. A few years later the event was commemorated in a more permanent form on the triumphal Arch of Titus, which stands in Rome to this day.

Titus left to the military governor the task of eliminating the last pockets of resistance. After the fall of Jerusalem the Zealots still had three fortresses in their control: Herodium, near Bethlehem, Machaerus, east of the Dead Sea, and Masada, to the south of En-gedi. Machaerus and Herodium were quickly captured but Masada held out until the year 73. This fortress stood on a steep and craggy eminence which rises from the western shore of the Dead Sea. On its eastern side a narrow track, known as the 'serpent path,' zig-zagged upwards for a distance of 2 miles. It was also possible to reach the summit from the western side, where the path was considerably shorter, though much steeper. The Maccabee Jonathan had fortified this eminence as far back as about 150 B.C. but the present fortress was the work of Herod the Great.

Along the rim of the plateau this monarch had constructed a wall which, according to Josephus, was 18 feet high and 12 broad. Its fortifications consisted of thirty-seven towers. An occupying force could hold out inside the walls for a considerable time. The plateau, covering an area of about 20 acres, was big enough to be brought under cultivation. Water was collected in reservoirs hollowed out of the rocky soil. When there was a shortage of rain on the plateau, water which had collected behind dams thrown across the wadis was carried in skins up the serpent path by mules.

The Roman commander, Flavius Silva, realized that a fortress like this, standing at a height of some 1300 feet, demanded elaborate tactics. He first of all threw a siege wall right round the hill, so that the nine hundred or so persons within the fortress could neither escape nor receive reinforcements. The wall was almost as long as the wall surrounding the old city of Jerusalem today, and it is still possible to follow the line of it. Protected by

Vespasian went to Rome, leaving his son Titus to capture Jerusalem.

The insurgents might have been expected to take advantage of this situation to reorganize their revolt, but they wasted time in petty quarrels amongst themselves. There were two factions in Jerusalem. On the hill in the south-western part of the city the aristocratic patriots, of whom Flavius Josephus had been one, were in control. Their leader was a son of the aged Annas, who some years before had been dismissed by the Romans from the office of High Priest. The eastern part of Jerusalem and the broad area of the Temple court were in the hands of the plebeian Zealot party, led by a certain John of Gischala. Both factions were trying to get the upper hand. The Zealots had called for help on a number of Idumeans, but with no success. The aristocratic party fetched Simon bar Giora, leader of a band of rebels in the Judean wilderness, to Jerusalem, but this move was equally unsuccessful. In fact, it soon became apparent that it was a great mistake. On the south-western hill he conducted a veritable reign of terror, and the more the situation deteriorated, the greater was his effrontery. Those who so much as mentioned the word 'surrender' were pitilessly murdered.

An old tradition has it that at the time of the first Jewish War the Christian congregation of Jerusalem fled to the town of Pella. The reason is probably to be sought in the situation just described. Pella lay to the north of Perea. Not many Jews lived there, and the Romans were in firm control of the area.

In the spring of 70 Titus advanced on Jerusalem. On the ridge north-east of the city, known as Mount Scopus, because it afforded a view of the whole of Jerusalem, he established his headquarters. First of all he built a siege wall right round the

184

their artillery, the Romans then built the siege-mound which would put the battering-ram on a level with the fortress wall. This was on the west side, where the difference in level between the fortress and the bed of the wadi was least. The insurgents were too few in number to prevent the mound being completed and the battering-ram soon breached the defences. It was not long then before the whole fortress was in Roman hands.

According to Flavius Josephus the rebels refused to be taken alive by the Romans and by unanimous agreement they put one another to death. Only two women and five children escaped this fate. Josephus concludes his story with some sentences reflecting a veiled admiration for his compatriots. "When the Romans saw so many dead, they felt no gladness, despite the fact that these were their enemies. They could not help expressing their admiration that so many people, with so great a contempt for death, had made and carried out such a resolution."

The fall of Jerusalem and the destruction of the Temple produced far-reaching changes for Jewry in particular and Palestine as a whole. Palestine now became an imperial province, under a military government, and the relative independence of the Jews was at an end. One warning symbol of this new situation was the tenth legion, encamped in Jerusalem, on the south-western hill. Jewry was thus deprived of its political power, and the Supreme Council disappeared from history. It is true that in the town of Jamnia, not far from the Mediterranean coast, a new Jewish body was soon constituted, but the only influence it wielded was in the strictly religious sphere.

A representative example of its activity was to be seen about the year 100, when, after a lengthy consultation, the Synod of Jamnia decided which of the religious books were to be accepted by Jews as Holy Writ. They rejected some which, through the influence of the Septuagint, had acquired a degree of authority among Christians. The Scribes also attempted to establish a single version of the text, drawn up from the various textual traditions in circulation. The extraordinary concern shown by the Jewish community for the text of their sacred books dates from this period. One notable result of this was the stimulus it provided to new Greek translations for the Jews of the Diaspora,

to take the place of the septuagintal texts increasingly used by Christians. All this accelerated the widening of the gap between Jews and Christians.

The destruction of the Temple put an end to the power and authority of the priestly class. The High Priest and his assistants became redundant now that the Temple cult could not be practised. And since the Jews no longer came to Jerusalem from every corner of the empire to keep the Feasts of Passover and Pentecost, the priests in general lost their influence over the people. Judaism became a religion of laymen, a 'religion of the book.' All this meant that the Jews were reduced to an ethnic group with certain religious ideas, but without a geographical centre. It also meant a change in their relations with the Christians. The Jewish leaders ceased to have any direct control over their compatriots, so that Christianity was free to develop independently and without fear of the Jewish authorities. At the same time it became easier for those Jews who wished to do so to associate themselves with the Christian movement.

The Jews were still to make several attempts to recover their political independence. About the year 116, during the reign of the emperor Trajan, a second rebellion broke out. Little is known about this uprising, which suggests that it did not take place on a very large scale. A much fiercer and more general conflict was that which occurred in the reign of the emperor Hadrian, in whose honour a triumphal arch had been erected at Gerasa in 130. More is known about this war, which lasted from 132 to 135. Jerusalem was captured and held by the insurgents, who even minted coins of their own, bearing such legends as 'liberation of Israel' and 'liberation of Jerusalem.' It is notable that coins have been found, belonging to the first year of the rebellion, with the inscription, 'the priest Eleazar.' This suggests that an attempt had been made to revive the cultus of the Temple.

The revolt soon collapsed, however, when the Roman legions were called in to deal with it. Only in the Judean wilderness did a few resistance-groups manage to hold out for a while against the imperial troops. Some recent discoveries have thrown new light on this period. One of the rebel bases was situated in the Wadi Murabba'at, about 12½ miles south of Qumran. In this

The Fourth Gospel relates various events of which the Synoptic Gospels give no account. This is the case in John 5, where the evangelist locates the story of the lame man at the pool of Bethesda. The pool is presently identified with a site north of the Temple court, where archaeologists have uncovered two adjacent water reservoirs. In the 5th century a large church (145 by 62 feet) was erected on the dam between the two pools, to commemorate the healing of the lame man. This church was destroyed in the 7th century by the Persians. The crusaders did not rebuild it, but erected a chapel on the site of the left-hand aisle of the original church. Of this, too, only some ruins remain. To the right is the church built by the crusaders over the cave alleged to have been the birthplace of Mary, the mother of Jesus. In the 19th century this holy place was thoroughly restored, but again suffered heavy damage in the Jewish-Arab war of 1967.

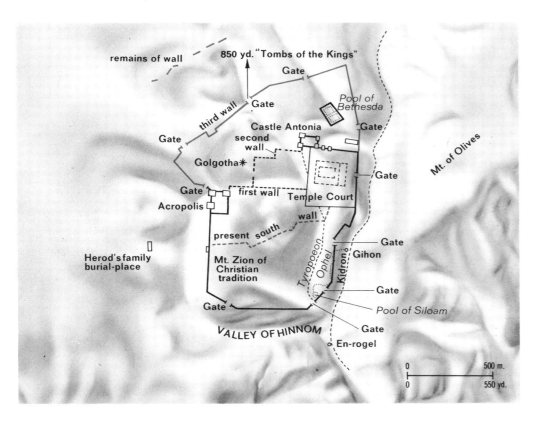

remains of wall — 850 yd. "Tombs of the Kings"
Gate
third wall
Gate
Pool of Bethesda
Castle Antonia
Gate
second wall
Gate
Golgotha*
Gate
first wall
Temple Court
Gate
Acropolis
Mt. of Olives
present south wall
Gate
Gihon
Herod's family burial-place
Mt. Zion of Christian tradition
Tyropoeon
Ophel
Kidron
Gate
Gate
Pool of Siloam
Gate
VALLEY OF HINNOM
Gate
En-rogel
0 — 500 m.
0 — 550 yd.

Jerusalem after its expansion under Agrippa I

King Agrippa (A.D. 41-44), by building the so-called third wall, extended Jerusalem to the north. This is an indication that, some ten years after the death of Jesus of Nazareth, the districts around Golgotha and the pool of Bethesda were built up sufficiently to justify their incorporation within the city. It is generally accepted that the line of this third north wall is that followed by the existing Turkish wall. It is, however, occasionally identified with the remnants of a wall discovered some 500 yards or so further north. In that case King Agrippa built a city wall around a virtually uninhabited piece of ground; and that seems unlikely. These latter remains may be what is left of the siege wall built by the Romans in A.D. 70. Such were the vagaries of fortune for Jerusalem that in the 16th century the Turks transferred the south wall of the city to the north. This meant that the Mount Zion of the Christians and the Ophel, the actual city of David, were situated outside the walls; and that state of affairs has persisted to the present day.

gorge, some 260 feet above ground level, there are several caves where a band of rebels remained in hiding. This has been revealed by the discovery of a number of coins and two letters written by the rebel leader, Simon ben Kosebah. The best known of these reads as follows:

> From Simon ben Kosebah to Joshua ben Galgolah, and to the men of your company. Peace!
> I call heaven to witness that if one of the Galileans whom you have taken under your wing should cause us any trouble, I will clap your feet in irons, as I did with the son of Aplul. Simon ben Kosebah, ruler of Israel.

Some 4 miles south of En-gedi runs the Wadi Habra, called by the Israelis Nahal Hever. There, in a cave, were found numerous skeletons of women and children, who probably died of hunger during the rebellion. The Romans had pitched camp on a rocky promontory dominating the area, so that escape was impossible. In another cave a leather bag was discovered, containing fifteen texts written on papyrus and one on a strip of wood. These too were letters from Simon ben Kosebah in Hebrew, Aramaic, and Greek, and mostly addressed to two men at En-gedi called Jonathan and Masabala, who are commanded, in a somewhat dictatorial fashion, to supply the leader with provisions and additional troops.

When this rebellion had been put down, the Romans took effective measures to ensure that it would not be repeated. Jerusalem was turned into a Roman provincial town and was given the name of Colonia Aelia Capitolina. On the Temple hill there rose a sanctuary in honour of Jupiter Capitolinus, and on the traditional site of Calvary a temple to Venus. The city was repopulated with Romans, Greeks, and orientals from other parts of the empire. No Jew was permitted to enter it on pain of death.

2. THE LATER WRITINGS OF THE NEW TESTAMENT

In the last three or four decades of the first century A.D. there came into existence those books which we now refer to as the Gospels. Originally, the word 'evangelion' simply denoted the 'glad tidings' of the salvation brought about by Jesus Christ, and the word is used in this way at the beginning of the Gospel according to St. Mark (Mark 1:1). However, as early as the second century the term was being applied to all the writings which dealt with the life and work of the man through whom these glad tidings were given to the world. Thus the testimonies of the four Evangelists came to be known as Gospels.

The earliest of the extant Gospels is undoubtedly the one which is known to us as the Gospel according to St. Mark. It is also the shortest. This book may have been written by the man known from Acts as John Mark, who, along with Barnabas, accompanied Paul on part of his first missionary journey, and was later with Peter in Rome (1 Pet. 5:13). At least, this assumption is supported by a passage in the work of a certain Papias, who was living at Hierapolis in Phrygia about the year 140. Papias says, "This also the presbyter used to say: Mark, who became the interpreter of Peter, wrote accurately, as far as he remembered them, the things said or done by the Lord, but not however in order. For he had neither heard the Lord nor been his personal follower, but at a later stage, as I said, he had followed Peter, who used to adapt the teachings to the needs (of the moment), but not as though he were drawing up a connected account of the oracles of the Lord: so that Mark committed no error in writing certain matters just as he remembered them. For he had one object only in view, namely, to leave out nothing of the things which he had heard, and to include no false statement among them."

It is no longer possible to say with any degree of certainty if

◁ The first disciples found support for their Easter faith—that Jesus of Nazareth was the Messiah—in the events of his earthly life. The account of his baptism in the Jordan was given its formal expression in terms of this conviction. The same applies to the account of the Transfiguration on a mountain (Mark 9 : 2-8). Christian tradition has localized this event on Mount Tabor which looks down over Nazareth. Because this mountain towers like a lonely giant above the plain of Jezreel, there had been an aura of 'sacredness' about it from ancient times (Hos. 5 : 1).

(Opposite, left) The valley of the Kidron still forms a natural defence ▷ for Jerusalem. An assault on the eastern wall of the city was therefore no light undertaking, even for the Roman legions, although the wall then may not have been as high as the present one which curtains off the two mosques (in the background). In the foreground, left, lies the sparsely inhabited Ophel, which ceased to be a residential centre after its devastation in the year 70. Against the eastern slope of the Kidron the village of Silwan preserves the name of the celebrated pool of Siloam (John 9 : 7).

(Opposite, right) The present courtyard round the Mosque of Omar (foreground) and the Mosque el-Aqsa (background, right) has more or less the same dimensions as the Temple court which Herod the Great built. In the Synoptic account, and especially in the Fourth Gospel, it was on this spot that the final break occurred between Jesus of Nazareth and the religious leaders of the Jewish nation.

the information given to Papias by the presbyter came from a reliable source. Papias's attempt to ascribe authenticity to the oldest of the Four Gospels by claiming that Mark wrote down what the apostle Peter had told him is not accepted today. The Gospel itself contains nothing which could be considered specifically Petrine in its handling of the traditional accounts of the sayings and actions of Jesus of Nazareth. It is sometimes argued from a number of points in the text that this Gospel originated in one of the non-Jewish Christian communities in Palestine, but Mark is traditionally thought to have written it in Rome about the year 65.

Whatever the truth of the case may be, the particular merit of its author lay in the fact that he was able to sift the various traditions current in the Christian communities of his nearer or wider acquaintance and weave them into a coherent and connected narrative (see Chapter Ten). The very way he selected and ordered his material gave to the whole an individual stamp. But in addition, he modified the texts he found in use amongst the various communities in such a way as to suggest that he had theological views of his own. The same may be said of the summarizing remarks which he interspersed between the traditional accounts he had already reworked into a connected narrative. In spite, therefore, of the traditional nature of his material, Mark proclaimed a personal message.

In Mark's eyes, Jesus is the chosen and obedient servant in whom God, in a hidden and yet visible manner, does battle with the powers of evil and overcomes them. The main outline of the narrative is probably based on some already existing scheme. The author takes as a convenient starting-point the ministry of John the Baptist, the baptism of Jesus, and his sojourn in the wilderness (Mark 1 : 1-13). Then comes Jesus's activities in Galilee, with the small town of Capernaum occupying a prominent place as the scene of much of the action (1 : 14–6 : 13). Next, a number of Jesus's journeys are described, including those to the eastern shore of the Lake of Gennesaret, to the neighbourhood of

Tyre, and finally to Perea and on to Jerusalem (6 : 14–10 : 31). The last episode deals with the events which took place in the holy city, and includes the entry into Jerusalem (11 : 1–13 : 37), the passion (14 : 1–15 : 47), and the discovery of the empty tomb (16 : 1-8). Whether the passage which follows (16 : 9-20) belonged to the original text of the Gospel is still a matter of debate, although the fact that it is not contained in several of the older manuscripts suggests that it was added at a later date. In this narrative, however short and fragmentary, Mark had created a work of literature that soon came to play an important role in the life of many local churches. It provided an assemblage of texts well suited to the purposes of preaching, instruction, and public worship, and it is therefore not surprising that it was soon transcribed many times over.

Not many years afterwards there appeared two other Gospels, both of which appear to follow the broad outline of Mark's narrative. These are the Gospels of Matthew and Luke. The similarity between Mark and Matthew is more striking than that between Mark and Luke, although the events narrated in Matthew begin earlier in time than those of Mark. Whereas Mark begins with the baptism of Jesus by John the Baptist, Matthew gives an account of the genealogy of Jesus, and then goes on to describe his birth. There is serious and well justified doubt as to whether the apostle Matthew was the author of the Gospel in its present form. An ancient tradition has it that he composed a gospel in Aramaic, but although the Greek work which is ascribed to him has been much influenced by Aramaic traditions, it is not itself a translation from Aramaic. An explanation which has been offered is that in the year 50 or thereabouts Matthew brought together some of the sayings of Jesus which were circulating in the churches of Palestine and wrote them down in Aramaic. Later on, perhaps in or about the year 75, an unknown author, following the lead set by Mark, composed a gospel in Greek for Jewish Christians. As this anonymous gospel contained a strikingly large number of the sayings of Jesus and was

perhaps indebted for these to Matthew's collection, which itself very soon disappeared, the book came to bear the apostle Matthew's name.

Another difference between the Gospels of Mark and Matthew is that the work of Matthew is more logically constructed. Time and again the author describes an action performed by Jesus and interrupts it to record one of his sayings. In this way he builds his narrative of events around six discourses which Jesus is represented as having delivered—the sermon on the mount (5:1-7, 29), the missionary charge (to the disciples) (10:1-42), the parables (13:1-52), the instruction given to the disciples (18:1-35), the denunciation of the Pharisees (23:1-36), and the discourse on the end of Jerusalem and of this world (24:1-25, 46).

Like the Gospel of Mark, this work also reveals a developed religious outlook on the part of its author. First and foremost, Jesus is presented as the expected Messiah, in whom the word of God as expressed in the sacred books of the Old Testament is eminently fulfilled. The Jewish leaders are seen as being chiefly to blame for the fact that this son of David was not accepted by his people—a thesis which makes it unlikely that the book was written before the breach had occurred between Judaism and Christianity.

The Third Gospel is attributed to Luke, who is also credited with the authorship of the Acts of the Apostles. Both works are dedicated to a certain Theophilus (Luke 1:3; Acts 1:1). Luke also relied heavily on Mark's work and at the same time he made use of the traditions reflected in the additional material which the Gospel of Matthew contains. In addition, however, Luke seems to have had his own independent sources, and it is these in particular that give his work its distinctive character. The universal validity of the Christian faith is more strongly emphasized than in the other two Gospels by the more frequent and explicit affirmation of Jesus as the Saviour of the whole of mankind. The poor and defenceless are seen as the particular objects of his love and concern, and special stress is laid on the efficacy of prayer,

the experience of joy, and the power of the Holy Spirit. These additional characteristics sufficiently explain why Luke should have chosen to write a new work, even though the two Gospels we know and others were already in existence.

Like the author of the Gospel of Matthew, he begins his account proper with an infancy-narrative (Luke 1:5–2:52), which, however, has a substance and purpose all its own. This he follows with the traditional triptych already familiar to us from the Gospel of Mark, consisting of the ministry of the Baptist, the baptism of Jesus, and his sojourn in the wilderness (3:1–4:13). The account of the public ministry of Jesus is then presented in accordance with the scheme to be found in Mark and Matthew, but the events have been modified to produce a shift of emphasis. Whereas Mark describes several journeys between Galilee, Jerusalem, and the neighbouring regions, Luke follows an account of Jesus's ministry in Galilee (4:14–9:50) with one of a lengthy but single itinerary culminating in the entry into Jerusalem (9:51–19:27). This is intended to show that in the whole course of events revolving about the person of Jesus Jerusalem occupied a central place, for it was in this city that the salvation of mankind was to be accomplished. In the final section of his narrative (19:28–24:53) Luke goes on to describe the events which took place in the Holy City—the passion of Jesus, his death, resurrection, and ascension into heaven.

The relationship between Luke's Gospel and Acts presents a thorny problem. Luke himself refers to the Gospel as his first book (Acts 1:1), and from this it has always been inferred that he wrote the Acts at a later date. In recent years, however, this view has been challenged. To judge from its contents, Acts must have been completed not long after 63. It would therefore seem reasonable to suppose that the Gospel was written in or about the year 60. But this is almost certainly too early a date for it. The highly developed nature of its theological argument, taken in conjunction with a number of other factors, point to a time somewhere about the year 80 as the earliest date at which it could have been

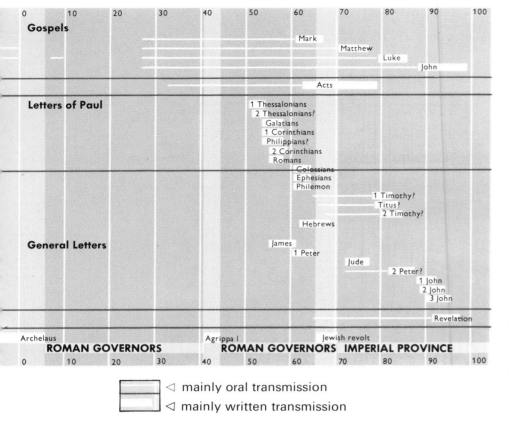

	0	10	20	30	40	50	60	70	80	90	100

Gospels

Mark
Matthew
Luke
John

Acts

Letters of Paul

1 Thessalonians
2 Thessalonians?
Galatians
1 Corinthians
Philippians?
2 Corinthians
Romans
Colossians
Ephesians
Philemon
1 Timothy?
Titus?
2 Timothy?
Hebrews

General Letters

James
1 Peter
Jude
2 Peter?
1 John
2 John
3 John

Revelation

Archelaus Agrippa I Jewish revolt
ROMAN GOVERNORS **ROMAN GOVERNORS IMPERIAL PROVINCE**
0 10 20 30 40 50 60 70 80 90 100

◁ mainly oral transmission
◁ mainly written transmission

Origin, growth, and revision of the New Testament books
This diagram shows that the New Testament emerged in quite a different way from the Old Testament (cf. p. 129). The process by which the New Testament books came into being took not ten centuries but only a few decades. Even so, this diagram presents only the broad outline, which takes little or no account of the connection *between* the books and of the many questions still awaiting a solution.

is now a generally accepted theory that these three Gospels go back to two main sources. According to this theory the Gospel of Mark is the oldest and was used by the other two evangelists as the basis for their work. Matthew and Luke must, in addition, have had access to a further source, which consisted mainly of sayings ascribed to Jesus. Moreover, each of these writers seems to have used material not available to the other, though there is no generally accepted theory as to how they may have come by it.

Traditionally, the Fourth Gospel has always borne the name of the apostle John, though there is nothing to prove that it could not have been written by another disciple of the same name. It must also be admitted that the work as it now stands shows signs of having been edited or revised, possibly by one of John's pupils. The closing sentences (John 21:24-25) and some other short passages cannot be accounted for in any other way. There are some curious differences between this book and the Synoptic Gospels. The writer mentions only a few events concerning Jesus, and these are for the most part not the same as those described by the synoptists. By far the greater part of the book is taken up with discourses, which are put into the mouth of Jesus. Their central theme is the mysterious relationship existing between Jesus and God. Themes such as the kingdom of Heaven and man's relation to God, which are all-important for the synoptists, here make way for the elaboration of the concept of eternal life and the contrast between belief and unbelief.

In the matter of chronology and geography, too, there are considerable differences. The simple scheme of events employed by the synoptists is more or less rejected. Instead, John concentrates on the activities of the adult Jesus, and describes him as making repeated journeys to and from Galilee and Jerusalem, so that his public ministry appears to last about three years. It is difficult to say how well the author was acquainted with the Synoptic Gospels, or even with the traditions on which they were based. The reasons for these marked differences should therefore perhaps be sought elsewhere. A possible explanation is that the subject-matter of the Fourth Gospel had its origins in the traditions of certain churches in Syria and Ephesus, where a group of Jewish and Gentile disciples were concerned to a greater extent than their fellow Christians in other parts with discovering the redemptive value and significance of all that Jesus had said and done. As a leader of such groups as these, John may have worked over and adapted the results of this kind of theological reflection, and one of his pupils may then have produced a final draft of the Gospel about the year 100, after John's death.

Closely related to the Fourth Gospel are three letters, known as the First, Second and Third Letters of John. Their terminology and the theological viewpoint adopted in them are closely related to those of the Fourth Gospel. Consequently we may assume that these letters, despatched by John to a number of churches in the region of Ephesus, contain the writer's original insights into the Christian faith which he later elaborated in his Gospel.

In addition to the Synoptic Gospels and the Johannine writings there is a group of letters, known as the Catholic Epistles, which also belong to this post-Pauline period of literary activity in the Christian Church. This group includes those letters which according to tradition were written by the apostles James, Peter, and Jude. They are not addressed to a particular community, as were the majority of the Pauline letters, nor to specific persons of

written. Acts, on the other hand, gives the impression of being more primitive, in that both its language and its theology appear to belong to an earlier stage. Yet if Luke did actually write his Gospel later, why does he say at the beginning of Acts, "In the first book, O Theophilus, I have dealt with all that Jesus began to do and teach, until the day when he was taken up, after he had given commandment through the Holy Spirit to the apostles whom he had chosen"? The answer to this problem may be that, using both oral and written traditions, Luke did in fact write Acts first, but only in broad outline. Later on, after having written his Gospel, he may have produced a final draft of the Acts, adding the above-mentioned introductory note.

In direct contrast to the Gospel of John, the first three Gospels reveal striking similarities in the presentation and arrangement of their contents. Scholars have long been accustomed to refer to these as the 'Synoptic Gospels,' because when the texts are placed side by side in parallel columns, it is possible to obtain a survey or *synopsis* of the similarities and differences in their treatment of what is essentially the same narrative of events. From the study of such a survey the following three main facts emerge. 1. Apart from a few unimportant exceptions, most of the subject-matter contained in Mark re-appears in the other two Gospels. 2. Matthew and Luke have a number of passages in common, and the majority of these consist of the sayings of Jesus. 3. Matthew and Luke also contain several passages which are not found in any other gospel, canonical or otherwise. There authority within the Church, as were the Pastoral Epistles of Timothy and Titus. On the contrary they were directed to the Church in its entirety, and are for this reason described as 'catholic.' These were probably written by Christians of the second or third generation, who simply issued them under the names of the apostles, though it is possible that the views expressed in them were traditionally associated with the men to whom they were individually ascribed. The Letter of James, for instance, is written in impeccable Greek. This would have been quite beyond the powers of the apostle himself, who was a simple Palestinian Jew. Moreover, it contains a number of maxims and exhortations which are more specifically Jewish than Christian in character. This suggests that it may have been based on an earlier Jewish writing which was subsequently worked over and given a Christian significance.

The First Letter of Peter must have originated at about the same time as the Letter of James. It is directed to the Christians in Pontus, Galatia, Cappadocia, and Bithynia, and appears to have been in its original form a baptismal address, which was only later expanded into a letter.

The short Letter of Jude was probably written during the 70's of the first century. Its author claimed to be the brother of the renowned James, who for about twenty years had been the leader of the church in Jerusalem. The document was addressed to the Christians in a place no longer identifiable, where the freedom for mankind proclaimed by the gospel was apparently being interpreted too broadly. This little letter is especially interesting because it illustrates so clearly how closely the Biblical authors were tied to the ideas and outlook of their age. The Christians of the first and second generation were no exception in this respect. The Letter of Jude reveals the strong influence of Old Testament writings and of later Jewish traditions. The author accepts, for instance, the belief that rebellious angels had been

cast into the nether world (6), that the angel Michael had contended with the devil for the body of Moses (9), and that Enoch, one of the patriarchs, had uttered prophecies (14-15). Extra-Biblical traditions of this kind are also to be found in, for example, Acts 7:3, 15, 53; Ephesians 1:21; 2 Timothy 3:8; 1 John 2:18; and Revelation 2:14.

Ten years or so later a Christian author used the Letter of Jude to counter a similar kind of 'latitudinarian' tendency. Into his own argument he inserted the greater part of the text of Jude, and to invest his teaching with yet more authority he issued his letter with the name of the apostle Peter attached to it. In the list of New Testament writings, therefore, his work has come to be known as the Second Letter of Peter. It was customary procedure for some centuries before and after Christ in issuing a new work, to use the name of some great figure of the past. Biblical books such as Ecclesiastes and Daniel, and other works such as the Book of Enoch, the Psalms of Solomon, the Assumption of Moses, and the Testament of the Twelve Patriarchs, which were all written near the beginning of our era, clearly demonstrate this habit.

3. CHRISTIANITY IN THE ROMAN EMPIRE

In the early period of the Church's history there was little conflict between the Roman state and the Christian communities. In fact, the peace, law, and order afforded by this world empire encouraged the spread of Christianity by making it possible for preachers and missionaries to travel about in safety and to propagate their doctrine over a wide area. The Roman authorities long continued to regard Christianity as a form of Judaism, and since the latter had enjoyed special privileges since the days of Julius Caesar, there seemed to be no reason for making an exception of the followers of the Jesus of Nazareth, who had also been a Jew. The leaders of the Christians, for their part, saw to it that this peaceful situation was maintained. Paul, for example, writing in the year 58, said to the Christians at Rome: "Let every person be subject to the governing authorities. For there is no authority except from God, and those that exist have been instituted by God." (Rom. 13:1) The ideas which Peter later expressed when dictating to Silvanus reveal a similar attitude (1 Pet. 2:13-14, 17).

Towards the end of Nero's reign (54–68) this peaceful state of affairs was suddenly disrupted, although the persecution which followed was ephemeral and local in character. No laws were promulgated against Christians in the empire as a whole. The emperor simply needed some way of re-establishing his gradually declining power and prestige in Rome, and he found suitable victims in the Christians, most of whom belonged to the lower levels of society. Furthermore, they were an unpopular group with many pagans on account of their ideas and their way of life. This was why there had already been several local outbreaks of persecution in Asia Minor (Acts 19:23-40; 1 Pet. 1:6; 4:12-19). Paul and Peter probably died martyrs' deaths during the brief persecution under Nero. A certain Clement, in a letter sent from Rome to the Christians of Corinth about 95, said that both apostles had died for their faith. As the Neronic persecution was the only serious conflict in Rome between Christianity and the

Traditions kept alive in the Churches and a lost book of the sayings of Jesus-referred to as *Quelle* or the Aramaic Matthew—formed the core material from which the Synoptic Gospels emerged.

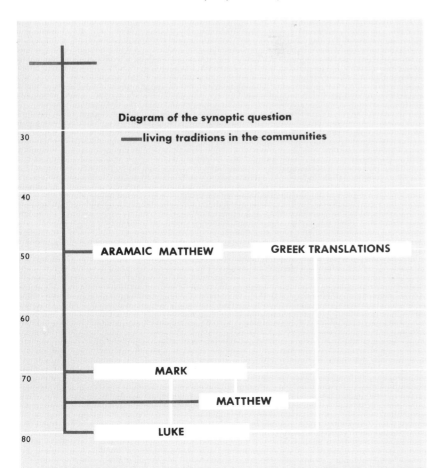

Diagram of the synoptic question
— living traditions in the communities

30

40

50   **ARAMAIC MATTHEW**   **GREEK TRANSLATIONS**

60

70   **MARK**

       MATTHEW

80   **LUKE**

state over many years, Peter and Paul probably died in or about the year 67.

The line of emperors which now occupied the throne–Vespasian (69–79), Titus (79–81), and Domitian (81–96)–did not follow Nero's policies with regard to the Christians. Moreover, the rebellion in Palestine (66–73) had brought no substantial change in the advantageous position enjoyed by the Jews of the Diaspora. And since, now that the Temple had been destroyed, it was more difficult than ever for an outsider to see the difference between Jews and Christians, the latter were also left free to grow and develop as a community. The good relations existing between the state and the Church at this time is evident from such passages as 1 Timothy 2:1-2 and Titus 3:1, where the readers are urged to pray for their rulers and to obey them. It may be assumed that under these conditions, which prevailed for about a quarter of a century, from 70 to 95, the increase in the number of Christians was substantial.

In the last years of the reign of Domitian the situation suddenly took a turn for the worse. For some years this emperor had been forced to concentrate all his energies on maintaining the imperial frontiers against invaders from the north and east. When at the cost of considerable effort he had at last restored peace in these areas, he set about consolidating his authority at home. He was an ardent upholder of the state religion, and saw the veneration of the tutelary gods of Rome as a means of ensuring peace within the empire and his own position as head of it. He was therefore hostile to any group which might in any way weaken this structure. As a result many highly-placed and well-known personalities suffered because of their liberal opinions.

Some Greek philosophers, too, whose attitude to the Roman gods had been somewhat sceptical, found themselves forced to conform. The persecution was directed most of all, however, against the Jews and the Christians, for they could accept neither the state religion nor the cult of the emperor. Domitian even went so far as to have his own brother, Clement, assassinated and Clement's wife, Domitilla, banished. Christian tradition has accorded these two the halo of martyrdom, but it is doubtful whether they were in fact Christians. Such little evidence as exists merely suggests that they were liberal-minded people who felt some sympathy with Christianity.

During these years there was an outbreak of persecution in Asia Minor also. One celebrated victim of the oppression was the Jew or prophet John, who is probably not to be identified with the author of the Fourth Gospel and the letters attributed to John. He was banished to the island of Patmos, west of Miletus, and according to an ancient tradition this enforced stay on the island induced him to put together a short book, which because of its opening sentences soon came to be known as The Revelation to St. John. It is written in the peculiar apocalyptic style so popular around the beginning of our era. Authors who cultivated this style of writing propounded their argument in the form of enigmatic visions, one purpose of which was to intimate the divine source or origin of their message. This is why it was necessary to employ the literary device of making an angel appear and reveal to the author and through him to the believer the symbolic meaning of these mysterious visions. Yet it was not the primary aim of these writers to impart hidden or esoteric knowledge, but rather to encourage and console their fellow-believers under

persecution. They proclaimed that, in spite of all appearances to the contrary, God was guiding history towards the final victory of good over evil.

Apart from such distinctively apocalyptic features, the Revelation to John teems with implicit and explicit references to passages in the Old Testament, which frequently make it very difficult to understand. In fact, on the meaning of many parts of the text there is extreme diversity of opinion. The book as it stands today was probably put together about the year 95, but parts of it may be based on texts of an earlier period. Writing from Patmos, John addressed himself to seven Christian churches on the mainland—to Ephesus, Smyrna, Pergamum, Thyatira, Sardis, Philadelphia, and Laodicea. His visions present the Roman state as a demonic power bent on the annihilation of the devout. The book was not actually a call to rebel against the authority of the state, but the author saw clearly that the attitude of authority which the Romans were adopting towards Christianity would result in open conflict in the not-so-distant future.

Generally speaking, the emperors who succeeded Domitian in the second and third centuries maintained the same policy towards Christianity. Trajan (113–120) is a familiar example. There is still in existence a famous series of letters between him and Pliny the Younger, a Roman official stationed in the province of Bithynia in Asia Minor. These letters discuss the problem posed by the Christians. Pliny explained in one of them how he tackled this problem: "I ask them if they are Christians. If they admit it I repeat the question a second and a third time, threatening capital punishment; if they persist I put them under arrest." It is clear that Pliny found it difficult to do justice both to

A general view of the sanctuary at Ba'albek. In the foreground is the hexagonal inner court. Behind it is the great forecourt with, in the centre, the remains of the monumental altars. In the distance rise the celebrated six columns, the remaining part of the arcade surrounding the temple proper. The scaffolding to their left was erected in the restoring of the building known as the temple of Bacchus. On the hazy horizon are the mountains of Lebanon.

◁ (Opposite) The temple complex at Ba'albek stood partly on a man-made mound. The dark doorway in the foreground leads to the basement. A corridor as broad as a street runs underneath the great forecourt. On the court itself one can pick out the remains of the monumental altars with, left and right, the water basins. Behind them are the hexagonal courtyard and the entrance to the temple complex. In the distance lie the village of Ba'albek, part of the plain of Beqa', and the first slopes of the Anti-Lebanon.

(Right) A fragment of the much discussed mosaic map of Madeba ▷ (Biblical Medeba). This piece of artistry was laid into the floor of a church during the 6th century. When this was destroyed by the Muslims in the 7th century, the map lay beneath the rubble until it was rediscovered at the end of the 19th century. The map probably included the whole of Palestine, but the greater part has been destroyed. This section of what remains shows Jerusalem in a particularly good state of preservation. On the left is the north gate. Behind it is an open space, from which two colonnaded streets run south. This layout has persisted to the present day in the Damascus Gate, the Street of the Valley (Tariq el-Wad) and the Great Suq (Khan ez-Zeit). In the centre of the city, on the straight street, stand the basilica of the emperor Constantine and the dome covering the Holy Sepulchre. The legends are in places difficult to read; they are done in a popular form of Greek and include numerous abbreviations and Bible quotations. Clearly inscribed over the east gate are the words: holy city of Jerusa[lem].

his official duty and to the Christians. They had committed no punishable crime. Moreover, he was embarrassed by the sheer number of them. This led him to write to Trajan saying, "The matter seemed to me to justify my consulting you, especially on account of the number of those imperilled; for many persons of all ages and classes and of both sexes are being put in peril by accusation, and this will go on. The contagion of this superstition has spread not only in the cities, but in the villages and rural districts as well." Trajan's reply was short and sharp. The Christians who renounced their faith might be set free; the others were to be punished.

The Roman rulers were concerned not so much with the suppression of Christianity as such as with the propagation of a state religion which would re-inforce their authority. The numerous ruins of temples dating from the second and third centuries show that Roman religion reached its peak of activity at this period. The most impressive remains are to be seen in Palmyra and Ba'albek.

Palmyra lies in the Syrian desert, about 140 miles north-east of Damascus. From the earliest times this oasis had been an important trading centre. The period of its greatest prosperity, however, did not begin until the early part of the second century A.D., when the Nabatean state became a part of the Roman empire, and its capital, Petra, was reduced to the status of a provincial town. Palmyra then became the principal centre for commercial traffic in transit. This economic progress coincided with a flowering of religious life, to which the famous temple of Bel, for example, bears eloquent testimony.

The remains of the temple complex at Ba'albek afford perhaps the best illustration of the revival of pagan worship in the earliest centuries of our era. The great temple of Jupiter must have been an imposing edifice. The entrance to the sanctuary was on its eastern side. A wide staircase conveyed the visitor to a flight of steps flanked with columns. It is still possible to detect on some of these columns traces of a Latin inscription of the emperor Caracalla (211–217). After this came a hexagonal forecourt, almost 200 feet across. Covered colonnades along the north and south sides protected the pilgrims from the heat of the sun and the cold winter rains. Behind this hexagon stood the forecourt proper, a spacious square, 440 feet long and 370 in breadth. Along the north, south, and east sides were yet more covered colonnades with richly decorated bays, some rectangular and some rounded, containing statues of the gods. Approximately in the centre of the square, on the longitudinal axis, were two immense altars. The larger one must have stood about 55 feet high, with broad steps leading up to the platform. The altars were flanked by two large water-basins for ritual ablutions, and the rims of these were ornamented with skilfully executed reliefs.

But the most imposing building of this whole complex must have been the temple of Jupiter which stood on the west side of the great forecourt and dominated all the other buildings as well as the immediate neighbourhoood. Fifty-four columns, each 65 feet tall with a diameter of some 6 feet, enclosed the sacral area, which covered a rectangular surface of about 280 by 150 feet. The famous six columns, which have remained standing to this day, give only a feeble impression of its vanished greatness. The building known as the temple of Bacchus, which stands next to it, on the south side, is in a better state of preservation. Although

Beside the ruins of two pagan sanctuaries at Ephesus lie the remains of the famous Church of Mary, where the third General Council of Christian bishops was held in 431. It was one of the many churches built within the Roman empire after the emperor Constantine had made Christianity a state religion in the 4th century. A pious tradition according to which Mary, the mother of Jesus, is supposed to have died at Ephesus, gave occasion for the building of this church. The baptistry, situated on the north side of the ruins, is undoubtedly part of the 4th-century church. It is a circular chapel with the baptismal font in the middle of the floor (see photo). The person to be baptized entered and left the basin by the small steps.

of more modest proportions, this structure enables us to obtain some idea of the magnificence of the Jupiter temple.

The ruins of Palmyra, Ba'albek, and other cities are a clear enough indication that the Christians were obliged to live out their faith on the fringes of public life. Persecution forced the congregations behind the walls of private houses and into the catacombs. This is why not a single Christian building of any appreciable size is known to us from this period.

4. THE EMERGENCE OF A NEW TESTAMENT CANON

Amongst the individual Christian communities, persecuted and hidden away as they were, the sacred books in which the history of the Chosen People stood recorded continued to be held in high esteem. They were found to provide support and confirmation for the belief that Jesus of Nazareth was the Messiah. For the purposes of preaching, instruction, and worship in the Christian congregations, however, they proved to be quite inadequate. For the profession of their own belief Christians were at first content to rely on the oral traditions kept alive in the local churches, but with the rapid spread of Christianity, there arose a demand, particularly amongst the more remote and isolated congregations, for an authoritative and permanent statement of doctrine. The disciples of the first generation were not always able to provide for this need. Moreover, their number was continually decreasing. It was as a result of this situation that the texts, some shorter and some longer, which dealt with the ministry of Jesus—the documents already mentioned—came into being. As soon as writers were able to collect and collate this material, it ceased to be a part of the life of the churches and was replaced by the Four Gospels.

Similarly, as Christianity spread from one town to another, it became necessary to make copies of Paul's letters, for the originals were preserved by the particular churches for which he had written them, and were read over and over again to the congregations. The author of the Second Letter of Peter must already have been familiar with a collection of Paul's letters, since he writes to his disciples, "So also our beloved brother Paul wrote to you according to the wisdom given him, speaking of this as he does in all his letters. There are some things in them hard to understand, which the ignorant and unstable twist to their own destruction, as they do the other scriptures." (2 Pet. 3:15-16) From this passage it would appear that even by the year 85 or thereabouts a collection of Paul's letters was generally available, and, furthermore, that people relied on them as a sure witness to the Christian faith.

What happened in the case of the other New Testament writings is not so clear, though the fact that the texts of them have been preserved in full suggests that they were held in great esteem and carefully looked after. Indeed, it is quite rare for first-century texts which the Christian community regarded as unimportant to have come down to us in their entirety.

There are various pieces of evidence dating from about 200 which show clearly enough that a list of sacred writings of the New Testament period had by then come into existence alongside the collected Old Testament texts. Various authors of this period, such as Irenaeus of Lyons, Hippolytus of Rome, Clement of Alexandria, and Tertullian of Africa, make mention of the Four Gospels, the letters of Paul, and a number of other writings, speaking of them as texts which were accepted as a norm of faith and were therefore read aloud to the congregations. The most striking evidence is offered by the Muratorian Canon. This is a detailed list of sacred books which was discovered and published in the eighteenth century by Muratori. The author of the list, which has been dated about 200, speaks with some authority about those books that were accepted by the universal Church and those that were not. To the former category he assigns most of the New Testament books we know today. He is silent only with regard to the First and Second Letters of Peter, the Letter of James, and the Letter to the Hebrews. With regard to some of the non-Biblical writings he is in doubt, and others he rejects with the comment, "one should not mix gall with honey."

Taking into account all the evidence available from the second and third centuries, it is probably correct to say that by about the year 200 the Four Gospels and the thirteen letters attributed to Paul were regarded as Holy Writ by the Christians in the eastern as well as the western part of the Roman empire.

With regard to the Letter to the Hebrews, the Revelation to John, and the Catholic Epistles (James, Jude, 1 and 2 Peter, 1, 2, and 3 John), however, some individual authorities or churches were in doubt. There was uncertainty, too about some other writings of a religious character, such as the Revelation of Peter and a little book called The Shepherd of Hermas. This doubt and uncertainty point to the fact that Christians were not yet being guided and governed by a strong central authority. The churches were under pressure and conducted their life in secret. As a result, it was difficult for them to reach general agreement on the individual value of these various writings.

By about 400, however, a Canon of Scripture had gradually emerged. This was made possible by the great change in the official attitude towards Christianity which had come about as a result of the efforts of the emperor Constantine. This ruler was sympathetic towards the new faith, and under the influence of his mother, Helena, he raised it to the dignity of a state religion. Christians were now free to make public expression of their belief, and this soon began to have a distinctive and abiding influence on the life of society. One fact illustrative of this newly-acquired freedom is that 'local habitations' were given to many of the traditions of apostolic times. Churches and sanctuaries were built at many places which according to one tradition or other were connected with the life or ministry of Jesus of Nazareth. For instance, a church was erected in Jerusalem on the spot where Jesus was believed to have died and to have risen from the grave. Bethlehem became the site of a Church of the Nativity, and on the Mount of Olives sanctuaries were built to mark the spot where Jesus's ascension into heaven was believed to have taken place, and where he was thought to have predicted the destruction of Jerusalem. The sixth-century mosaic of Madeba bears witness to the spate of church building which was then taking place not only in Jerusalem, but throughout the Holy Land.

This official change of attitude also made it possible for a stronger central authority to develop within the Christian community. Contacts between one place and another became closer and more frequent, now that they could be conducted in the open. The general councils of the church which were held at Nicea, Constantinople, and Ephesus show how much the situation had altered since the times of Nero. All these factors were conducive to the general acceptance of one and the same list of sacred books and the establishment of a fixed canon of New Testament writings. There was occasionally still some doubt expressed as to the authority of certain works, such as the Letter to the Hebrews, the Revelation to John, and some of the Catholic Epistles. Nevertheless, it is fair to say that by about the beginning of the fifth century the list of twenty-seven New Testament books had won almost universal recognition.

EPILOGUE BY LUCAS H. GROLLENBERG

On not a few occasions the author of this book has discussed in more or less detail the religious outlook of those who brought the books of the Bible into existence. At the close of this fascinating story the reader may feel that he needs some kind of summary statement of the vision behind their achievement. He may perhaps have wondered whether, despite all the changes in, and enrichment of, that vision down the centuries, it has remained fundamentally the same. The question may even have presented itself in this form: in the long-drawn-out process by which the Bible came into being is it possible to point to a governing principle? The purpose of these concluding pages is to offer the reader some thoughts which he may perhaps find useful in formulating his answer to such questions.

1. EXODUS AND COVENANT

Now that we are able to compare ancient Israel with her predecessors and neighbours, it has become possible to recognize certain characteristic features that were peculiarly her own. They are by now matter of common knowledge. In the ancient world Israel stood alone in worshipping a deity who did not countenance the recognition of other gods, who had no female consort, and who could not be represented or portrayed in any form. Israel was the first nation in the world to produce any real historiography; and she evolved an attitude of expectancy regarding the future which had no parallel. These and other characteristics would all appear to be rooted in a quite distinctive way of apprehending and experiencing the nature of reality. One might describe this, in broad outline, as follows.

The oldest title accorded to Yahweh—and that which occurs most frequently—is "He who brought us out of Egypt." Israel owed her existence to an act of deliverance. If Yahweh had not intervened, she would not have been. On his own initiative he had saved a group of people from annihilation and in so doing had brought them into a new mode of existence—the existence of those delivered by him. It made the group his possession, his people. Israel was a creation of his and belonged wholly to him, to him alone.

Israel gave expression to this fact and made it a living experience in the notion of the Covenant which Yahweh was believed to have concluded after the Exodus and in consequence of it. In that Covenant the new relationship was ordered and regulated: "Henceforth I am your God and you are my people." It meant that a reality from the world of human relations—a contract, treaty, covenant—was thus transferred to the plane of the relation between man and deity; and this was something without parallel anywhere among the religions.

The past few years have acquainted us with specimens of the treaties, highly specific in content, which powerful rulers in the ancient Near East concluded with minor princes on whom they had conferred some favour (cf. above, p. 56, where the Hittites are under discussion). The treaty into which Yahweh entered with Israel exhibits striking similarities with those 'vassal treaties,' as they are so appropriately called. In a great variety of Biblical passages, not only in the Prophets and the Psalms but in the Law as well, the deliverance from Egypt forms the basis of the exclusive attachment demanded of his people by Yahweh. It is from this that other more detailed stipulations derive their authority, and it is all underpinned by sanctions, the blessing and the curse.

We shall never know precisely when and by whom this institution, which formed part of the international legal system, was applied to Israel's experience of God, nor to what extent there was a connection with the vassal treaties with which we are now familiar. What is certain is that the parallel has served to fasten attention more sharply on a number of features present in Israel's experience from the very beginning.

Conspicuously prominent among them is the fact that besides requiring respect for himself, Yahweh demanded it also for human beings. Because Israel owes her existence to an act of deliverance from distress, an Israelite sins against his own existence, so to speak, whenever he inflicts distress upon someone else. He then goes clean against the nature of Yahweh, who is precisely the deliverer. An offence committed against another human being is an offence against Yahweh. Of the many ancient texts which illustrate this notion, the Ten Commandments —otherwise known by the Greek term the 'Decalogue'—is the best known.

The sovereign Lord of Israel begins with a reminder of his beneficent act: "I am Yahweh who brought you out of Egypt"; and he then proceeds to summarize his claims. The Israelite must not acknowledge any other power besides him. He must not make an image and so engender in himself and in others the idea that he can exercise some sort of control over Yahweh. He would be doing the same thing if, like the heathen, he were to employ Yahweh's holy name for purposes of magic. He must devote one day of the week—the Sabbath—to Yahweh in order to express the truth that all time, and therefore the whole of existence, belongs to him. And he must revere his parents, through whom Yahweh gave him life; for parents are not just like other people—they are part of the divine order. Other people as such come into the picture in the last five commandments: "thou shalt not kill," and so forth. When we bear in mind that 'kill' in this passage does not refer to killing in war, nor to the death penalty in the due process of law, but only to wilful murder; and furthermore that 'stealing' probably refers only to the seizure of another person with the intent to enslave him; and finally that 'coveting' in ancient Hebrew includes the act of confiscation, then we can see that Yahweh is stating here, as being in line with his own rights, five fundamental rights of man: man's right, that is, to life, conjugality, freedom, good name, and property.

This is a true reflection of Israel's experience. One has only to read the nineteenth chapter of the Book of Leviticus. Again, where the rights of the poor and of the stranger are concerned, the commandments are punctuated again and again by the statement: "I am the Lord your God [Yahweh]"—a plain assertion that in him is to be found the real ground of just dealing between one man and another, and indeed of more than that. "I am the Lord. You shall do no injustice in judgment; you shall not be partial to the poor or defer to the great, but in righteousness shall you judge your neighbour. You shall not go up and down as a slanderer among your people, and you shall not stand forth against the life of your neighbour: I am the Lord. You shall not hate your brother in your heart, but you shall reason with your neighbour, lest you bear sin because of him. You shall not take vengeance or bear any grudge against the sons of your own people, but you shall love your neighbour as yourself: I am the Lord."

As the translation brings out, it is the individual Israelite who is addressed in the passage just quoted. Other passages where the general tenor is the same sometimes employ the plural. The singular is often applied to Israel as a whole. Such facts as these disclose a profound respect for the individual human being. The people of Yahweh do not constitute a mass at Yahweh's beck and call. Along with Israel as a whole Yahweh addresses himself to each Israelite personally, as a responsible individual called upon to make repeated choices. "Behold, I set before you this day a blessing and a curse: the blessing, if you obey the commandments of the Lord your God...and the curse, if you do not obey..." (Deut. 11:26-28); or in the singular: "See, I have set before you this day life and good, death and evil... therefore choose life..." (Deut. 30:15-19) Even though the deliverance from Egypt and the consequent absolute sovereignty of Yahweh are something given, de facto, every member of the nation must constantly reaffirm the situation thus created.

Leading experts on Israel's very early history are of the opinion that only a relatively small group underwent the experience of the Exodus. This group is thought to have settled somewhere in central Palestine, in the neighbourhood of Shechem. There a number of other tribes joined them; and they did so by opting for Yahweh—"He who brought us out of Egypt"—as their God also, and by rejecting in that way all their previous gods. The core of Joshua 24 is thought to enshrine the recollection of this agreement. This hypothesis, although not as yet universally accepted, may well serve to elucidate what we have just been saying. The covenant relationship calls for free acceptance, constantly reaffirmed, from those who are party to it. The basis for membership of this community of persons, of Israel, the people of Yahweh, is this personal assent, and not one's ancestry.

As for Israel's extraordinary historical consciousness, that too would seem to have issued from the pattern of Exodus and Covenant. When a powerful ruler made a treaty with a vassal, he involved himself in the future history of the other party. Loyal observance of whatever stipulations the treaty might contain he would reward with further benefactions—disloyalty he would punish. That was all part of the agreement. In conceiving her relation with Yahweh in terms of this kind of covenant Israel knew very well that she was bound to him in respect of whatever her further history might be. She therefore interpreted her good fortune as a benefit which he conferred, her misfortune as a chastisement; and this enabled her to see a coherence in events that would otherwise have passed for the vagaries of accident.

This accounts for the fact that Israel was the first nation in the ancient world to practise the writing of history. Among the other peoples of the ancient Near East, even the most civilized, such a development could not occur; for they recognized a large number of gods who could interfere capriciously in mundane affairs and were motivated often enough by quarrels among themselves. It simply was not possible for any coherence to be detected in whatever occurred in the plane of natural events and of history. Admittedly, there were sporadic attempts to attain to some degree of insight into the course of this or that series of facts; but nowhere was anything produced that was remotely comparable with works of history like the one which treats of the Davidic succession or that of the Yahwist (see pp. 67 and 72).

The latter work combines with the notion that Yahweh governs the course of history and is constantly engaged in fulfilling his own utterances ('promises') a lively interest in 'the phenomenon of man'—an interest undoubtedly grounded in the respect of which we spoke above. Once she had become a state, numerous foreign peoples loomed up upon Israel's horizon. The Yahwist sees them all as one big family, as 'Adam'; and he sets this Adam in a sort of covenant-situation: Yahweh creates him, puts him in a garden, lays an injunction upon him and confronts him with the choice—life or death... That the human family in fact comprises so many races, each speaking its own language and being unable to understand the rest, the Yahwist 'explains' with his story of the Tower of Babel. And he uses that as a background for the call of Abraham, whereby God's voice summons into being, in a mankind divided and separated by pride, a principle of unity, the obedient Abraham, through whom he will re-unify all peoples under his blessing.

2. THE PROPHETS

As this book has shown already in considerable detail, it was possible for the earliest historical writings to emerge only after Israel had become an organized state, a monarchy (see pp. 65-72). Yet it was this very state that constituted a danger to that which was uniquely distinctive about Israel: her life under the Covenant. For in the Near East of that time the king was usually regarded as the son, in bodily form, of one of the national gods. That is why he could on the one hand exert an influence on the god in question and on the other hand enjoy privileged claims of one sort or another over his subjects. Furthermore, monarchy required a court, officials of high standing and a state system with different classes, higher and lower, rich and poor. All this was hard to reconcile with the structure of the Covenant; for that seemed better suited to the situation of the original tribes—that is, of small groups of stock-breeding nomads—in which everybody shared in the tribal property, in which there were no rich and poor, no classes, in which each man enjoyed as many rights as the next, and in which the deity was worshipped as the invisible chief shepherd, a 'mobile' god without priests or temple, who through a revelation to the head of the tribe would give the command to seek new pastures—a god whom men 'served' by obeying his voice and responding loyally to his call.

Even so, Israel's advance to statehood was an inevitable process; and after that the prophets appear, in their role as spokesmen of the Covenant-God, making his claims and utterances heard.

Leaving aside the objections which Samuel is said to have raised against the institution of the monarchy, one may point to two characteristic protests voiced by the prophet Nathan against King David. In the name of Yahweh he opposed David's plan to build a temple alongside his own palace. Was it the King's idea to obtain a measure of control over the Lord of Israel in this way? Yahweh had always been an itinerant God; and, said Nathan, as sovereign Lord he will not let himself be incapsulated in any monarchic structures of yours. Nathan again reacts violently when David trespasses against the second part of the Ten Commandments and murders a man who, albeit a Hittite, is a loyal member of Yahweh's people, so that he can get possession of the victim's wife (2 Sam. 7:7-8 and 12:1-10).

Two episodes in the life of Elijah are particularly well known: the sacrifice on Mount Carmel and Naboth's vineyard. The issue again concerns the rights of God and of the human person. Because she is now given to land cultivation, Israel thinks that like the Canaanites she must turn to the local Baals for the gifts of fertility and rain; and so she recognizes other powers besides Yahweh and wavers between this and that opinion. Elijah's other protest is directed against King Ahab, who has taken it upon himself to put a compatriot to death in order to appropriate the man's property to his own use. That is not admissible. In Israel a person is appointed king to maintain justice and above all to conform to it himself. He is not more than another man (1 Kings 18:20-39 and 21:1-19).

The 'writing prophets' likewise speak up for a way of life that is true to the Covenant and so for the exclusive claims of Yahweh on the one hand and respect for the rights of one's fellows on the other. Hosea puts most emphasis on the former aspect. Like Elijah he has to deal with an Israel owing—as she thought—the fruits of the land, corn and flax, oil and wine, to the local Baals, the 'paramours' of Israel, their mistress. In this she injures the affection of Yahweh, her first and only 'Baal,' which is to say, her lord and husband. Yahweh must now bring calamities upon her, must lay waste her land, so that in that 'wilderness situation' he may restore her to her first love.

Thus Hosea makes clear the essential character of the One who on his own initiative delivered from Egypt the group whom he purposed to make his people, wedded to him alone. The prophet represents Yahweh as a passionate and 'jealous' lover; but along with that he employs the image of the father who has been at pains to feed and nurture Israel, his son. Although this son of his is recalcitrant and ungrateful, he cannot find it in his heart to let him go. Hosea then confesses that all images drawn from the world of human relations, even the most intimate, are inadequate to describe the love of Yahweh for his people: "for I am God and not man, the Holy One in your midst." (See, e.g., Hos. 2:4-17 and 11:1-9.)

Alongside Hosea the prophet Amos does battle with incredible ferocity for the other element in the Covenant: the rights of the human being. That by reason of their special relationship to Yahweh, their 'election,' Israelites should look for blessing and good fortune at his hand, whilst they exploit and trample on the poor, Amos regards as worse than lunatic.

It leaves him lost for words. If Yahweh did indeed lead Israel out of Egypt to link himself with that people in a special way, then she must expect to be punished more severely than other nations for social injustice. Amos goes further than that. He is bold to ask whether in the sight of Yahweh Israel is necessarily something more than the black people of Ethiopia. The Israelites appeal to the fact that he has brought them out of Egypt. True; but Yahweh was at work in the migration of other peoples too: "Did I not bring up the Philistines from Caphtor and the Syrians from Kir?" Amos, then, sees him as the God of all the nations and in particular as the universal protector of human rights. And if those rights are infringed within his own people, he will have no compunction about destroying them (Amos 3:2 and 9:7).

Not long after Amos the great figure of Isaiah is both eloquent and dauntless in defence of the Covenant in both its aspects, even though he nowhere uses that ancient term. In his day the energetic state of Assyria, emerging from the mass of neighbouring peoples, sets rapidly and effectively about the task of making itself the ruling power in the world; and so there looms for the first time before Israel and Judah the prospect of a single dominant authority. What to make of this? For the people of Yahweh are to countenance no other power beside him. At this juncture Isaiah declares what he has seen in the Temple: he has seen Yahweh seated aloft on a throne as *the* king, the sole ruler over all. What, then, is Assyria's position? Assyria, says Isaiah, is in the service of Yahweh; and he makes a number of bold comparisons: it is the rod that Yahweh wields in order to chastise his people, the razor that he has hired from Mesopotamia to shave the land of Israel. For his people have not known him aright. Instead of the justice and righteousness he had looked for, what he saw was justice violated and what he heard were the cries of the downtrodden in their distress.

Isaiah threatens with fearsome curses those Israelites who steal, one after another, the houses of the poor and 'add field to field' so as to make themselves sole owners of the land. There is no future for *that* Israel. Only those who make their choice for 'Yahweh will continue to exist. In emulation of Elijah, with his seven thousand men who refused to bow the knee to the Baals, all the prophets called for a personal decision on the part of every Israelite. But Isaiah appears to have been the first to use the word 'believe' for that act of choosing Yahweh as the one and only Lord. Those who believe constitute the true Israel, the 'remnant,' with whom Yahweh will proceed for the future. (See, e.g., Is. 6:5; 10:15; 7:20; 5:1-8; 7:9; and 30:15.)

In the richly diverse collection of prophetic utterances that make up the Book of Jeremiah one can quickly recognize the two great themes of the Covenant. In line with Hosea, Jeremiah portrays the God of Israel as a lover tirelessly soliciting the affection and loyalty of his people, and at the same time as a father hoping that his children will look to him alone for all that is good. Jeremiah seems to feel something of Yahweh's anguish, as he (God or Jeremiah; it is often difficult to say) sees his people running after worthless and powerless idols and false gods who can impart no blessing but only disenchantment. As always, such defection from Yahweh goes hand in hand with offences committed against men. One can detect something of Amos's indignation in the vehement tones in which Jeremiah ridicules the nation's obtuse confidence in Yahweh's habitation:

"Will you steal, murder, commit adultery, swear falsely, burn incense to Baal, and go after other gods that you have not known, and then come and stand before me in this house... and say, 'We are delivered!'?"

The prophet rebukes King Jehoiakim for making his compatriots toil at beautifying his palaces without paying them any wages and further for the fact that he had an eye only to his own advantage, not scrupling to use violence and to shed innocent blood. Take his father, Josiah. He indeed had lived like a king—but like a king who 'knew Yahweh'; and Jeremiah tells us what that implies: "He did justice and righteousness, and judged the cause of the poor and needy." Finally, be it noticed that Jeremiah speaks with the same voice as Isaiah when it comes to the world power with which the Judah of his day had to deal, Babylon. He sees their great king, Nebuchadnezzar, as one whom Yahweh is working into his plans; this mighty ruler is "the servant [or slave] of Yahweh." (See Jer. 2:1-13; 3:19-20; 7:9-10; 22:13-16; and 27:6.)

The reader will certainly have gathered from these cursory observations about the prophets as champions of the Covenant and of a way of life based upon it how very strongly they were all imbued with what was earlier described as 'the sense of history'—the historical consciousness given along with the Exodus and the Covenant. None of them proclaimed eternal 'truths' or stated 'principles' that were valid for all time. Each in his situation let his compatriots know how the sovereign partner to their Covenant would react to their conduct. In that sense the prophets 'foretold' the future: not from a mysteriously imparted knowledge of facts which would come to pass at some later date, but on a basis of their intimacy with Yahweh, acquired in personal intercourse with him, in accordance with the image presented of him by the oldest traditions. Whether by chastisement or by forgiveness or by some other means he would eradicate all injustice, so that in the end he might live in union with a community of people who, being wholly oriented to him, would be a perfect brotherhood, a 'holy nation.'

The Book of Deuteronomy was apparently meant to provide a kind of programme to this end. At any rate the legislative part of it, in which a good deal of older material has been incorporated, is strongly marked by a humanitarian strain. Much thought is given to the well-being of each and every member of the nation, especially the poor, the widowed and fatherless, and strangers; further, it is urged that animals be well treated. All this is evidently and closely linked with the requirement of total and exclusive orientation to Yahweh, the celebrated commandment in the introduction to the legal code: "Hear, O Israel: the Lord is our God, the Lord alone; and you shall love the Lord your God with all your heart, and with all your soul, and with all your might." Chosen through a completely unmotivated preference on Yahweh's part from among a whole multitude of peoples, Israel is required, in each one of her members, to offer this one Lord one rite of worship at one place of sacrifice and, unsullied by any practice of the idolatrous world, to devote herself to him in singleness of heart and in perfect brotherhood. That, more or less, describes the ideal presented in Deuteronomy. Impressive though it is, it tended to obscure an essential aspect of the Covenant illuminated centuries before by the Yahwists: its significance for mankind as a whole.

3. THE CRISIS OF APARTHEID

It is not long since a commentator on Deutero-Isaiah (Is. 40–55) put forward the following simile: if one envisages the experiential witness of the Bible to God as a broad arch stretched out between two main pillars—the Exodus from Egypt and the death and resurrection of Jesus—then it is possible to regard Deutero-Isaiah as a kind of central pillar. Anyone who steeps himself in these sixteen chapters will understand how this piece of imagery could suggest itself. On the one hand they appear to sum up the whole past experience of God and on the other they offer a compelling prospect of the future. The Yahwist's God, who formed mankind, who overwhelmed the world with the flood from which he rescued Noah, who made Abraham a principle of blessing for all peoples, and who for his progeny's sake overthrew the Pharaoh and parted the waters—he fulfils the message of Deutero-Isaiah as 'the First and the Last,' the absolute Lord of history and of the cosmos in which it is enacted.

At the same time he is the God of the Covenant, the deliverer, the creator, the shepherd, the father and husband of his people—even now, now that nothing remains of that people save a tiny remnant of Jewish exiles in Babylon. They have paid with interest the penalty for all their sins. Now Yahweh prepares to make a new beginning. As he had used Assyria as a rod with which to smite Israel, and the mighty Nebuchadnezzar to execute his judgment, so now he summons a still greater ruler—Cyrus the Persian—on to the stage of history, but this time in order to save his people. And this deliverance is to follow the ancient pattern: an exodus from Babylon, right across the wilderness to a Jerusalem restored in all her splendour. The prophet adjures the exiles to forget the old Exodus only in order to prepare themselves fully for the new one.

Even so, the prophet evidently found it impossible to envisage this new Exodus without an intermediary figure, in the style of Moses. At all events in chapters 42, 49, and 50 a person emerges who is represented by Yahweh to be his consecrated 'servant.' This man testifies himself to the resistance that he encounters when he sets out to bring Israel to a true faith in Yahweh and to accomplish his further task: to be a light to all peoples and to extend the salvation of Yahweh to the ends of the earth. In the 53rd chapter is described in mysterious terms how after his violent death this servant succeeds in leading countless people to a right attitude to God. Each of these 'servant songs' is preceded and followed by enraptured prophecies of the new Exodus, which will result in the restoration of Zion on a magnificent scale. At the same time this saving activity, by which Yahweh restores his dead people to life, is seen as the definitive, worldwide manifestation of his nature. 'All flesh,' that is, the whole of mankind, will behold his salvation, and every knee will bow before him.

So far as visible circumstances were concerned, this all-embracing vision on the part of Deutero-Isaiah had nothing to support it; for the group from which he came and to which he addressed himself had lost everything that provided a firm basis for its religion: country, monarchy (political independence), and Temple. Could it have been that such an exceptional posture of faith attracted the attention even of some of the Babylonians? It is a fact that a slightly later Biblical passage makes reference to "foreigners who join themselves to the Lord, to minister to him, to love the name of the Lord." (Is. 56:6) It was probably accessions of this sort which prompted Zechariah, soon after the year 522, to utter his prophecy regarding the "ten men from the nations of every tongue" who "shall take hold of the robe of a Jew, saying, Let us go with you, for we have heard that God is with you." (Zech. 8:23)

Soon afterwards that universal vision was replaced among the majority of Jews by an increasingly narrow-minded view of their God's intentions. Circumstances forced them as a community to give ever more intense expression to their 'apartheid,' for they formed a negligible minority group among the peoples governed by the Persians. Such a group is generally able to maintain its existence only by insisting on certain distinctive customs which distinguish its members very clearly from 'the others' and serve to knit them closely together. Ezra elevated the Law of Moses to an exclusive rule of life, which of course soon made it necessary to spell out many things in precise detail, with an authority equally absolute. With 'Deuteronomic' zeal, all women of non-Jewish origin were ejected from the community together with their children. The intention was of course to debar idolatrous practices; but it opened the door to a concern for the purity of the race and so to a degraded view of the Covenant. (See, e.g., Neh. 8, Deut. 13, and Ezra 9.)

It was this atmosphere that gave rise to many of the 'divine utterances against the nations,' which were incorporated into the collections of prophecies. Most of them consigned the Jews' neighbours, whether near or distant, to unqualified annihilation. Many Jews saw a world coming in which there would be room only for the Chosen People. But not all of them did that. Ancient texts continued to have their effect, especially accounts of noble non-Jews, from the story about David and Bathsheba, in which the only 'good' character is Uriah the Hittite, to the one about Jeremiah being rescued from a gruesome death by suffocation by a negro slave.

And to these, new stories of a similar import were added. Very tenderly written was the one about the noble figure of Ruth, the Moabitess, member of a people who according to the oracles of God deserved total destruction. Ruth was supposed to have been an ancestress of no less a person than King David. In the imposing short story about Jonah, the sailors are God-fearing men; and the people of Nineveh are evidently prompt to repent. The only repellent character in the story is the Jew, who tries to evade his mission to the heathen and becomes furious when Yahweh does not exterminate them. Any sharper criticism of Jewish 'apartheid' it would be hard to conceive. (See 2 Sam. 11; Jer. 38:7-13; Ruth 4:17; Jonah 4:2.)

Others chose the prophetic style to give expression to the universality of their outlook. Two collections included the splendid utterance about the mountain of the house of Yahweh —the hill of the Lord to which at the close of the age all nations will ascend, to be taught by him how they are to live together; then they will beat their weapons into tools of prosperity and peace. There is also the vision appended to one of Isaiah's pronouncements: Egypt and Assyria, those arch-enemies of earlier days, will turn as brothers to Yahweh; and Israel will be the third party to this alliance, "a blessing in the midst of the earth." (See Is. 2:2-4 = Mic. 4:1-3; Is. 19:23-25.)

But it would seem that all visions of this sort met with no response. The very fact that the Maccabees fought so stubbornly and successfully to preserve their own Jewish customs served to foster in the pious a negative attitude toward all who were outside their circle. When at the start of our era misgovernment on the part of the Romans and their underlings resulted in a very critical situation, the marked resurgence of hopes and expectations concerning the future was concentrated entirely upon their own Jewish group. Whilst the nationalistically-minded pinned their hopes on a Messiah who would overthrow the Romans by force and would subjugate all the nations to Israel, those who lived punctiliously according to the Law looked for God to intervene in a way which would bring eternal salvation to their own group and eternal perdition upon all who disobeyed the Law, even if they were strangers to it.

4. JESUS – GOD FOR ALL

In a manner that was wholly unexpected, the crisis mentioned above reached its climax and its solution in Jesus of Nazareth. The movement which originated with him displayed the structure of the Covenant. It saw itself as the continued unfolding of what God had initiated in Israel; and that was the reason why the Jewish Holy Scriptures became an essential part of the Christians' Bible. These assertions can be elucidated to some extent on the following lines.

There is a growing consensus among modern students of the Gospels that the most distinctive feature of what Jesus said and did during his ministry was the absolute character of his claims. Whereas the prophets had always prefaced their sayings with the formula, "Thus says Yahweh...," or had concluded them with "Oracle of Yahweh...," Jesus never did so. He often prefaced his own sayings with an authoritative "I say to you...," sometimes reinforcing this with the solemn 'Amen' of the Hebrew liturgy: "Amen [truly], I say to you..." To his own mind he was evidently not in the service of God as the prophets had been; and he felt no need to appeal to a commission or mandate.

The assertions he made with this unsurpassed authority related as a rule to the consummation of history, which the Jews longed for more ardently than ever before. In that connection he made use of the rich variety of terms and images current at the time. But the really unique element in his 'teaching' about this was the unprecedented claim that the eagerly awaited definitive action on God's part was actually happening in what he himself was doing and saying. He felicitated the people who encountered him personally: "Prophets and kings have yearned to see what you see, to hear what you hear..." Many Jews were expecting that the prophet Elijah, who long before had been carried up into heaven, would return to herald the great 'day of Yahweh,' on which his kingship would be publicly revealed. According to Jesus, Elijah had come already, in the person of John the Baptist.

Many believed, basing themselves on the Book of Daniel, that 'one like a son of man' would execute God's final judgment. Without ever declaring plainly who he himself was, Jesus said: "Whoever accepts me will be accepted by that son of man, and whoever rejects me will be rejected by him." Thus the attitude taken towards Jesus would in fact determine the later destiny of every individual Jew and of the community as a whole. Jesus pronounced God's sentence of annihilation upon whole towns such as Chorazin, Beth-saida, and Capernaum because they had rejected his call to repentance. He addressed that call to every Jew, to 'all Israel'—and indeed exclusively to her. Of other peoples he spoke only when his summons took the form of a threat: if those specially invited to the wedding refuse to come, the host will fill his banqueting-hall with the riff-raff of society; they will come from east and west and north and south and in company with Abraham will enjoy everything that the 'sons' have forfeited. In saying this Jesus was also doing something else. He was condemning the discrimination which officially obtained between the 'righteous' and 'sinners,' something that permeated the whole of Jewish society. According to him the former were required to repent just as much as the latter. He regarded the whole system—forming a judgment of oneself and of others on the basis of obedience to the Law—as a fundamental misapprehension of what God really wanted.

With all these shockingly presumptuous actions of his Jesus put himself beyond the pale, the more so in that he always refused, in any case, to establish his identity. When the conflict between him and the Jewish leaders had reached its climax, as a good Jew he still made the pilgrimage to Jerusalem at the time of Passover. From among his followers he had constituted a special group of twelve, just as Yahweh had once chosen twelve tribes to constitute his people. These twelve he took with him. They knew him better than did other men. They had noticed, with all those staggeringly presumptuous words and deeds, how unpretentious he always was. On occasion he even went so far as to wait upon them at table, like a house slave. They knew, too, how he prayed to the God of Israel. It was Jesus's custom to address him with a word used by children: 'Abba,' which means something like 'daddy.' When he spoke of him to others, it was usually as 'your Father in heaven.' He evidently felt that the infinite distance between God and other people did not exist in his own case. He sometimes referred to himself as 'the son.' Thus he had said on one occasion, regarding the point in time at which history would be consummated, that no man knew anything about it, 'neither the angels in heaven, nor the son, but only the Father.'

The twelve also knew what he was expecting to happen in Jerusalem, the city that had been wont to kill prophets. He would press on, undaunted, with the proclamation of his message, which faced the Jewish community so clearly with this dilemma: either to accept him or to perish. The Jewish leaders had no alternative, therefore, but to effect his removal. In alluding to his approaching death he had himself used this remarkable metaphor: "The baptism wherewith I must be baptized..." Did not baptism serve as initiation into a new life with God, in a new community? During the final meal with his disciples he used yet another figure of speech to illustrate how he understood his death: in the bread broken and the wine outpoured he gave himself, in order, by so doing, to institute a new Covenant.

When after the Passover the disciples had obtained the assurance that God had raised him from the dead and so had ratified all his 'presumptuous' claims, Jesus became once and for all their 'Lord'—Lord, that is, in the total sense in which Yahweh had made himself known as the absolute, sovereign Lord of Israel. Whereas that mighty and invisible One had addressed himself to his people over all those centuries through the medium of legislators, priests, and sages, and above all through prophets who declared how the divine mind was revealed in particular circumstances, Jesus was accepted by his disciples as Yahweh speaking in his own person, as Yahweh's 'word become man.' His whole life was centred in this and was devoted to it. The factual content of what he proclaimed and his acts of service, his death and his resurrection were seen as the definitive disclosure of how God is disposed toward men.

Thus it was that the rapidly expanding group of disciples centred on their 'Lord' came to envisage themselves as the continuation and development of the old Israel. Just as that people had again and again been called upon to heed the voice of Yahweh, to 'follow' him, as the expression sometimes was, and not to run after strange gods, so Jesus had uttered, just as unconditionally, the command to 'follow after' him—to follow to the end his path of consecration and self-giving. Admission to the group which confessed him 'Lord' was effected in baptism, as a rite expressing complete involvement in his person, his life, and his destiny. Just as in Israel the Covenant was continually renewed through commemoration of the Exodus in virtue of which Yahweh had become sovereign Lord, and also through assent to his claims, so the Church celebrated 'the Lord's supper,' as both a memorial of Jesus's saving action and a means of symbolizing in action the involvement of all in his person.

Israel had been known as 'the people of Yahweh.' The new community of believers called itself 'the Church of Christ.' We saw that Hosea represented the living fellowship between Israel and Yahweh as that between loved one and lover, woman and man. It was in that vein that believers spoke of the Church as 'the bride of Christ.' But now that the divine partner had given shape and form to his love in a tangible human being, the metaphor could be taken even further. Christians for whom the living communion of each and every member with Jesus was an intense personal experience came to speak of the Church as 'the body of Christ.'

Furthermore, it was a distinctive feature of this life under the new Covenant that it was no longer restricted to a single people. Jesus had thrown his life into the struggle against the discrimination, officially encouraged, between 'sinners' and 'the righteous.' He had set his own authority above that of the Law. It was not a total adherence to the commandments that would decide a person's future, but his attitude toward him, Jesus. He had brought the definitive revelation of the mind and will of God; and he was in his own person the palpable expression of God's sovereign claims. With all this Jesus put an end to the privileged position of the Jewish people, which it enjoyed especially in its possession of the Law. Because God had now declared himself fully in a human person, he addressed himself to all men without distinction. All this became apparent after Jesus's withdrawal; but it was to take a Paul to see clearly all that flowed from it and to bring home to the Jewish disciples of Jesus at the practical level all that their recognition of him as 'the Lord' implied.

Jesus had demolished every dividing wall between men. Jew and Gentile, Greek and barbarian, freeman and slave, male and female—all alike were 'implicated' in Christ. Hence the figurative notion of 'the body of Christ' as something that is growing all the time, and will so continue down the centuries. This in turn has served to impart broader dimensions to that way of thinking which is oriented towards history and to an expectant view of the future—elements which are themselves inextricably bound up with the experience of life lived under the Covenant. But these are matters which the reader must work out for himself; for there is still one more question to be considered.

5. THE GOVERNING PRINCIPLE

Professional students of religion tell us that the phenomenon has its source and origin in 'religious experience'—by which they understand something like this: all human beings have a vague apprehension of 'the mystery of existence,' and this may suddenly present itself with overwhelming force. It is revealed as both terrifying and fascinating. The person concerned wants to run away from it and yet is also irresistibly attracted by it. In experiences of this kind, it is said, every religion has its roots.

If one accepts this view of the matter, the special characteristics of the religion of the Bible may be described in the following terms. More strongly than was the case anywhere else, the founders of this religion experienced the mystery in question as a 'someone.' The element of fascination consisted in the fact that the mystery manifested as 'personal' made itself known as 'life-giving,' as 'saving,' while the terrifying aspect found expression in the absolute and ineluctable character of its claims. A no less distinctive feature was that it 'laid claim' to those concerned not simply as individuals but also as people-existing-together-with-others. Of genuine 'mysticism,' as a mode of being in which the individual is 'swallowed up' in the divine, there is hardly a trace in the religion of the Bible. There, whoever has had 'experience' of God is by that very fact constituted a witness, an emissary with a message for others. For the people of the Bible any religious experience is inchoate, it would seem, and in a sense unreal, so long as there are no other people implicated in it.

Whatever may be thought of this view, one thing at any rate is certain: all the people who in one way or another have something to say in the Bible acknowledge 'a personal God' as actively and dynamically involved in things as a whole. They would probably object to the non-Biblical word 'personal,' in so far as it is an attempt to define or delimit God; for they are keenly aware that he is not to be comprehended within any single concept. But the term might well be acceptable to them if it is meant simply to indicate that man is essentially a being who is 'addressed' and who gives expression to his existence by responding. He is a being who is responsible in respect of the existence which has been given him and which he fulfils together with others, responsible in respect of those others to the Other. Those who hold the faith of the Bible see in that God the governing principle of history. He is mysteriously implicated in the doings of all men, giving them freedom and at the same time guiding and directing them. He is bent on realizing what has turned out, especially since Jesus, to be his ultimate purpose: the perfect fellowship of all men in him.

This principle they have seen at work also in the process that gave rise to the Bible. As more and more texts comprising the 'words of God' were conjoined to form 'Holy Writ,' believers have recognized their God at work in that phenomenon too, engaged in producing a community, a fellowship. One of the terms by which they were pleased to denote that activity was 'the spirit of Yahweh' or 'the Holy Spirit.' In their language the word could mean either 'blowing' or 'breathing'—'wind,' therefore, as well as 'breath.' Both these things people found mysterious: the wind can have a very powerful effect without ever being seen; and breath is the unmistakable sign of the mysterious energy operative in man and animal. Hence men spoke of the wind or breath of Yahweh—'the spirit of Yahweh,' that is—in cases where he had moved great heroic figures to deliver his people or had caused prophets to address them with authority and power. At a later period, when the hope was expressed that the heart of man, steeped as it was in self-centredness, might be created anew as a heart desirous of fellowship, this too was ascribed to the spirit of Yahweh or 'the Holy Spirit.'

It will be readily understood that this term straightaway became common currency among the disciples of Jesus. God had made of him a new rallying-point: he was like a powerful magnet, drawing to himself, and so to one another, people of every variety of temperament, status, education, language, and nation. Never before had God's fellowship-creating activity, and therefore his 'Holy Spirit,' been so plain to see. That is why people came to see Jesus himself as 'moved' by and 'filled' with that spirit, and even as begotten by that Holy Spirit of God in his mother's womb.

As the Jewish sacred writings continued to play such an essential role in making people aware of what the appearing of Jesus meant for the unification of mankind, they too began to be regarded as the work of the Holy Spirit—and in a much more explicit fashion than had previously been the case among the Jews themselves. The 'wind' or 'breath' of God had 'instilled' into the authors of Scripture—into Moses, David, and the prophets, and later also into the evangelists and the writers of the epistles—what they had put on record. Thus there came into use the term 'inspiration,' the Latin word for 'breathing into.'

Whatever may have been inferred from this term at a later time, the way in which it was used originally may well afford us clues to the proper function of the Bible as a holy book. If with those who held the faith of the Bible one is prepared to admit the universal governing principle as we have already described it, then a Biblical passage is being put to its proper use only when through it people find one another in Christ. If individuals or groups seize upon a text for their own ends, or to prove themselves in the right, or to validate their own rights and pretensions, or to confirm their own superiority, then that must be branded as an abuse of it, because in conflict with 'the Holy Spirit' as the governing principle. The faith of the Bible entails the recognition that God's fellowship-creating activity knows no bounds. It is not tied to that one book, nor to the religious community in which it originated and continues to function now. We must recognize, therefore, the nature of the value of the Bible and its underlying purpose. It will have fulfilled that purpose when that is achieved which has been above indicated as its real end: the perfect fellowship of all in God.

INDEX

Numbers in italic type indicate captions to photographs and maps.

ACKNOWLEDGMENTS

The publishers wish to acknowledge their indebtedness for permission to reproduce copyright material as follows: lines on pages 36, 37, 38, 39, 40, 41, 46, 48, 53, from *Ancient Near Eastern Texts Relating to the Old Testament*, edited by James B. Pritchard (Rev. edn., Princeton University Press, 1955), reprinted by permission of Princeton University Press, and Oxford University Press, London; lines on page 16, from *The Monks of Qumran* by E. F. Sutcliffe, published by Burns & Oates, London, and Paulist-Newman Press, New York, © Edmund F. Sutcliffe 1960.

PHOTOGRAPHS

(t. = top; m. = middle; b. = bottom; l. = left; r. = right)

Bad. Landes Museum, Karlsruhe 139; Bibliotheca Ambrosiana, Milan 13; Bibliotheek der Rijksuniversiteit, Leiden 12 (b.); Bodleian Library, Oxford 11 (both), 12 (r.t.); British Museum, London 14 (l.b.), 22, 26 (b.), 28 (b.), 33 (b.), 41, 49, 92, 105; Prof. G. G. Cameron, Department of Near Eastern Studies, University of Michigan, Ann Arbor, Michigan 112; N.V. Drukkerij de Spaarnestad, Haarlem 27; Elsevier-archief 9, 10, 14 (r.b.), 15, 16, 17, 28 (l. and r.t.), 33 (l.t.), 36, 40, 42 (t.), 44 (both), 45, 58, 59 (r.b.), 118, 129 (b.l.), 136 (t.), 160, 176; Foto-Enit-Roma 178; Drs. A. A. M. v. d. Heyden, Naarden 66, 91, 110, 130, 149, (t.), 152, 159, 164 (b.), 165, 168, 172 (b.), 177, 186, 187 (both); Hirmer Fotoarchiv, Munich 119; Israel Museum, Jerusalem 136 (b.); The Jewish National and University Library, Jerusalem 12 (l.t.); Paters Montfortanen, H.-Landstichting, Nijmegen 62, 68, 69, 98 (both), 99, 102, 103, 108, 115, 123, 134 (t.), 147, 150, 151, 154, 163, 166, 167, 169 (both), 171, 172 (t. and m.), 175, 181, 182, 183, 184, 192; Ned. Organisatie voor Zuiver Wetenschappelijk Onderzoek 34 (l.); Drs. J. H. Negenman, Nijmegen 59 (l.), 90, 121; Palestine Archaeological Museum, Jerusalem 78, 146; Palestine Exploration Fund, London 35; Revu Biblique, Jerusalem 134 (plan); Rijksmuseum van Oudheden, Leiden 34 (r.); Sam Wagenaar 30, 89 (t.); H. Sibbelee, Maartensdijk 20; University Library, Cambridge 19; Ad Windig, Amsterdam 21, 22, 26, 29, 32, 42 (b.), 54, 55 (both), 57, 60, 61, 63, 67, 70, 73 (both), 74, 75, 77, 79, 84, 85, 86, 87, 89 (b.), 93, 94, 95, 96, 100, 111, 113 (both), 120, 124, 127, 131, 133, 135, 140 (all), 141, 144 (b.), 145, 149 (both), 156, 157, 161 (both), 164 (t.), 190, 191 (both).